The Disinherited

The Disinherited

THE POLITICS OF CHRISTIAN CONVERSION IN COLONIAL INDIA

Mou Banerjee

HARVARD UNIVERSITY PRESS
Cambridge, Massachusetts, & London, England
2025

Printed in the United States of America

First printing

Library of Congress Cataloging-in-Publication Data

Names: Banerjee, Mou, 1985– author.
Title: The disinherited : the politics of Christian conversion in colonial India / Mou Banerjee.
Description: Cambridge, Massachusetts ; London, England : Harvard University Press, 2025. | Includes bibliographical references and index.
Identifiers: LCCN 2024004997 (print) | LCCN 2024004998 (ebook) | ISBN 9780674268036 (cloth) | ISBN 9780674298101 (pdf) | ISBN 9780674298118 (epub)
Subjects: LCSH: Religion and politics—India—History—19th century. | Christian converts from Hinduism—India—Bengal—History—19th century. | Christian converts from Islam—India—Bengal—History—19th century. | Religion and sociology—India—History—19th century. | Evangelistic work—India—History—19th century. | Conversion. | India—Religion—19th century. | India—History—19th century.
Classification: LCC BL2007.5 .B36 2025 (print) | LCC BL2007.5 (ebook) | DDC 322/.1095409034—dc23/eng/20240422
LC record available at https://lccn.loc.gov/2024004997
LC ebook record available at https://lccn.loc.gov/2024004998

For MIMI BANERJEE and MADHUSREE CHATTOPADHYAY

In loving memory of BINA BANDOPADHYAY and KRISHNA BOSE

Contents

Note on Translation

All translations in this book are by me unless indicated otherwise. Poems, quotations, and titles in Bengali are rendered phonetically into English, as they would be pronounced, and do not follow the Library of Congress style of romanization or transliteration.

Introduction

On September 20, 1882, *The Statesman* newspaper published the news of the majestic last rites, known as *Dansagar,* of a lady belonging to one of Calcutta's most aristocratic families:[1]

> The *sraddha* ceremony or *requiem* service of the Dowager Maharani presented the unusual spectacle of a stately ritual.[2] . . . In the evening, some ten to twelve thousand beggars received charity. On the second day, over 2,000 Brahmins were feasted, on the third day the Kayasthas had a feast while some 3,500 ladies partook of a banquet on the fourth day.[3]

The Dowager Maharani, widow of Raja Kalikrishna Dev, belonged to the Sovabazar Raj family, and her *sraddha* ceremony had been celebrated with imperial pomp three days earlier on September 17.[4] The list of honored guests at the *sraddha* was a veritable compilation of the richest and most influential of the Bengali elite and intelligentsia.[5] Famously, the Sovabazar Raj family was itself a product of entrepreneurial connections between the Bengali service class and the British East India Company. The founder of the Sovabazar family's fortunes was Nabakrishna Dev, renowned as Robert Clive's *munshi* or man of business—the same Clive who was the treacherous architect of the British colonization of India through his conquest of Bengal in 1757.[6] Nabakrishna Dev earned enormous riches through his connections to Clive. Based on this wealth, the influence of the Devs spread across Bengal, and he and his descendants cemented their position as the factional leaders of the Kayastha caste group in Calcutta. This role then mutated into being widely accepted as the leaders of a conservative ideological lobby that was orthodox in its approach toward the upkeep of the sanctity of a Hindu Bengali way of life, or *Hinduani,* as it was referred to in the archives.[7] The family, despite their prominent role as interlocutors of the British administration and partners in the empire, were therefore strongly antagonistic toward any evangelical effort to convert Bengali subjects. They were often at the forefront of anti-missionary movements in Bengal in the nineteenth century. Nabakrishna's most famous descendant was his grandson Raja Radhakanta Dev, who emerged as the leader of Calcutta's orthodox Hindus by 1816. He was the chief adversary to Raja Rammohan Roy during the debates on the banning of *sati* in 1829, which led him to found the association of orthodox Hindus, the Dharma Sabha.[8] The Dev family and the Dharma Sabha played an important role in the 1840s and 1850s, aiding the concerted effort led by Debendranath Tagore of Jorasanko, in combating the pernicious effects of "missionaryism"—conversions of minor schoolboys in Bengal by their missionary preceptors. The Dowager Maharani's husband Kalikrishna Dev himself had taken part in these anti-missionary activities alongside his cousin Radhakanta Dev, especially between 1830 and 1863. The Devs used their status as the leaders of the conservative faction of Calcutta's elite to consolidate public opprobrium against British missionaries and their pedagogical activities during the controversies surrounding Gyanendramohan Tagore's conversion in 1851 as well. Their anti-missionary feelings went so far as to hire mercenaries to beat up Rev. Alexander Duff.[9]

Calcutta's Christian missionaries, irrespective of their affiliations, were understandably not enamored of the Devs and their socioreligious performances, which were aimed at upholding exactly those values in Hindu society that were seen as the most regressive and superstitious by evangelical missions. Thus, the occasion of the Dowager Maharani's *sraddha* was an opportunity for retaliation by the missionaries. The *sraddha* gave rise to a vicious epistolary battle between the missionaries and the Bengali intelligentsia, represented by Rev. William Hastie on one hand and the pioneering Bengali novelist and political theologist Bankimchandra Chatterjee on the other. This apologetic debate was a bitter battle to define what Hinduism meant to believers in Bengal and to decide how far ritualistic performances shaped the contours of its popular practice. It is not surprising that Bankimchandra Chatterjee's war of words with Hastie began with what he saw as the irascible missionary's misunderstanding and misrepresentation of private practices of Hindu piety. He rightly critiqued Hastie for his lack of tact and tastefulness in criticizing the *sraddha,* which was ostensibly a private act, even though it was celebrated on a grand public scale by the Devs. However, the occasion clearly pointed to the deeply held religious convictions of even *progressive* Indian men. There was a coexistence of their rational, modern, educated public personas, and their deeply pious and observant private selves, without any seeming contradictions between these two positions. For Hastie, this seemingly paradoxical coexistence of Western "rationality" and "Eastern" superstition was embodied in the overt idolatrous practices of the Devs of Sovabazar and legitimized by the respectful obeisance paid to the idol by the Bengali intelligentsia.

To Hastie, this was an unbearable hypocrisy that needed to be challenged. His assessment, closely following the template of apologetic debates between missionaries and Indians for a century, was in many ways the final such attempt at a theological critique of Indian faith systems in Bengal. According to Hastie, it came as a shock that the ceremony was so openly idolatrous. Hastie was perplexed, he said, by a singular problem: "It is the problem of the relation of our English education and civilization to the traditional Idolatry, and more particularly the question of the moral and personal responsibility of the educated and enlightened heads of the Hindu community for its continued countenance and perpetuation."[10] Hastie's aim was to arouse a reaction from Calcutta's Hindu Bengali society regarding their incompatible views on faith and progress. It was a faith that had not been shaken even on close contact with evangelical efforts for over a century. The Bankim–Hastie debate occurred at the noon of imperial glory, at the moment when Victorian belief in the untrammeled progress of science and capitalism, undergirded by a strong Protestant ethos, held sway over half the world. Therefore, Hastie personified the mystification that most British commentators experienced in confronting the staunch idolatry of Indian Hindus. Hastie's chief critique of Hindu Bengali leaders was that they refused to let go of their Hindu beliefs and the customary rituals and daily practices of piety. They had all received the benefits of English pedagogy; had nurtured close social ties to the British establishment through their participation in the commercial, political, and administrative services; and had enjoyed close ties of friendship with British civilians. And yet, in their private lives, they refused to turn away from the "superstitions" of the Hindu faith. It seemed clear to Hastie that when these men participated in Hindu religious ceremonies, it could only be out of communitarian social compulsion, not out of true religious belief.[11] And as long as Hindu idolatry flourished in India, supported by the so-called modern and progressive leaders of the Bengali public sphere, the community as a whole was bound to be corrupt and weakened. Therefore, it would fail to partake of the march of progress that a century and half of the civilizing influence of colonialism promised.

The reaction to Hastie's accusations was explosive and largely scathing. Both Indian and British respondents sent letters to the editor of *The Statesman*. The most vituperative letter was from a man writing under the nom de plume Ram Chandra, the great god-hero of the Indian epic *Ramayana*. Ram Chandra's first letter to the editor, published on October 6, 1882, was a sharp rebuke of Hastie's apologetics: "Will you allow me to suggest to Mr. Hastie, who is so ambitious of earning distinction as a sort of Indian St. Paul, . . . that he should render himself better acquainted with the doctrines of the Hindu religion before he seeks to demolish them?"[12]

As we now know, this Ram Chandra was none other than Bankimchandra Chatterjee, writing from what was a barely disguised punishment posting at Jajpur in Orissa.[13] As Chandra Mallampalli shows, just as Hastie had accused the Bengali elite and the intelligentsia of hypocrisy and thoughtlessness, Bankimchandra accused Hastie and other missionaries of willful ignorance of the tenets of Hindu religious philosophy and the cultural practices of Hindu piety.[14]

In accusing the most progressive Bengali men of letters of religious hypocrisy, Hastie was also making a more troubling point. If these Indian men still held on to their ancestral beliefs, even after more than a century of colonial pedagogical, social, and political influence, it showed that they, and Bengalis in general, could never be civilized by European norms. For such men, Christian conversion and a turn away from Hindu superstition was the only possible route to salvation. Their recalcitrance was a sign of the corruption and immaturity of their selves and their communities. In a sense, the religious piety of Bengali Hindus justified the civilizing mission and British colonial rule. In other words, Indians, even of the most elite socioeconomic class, still needed to bide their time in the "waiting room of History" before they could be seen as social, racial, and political equals of the British and therefore considered capable of ruling India by themselves.[15] Partha Chatterjee, in defining the conditions necessary for the "moment of departure," claimed that "the Hindu is defined by those who are not Hindu. He is also defined by a *difference*, as possessing in common with all other Hindus something that was essentially different from all other religions."[16] Given the historical context, it became necessary for intellectuals like Bankimchandra to consider Christianity seriously on its own terms—as a religion but more importantly as a denominator of racial and social difference for Hindu Indians who engaged with it.

The Bankim–Hastie debate was, in many ways, a first step in Bankimchandra Chatterjee's conception of a Hindu political theology, an "uncompromising avowal of faith in Hinduism."[17] Bankimchandra's influential anti-Muslim rhetoric would eventually be accepted as an indispensable component of Indian nationalism in the late nineteenth century. The affective expression of this nationalism would also be deeply dependent on Hindu religious and sociocultural imagery. This step toward normalizing Hindu cultural understanding of nationalism as the only legitimate form of anticolonial resistance is often described as the fruit of Bankim's poison tree.[18] It resulted in increasing divisions between communities of faith, which accepted religion as a marker of political identity in order to stake political claims in India.[19] The virulent anti-Muslim rhetoric that infused Bankimchandra Chatterjee's work—and that ostensibly inspired the nationalist binary of communal violence between Hindus and Muslims in India in the next eighty years, leading to the Indian Partition in 1947—was presaged in the Bankim–Hastie debate. Some of the deeply negative judgments that Bankim made about Christianity and Christian ethics—as profoundly alien to authentic Indian sensibility and tradition—in his war of words with Hastie foreshadow his anti-Muslim rhetoric. Assigning inauthenticity to Christianity (and Islam) as Indian faith systems created rigid definitions of both private and political identity on a religious basis. It also eroded the space for the creative accommodation of differences that had existed between such communities of faith in India for millennia.

The Bankim–Hastie controversy is a snapshot, a microhistorical illustration, of the theological debates that had been occurring between Bengalis and evangelically minded British men and women for at least sixty-five years at this point. The Bankim–Hastie debate also came at the tail end of increasingly fractious apologetics that had spilled over into the Indian public sphere. These conflicts began in the second decade of the nineteenth century, with Raja Rammohan Roy's apologetic entanglements with the Serampore Baptists on Christian theology, Christian ethics, and Hindu philosophy. From the Serampore Baptists to Alexander Duff of the Scottish Free Church in the 1830s, down to Hastie in the 1880s, Protestant Christian missionaries were convinced that the moral and material progress of Bengal, and of India more broadly, depended on the spread and success of the evangelical mission—and on the conversion of Indians to Christianity. They were constantly stymied, however, by the conditions of colonial rule and the sustained opposition of Indian intellectuals like Bankim Chandra Chatterjee to Christian evangelism. First, the British administration's professed public stance was one of noninterference in the religious practices of Indians, and they were careful about not upsetting the religious sensibilities of their fractious subjects. This noninterference policy was reiterated several times between 1781 and

1858. Second, these apologetic debates, instead of establishing the supremacy of Christianity as the missionaries wanted, would go on to shape the history of marginalization of minorities in India and incite a pattern of terrible violence—social, political, and legal, in both colonial and postcolonial India.

Missionaries were also challenged about their spiritual beliefs and social and racial policies, theologically and socially, by a host of Indians from every stratum of society, from the profoundly elite to the abjectly subordinated and impoverished. Bankim and Hastie were both aware that the apologetic critiques each leveled at the other's faith were nevertheless closely tied to contemporary debates in the Indian and British public spheres about the legitimacy of the British Crown's rule of India. The effects of the failed civilizing mission in India that Hastie was pointing out and that Bankim was responding to was evident in the duplicitous characters of Calcutta's Hindu elite. And it was a critique of colonial governance. The Bankim–Hastie debate was ultimately about the racial fitness of Indians to accept enlightenment and in turn to be accepted as equal partners in a rule of law. The rule of law and commerce, first by the East India Company and then by the Raj after 1857, was executed by British colonial administrators and supported by the cooperation of the nonofficial British population in India. These men and women were Christian, largely Protestant, and though their religious attachments varied they deeply identified the justifications for colonialism with Christian superiority over the *heathen*, the superstitious and morally corrupt Hindus and Muslims. Members of the Indian intelligentsia, Bankimchandra among them, resisted the discourse that made "enlightenment" a prerequisite for assimilation and accommodation within the accepted hierarchies of colonial rule. Their distaste for evangelism and Christian conversion programs remained deep-rooted, even when they were educated according to English pedagogical norms and partook in debating the intellectual and political ideas that circulated between the metropolis and the colonial public spheres.

The many valences of religion—as a material practice of daily piety, a form of communitarian affiliation, and a political identity—made dialogue on the matter of Christian conversion extraordinarily difficult in Bengal. The specter of Christian evangelism haunted many Bengali intellectuals. While elite Bengalis were justly proud of their own moral and material progress under British rule and often identified with the high-minded rhetoric of enlightenment and liberalism in India, this enlightened liberalism also entwined with suspicion and even hatred toward religious minorities, exemplified by Bankimchandra's attitude toward Christianity and Christian converts (and toward

Muslims, more famously). When missionary apologetics stressed the inner corruption of Hindu and Muslim material practices and religious philosophies, Hindus as well as Muslims turned to a particularly rigid definition of the Indian political self and community: this Indian identity was very strongly defined by religious faith. Bankimchandra's rigid stance that the Hindu way of life was the only historically and culturally authentic expression of Indian belonging became increasingly popular among the majoritarian Hindu community in Bengal and widened the gradual rift that had been opening up between members of different Indian faiths since at least the second decade of the nineteenth century.

As such, the debate between Bankim and Hastie encapsulates the nature of apologetics in India over the course of the long nineteenth century and also predicts the tragic inheritance of communal tensions characteristic of the history of the postcolonial South Asian nations of India, Pakistan, and Bangladesh. Therefore, the apologetic debates—these learned, fractious, controversial, and often violent exchanges—were an indicator of both the long life of the civilizing mission in India and also the ways in which Hindus and Muslims constantly fashioned and defined their political identities around the threats to their religious faith that they saw coming from evangelical Christian conversion programs. Indian attitudes toward Christian conversion efforts in Bengal raised significant questions about the braided nature of private faith, public identity, and the rights of individuals in the Anglo-Indian administrative and legal system. How did the processes of conversion harden Hindu and Muslim definitions of individual and communal identity and reconfigure the relationship between personal faith and political affiliation? How did Bengalis who were combative toward Christian conversion interact with both Christian converts and the colonial state? I analyze these questions from the perspective of those who resisted conversion and rebelled against Christian evangelism, as well as Christian converts themselves. This book therefore aims to recover the fractious history and tragic outcomes of these apologetic debates to shed light on an alternative history of the origins of communal tensions and marginalization of minorities in India.

THE RISE OF CHRISTIAN CONVERSION "PANIC"

In the nineteenth century, the stabilization and expansion of the British Empire in India meant that colonial pedagogy increasingly purveyed an Enlightenment ethos and milieu that was in turn "cannibalized," to use C. A. Bayly's phrase, by the nascent Indian intelligentsia. It also meant a significant expansion of missionary activity in India, due to a rekindling of evangelical Christian zeal that spread from Britain to the British-Indian domains in the second half of the eighteenth century.[20] This zeal was evident not only in missionary activity by different evangelical societies in the British colonies but also in the liberal utilitarian principles of British administrators. These principles were deeply infused with the evangelical attitudes of the Clapham Sect and its followers at Haileybury, where young British civilians were educated in the art of governing the British-Indian colony. Despite the British colonial administration's professed commitment to noninterference in the religious beliefs of Indians, colonial administrators were often noted for the personal zeal that—channeled through their professional administrative power—made them the most effective agents in attempts to reform or convert "superstitious" Muslim or Hindu subjects.[21] Any discussion of utilitarianism, free-trade reforms, or even the introduction of liberal-paternalistic forms of colonial governance in colonial India remains incomplete without a thorough investigation into the close ties between these popular historiographical themes and the evangelical principles that swept Britain in the latter half of the eighteenth century.[22] Enlightenment ethics, commercial free-trade principles, and reformist Protestant evangelicalism were equally important to the creation of the concept of "moral capital," which lent to imperial colonialism many of its legitimating ideologies, including that of the "civilizing mission."[23]

A major shift took place in 1813, however, when the renewal of the Charter of the East India Company finally granted *legal* permission to evangelical groups to preach in the British-Indian domains. In this decade, Britain consolidated its hold over India with the defeat and pacification of the Marathas after the third Anglo-Maratha War in 1817. The Charter of 1813 is primarily known for ending the East India Company's monopoly on Indian trade. However, the evangelical lobby—spearheaded by the great abolitionist and British politician William Wilberforce—used this occasion to push through legislation allowing Protestant evangelism and conversion efforts in the Indian Empire. Thus in 1813 ending the "spiritual slavery" of Indians through evangelism became a political objective for the first time in the history of the Company Raj. The consolidation of British hold over India also paved the way for the work of missionaries and provided substance and support to the civilizing mission. During this period, the inherent tensions between Christianity, Hinduism, and Islam fostered a discourse of exclusion in Bengal. From the second decade of the nineteenth century, Hindus and Muslims generally accepted the moral merits of Christianity as a code of ethics centered on the worship of one God. However, many majority faith communities also expressed deep anxiety about the conversion efforts of British Protestant missionaries. Contemporary chroniclers in Bengal, such as Kālīprasanna Siṃha, defined conversion not as a deeply spiritual inward process but as a momentary fashion, a *hujoog* or crazy fad.[24] These commentators saw conversion as a spectacle embraced by converts and their mentors, one that shamed the Hindus and Muslim communities to which the converts originally belonged. They framed conversion as a choice driven by inherently materialistic motives, rather than one based on spiritual or theological conviction. These competing senses of what conversion meant marked the event of conversion and baptism as profoundly political and traumatic. Conversions in Bengal in the decades between 1830 and 1865 were a public spectacle on a grand scale, celebrated by missionaries and supported by British administrators as a sign of the civilizing mission's success in India. Opposition to the conversion fad resulted in conspicuous political mobilization within Indian communities of faith, which began hardening the boundaries of their own identities and faith practices in response to the evangelical challenge. The Indian response to Christian evangelism was political from its inception and marked by suspicion, which frequently defined the debates on conversion in the emergent public sphere. I argue that this narrative of suspicion defined Christian converts as traitors, outsiders, or interlopers to Hindus and Muslims alike.

The threat that Christian conversion, real or imagined, posed to Hindu and Muslim Indians had an outsized and profoundly transformational effect. Their anxiety far exceeded the statistical significance of conversions, given that the number of Christians in the Indian census data remained steady at a mere 1–1.5 percent across the nineteenth century, and this is true of Bengal as well.[25] In this sense, Bengal suffered from a conversion panic more than a conversion crisis. But these anxieties did powerful political and intellectual work, laying the groundwork for Christianity to emerge as an oppositional and threatening "Other" to both Hinduism and Islam. The curiosity of evangelical influence in colonial Bengal is that it was largely disconnected from the actual spiritual dimensions of religious conversions, namely, the transformed relationship of the believer to herself, to her world, and to a higher power. Rather, evangelism was far more influential as a symbol and a specter in Bengal's emerging secular sociopolitical imaginary.

In this sense, the history of Christian conversion belongs in dialogue with the vast body of scholarship on communal violence between religious communities in colonial South Asia. This violence has generally been periodized to the decades after the Mutiny of 1857, framed as a result of the emerging political divisions between Hindus and Muslims in the mid- to late nineteenth century. The centering of the Hindu-Muslim binary has been amply and decisively substantiated by eminent scholars of South Asia, including but not limited to the late C. A. Bayly, Susan Bayly, Ayesha Jalal, and Sugata Bose.[26] Christian conversion, meanwhile, has typically played rather a different part in the historiography of religious and communal identity. Gauri Viswanathan, Chandra Mallampalli, Shabnum Tejani, and Nandini Chatterjee, among others, have suggested that Christian conversion was a destabilizing force that shattered accepted definitions of religious and communal identity and acted as a pervasive ideological current that shaped British interactions with Indians.[27] They have argued that the emphasis on secular liberalism as a guiding principle, in both colonial and postcolonial India, first by the British government and then by the independent Indian state itself, resulted in the government always maneuvering a difficult and tense relationship with the religious faith of its subjects and citizens. As Gauri Viswanathan stated in her seminal 1998 study of conversion, *Outside the Fold*, "By undoing the concept of fixed, unalterable identities, conversion unsettles the boundaries by which selfhood, citizenship, nationhood, and community are defined, exposing these as permeable borders."[28]

However, the history of Christian conversion in Bengal shows that the boundaries of religiopolitical identities in India began to meaningfully cohere at least forty years prior to the Mutiny of 1857—and in direct response to Protestant evangelism. In India, the emergence and sharpening of political consciousness based on religious identity began as early as the second decade of the nineteenth century. I argue that it was the perceived threat of Christian conversion, and the apologetic debates regarding conversion, that spurred the creation of nationalist narratives of cohesive Hindu and Muslim identity, hardening the sociopolitical stakes around religious identities and affiliation in South Asia. These apologetics, centered around the political and intellectual contexts of religious identity, can be traced as far back as the second decade of the nineteenth century, when Indian intellectuals like Rammohan Roy engaged in contentious apologetic exchanges with Protestant missionaries in Bengal and protested against Christian conversions. As a result of these apologetic debates, the figure of the convert emerged in the Bengali and the Indian imaginary not as a person with double affiliation to both their natal faiths and their subsequent faith of choice (although, as we will see, this was attempted by figures such as Krishnamohan Banerjee, Gyanendramohan Tagore, and Brahmabandhab Upadhyay) but as a person with no discernible affiliation at all, in the eyes of society or in the eyes of the Anglo-Indian legal system. Their identities remained, to all intents and purposes, negatively associated with the faith they had left, and as a result of their conversions, they were treated as traitors, outcasts, and pariahs. Christian converts suffered a violent unmooring from their own understanding of who they were and where they belonged within the social and political matrix of India. To draw attention to the sociopolitical ostracism and disenfranchisement of Christian converts in Bengal from the majoritarian nationalist discourse can therefore challenge the historiographical narrative of the secularization of the Indian public sphere. Centering the liminal figure of the Indian Christian convert at the heart of apologetic debates—both elite and vernacular, intellectual and quotidian—shows us instead the ways in which a minoritarian religious affiliation disadvantaged and disempowered them. These apologetic debates also illustrate the ways in which the thin veneer of enlightened progress in colonial India obscured the increasingly wide fault lines around the question of religious identity and national belonging.

In Bengal, the close connections between evangelical Christianity and British imperialism—emphasized by conversions conducted with great public spectacles of baptism at Calcutta's churches by evangelically minded British administrators and missionaries—created a specter of forced mass conversions in the minds of both Hindus and Muslims. It also triangulated the relationship between Hinduism and Islam, so that Hindu and Muslim identities in India developed in direct response to the threat of Christianity. A series of high-profile conversions in the 1830s and 1840s resulted in profound public anger at the missionaries for luring young boys and men outside the fold, and at the British administration over the support the missionaries received from sympathetic bureaucrats and officers in their conversion programs. The fall of the Sikh Empire in 1849 and thereafter the conversion of the barely fourteen-year-old heir, Prince Duleep Singh, in 1853 were devastating occurrences that confirmed Indian suspicions of British motives regarding mass conversions of Indians. It seemed to Indians that their religious rights were in danger from the constant interference and encroachments by the Company Raj. During the Mutiny of 1857, Indian soldiers in the British army suspected the British administration of a dishonorable and covert attempt to convert them en masse by decreeing the use of bullets smeared with pig fat, the ingestion of which was forbidden in both Hindu and Islamic practices.[29]

The widespread disaffection in Northern India and in Bengal against evangelism was one of the major reasons for the Mutiny of 1857, as Sir Syed Ahmed Khan pointed out in his pamphlet on the causes of the revolt, *Risala Asbab-e-Baghawat-e-Hind:*

> It has been commonly believed that the Government appointed Missionaries and maintained them at its own cost. . . . The covenanted officers assumed the Missionary functions. Many covenanted officers, and many military men, have been in the habit of talking to their subordinates about religion. . . .
>
> The missionaries moreover . . . took to printing and circulating controversial tracts. Then Missionary schools were started in which the principles of the Christian faith were taught. . . . This again added to the prevailing ill will.[30]

Once the Mutiny had been brutally suppressed and India became a possession of the British Crown in 1858, this Indian anger about evangelism and conversion efforts had to be politically assuaged. Queen Victoria declared in her Proclamation:

> We disclaim alike the right and desire to impose our convictions on any of our subjects. We declare it to be our royal will and pleasure that none be in anywise favored, none molested or disquieted, by reason of their religious faith or observances. . . . We do strictly charge and enjoin all those who may be in authority under us that they abstain from all interference with the religious belief or worship of any of our subjects.[31]

The events of 1857 were a watershed in terms of the evangelical civilizing mission in India. They demonstrated the long-standing and profound anxiety that Indians felt about forced mass conversions, which has periodically bred paranoia and resulted in political violence in South Asia. After 1857, British administrators and the Anglo-Indian legal and judicial establishment became far more circumspect when dealing with tensions between missionaries and Indian Hindus or Muslims. Although the beginning of the Indian decennial census in 1872 once again made religious identity central to the way in which Indian communities were statistically enumerated, the suspicions about the threat that Christianity and Christian conversions posed to Indian communities of faith never abated in India.

The majority of Indians in the nineteenth century viewed conversion as the result of some perceived lack, material or social, that could be alleviated by the material gains promised by missionaries. Thus, a hollowing out of the actual significance of conversion—both as a spiritual awakening and as a socioreligious event commemorating the believer's transformed relationship to God—occurred in Bengal from the beginning of the century. Conversion, within this emerging worldview, could only promise a radical and disenchanting inheritance of loss—loss of identity, family, property, and legal rights—for the converts. The native communities of faith they left behind were enraged by the perceived familial and communitarian abandonment and betrayal they saw in the act of conversion, and they were further disturbed when it seemed that missionaries and the colonial state joined hands to safeguard the rights of converts while encroaching constantly upon the religious and legal rights of Hindus and Muslims. From the 1830s, conversions to Christianity in Bengal resulted in the converts' disinheritance and expulsion from their families. Under customary practices of Hindu legal traditions in colonial Bengal, based on a treatise called *Dayabhaga,* a convert could be disinherited from both ancestral and paternal property, since the act of conversion meant the person was deracinated, spiritually dead to the family and community of birth. The British administration and missionaries both recognized early on that prevalent inheritance laws in Bengal were a major impediment to missionaries' evangelical conversion efforts. In response, the administration passed legislation that attempted to safeguard converts' rights to inheritance: Regulation VII of the Bengal Code of 1832, followed by the Caste Disabilities Removal Act (Act XXI) of 1850, which would, ostensibly, safeguard the right to inheritance for Christian converts. Indian critics worried that India's administrative, judicial, and legal systems were being manipulated by the British in a display of nonofficial soft power designed to create a class of Indian converts who betrayed the aims of Indian political resistance to British imperialism. Yet Bengali Hindus would also find ways to use the apparatus of law, as we will see, to contravene legal safeguards afforded to native converts under the Anglo-Indian legal system.

Before the colonial and evangelical challenge, both Hinduism and Islam depended on local customary practices of piety, and legal decisions to decide disputes were undertaken based on local precedence. Only with the advent of colonial reformism, influenced by evangelical attitudes, did Indian identity begin to become homogenized in both the legal and social domains. This was visible in the evolution and establishment of a code of laws to regulate Hindu and Muslim societies and families, as well as in deciding a nomenclature of political affiliations based on religious faith. Therefore, one consequence of the evangelical mission and conversion programs in Bengal was a concerted hardening of the boundaries of identity for both Hindus and Muslims—not only in Bengal but also across India. The perceived or real threat of conversion to Christianity pushed Hindu and Muslim communities to band together and put up a unified front against the infection of Christian evangelism that was spreading religious contagion. What emerges in this story of reform, then, is the formation of a majoritarian Indian identity, which was excised of any true liberalism when it came to matters of faith and religious identity.

From 1813, when legislation for the first time allowed Protestant evangelism and conversions in the Indian Empire, through the early twentieth century, Indian responses to Protestant Christian conversions helped transform matters of private religious faith into widespread—and very public—categories of political and social identity. What emerges from these critiques is not only a fascinating picture of the heated debates over the meaning and implications of Christian conversions for public life in colonial India but also, and more broadly, a powerful narrative of the evolution of religion as the primary category of political identity in South Asia. Ultimately, the perceived threat of Christian conversion gave powerful shape and coherence to Hinduism and Islam, thus hardening the sociopolitical stakes around religious identities and affiliation in South Asia. In this sense, a Habermasian interpretation of the emergent "public sphere" as postsecular in modern civil societies is profoundly inadequate in the case of nineteenth-century India. While Jürgen Habermas characterized the modern public sphere by a hardening of the borders between private and public, the furor over Christian conversion powerfully transgressed such borders: religious identity became central to the way in which the Indian imaginary, the Indian nation, and national belonging were defined. For the majority communities of faith in colonial India, the specter of conversion raised the specter of deracination: a convert was supposed to be betraying both his native identity and his duties toward his family and his social matrix. This was spiritual death in a religious sense as well. According to Hindu and Muslim personal law, one who had converted or apostatized from their religion of birth was supposed to have committed spiritual suicide. It also meant lineage and community deaths of entire families and clans, since converts could no longer perform the hereditary religious rites and rituals of their natal families, including last rites for parents. This meant that parents were deprived of the merits accruing from their children's performance of *sraddha* rituals, which were necessary for them to attain heaven after death. The devastating cosmological nature of this permanent severance helped to fuel widespread conversion panic.

Conversion to Christianity, therefore, did not enable Indians to overcome the racial and religious barriers that British colonial officials imposed on them. Instead, it led Indians from majority communities of faith to harden the logics of exclusion practiced against those who transgressed religious boundaries through conversion. Moreover, it led to converts' liminal status within the social and political milieu of the Indian nationalist movements that increasingly gained force in the second half of the nineteenth century. In other words, although the logic of conversion might have momentarily destabilized boundaries of religious, political, social, and legal identities in an abstract sense, it ultimately reinforced and ossified those very same boundaries in historical context.

THE DRIVING FORCE OF APOLOGETIC DEBATE

In both public and private, the actors in this book vigorously debated the ethical and religious merits of Hinduism and Islam as measured against those of Christianity. I characterize these kinds of debates as apologetic in both nature and content. Apologetic debates occurred within an established lifeworld in India where disputation on religion was a philosophically and ethically discursive enterprise. But in the new colonial atmosphere, these theological debates were also, invariably, deeply braided with and entangled in the notions of the lived life—in its pious, private, social, cultural, and political dimensions. I use the term *apologia* therefore as a conceptual category, considering the many ways in which it was deployed in defending and also homogenizing political identity based on religious faith in colonial India. In so doing, I distinguish between two words that evolve from the same source, the Greek ἀπολογία. The original meaning of *apologia* has the sense of "a formal written defense of one's opinions or conduct."[32] The word *apology*, however, came to mean something very different from the mid-sixteenth century in English: a regretful acknowledgment of an offense or failure.[33] The former is a positive rhetorical endeavor, while the latter has a distinctly negative usage. It is the first meaning of the term that is used in practices of both philosophical and theological justifications of one's position regarding one's ethical, religious, and doctrinal beliefs. An apologia always emerges as a response to some perceived misapprehension regarding one's faith and rational capabilities, and it is meant as a corrective. In the second case, however, it is clear that one accepts one's shortcomings of conduct or opinion, and as such, an apology in this sense also requires an abasement of the self before the other.

In this book, I return to the original, positive meaning of both *apologia* and *apologetics* in describing the content, tone, and tenor of adversarial religious debates in Bengal. I illustrate, through these variously "robust, raucous, rowdy, reflective and learned" debates, the ways in which religious identities in Bengal were consolidated against the perceived threats of Christian evangelism. Christianity's ethical framework was seen as worth emulating in reform movements within Hindu and Muslim communities. These apologetic debates, strongly critical of missionaries and conversion efforts, also led to empowering moments of reflection by critics of Christian conversions on the ways in which ideas about the ideal pious self and the ideal community were bound up together and reinforced each other.

Indeed, the Indian critics of Christian evangelism and conversion who I study in this book often had to examine their own allegiances and affinities as they found themselves caught between two cultural, social, religious, and philosophical traditions: one their own, and another they engaged with as part of their colonial subjecthood. The question of political allegiance and affinities grew even more fraught when religion and conversion, especially conversion to Christianity, became variables in the complex life-world they inhabited. These Indian intellectuals who engaged critically with both the realities of British colonialism and the ways in which the civilizing mission remained braided with evangelical concerns would, over the course of the nineteenth century, go on to play a decisive role in the creation of a modern Indian public sphere. This public sphere of course evolved out of what C. A. Bayly termed the "Indian ecumene."[34] Therefore, the ways in which Christianity was approached, examined, and theorized by a spectrum of Indian intellectuals, from Ram Mohan Roy in the early nineteenth century to Brahmabandhab Upadhyay in the early twentieth, reflect the development of overt repudiation of the evangelical conversion programs associated with it while maintaining at the same time a covert fascination with its ethical content.

Critics of the evangelical mission in India were deeply suspicious of both the rhetoric and the political realities that undergirded conversion efforts. Such critics argued that only religious, familial, and social relationships inherited and nurtured from birth were sincere and authentic and consequently deemed converts illegitimate. Most of these Indian critics, beginning with Rammohan Roy, were otherwise liberal in their personal and political outlook. However, they considered the religious identities that individuals assumed through conversion to be superficial and insincere. Conversion, they thought, could only be undertaken for material gain—not for spiritual reasons. To analyze the phenomenon of Christian conversion from the standpoint of those who resisted it, in addition to that of missionaries and converts, is to illuminate the contours of an intellectual and political debate in India that created a template of sociopolitical proscription and leeriness of those who chose to adopt a religion different from the one that they were born into. I argue that Indian critics of British evangelism in nineteenth-century Bengal so strongly emphasized the artificiality of conversion because they perceived conversion itself as a threat to Hindu and Muslim communities. Religion in colonial India was never merely about belief or faith but was intimately connected to a ritualistically ordered social fabric. In this hierarchical matrix, many Hindu and Muslim critics saw conversion to Christianity as a threat to existing ways in which religious practice mediated social and political life.

Many of those who resisted Christian conversion in Bengal—from Rammohan Roy, to Debendranath Tagore, to the once widely recognized and now forgotten Muslim tailor and apologist Munshi Meherullah—were driven by an ideological commitment to transform their own religions. Whether Hindu or Muslim, they believed that their religious traditions had been corrupted through centuries of idolatrous, superstitious, and even polytheistic customary practices and rituals and sought to restore them to their original, uncorrupted state of rational, unitarian faiths. Faced with the threat of Christian conversions, this reformist impulse became especially urgent: reform within a community, spearheaded by the leaders at both the elite and the subaltern level, was far preferable to being converted. The reformist programs within Hindu and Muslim communities were also meant to appease young members. This new generation of Bengalis, having encountered the modernizing ethos of the British Enlightenment through their exposure to English pedagogy, were often deeply concerned by the moribund and ritualistic elements of their natal faiths, which to them were at cross-purposes to the new and modern colonial world they inhabited. The orthodox and older generation, in response to these concerns from their children, believed that the performance of reform could prevent conversions and keep the youth within the matrix of their communities. It was infinitely better to illustrate to them through apologetic debates that their own faiths were preferable to the uncertain and outcaste life that conversion to Christianity could result in.

THE IMPACT OF BENGAL'S CONVERSION CONTROVERSIES

An older and more pervasive Catholic influence had prevailed in Southern India since at least the fifteenth century. The historiography on Christianity in India is largely centered on the latter region, which had the largest population of native converts and is still home to the largest portion of India's native Christians, although there is a rapidly expanding Christian population in India's northeastern states.[35] However, the case in Southern India—and to an extent, the Punjab—is quite different from the case in Bengal for a number of reasons.[36] First and foremost, Southern India is characterized by a much longer history of Christian conversion than Bengal. While Thomas the Doubter supposedly landed in India in AD 52 and immediately converted aristocratic communities who then identified themselves as Nazarene or Syrian Christians, Catholic evangelism and the conversion project in Southern India began in earnest with the arrival of Vasco da Gama in 1498 and the beginning of the Portuguese *Padroado*.[37] From the beginning, Catholic missionaries in Southern India also oversaw mass conversions of entire communities—often artisanal, lower-caste, and non-elite.

This approach, along with the entrenched presence of the church in the region, meant that conversion had a very different impact on existent socioeconomic and political structures than it did in Bengal. The Catholic Church was also far more accommodating of syncretic practices and often tacitly allowed Hindu and Muslim caste and kinship hierarchies to remain undisturbed when communities as a whole converted to Christianity. Community conversions even enabled upward sociopolitical mobility among Southern India's convert groups in a way that was impossible for converts in Bengal. From the late eighteenth century, missionary activity in Southern India occurred primarily in the princely states, where the center of power was an Indian prince. In many cases, princes directly employed missionaries in their administrations and worked closely with them in ways that were not possible in domains under direct British rule, like Bengal. In these princely kingdoms, the relationship between the missionaries, the administration, and the native communities was marked by a different set of maneuvers and contestations than those regions, like Bengal, that were at the center of British power in India.[38]

The situation in directly administered Indian territories was vastly different politically. The story that this book tells is particular to the colonial province of Bengal and tethered to a set of circumstances particular to Bengal. Yet, at the same time, the implications of these Christian conversion controversies reverberated far beyond the bounds of the Bengal Province: Bengal was the British bridgehead from 1757 and Calcutta the colonial capital from 1772 to 1922. From the multiple institutions of higher learning where education was provided on the British model and English was the language of instruction, to the courts of justice, including the Calcutta Supreme Court and then the High Court, and as a commercial and intellectual center of the British Empire in the world, Bengal was the crucible. This is where issues of importance were debated, with ripples moving outwards into the entire empire and even to London. The social, legal, and political implications of Christian conversion controversies in Bengal affected the debates on Christianity and the civilizing mission across the British Empire. Bengal's conversion panic, therefore, impacted political mobilization across India more broadly. This political mobilization was uniquely provoked by the circumstances surrounding conversions in Bengal. For one, serious evangelical efforts began in Bengal only from the last decade of the eighteenth century, nearly 400 years after the first wave of community-wide conversions in South India. Bengal also saw a far greater involvement of Protestant missionary groups, especially the Baptists, the Scottish Free Church, and the Anglican Church Mission groups, which created a strong impression among Hindu and Muslim Indians that Christianity was the colonizers' religion. The fact that many liberal, evangelically minded colonial officials backed conversion both covertly or openly—even after the Queen's 1858 pronouncement of noninterference in her subjects' religious prejudices—only reinforced this impression.[39]

In Bengal, the capital of British India, the force of public anger against Christian evangelism resulted in a staggering outpouring of dissent. Elite and individual conversions in Bengal had threatened destabilization and had challenged existing social and religious community affiliations in a radical way. Since the act was seen as a disavowal of the religious rites and duties the converts owed to their family and community, and since the British administration was seen as implicated in these conversions, the tide of anger turned against the administration. Elite conversions highlighted the failure of Hindu and Muslim communities to keep their members within the fold—as well as the failure of familial and communal bonds. They also highlighted the lack of governance, control, and surveillance these communities exercised over younger members who chose to convert.[40] Thus individual (and elite) conversions evoked overwhelming fears of colonial interference and repression, and the erasure of indigenous identities and histories, because these conversions were a direct challenge to caste and community laws that were seen to be immutable and the only sacrosanct domains of national affective identities. For elite converts and elite commentators on Christianity, like Krishnamohan Banerjee and later Brahmabandhab Upadhyay, the loneliness engendered by social and communitarian boycott and severance of family ties through conversion led to an increased desire for social engagement and a desire to bridge the gap between their faith of choice and their community and culture of birth. Their sense of mutilated bonds and unmoored social, political, and legal existence was a reaction to the violence that conversions inevitably engendered. They sought resolution and psychic healing in claiming an immutable bond of love with their country, but their convert status made even this form of engagement difficult and tense.

For these reasons, conversions in Bengal were uniquely positioned to engender anxiety among majoritarian faith communities. In turn, these anxieties created a narrative of profound suspicion and anger, not only against missionaries, who were the face of conversion programs, but also against Indian Christian converts, who were seen as traitors to their natal faiths and their communities. In turn, this narrative led to increased violence and marginalization of minority communities of faith in India, leading to devastating consequences—a carnage of communal violence during the Partition of India in 1947, continuing in religious riots in the seventy-five years since. Bengal was the focal point of British colonial power in India during the nineteenth century. Throughout the century, Calcutta was the capital, the second city of the British Empire and its most important transnational trading hub. Whatever happened in Bengal politically, religiously, and socially indisputably had a ripple effect on events elsewhere in India and across the British Empire. The events in this book, while they took place in the Bengal Province, were reported widely and impacted legal and political developments across India. For example, the famous Great Tagore Will Case—a legal battle fought between two members of the prominent Tagore family, Prosonnocoomar Tagore and his convert son Gyanendramohan—would redefine the Anglo-Indian legal system's approach to converts' inheritance rights across India. Bengali Hindu parents' legal challenges to the conversions of their school-age sons, meanwhile, changed the legal definitions of both age of discretion and age of maturity across the British domains in the subcontinent. Even more importantly, however, the backlash against Christian conversion in Bengal consolidated Hindu and Muslim identity—and nationalist claims-making—across India. The political impact of Christian conversion, while it created the most panic in Bengal, could be felt across India in an amplified form. Questions about the relationship between religious faith, patriotism, and nationalist claims-making continue to be debated into the twenty-first century across India. The place of Christianity as an authentic Indian religion, and Christians as authentic Indian subjects and citizens, remains a flashpoint of political violence. Bengal in the nineteenth century is the *origin* point for a story that is still unfolding across India today.

CHRISTIAN CONVERTS IN THE ARCHIVE

This book draws upon several years of research in India, Bangladesh, England, and the United States, and on material written in Hindi, Urdu, Bengali, and English. I use historical, ethnographic, literary, and legal historical methodologies to reconstruct the liminal life-worlds of Indian Christian converts from a range of fragmentary, incomplete archival minutiae. Each chapter tells a richly emotive story of the entanglements between converts and their interlocutors from across elite and vernacular milieus. These fragmentary life-worlds are reconfigured using legal and administrative documents such as wills and inheritance disputes, as well as from stray references in vernacular pamphlets, newspapers, chapbooks, satires, scandal broadsheets, parodies, and plays. Each of the case studies either uncovers fresh archival material or brings a new lens to events partially discussed in existing historiography. They collectively lay bare how Christian conversions shaped the history of Bengal, in ways that are deeply relevant to the sectarian violence haunting India today.

Most of the historical work in this field in the last thirty years has been largely based on missionary archives. Perhaps as a result, there has been too much reliance on the colonial and evangelical point of view in categorizing change wrought by evangelism and the civilizing mission in India over time, and in political, social, and legal institutions in the British-Indian colony.[41] Most discussion of these changes, moreover, centers the experiences of missionaries and Indian converts in navigating the evolving Anglo-Indian administrative and politicolegal system over the long nineteenth century. Historians of the British Empire have written extensively on the relationship between colonial officials and missionaries, and on the impact of such collaborations, which have been seen as producing ideas and legitimizations for buttressing the empire. Other historians have deconstructed the monolith of empire by describing colonial responses to nonofficial white violence in India.[42] To this end, most recent historiography has focused on colonial officials and nonofficial whites and evangelicals.[43] Therefore, this book is also in conversation with the rich tradition of scholarship on Indian Christianity, including the work of Robert Eric Frykenberg, Penelope Carson, Geoffrey Oddie, and Eliza Kent.[44] These scholars have sensitively analyzed the experiences of Indian Christian missions, missionaries, and converts to delineate the complex histories of Christian traditions and experiences in Central and Southern India. My research, which is based on Bengal, takes seriously the reactions of those who are often overlooked in the majority of mission-archive-dependent scholarship on the southern regions of India: namely, Bengalis who critiqued and opposed Christian conversions, in counterpoint. I have consciously exerted care in my use of missionary archives and sources to avoid mirroring many of the established mission narratives about the successes of conversion efforts, which are not borne out by the archival evidence for Bengal that I have consulted.

Instead, I seek to privilege the many Indian interlocutors—both in the elite as well as the vernacular public sphere—who participated in the critical debates about conversion. To this end, I examine legal disputes and court cases involving questions of inheritance, as well as literary and political sources. I demonstrate the multiple registers in which the conditions of political identity, belonging, and exclusion were debated in the Indian public sphere. While this book engages with the perspectives of evangelical missionaries and colonial officials, I ultimately seek to recover—to the extent possible—the voices and experiences of Indian interlocutors and Indian converts. Many of these voices were based in Calcutta, the capital of British India and the center of colonial power. Home to the Council of the Governor-General of India and the viceroy's seat, Calcutta also saw the burgeoning of institutions like the Hindu College (founded in 1816) and missionary schools like the General Assembly's Institution (founded in 1830). It was home, as well, to important and pioneering Indian intellectuals like Rammohan Roy and Dwarkanath Tagore, Hindu elites like Radhakanta Dev and Ramdulal De, and the institutions of the Brahmo Samaj.[45] This book seeks to privilege the perspectives of some of these individuals, who observed the rapid change that Calcutta (and Bengal) underwent as a result of British colonial control. They found themselves at the center of the political, social, and religious tensions that gripped the region because of these rapid changes as well as the intimacies between the colonial administration, the evangelical establishment, the nonofficial white population, and the Indian subjects themselves. These intimacies encompassed social, economic, and political connections in the public domain and sometimes encroached into the inner domestic world as well.

Therefore, this book also seeks to bring forward, as much as possible, women's voices and the possibility of women's agency in choosing their personal faith—a subject rarely considered in scholarship on Christian missionary activity in Bengal, which I address in Chapters 3 and 4.

This is not, however, only a story about Calcutta. The networks of some Calcutta-based Indian intellectuals, like Rammohan Roy, spread across the globe. Other interlocutors, meanwhile, were quintessentially rural or *mofussil* in their milieus: Chapter 5, for example, will examine how impoverished peasants in eastern rural Bengal, following the lead of a charismatic preacher, began defining their identities as good Muslims against the threat of Christian evangelism. Even their networks spread out across Bengal, from rural eastern Bengali districts like Jessore and Barisal to Dhaka and even to the metropolis of Calcutta. Too often, the historiography on Indian intellectual and religious reformism has focused almost exclusively on elite, male, urban high-caste Hindu. To fully understand the facets of anxiety about Christian conversion among majoritarian faith communities, however, we must look to the hinterlands and rural milieus.

The apologetic debates examined in this book played out in the public sphere in the form of pamphlets, petitions to the colonial government, letters, circulated speeches, and biographies—but also, most importantly, through the newspapers and journals that acted as the mouthpieces of different religious and political groups, both among the Indians and the British populace.[46] These debates and the Indian actors who took part in them embodied the highly contested zone of identity formation and self-fashioning of the colonial subject.[47] In order to really understand the conversion panic in Bengal in the nineteenth century, and the ways in which it affected how people thought of sociolegal identity, I study the everyday life of Indians through a variety of sources, including legal ones, which contain voices of converts otherwise erased in standard sources like family genealogies.

These microhistorical narratives of Christian conversions, I argue, help to decenter the commonplace binary of Hindu-Muslim oppositional relationships in colonial India. Tracking converts' experiences of ostracism as well as the perceived betrayal felt by the members of their natal communities, I chart the catalyzing influence of religious faith as public political identity in colonial South Asia. Since the identities of converts often were effaced from their families' genealogical records and from vernacular memory, the work of reconstructing these histories has proven particularly difficult. Indian converts mostly exist only as sites of negative speculation and debate in both the public sphere and the archives. As a result, they leave fragile, incomplete traces. To write about their inner lives and the social milieus they inhabited requires constant negotiation of silences and absences. The methodologies of microhistory have helped me to historicize liminal lives, with a focus on the fragmentary traces they left behind in colonial archives and in secular historiographies of South Asia.

As the eminent practitioner of microhistorical methodologies, Carlo Ginzburg, pointed out in a 2022 interview, "In history as in cinema, every close-up implies an off-screen scene. . . . In any close-up, the global perspective is implicit. Every singular case assumes the possibility of a generalization, and there is back and forth between the one and the other."[48] Francesca Trivellato has also argued that microhistories have global and macroanalytical scope, featuring individuals who suffer geographic and cultural dislocations. Trivellato cautions us, however, that the historian must be profoundly mindful of what archival sources reveal, conceal, and distort.[49] In exploring these life-worlds, and reimagining the relationship between religious faith and social identity, I have been influenced by Saidiya Hartman's poignant use of the concept of "waywardness" to speak of "intimate histories of social upheaval."[50] Marginal lives, Hartman shows us, are theorized and historicized within negative paradigms and are often erased and silenced. The social and political changes that affected the ordinary private lives of Indian Christian converts made them traverse multiple religious, linguistic, and political boundaries, changing the ways in which each individual interacted with their society and vice versa. Over the course of the nineteenth century, Indian Christians found themselves erased from the political discourse of nationalism as a result of this persistent adversarial critique. The histories of native Indian Christians, I argue, were unique in that a wayward irregular irruption of their voices occurred within the Anglo-Indo-Islamic public sphere. In Saidiya Hartman's words, this was "a social poesis that sustains the dispossessed."[51]

Ultimately, this book is a historical narrative of disinherited, dispossessed, forgotten, and erased people within the broader contours of the Bengal Renaissance. Their lives and struggles anchor my analysis, while well-known figures like Bankimchandra Chatterjee and Rabindranath Tagore—who together often seem to define both Bengal and its historiography—appear only on the margins of this book. These acts of close reading, of critical fabulation, of reconfiguring individual lives from fragmentary archival material, have clear macrohistorical repercussions. The lives of Bengal's disinherited Indian converts, and the narratives of suspicion and paranoia to which they were subjected, offer a meaningful prehistory of the communal tensions that continue to flare up around religious conversions in India. They lay bare the genealogy of violence that India's minority communities have suffered over the last two centuries.

THE STRUCTURE OF THIS BOOK

This book maps how conversion controversies became the central flashpoints in the intellectual debates that shaped public discourse on political identity in colonial India, through a social history of individual and communitarian encounters between Indian interlocutors, missionaries, the British legal system, and the colonial state. Each chapter is framed around case studies of such encounters, with three aims: (1) to demonstrate the deepening reach of Christian conversion controversies in everyday life; (2) to uncover how the Indian public sphere and the modern Indian self were transformed over the course of the nineteenth century as a result of apologetic debates; and (3) to chart the violent reformulation of what it meant to be a "good" Hindu or Muslim over the course of the century, defined against the liminal image of the Indian Christian convert—the Other to authentic Indian selfhood, as it were, in a mirror darkly.

Chapter 1 investigates the birth of modern apologetics in colonial India. This was the earliest phase of socioreligious polemics by Indian intellectuals, the first instance being Rammohan Roy's debates with the Serampore Baptists from 1820 onward. The contours of these debates are well known. Yet I argue that although religious controversies made Rammohan Roy's global reputation as the father of Indian modernity, the by-product of his arguments with the missionaries was that he originated a series of negative stereotypes about Indian Christian converts that would prove to be enduring and inescapable. Rammohan's accusation that native conversions were not sincere but motivated by material gain would permanently damage the credibility of both missionaries and native converts for two centuries afterward.

A second, more vicious wave of apologetics, resulting in violent antimissionary propaganda by Indians, began with the arrival of the Scottish missionary Alexander Duff in Calcutta in 1830. Duff was strongly invested in a conversion program aimed at high-caste Hindu men and women. He was also one of the first missionaries to realize that pedagogical efforts could ensure new intimacies between missionaries and young Hindu men that paved the way for Christian conversion. Chapter 2 examines the growing unease in

Calcutta's Hindu elite society over the power of the missionary as teacher, using his moral authority to encourage conversion among young high-caste Indian schoolboys. In Bengal, parents increasingly found it necessary to send their sons to missionary-run schools to learn English, the new language of enlightenment and social mobility. However, they feared that missionary preceptors would also use English to teach the precepts of the Bible and encourage schoolboys to accept Christianity. A series of high-profile conversions by high-caste Hindu youth between 1830 and 1865 fueled these fears into an inferno of Bengali anger and dissent. The tussle between Bengali Hindu parents and Christian missionaries regarding the souls of schoolboys culminated in a series of habeas corpus cases in the Calcutta courts. These cases hinged on questions of self-determination, and specifically the question of when a young Bengali boy was old enough to conscientiously choose to convert to Christianity. Religious apologetics spilled over into the domain of Anglo-Indian law in Bengal at the Calcutta Supreme Court and resulted in a definitive change of legal opinion on the age of discretion and maturity in India, as well as the question of parental rights to education and custodial control of young children.

Chapter 3 examines the so-called Great Tagore Will Case, a legal inheritance dispute between two of the richest and most influential members of the Pathuriaghata Tagore family of Bengal. Prosonnocoomar Tagore, the first Indian member of the Viceregal Legislative Council, disinherited his son and heir Gyanendramohan Tagore, the first Indian barrister, because of Gyanendramohan's conversion to Christianity in 1851. This conversion was preceded by the private apostasy of Gyanendramohan's first wife, Bala, who chose Christianity as her faith and was often held up by missionaries as an exemplar of the high-caste *zenana* (Urdu for "women," but also the secluded inner quarters of a home where the women lived) convert. Her relationship to her husband was a central factor in the scandal of Gyanendramohan's very public conversion and baptism, and it illuminates the importance of female voices and agency in conversion controversies. Distraught by his son's conversion and in direct contravention of the Lex Loci Act of 1850, Prosonnocoomar left his property to his nephew Maharaja Jatindramohan Tagore of Pathuriaghata. Gyanendramohan contested his father's will, and the resulting case—which spanned from 1868 to 1872—went from the Calcutta High Court all the way to the Privy Council in London. The Great Tagore Will Case played an important role in establishing the primacy of Hindu laws of inheritance in disputes between family members, especially in cases of conversion to Christianity by male heirs, and proved that the right of disinheritance still lay in the hands of the Hindu fathers. Christian converts had no place of legal safety in British India.

Chapter 4 turns to the case of the Baropakhya Christian converts, a group of rural peasants who experienced brutal violence at the hands of their British planter landlord and his Indian associates in 1856. By midcentury, legal, social, and physical violence against Indian Christian converts had become an increasingly recognizable hallmark of the colonial political landscape. This cycle of violence was enacted against converts by the British government, by the white nonofficial population, and by their Indian neighbors. Racism and sociolegal inequality between Indian and white British subjects dominated the public sphere. Evangelical missionaries and the Indian intelligentsia at once forged close alliances and furthered extreme ideological divides. Conversions increased the fractiousness of religious apologetics that contested evangelism, and apologetics in turn fanned fears of unrest and mass conversions among Hindus and Muslims, which resulted in physical and mental violence against Christian converts. This especially affected the relationship of the British executive and judiciary with the landholding white planter classes. This case reflects the emerging role of missionaries in facilitating discourses of social change: to safeguard against the violence and exclusion faced by converts. It also reflects how the realities of colonial rule, as well as caste hierarchies, frustrated their efforts at reform in rural Bengal.

In Chapter 5, I analyze a selection of apologetic pamphlets authored by an itinerant tailor called Munshi Meherullah, who spearheaded the *atrap* Bengali reaction against missionary efforts. Rural Muslim *atrap* (peasant and non-elite) communities in the eastern part of the colonial Bengal Presidency were the target demographic of Christian conversion efforts in the last decades of the nineteenth century. Debates (*bahases*) between Muslim preachers and Christian missionaries, as well as religious meetings (*waz-mahfils*), characterized these apologetics. Disseminated through street-market chapbooks in Musalmani Bengali or *dobashi* Bengali, such polemics translated the cultural valences of Christianity and Islam both as personal faith and as communitarian identifying markers. As this chapter demonstrates, Meherullah's distinctive approach toward social reform, religion, and religious identity played an important role in defining the parameters of what it meant to be a good Bengali Muslim. Religious conversion, as a result of Meherullah's intervention, enabled self-examination and analysis of their immediate social milieu for Bengal's Muslims, in order to resist colonial religious and political subordination.

Amid the gathering momentum of nationalist mass movements in the first decade of the twentieth century, the necessity of maintaining a public and inalienable Hindu identity in politics—as opposed to Christian faith in salvation—resulted in a crisis of the soul. This crisis played out in the context of the radical nationalist politics of the *swadeshi* movement in the life of Brahmabandhab Upadhyay, the subject of Chapter 6. Brahmabandhab converted to Catholicism but maintained a public identity as a Hindu nationalist. In his varied careers as social reformer, political radical, heretic theologian denounced by the Catholic Church, and revolutionary against the British government, he embodied the tensions between a public identity as a Hindu nationalist and private identity as a Christian believer. He was one of the last and most important apologists of a cultural Hindu nationalism in the story I tell. His life was riven in half—he publicly performed the role of a Hindu ascetic, wrote rousing apologetic editorials and articles espousing armed extremism against the British administration, and inspired the Bengali revolutionary violence of the *swadeshi* era, but he was also a deeply private and devout Catholic Christian. Upadhyay's intellect, apologetic political ideology, and enigmatic life fascinated his contemporaries, including the polymath and future Nobel Prize recipient Rabindranath Tagore and the veteran Indian Congress politician Bipin Chandra Pal. As I demonstrate in this chapter, the erasure of his memory from the narrative of nationalist historiography—and the many attempts to appropriate the legacy of this elusive man—point to a collective failure to resolve the ways in which an individual's privately held religious beliefs affected their political, legal, and social belonging within the imagined community of the Indian nation.

CHAPTER ONE

Conversion and the Birth of Modern Apologetics in India

Calcutta, the second city of the British Empire and capital of British India, was reclaimed from the swampy grounds around the natural port of the River Ganges in the lower reaches of the Bengal province in the late seventeenth century. Although initially renowned for its heat, dust, and cyclical epidemics, especially cholera and mosquito-borne diseases like malaria, by 1813 the city had been transformed into an international, cosmopolitan space. Ships from Bristol, Liverpool, and other British ports competed with those from Boston and Philadelphia.[1] From the port to the esplanade and parks of the European neighborhoods to the so-called Black Town where Indians lived, Calcutta was a bewildering, enchanting, and occasionally violent city of marble palaces and mansions, mixed with huts and temples, churches, synagogues, and mosques. Hindus, Muslims, Armenians, French, Danish, British, Americans, and a small but thriving population of Chinese and Jewish peoples made up the city's population. Calcutta was a hub of international diplomacy and trade and the central node for the emerging vernacular Indian public sphere, which flourished as Indians increasingly vocalized their opinions about British policy in India. The renewal of the Charter of the East India Company in 1813, which introduced free trade in India and abolished the monopoly the Company enjoyed, led to a commercial and political upheaval. Private trade essentially heralded an age of booming economic profits for the metropole. Calcutta had become the seat of Kamala or Lakshmi, the Hindu goddess of wealth.[2] At the same time, the "Pious Clause" inserted into the Charter of 1813 provided missionaries and evangelical institutions with official access to the British-Indian Empire. Previously, these entities had operated only in an unofficial capacity from the hinterlands of Calcutta, often with bases in Danish, Dutch, or French colonies along the River Hooghly.[3] In the aftermath of the Charter, a great religious and political debate unfolded in the public sphere, in ways that had lasting ramifications

"Missionary Influence or How to Make Converts," from the satire by Thomas Rowlandson, *The Grand Master: Or Adventures of Qui Hi? In Hindostan* (London, 1816). The illustration caricatures Christian evangelism and conversion programs practiced in colonial India.

Robert J. Del Bontà / National Museum of Asian Art Archives, Smithsonian Institution, Robert J. Del Bontà Collection, FSA_A2014.06_1.22.

for Indian Hindus, Muslims, and convert Christians alike. It set the stage for a debate about religion and religious identity, which led to the birth of modern apologetics in India. Furthermore, this modern apologetics created a template for religious tensions that converged around the question of conversion, and especially conversion to Christianity. Ultimately, this led to a social, political, and legal discourse of suspicion about converts and the motives for religious conversions and paved the way for the eventual and violent disinheritance of not merely Christian converts but also adherents of all minority communities of faith in India from the mainstream of nationalist belonging.

The old maxim that colonization and missionary activity were coeval was never quite true in the Indian context. This vision of British colonization with sword in one hand and Bible in the other would be challenged repeatedly, even from within the British establishment, especially in the early stages of its extension of active colonial control between the Battle of Plassey in 1757 and the 1830s. During this period, the British establishment was careful to maintain a pose of religious neutrality with regards to India, and British administrators often explicitly denounced the idea that the East India Company would completely convert all of India's population to Christianity. British belief was deeply entrenched regarding the tenacious attachment of Indians to their respective faiths, and aggressive territorial expansion by the East India Company often went hand in hand with assurances to the Indian princes and peoples that their freedom to worship as they wished would not be interfered with, all through the second half of the eighteenth century. This was partly because the British administration needed to keep its Indian army, the largest in the world at the time, happy and loyal. This was also because the East India Company was deeply aware of the profound numerical discrepancy between the white population in India, which numbered a few hundred thousand, and the millions of Indians they ruled over.[4] An old Company official said with regard to allowing Christian proselytism in India that "indignation will spread from one end of Hindustan to the other, and the arms of fifty millions of people will drive us from that portion of the globe."[5] British Christian missionaries were aware of this deep-rooted political belief among the older generation of the East India Company's officials and were deeply frustrated by this reluctance and opposition to any prospect of supporting evangelism and Christian conversion programs in the British-Indian domains: "Our brethren found the government of India decidedly inimical to the introduction of missionaries. They predicted nothing short of the loss of the country, if the prejudices of the natives were interfered with."[6] This openly adversarial relationship was softened, however, by the entangled nature of the collaborations between the British administration and missionaries. The collaborations occurred in many different ways—through pedagogy, printing, translation, ethnography, and most importantly in gathering and recording information, in gaining a thorough command of Indian languages and indigenous knowledge systems, and in aiding the surveillance efforts of the East India Company over their Indian subjects by categorizing this information.

Therefore, this chapter explores a phenomenon that was deeply entwined with the complicated project of Protestant evangelism and Christian conversion in the Indian Empire, from the time of the 1813 Charter to the abolishment of the custom of Hindu widow-burning or *sati* in 1829. Specifically, this period saw the birth and consolidation of a particular kind of religious debate: apologetic exchanges about the relative merits of Hinduism, Islam, and

Christianity, relating to the individual potential each of these religions exhibited in terms of civilizational, enlightenment, and salvific benefits. These apologetic debates took place between Christian missionaries, evangelically minded British administrators, and Indian intellectuals. This new colonial apologetics differed significantly from earlier precolonial forms of religious debates in India, such as the Hindu-Sanskritic form of *tarka* or the courtly Indo-Islamic *bahas* in Northern Indian aristocratic and theological circles. These debates occurred between scholars and theologians from all religions. One of the most famous examples of this *bahas* was the culture of religious apologetics at the court of the Mughal emperor Akbar, where Hindus, Muslims, Jesuits, and Zoroastrians all engaged in learned disputation, with the emperor and his aristocratic courtiers as the audience.[7] In the earlier forms of debates in the Indian ecumene, there were common practices of engagement and disputation that could be adopted depending on the context—and these patterns of participation were based on the idea of *akhlaq* or ethical considerations for the betterment of humankind. The disputation was structured around that precedence and adhered to a usually strict code of civility between the debating parties. There was a shared space of philosophical and theological exchange, dependent on a core of sacred or literary texts and guided by norms of civil exchange of opinions. Thus, the participants in such debates, particularly those focused on textual differences across various editions of religious or "sacred" texts and their commentaries, relied on the commonality of experienced life-worlds to discuss—in a social context—the connections between faith, ethics, and politics. As Avril Powell points out in her seminal study of colonial Muslim-Christian debates in Northern India, a millennium of these precolonial forms of *bahas* and *munazara* were predicated on shared life-worlds between Muslim believers and the *zimmi/dhimmi* Christian communities, who enjoyed protected status in Muslim empires across Asia, from the Ottomans to the Safavids to the Mughals.[8]

However, the knowledge and memory of these encounters—especially those pertaining to the sixteenth-century Mughal world in India, such as the apologetics between Muslims and Jesuits—were only textually retained. They were not transmitted across other Christian sectarian circles or in the Indian ecumene during the age of decentralization and decline in the eighteenth century. And in the nineteenth century, these older forms of religious apologetics had to adapt to a new colonial reality. After 1813, British Protestant evangelical policy refocused on renewing these religious debates to advance their program of evangelism and to counter the merits of Hinduism and Islam.

This renewed effort was essentially a fresh attempt at colonial apologetics. Yet by the early nineteenth century India had undergone a century of decentralization and colonial wars of expansion. The norms of civility and the shared experiences of life-worlds that had been embodied in the earlier apologetic debates of the Mughal world had either been lost entirely or remained only in vestigial forms in shared communal memory. What took their place within the structures and institutions of the Enlightenment's civilizing mission were the attendant racial, religious, and colonial hierarchies that were parlayed into colonial apologetics and resulted in exclusionary politics within Indian communities.

The evolution of a particular template for the rhetoric of exclusion and marginalization, especially one that targeted India's native Christian communities, was one of the unintended consequences of Britain's imperial and evangelical policies in India. Protestant missionaries had an implicit racial bias when they preached conversion to their audience in Bengal. They saw their mission as not only to establish the supremacy of the Bible over Hindu and Muslim sacred texts but also to establish the supremacy of Christianity over Hindu and Islamic belief systems, and by extension, the supremacy of white Britons over the native Indian population. The evangelical project in India was thus deeply political from the start, directly entangled with the project of establishing the supremacy of the British over Indians and providing legitimacy to the colonial project. Indian interlocutors made a robust defense of their faith and religious communities, drawing on past precedent, wherein disputation on religion was a philosophically and ethically discursive enterprise. But in the new colonial context, theological debates were also invariably entangled in notions of the lived life—in its pious, private, social, cultural, and political dimensions. In the new colonial form of apologetics that evolved in Bengal, verbal disputations gave way to textual and printed exchanges—which, in turn, allowed apologetics to ebb from the realm of religion into the social, political, and legal domains in surprising ways. Textual criticism of religious texts, and apologetics based on textual analysis, became one of the great tools of debate and discussion in the Indian ecumene. Both the newly emergent print media and the oral forms of scribal transmission in a literacy-aware society aided in wide dissemination of these debates.[9]

The unique political and social circumstances in Bengal, and especially in Calcutta, after 1813 made this new flowering of religious apologetics possible. In turn, these debates made possible the displacement of Christian converts to the margins of protonationalist debate on the religious and legal rights and privileges of British-Indian subjects. This chapter argues that early nineteenth-century apologetic debates between British Protestant missionaries and Indian intellectuals created a rhetorical template for the disinheritance of India's convert Christians. Specifically, the origins of this template are a series of apologetic debates between the pioneering reformer and intellectual Rammohan Roy (1772–1833) and a group of missionaries known as the Baptists of Serampore. Between 1815 and 1823, Rammohan was increasingly drawn into the social, administrative, legal, and political ramifications of evangelical influence in British domains in India, especially Calcutta and its hinterlands. Yet he was also drawn into philosophical and ethical debates about Christianity as it pertained to India and Britain's Indian subjects. Although the scholarship on Rammohan's entanglements with Christianity is extensive, there is perhaps more to be explored about his relationship with the Serampore Baptists.[10] The debates with the Serampore Baptists were a prelude to the controversies and apologetics surrounding the debate on the ban on *sati* (the practice of self-immolation of Hindu widows on the funeral pyres of their deceased husbands) in 1829 and prepared the ground for Rammohan's preeminence as the pioneering Indian intellectual and reformer of his age, in the eyes of both the British administration and his Indian contemporaries. While Rammohan and the Serampore Baptists at first collaborated on his efforts to criticize the practice of *sati,* they soon became embroiled in a series of acrimonious debates about the ethical and rational content of the Bible. Rammohan was deeply invested in understanding how the message of the Bible could be interpreted for Indians as a moral code to live a good life. At the same time, he was deeply disconcerted by the methods missionaries in India were using to evangelize and convert Indians to Christianity. Rammohan's stated position on missionary activity in India and the character of Indian Christian converts would shape public opinion for the next two centuries.

As I argue here, the effects of Rammohan's views on conversion set the colonial template for the exclusion and effacement of converts from Hindu and Muslim discourse on national belonging, both in and beyond Bengal. Between 1813 and 1829, these apologetic debates also inaugurated a form of effacement of those Indians who changed their own natal faiths and chose to convert to Christianity. Converts were excommunicated from their communities of birth. But also, as we will see, Indian intellectuals, beginning with Rammohan, believed that converts did not deserve any preferential treatment over Hindus and Muslims pertaining to legal rights just because they had accepted Christianity as their personal faith. A certain discourse of suspicion about the motives of converts began to take hold among both Hindus and Muslims. On one hand, Hindu and Muslim communities preferred to deracinate and publicly excommunicate those members who abandoned their faith through the public spectacles of baptism. On the other hand, the leaders of Hindu or Muslim ecumenes also laid out the social, political, and legal arguments for why these converts should be disinherited from any social or moral capital to which they could lay claim as their birthright. Yet in order to understand the characteristic virulent anti-missionaryism among Calcutta's native Bengali intelligentsia after Rammohan's first public debates with the Serampore Baptists, we must first look back to the earlier period of evangelical activity in Bengal and its connections to the increasing concern among prominent evangelical groups in England about the necessity of saving the souls of Indian subjects and the means and methods through which this civilizing endeavor might be successfully carried out. These are the connections we will trace in the next section.

THE CLAPHAM SECT AND THE SERAMPORE BAPTISTS

The foundations of the project of evangelizing India were laid long before the Charter of 1813, with the formation of the Clapham Sect in London.[11] Politically conservative and associated with leading politicians and financiers, the Clapham Sect were prominent in England's sociopolitical, religious, and financial life from about 1790 to 1830, promoting abolitionism and missionary work both at home and abroad. Among its founder members was the abolitionist William Wilberforce, who began actively promoting the Protestant evangelical care of Indian subjects in 1793. His efforts, which culminated in a speech in Parliament on June 22, 1813, exhorting the necessity of evangelism in India, led to the inclusion of Resolution XIII, the "Pious Clause," in the Charter of 1813.[12] Other members of the Clapham Sect also had active careers in India, including John Shore, Lord Teignmouth, who was governor-general of India from 1793 to 1797. He was a friend and biographer of Sir William Jones, the great philologist and linguist, and founder of the Asiatic Society. Shore was also one of the unofficial patrons of the Serampore Baptists. The Clapham Sect's membership also included Henry Thornton, of the Thornton-Sykes banking family, whose father John and brother Samuel were both directors of the Bank of England. All of these individuals' interests converged at the intersection of free trade, free commerce, and free Protestant evangelism: the Clapham Sect and their allies in England wanted to mold the East India Company's policies in India to suit their own ideological, commercial, and theological aims. It is no coincidence that the evangelicals who most influenced colonial policy in India were, or had been at one time, influential figures in British politics and finance, as well as active members of the English East India Company's administration.

The most important member of this group was undoubtedly Charles Grant, former trade superintendent of Bengal and member of the board of trade under the governor-general Lord Cornwallis. It was his 1792 tract *Observations on the State of Society among the Asiatic Subjects of Great Britain* that first put forward a cohesive program for the need for a civilizing mission to which the British colonial powers had to adhere as a sacred duty. The idea was that partial diffusion of Christianity as well as partial influence of moral improvements would construct what Homi Bhabha calls "a particularly appropriate form of colonial subjectivity."[13] This kind of subject formation would not only improve India's men and their morals but also help to cultivate the kind of laborers at the lower rungs of the administrative machinery that the colonial power desperately needed for the expansion of its commercial interests.[14] "Truth," in colonial discourse, was a weighted term with both philosophical and theological implications. Politically, the imperial project usually depicted Indians as infamous liars and perjurers. Yet the propagation of "Truth," written by British administrative officers and British missionaries, was also closely associated with the dissemination of Christianity. Grant's 1792 tract is the most famous example of this discourse around truth.[15] There are at least thirty-five instances of the word *truth* in this text, and in almost all cases, it is contrasted with the immorality, venality, and superstitions of the Hindus and Muslims. A characteristic example reads, "Of the Bengaleze, then, it is true most generally that they are destitute to a wonderful degree of those qualities which are requisite to the security and comfort of society. They want truth, honesty and good faith, in an extreme."[16] Elsewhere in the text, Grant elaborated on a similar theme:

> *False religion* shuns fair examination; before this test it cannot stand. Such is *the force of truth* that on the first promulgation of Christianity it prevailed against all the deceits, impositions, ignorance, prejudice and prescriptive authority of the ancient superstition. . . . *The Brahmins will not possess the instrument most effectual for the support of religious error and imposture, this is the power of the sword.*[17]

Grant's influence in Indian policies would only be superseded by James Mill's *The History of British India* (1817), which was the first and most important official history of the British conquest of India and the justification of the conquest as a civilizing mission.[18] In fact, Grant's *Observations,* Mill's *History,* and the Serampore Baptist William Ward's *Account of the Writings, Religion, and Manners of the Hindoos* (1813) were three of the most important influences on British colonial policies in India between 1800 and 1830.[19] Thomas Babington Macaulay, whose famous "Minute on Education" would change the landscape of pedagogy in India in 1835, in fact borrowed strongly from the language of "Truth" pioneered by earlier texts, including Grant's tract. The colonial ethnographic project, almost half a century old by the time Macaulay wrote his "Minute," remained the subtext of most works on British India that championed the civilizing mission through the nineteenth century. It should not come as a surprise then that the views of evangelically minded British administrators, from Charles Grant to Macaulay, were also echoes of opinions held by the missionaries who operated in Bengal—especially William Carey and the Serampore Baptists.[20] The relationship between the British administration in Bengal and the missionaries, it should be clear, was anything but straightforward prior to 1813. These entanglements between the missionaries, the official British administration, and the Bengali Hindu and Muslim *bhadralok* or gentry were, from the political perspective of the East Indian Company, deeply dangerous.

While Europe experienced an age of evangelical awakening in the eighteenth century, political circumstances in India posed challenges to the work of missionary preaching.[21] The great evangelical revival was widespread in English society and cut across the barriers of class. Even if the government did not officially approve of evangelism and conversion in the new Indian Empire, in reality almost all British administrators in India held strong evangelical beliefs and sympathized with missionary activity. On the other hand, because they were not legally admitted to the Company's Indian domains, missionaries had to carry out their evangelical activities in Bengal from bases in neighboring colonial holdings of other European powers like the Dutch, the French, and the Danish. For example, the Baptist Mission operated out of Serampore, a Danish settlement, upriver from Calcutta. Established by Carey in 1798, the Serampore Baptist Mission in many ways provided the blueprint for modern Protestant missionary activity in British India. The mission established its strong presence and secured patronage by inextricably entwining itself with unofficial and semi-official services provided to the East India Company's administration. But Carey, the most important Christian missionary in Bengal from 1796 until his death in 1834, also moved freely between Calcutta and Serampore. This was possible because missionaries, men and women, enjoyed free mobility within the British colony as linguists, ethnographers, preceptors, doctors, and nurses, among other occupations. As long as they did not mention "missionary" as their primary identity and occupation, they were free to travel and also largely free to proselytize within Bengal.

Evangelical missions expressed publicly what many British administrators felt privately—that saving the souls of their Indian subjects was an important part of the imperial project. Setting an infinite value on men's souls meant working for their salvation, which for the missionaries meant converting them to Christianity at any cost. Though one of the avowed aims of the Covenant of the Baptist Mission in India was to abstain from doing anything that could deepen Indian prejudice against the gospel, this wish was a facile cover to appeal to the public policies of the East India Company. It directly opposed the primary aim of the evangelical project: preaching Christianity, converting the heathens, and thereby freeing the minds of Indians from the snares of false religions like Hinduism and Islam. For evangelicals like the Serampore Baptists, the study of Indian people and Indian manners was also a study of their ways of life. This concern with moral uplift in the Indian domains was important because it changed how Britain and Britons viewed the imperial policy both at home and abroad. As Eric Stokes noted in his classic study *The English Utilitarians and India* (1959), "The improvement in moral tone . . . wrought in the character of the Englishman at his center . . . the emergence of a new ethic for a new society."[22] Transformed by the ingress of industrialization and imperial consolidation on one hand and the prolonged domestic and commercial uncertainty occasioned by the Napoleonic Wars on the other, British society looked for a new ethic of morality in the resurgence of evangelism and a new commercial ideology in free trade. As Stokes said, "Evangelism, the rock upon which the character of the nineteenth century Englishman was founded, owed much of its impetus to the Indian connexion. . . . The militant, aggressive Christianity of Clapham became a force in public life as much through the cause of Indian missions as through the campaign against the slave trade."[23] The ideology of free trade strongly opposed the vaguely mercantilist and monopolistic policies that the East India Company still followed, which had been roundly condemned by, among others, Adam Smith in *The Wealth of Nations* (1776). The laxness of the early East India Company policies regarding the religious morals of their heathenish Indian subjects was a cause of great disaffection too in the newly emergent evangelical perspective of the late eighteenth and early nineteenth centuries. It was also opposed to the way the evangelically inspired new British administrators saw themselves in relation to their chosen worldly vocation of ruling over Indians: actions performed in the world reflected on their personal ethical ideology, and therefore saving the souls of their Indian subjects was an issue of concern and demanded urgent resolution.

The goal of evangelism was understood to be a complete transformation of the soul, enacted through a deeply realized sense of repentance of sin and being saved through faith. The experience of being saved resulted in the sudden illumination of the state of one's soul and a realization of the path of duty to be enacted through "industry, frugality and perseverance." At the same time, this work would provide a sense of being graced with God's favor through worldly success realized in material terms.[24] These material benefits could of course then be channeled to evangelize and further the kingdom of heaven on earth. Although the East India Company's older colonial policies continued to be enacted in a new and unstable colonial possession, the reality on the ground shifted tremendously both at home and in India during the nineteenth century. The evangelical rhetoric of the civilizing mission was seen as far more appropriate to justify the expansions in the Indian Empire and to establish the Company's right to rule India without contest. By the 1810s, the Indian Empire was also far more stable and established, and the evangelical experiment could commence in order to usher in an age of reform in the colony.

This was done in such a way that the threadbare fiction of British administrators' noninterference in their subjects' religious practices could, with some strain, be maintained—at least until the Indian Mutiny of 1857, when it shattered completely. Carey was a Baptist missionary, whose sphere of work, for the duration of his life in India, was centered at Serampore—a choice necessitated by the ban that kept missionaries from preaching on British colonial soil. In his extraordinary account of the religious ferment in nineteenth-century Bengal, *Ramtanu Lahiri o Tatkaleen Bangasamaj* (Ramtanu Lahiri and Bengali society of the past), the Bengali educator and reformer Shibnath Shastri mentioned that the lawmakers of the fledgling British Empire in India did not allow missionaries to reside in Calcutta because they feared offending the religious sentiments of their new subjects. Shastri wrote:

> It was at this time that three European missionaries named Carey, Marshman, and Ward were living in Serampore town, a few miles north of Calcutta.

> During those days, Serampore was a Danish colony. The British government, newly in possession of their Indian domains, lived constantly in fear that if they allowed Christian missionaries to preach and evangelize in their lands, the fire of Indian revolution would flare up. It is due to this reason that the three missionaries had not been allowed to conduct their work in Calcutta.[25]

Between 1798 and 1812, an older generation of British civilians attempted to halt all missionary endeavors in India. They argued that missions posed a threat to British rule by inciting a spirit of religious animosity. This is corroborated by William Carey in his journal in 1799: "At Serampore we may settle as missionaries, which is not allowed here; and the great ends of the mission, particularly the printing of the Scriptures, seem much more likely to be answered in that situation than in this."[26] Carey was a fascinating historical witness to the strange and complicated relationship between the imperial British power and the great wave of missionary activity that began in the last half of the eighteenth century with the aim of "moral and material progress in India."[27] The legacy of Carey and his cofounders, William Ward and Joshua Marshman, popularly known as the Serampore Trio, was that they were the unlikely pioneers of "the conquest of India [through] a conquest of knowledge" rather than as evangelicals.[28] Away from the British capital city of Calcutta, they led a unique experiment in evangelism in Serampore.[29]

The East India Company's professed stand of religious noninterference continued to come into conflict with the need that many pious administrators felt for evangelical activity in India. These tensions can be seen in the British response to the Vellore Mutiny of July 1806, which was the first instance of violent uprising by native Indian soldiers against British officers. It led to the recall of William Bentinck, then governor of Madras, to England. (Bentinck would later return to India as governor-general in 1828, when he would helm the age of reform and oversee the legal ban on *sati* in 1829.) The mutiny also fueled alarm and anger in Britain, becoming a focal point of discussion for both proponents and opponents of evangelicalism. As chairmen of the East India House, Charles Grant and Edward Parry, the "pious chairs," had sent a number of clergymen to India, including Claudius Buchanan, the Calcutta chaplain and vice principal of the Fort William College.[30] William Carey was attached to the college as preceptor in Bengali, and he and Buchanan shared a mostly amicable relationship. Those who opposed allowing proselytization in India claimed that both men had incited the Vellore Mutiny by raising native fears of conversion to Christianity. Similar claims about missionary culpability, as we will see, recurred years later after the Indian Mutiny of 1857.

In the immediate wake of Vellore, George Barlow—the protégé of Grant and Parry, who was also considered favorable to missionaries, and was the Grant–Parry faction's chosen candidate for the governor-general in Calcutta after Cornwallis's death—wrote to the president of the Board of Control, Thomas Grenville: "Preaching Methodists and wild visionaries disturbing the religious ceremonies of the Natives will alienate the affections of our native troops and lead to the loss of India."[31] He also claimed that Carey had, in his preaching tours in Bengal, previously destroyed some Hindu idols—which so infuriated the native worshippers that Carey was apparently in danger of losing his life.[32] Such compulsive action, Barlow said, reflected poorly on the Company's much vaunted promise of nonintervention in the religious lives of the Indians. Such views were not uncommon. A large majority of the older generation of East India Company civilians, who had served in India since the conquest of Bengal at Plassey in 1757 or earlier, strongly opposed any effort at evangelism and conversion. They found support from the group led by Francis Baring, director of the East India Company since 1779 and cofounder of the Baring bank. Baring's group dissented against the platform of free trade and free evangelism in India supported by the dominant clique of Clapham Sect members like Grant, Wilberforce, Parry, and Thornton. Conservative older Company civilians thought that any attempt to convert Indian natives, seen to be supported by the Company-state, would lead to an uprising and loss of Britain's domains and trade in India.[33]

In 1805–1806, the Scottish theologian and Church Missionary Society missionary Claudius Buchanan published a pamphlet urging the government to set up an ecclesiastical establishment in British India. A principal agitator in India for the freedom to evangelize and convert, Buchanan favored an approach of mass conversion of Indians to the true faith. He had written widely on these beliefs. In an essay titled "Is an Ecclesiastical Establishment Necessary? Our Commercial Indian Empire Has Done Hitherto without It," Buchanan opined:

1. We know that the moral principles of our countrymen were, for many years, in a state of public trial . . . in relation to this commercial empire; and that Indian immorality was for a time proverbial.
2. It was observed in extenuation, . . . that India was remote from national observation and that seducements were powerful and numerous. . . . We are the only nation in Europe having dominions in

> the East, which being aware of these evils, declined to adopt any religious precaution to prevent them.

Buchanan had been frustrated by the imperviousness of Bengali Hindus to the light of Christ. "A wise policy seems to demand that we should use every means of *coercing this contemptuous spirit* of our native subjects," he noted.[34] This one comment in the book, coupled with his remonstrations on the lax private ethics of Company officials, merchants, and soldiers, infuriated old East India Company civilians and opponents of evangelism.[35]

One of them, Thomas Twining, actually precipitated the intense debate on Christianity and its effects on the political and commercial future of the Company in India. In an open letter to Parry in 1807, Twining castigated Buchanan's proposed plan to use force to convert natives, as well as the covert and overt support that people like John Shore and Grant gave to missionaries, which caused Indians to mistrust the Company's intentions.[36] A member of the Twining Tea Company family and an old Indian civilian, Twining objected to Buchanan's view that forced and compulsory conversion of native subjects was the East India Company government's ethical duty as Christian rulers of heathen India. For Twining, it was patently absurd to think that Indians would mildly accept such application of force:

> Notwithstanding the extraordinary observation of Mr. Buchanan, that the natives are not particularly attached to their religious opinions, I will venture to say that there is not, in the world, a people more jealous and tenacious of their religious opinions and ceremonies, than the native inhabitants of the East. Sir the people of India are not a political, but a religious people. They think as much of their Religion as we of our Constitution. They venerate their *Shastah* and *Koran* with as much enthusiasm as we our Magna Charta.[37]

In equating the veneration of Britons' political and civil liberty with Indians' freedom to observe their own religious rites and rituals, Twining was making a political comment about the duties of a colonial government headed by a commercial joint-stock trading company. Such a government had to pursue tolerant noninterference in the civil and religious rights of colonial subjects. Pointing out that the religious was political in India, Twining favored the old Company policy of concentrating on commercial and administrative dominance rather than ethical paternalistic duties of improving the colonized subject's lot.

But there was a deeper problem in his use of this comparison. By equating the religious freedom of Indians to British civil rights, he was collapsing the legal rights pertaining to Indians as British subjects to one factor: religious allegiance and observations of their rituals and customs, dependent on tolerance and noninterference from the colonial government. However, the proponents of evangelism and conversion argued that the Company's noninterference in the religious rights of the Indians was untenable as it harmed the moral duty of the British Empire toward their subjects. Britons should save the souls of their heathen Indian subjects, which could only be done by converting them to Christianity with the tacit support of the state. But this argument meant that the right to religious freedom, the only category under which Indians had enjoyed similar subject rights to British-born men and women, was whittled away and emptied of significance in the first half of the nineteenth century due to the increasing evangelical influence that could be observed in the British administration, in new institutions of English pedagogy, and even in the domain of Anglo-Indian law. Missionary apologia in favor of converting Indian subjects aroused suspicion, anger, and fear not merely among Indians but also among older and more conservative British administrators and other influential Britons in India. This apologia was clearly considered to be politically dangerous and a threat to the future of the empire. It also raised apprehensions about the disaffections of Indian subjects, which would turn out to be a justified fear.

In response to the activities of the Serampore Baptists, the interim governor-general of India, Sir George Barlow, issued a panicked ultimatum requesting that Carey stop publicly preaching without a license. The East India Company would not, of course, provide the license in any case. Carey was also asked to cease sending native preachers into British-Indian domains, chiefly into Calcutta. In addition, Barlow sought to repatriate Joshua Marshman and another missionary to England, an effort that generated the possibility of international scandal—involving Britain, Denmark, and the United States—on the legal question of rights of jurisdiction over domiciled subjects.[38] Joshua Marshman's son, John Clarke Marshman, would later assert the missionary point of view regarding this controversy. John Clarke Marshman was an important member of the Anglo-Indian evangelical establishment in his own right, the author of an influential history of India and the editor of *The Friend of India,* one of India's longest circulating newspapers. In his 1859 book *The Life and Times of Carey, Marshman and Ward,* he strongly refuted the view of missionary culpability in the Vellore Mutiny.

Marshman, who would also go on to author an influential history of India in 1869, wrote:

> Before the real cause of the mutiny was ascertained by investigation, it was ascribed to the wanton and needless violation of the religious usages of the natives by the Madras Government, and this opinion appears to have been adopted without inquiry by the Supreme Government in Bengal and at India House. The alarmists obtained an ascendency in the Supreme Council at Calcutta, and the missionary undertaking was denounced as the inevitable forerunner of rebellion and massacre.[39]

Undaunted by the East India Company's efforts to restrict preaching and evangelical activity, the missionaries took other steps at Serampore to advance their evangelical efforts—steps that would have much farther-reaching effects than their preaching in the streets and markets of Bengal.

THE LANGUAGE OF COMMAND AND THE LANGUAGE OF CONVERSION

In his foreword to Bernard Cohn's magisterial book *Colonialism and Its Forms of Knowledge* (1996), Nicholas Dirks commented that for the British, in India, "language was to be mastered to issue commands and to collect information."[40] Bengal was the province where the British imperial project started to take shape after 1757. In 1800, Lord Wellesley established the Fort William College to train young British administrators in the languages of command—and to create the ethnographic colonial knowledge production and collection project that Bhavani Raman has elsewhere called the Document Raj.[41] The Fort William College, which became the seat of training young British administrators in Calcutta, was fundamentally important in the evolution of the Bengali language: teaching Bengali to young civilians necessitated the production of the first Bengali language primers and dictionaries, undertaken by Carey and his Indian interlocutors at the college. In turn, these printed primers, many of which remained in use until the 1870s, led to the Bengal Renaissance of the nineteenth century and contributed to the extraordinary political and literary revolution that defines Bengali culture and the Bengali love of their mother tongue to this day. The oddness of the British evangelical influence in Bengal is that it led to a reformation of Indian religions, languages, and cultures rather than any momentous change in religious demography through conversions. The colonial project of archiving and recording all knowledge instilled a strong, almost Protestant, belief in textuality. One important guiding ideal for Lord Wellesley, governor-general of India, when he established Fort William College has now been forgotten: "To maintain and uphold the Christian religion in this quarter of the globe." Although the college was staffed by both British teachers and Indian *munshis,* with Muslim *qazis* and Hindu *pandits* to support them, all professors and lecturers had to swear an oath that they would not teach anything contrary to the Christian faith. It is perhaps not surprising, then, that the "*sahibs*" at Fort William were devout Christians or missionaries or both. The most famous of these *sahibs* was William Carey, who would be known to posterity as the "Father of Modern Missions." Given their close connections to evangelically minded British men, it is also not surprising that Indian teachers at the college, like Carey's *munshi* Ramram Basu, often showed deep interest in Christianity.

The simple truth is that evangelical missionaries came to India with the idea of converting Indians to Christianity. This conversion project, they assumed, would be best served by translating the Holy Word into the Indian languages and disseminating the principles of Christianity in preaching and in print, as the situation allowed. This led many missionaries to the enormous project of beginning to learn and analyze Indian languages. The Serampore Baptists embraced this project, beginning with Sanskrit and Bengali. They ended up writing new grammars to facilitate the translation and cultivating close ties to Indian intellectuals, which led to exchanges of ideas about the major Indian religions like Hinduism and Islam.[42] To disseminate this knowledge widely, Carey's associate, the printer William Ward, set up a pioneering printing press at Serampore. The most important technician at this press was Panchanan Karmakar, master typemaker and printer, who had assisted the British typographer Charles Wilkins in creating the first wooden Bengali typeface to print the first Bengali grammar by Nathaniel Brassey Halhed. Halhed, in turn, had translated the *Vivadarnavasetu* into English as *The Code of Gentoo* (Hindu) *Laws, or Ordinations of the Pundits* (1776). *The Code of Gentoo Laws,* commissioned by India's first governor-general, Warren Hastings, was the first attempt to understand Hindu precepts as they applied to the domain of legal disputation. Carey and Ward convinced Panchanan Karmakar to join them at Serampore in 1799, and he created another Bengali typeface for Carey's Bengali translation of the New Testament in 1801. In thirty years, only briefly interrupted by the great fire of 1810–1811, the Serampore Mission Press printed over 200,000 books in more than forty Indian languages, including

Bengali. These included missionary pamphlets, dictionaries, Bible translations, translations of Sanskrit and Persian epics, and textbooks used at Fort William College—all part of the evangelical apologetic program. But the Serampore Press also printed a large number of official documents for the East India Company's administration, including proclamations, codes and regulations, and correspondences. The press's commitment to such publications reflects the entanglements between the evangelical establishments and the administrative spheres of Company rule in the early nineteenth century in Bengal. The missionaries inaugurated the great age of print revolution in India and were instrumental in creating a public sphere where British policies were debated by Indians. Many of the important teachers and officials at Fort William College figured prominently in public sphere apologetic debates between 1810 and 1830. For example, Mrityunjay Bidyalankar, who left Fort William College in 1816 to become the Hindu *pandit* at the Calcutta Supreme Court, was a leading critic of the *sati* ritual. His written opinion in 1817, to the chief justice of the Sadr Diwani Adalat (Revenue and Civil Matters Court) at Calcutta, can be considered the first protest against *sati* by an Indian intellectual. This opinion is also the unacknowledged inspiration for the much more widely remembered pamphlets against *sati* written by Rammohan Roy, published in 1818 and 1820.

From the Serampore Baptists onward, in the period between 1800 and 1830, missionaries began to pay increased attention to cultivating Bengali, the language of the milieu they inhabited. British administrators also understood that if they were to have any success in exercising command over their Indian subjects, they would have to learn Indian languages, including Bengali. Therefore, what began as an evangelical Bible translation project soon evolved into a project to know Indians and their *dharma* better. This colonial project of knowledge-gathering was initiated so that the missionaries had better strategies to gain access to the souls of Indians and influence them to convert to Christianity, and so that British administrators could rule their Indian subjects in a more effective manner. It came to involve the close study of religious texts, epics, and mythologies, so that they could confidently answer any question a native inquirer might ask about why Christianity offered a better chance of salvation than Hinduism or Islam. Both missionaries and European Orientalists undertook the translation of Hindu and Islamic texts, as well as close study of the manners, customs, rituals, and lives of native subjects. These efforts led to the codification of ideas about India and Indians in the European mind, which would acquire monolithic status as time passed, becoming the pretext for continuing imperial domination in India.

Therefore, as the "Father of Modern Missions," William Carey with his colleagues left behind a blueprint for British cultural and political control of Indians. The evangelical character of their enterprise was contaminated and complicated further by the fact that Carey was at various times employed by the government (most prominently as a teacher at Fort William College), which all the while denied the missionaries legal status in India. Carey, Ward, and Marshman were active ethnographers and the propagators of colonial rule through appropriation and classification, always based in an idea of the subject as "Other." To reform, in other words, one needed a subject in need of that reform. Ward, Carey, Marshman, and their colleagues engaged in vigorous ethnographical, botanical, and historical research, which became a template for future endeavors by missionaries in India. The Serampore missionaries thus became part of the British colonial project by taking an active part in recording, classifying, and archiving information about Indian subjects, and by acting as enlightened paternalistic interpreters of colonial history and culture, subsuming the ungovernable, primitive, superstitious Indian natives into the narrative of the civilizing mission. With the innovations in print techniques ushered in by the Serampore Baptists, especially through the efforts of William Ward and Panchanan Karmakar, during the first fifteen years of the nineteenth century, the domain of apologetic disputation shifted decisively from the oral to the textual medium.

However, Indians would soon learn the language of modern colonial apologetics and use it to robustly defend their own faiths. In the 1810s, an important Indian actor stepped into the limelight: Rammohan Roy, perhaps one of the first global public intellectuals of the nineteenth century.[43] Rammohan Roy debated the Serampore Baptists on both Christian Trinitarian theology and reforms of Hinduism—a set of engagements that reflects the greater involvement of the Serampore Baptists in the political and social milieu of the times. And yet, there are latent linguistic and political tensions in the textual apologetic mission of the Serampore Baptists. Their venture depended on the dissemination of the printed text of the Bible in a highly distinctive Bengali idiom—with words often assigned new meanings, and new words coined to explain the basic tenets of the Scriptures—to a native Indian population of the unlettered or semiliterate. They paid somewhat less attention to the fact that this target population would find the language and the precepts strange and incomprehensible. Therefore, there was already a sense of unease among Indians about this colonial and evangelical effort at the command of Indian languages and, through it, of the souls of Indians.

Rammohan Roy's perceptive analysis posited a sharp difference between the belief in Christ and the ethical content of the Christian faith. The moment of encounter between Rammohan Roy and the Serampore Baptists was a direct result of the colonial and missionary desire to have a subject to reform. But this recalcitrant subject of attempted reform learned to speak back to missionary apologetics, as Rammohan illustrates in his own debates with Marshman and others. Unlike a Caliban, Indian intellectuals like Rammohan learned how to deal not in curses but with the same elegant tools of the textual analysis of sacred texts aided by rationalist deconstruction of the evangelizing colonial mission. Even for Rammohan Roy, command of English and analysis of Christian ethics were therefore absolutely necessary and formative in interrogating his own identity and his spiritual beliefs in the context of colonialism.

THE BIRTH OF APOLOGETICS IN COLONIAL INDIA

The Charter of 1813 revolutionized the East India Company's administrative function and commercial capacity in the British-Indian domains. By abolishing the Company's monopoly on trade, the Charter redefined it primarily as an administrative body, governing India under the strict oversight of the British Parliament. The Charter's "Pious Clause," meanwhile, legally allowed missionary activity in Calcutta and surrounding British-Indian domains for the first time. According to Penelope Carson, whose work has in many ways reshaped our understanding of the religious component of the East India Company's colonial project and civilizing mission, "The Company's 1813 charter was a significant turning point. . . . It was now required to provide for the 'religious and moral improvement' of its Indian subjects."[44] The decade after 1813 was one of great political, social, and religious ferment in Calcutta, and in Bengal—a period in which modern apologetics took shape. It is to this post-1813 moment that we will now turn.

Anyone with an interest in trade and commerce but also in the great religious ferment emerging in the new colonial capital—indeed, anyone who wanted to carve out a definitive place for themselves in these corridors of power—flocked to Calcutta in the early nineteenth century. These are the reasons that must have influenced Rammohan Roy, father of Indian modernity, to relocate to Calcutta permanently in 1814. Rammohan, the pioneering religious and social reformer, founder of the Atmiya Sabha (which later transmuted into the Brahmo Samaj), and moving force behind the ban on *sati*, arrived in Calcutta in 1814, a year after the renewal of the East India Company's Charter.[45] Rammohan moved to Calcutta at a time of great changes—intellectual, religious, and commercial—in the British administration as well as in Indian society. Having previously worked as a *dewan* or financial officer in charge of revenue under a number of British administrative officials in northern and eastern Bengal, Rammohan had a strong understanding of the British-Indian administrative system, a uniquely strong grasp of the English language and the nascent system of Anglo-Indian legal apparatus, and an influential network of connections with British officials and also with Indian elite entrepreneurs like Dwarkanath Tagore, Prosonnocoomar Tagore, Radhakanta Dev, and others. Indeed, he exhibited an attractive combination of practical experience working for the East India Company's administrative officers, linguistic prowess, and an intellectual bent toward theology and religious apologetics. This meant that he was able to speak to both the official and nonofficial British population of Calcutta in ways that were meaningful to them, addressing their concerns about the spiritual and religious uplift of "superstitious" Indians. At the same time, he was well positioned to engage with Indian interests in the British administrative policies shaping India as a colonial domain. This meant that as soon as he had settled into his residence at Calcutta, he found himself at the center of some of the debates that were roiling the nascent Indian public sphere.

Rammohan soon distinguished himself in both elite Bengali as well as Anglo-Indian society in Calcutta. By his own admission, he had received a thorough education in Persian and Arabic befitting the scion of a Brahmin family that had traditionally served as officials for the great landowning aristocratic families in Bengal. He also received instruction in Sanskrit sacred texts and literature as a high-caste Brahmin.[46] He had thoroughly studied the Quran, which served as the basis for his sustained interest in monotheism and Christian Unitarianism. His interest in Christianity was perhaps the result of his long service in the Murshidabad and Rangpur districts of Bengal under British civilians, a period of his life that has only recently started receiving the sustained interest it deserves because of how it shaped his attitude toward religion and religious scriptures. Brian Hatcher, following Shomik Dasgupta's intervention, has opened up the world that Rammohan inhabited before he arrived in Calcutta. During this formative period, he spent time at the frontiers of Bengal and at the margins of the East India Company's early empire.[47]

Rammohan's last assignment for his employer, John Digby, was a diplomatic mission to Bhutan in 1815, after which he mostly stayed in Calcutta, where he cultivated connections with influential members of Calcutta's elite Indian and British population. Among them were members of the Tagore families of both Jorasanko and Pathuriaghata, who would leave a lasting mark on Bengal through their philanthropy and cultural contributions. Two of his closest friends were Dwarkanath Tagore and Prosonnocoomar Tagore, and he acted as a mentor to Dwarkanath's heir Debendranath as well. He also developed close friendships and collaborations with the Unitarian minister William Adam, the educationist David Hare, and William Yates, who translated the Bible into the Bengali language. He simultaneously connected with a network of collaborators at Fort William College, who introduced him to the missionaries at Serampore.

Rammohan's relationship with the Serampore Baptists gave rise to a series of extraordinary exchanges—in essence, the first modern Indian apologetic debates, concerning the true nature of the divine in Christian theology. Rammohan's early fame spread through his pamphlets on translations of Indian sacred texts and his apologetic work on Christian theological texts, especially the Bible. His views on Christianity brought him into the limelight in Calcutta, which roiled with religious controversies after the Charter of 1813 allowed free evangelical activity in British-Indian domains. It is often forgotten that Rammohan earned his public prominence and authority in India through religious apologetics. He later parlayed this authoritative position into social and political reform, championing an indigenized Indian political thought that was a form of what C. A. Bayly has called "constitutional liberalism."[48]

By John Clarke Marshman's account, Rammohan first met William Carey and the Serampore Baptists in 1816, when he was about thirty-six years old. The missionaries—and the British ecclesiastical establishment at large—initially noticed Rammohan after the publication of his English translations of the *Kenopanishad* and the *Ishopanishad,* due to his unsparing attack on Hindu idolatry in the preface.[49] The Serampore Baptists printed Rammohan's early pamphlets against the practice of *sati* in 1819 and brought his work to the notice of the British public.[50] Rammohan's close association with the Baptists of Serampore and Calcutta included personal acquaintance with William Carey's nephew Eustace Carey, as well as with a young William Yates, whom he aided in the Bengali translation of the New Testament. A number of Rammohan's essays in English, including those on the issue of *sati,* were printed by the Baptists at Serampore or Calcutta.

Sophia Dobson Collet, one of Rammohan's acquaintances in London and later his biographer, quoted extensively from his preface to the translations of the Vedas. It is evident that he already had a clear vision of the kind of socioreligious reform that Hindu Bengali society required in order to modernize itself. And he made this claim for his own religious authority, based on his powers of textual exegesis:

> I have never ceased to contemplate with the strongest feelings of regret, the obstinate adherence of my countrymen to their fatal system of idolatry, inducing, for the sake of propitiating their supposed Deities, the violation of every humane and social feeling. And this in various instances but more especially in the dreadful acts of self-destruction and the immolation of the nearest relations under the delusion of conforming to sacred religious rites. I have never ceased, I repeat, to contemplate these practices with feelings of regret, and to view in them the moral debasement of a race.[51]

Rammohan ascribed immense importance to a system of social and moral reform, enacted through an iconoclastic insistence on the authenticity of the texts of sacred scriptures, rather than religious rituals and customs sanctioned through immemorial use. This must have seemed very familiar to proponents of evangelization, who aimed to destroy the "heathenish" superstitions that had led to the supposed decay of a once glorious and ancient civilization. The translation of the *Vedantasara,* or the *Abridgment of the Vedas* was reprinted in England by Mr. John Digby, the British civilian under whom Rammohan had served for many years in Rangpur. It attracted instant and widespread notice, beginning with the *Periodical Accounts of the Baptist Missionary Society* and the Church of England's *Missionary Register.* The editor of *The Times* in India, a certain Mr. D'Acosta, forwarded the translation to Abbé Gregoire, the bishop of Blois, which led to a correspondence between Rammohan and the bishop and an enduring connection with French intellectuals. Another of Rammohan's correspondents, George FitzClarence, 1st Earl of Munster and the illegitimate son of William IV, wrote about Rammohan in his travelogue:

> From his having observed the number of different modes of addressing and worshipping the Supreme Being, he naturally turned to his own faith with

> an unprejudiced mind, found it perverted from the religion of the Vedas to a gross idolatry, and was not afraid, though aware of the consequences, to publish to the world in Bengali and English his feelings and opinions on the subject.[52]

Rammohan was an instant sensation, and speculation abounded regarding the chances of his conversion to Christianity.[53] For example, in an appreciative American notice on Rammohan's publications, we find these comments:

> The author's great objective seems to be, to do away the worship of idols and introduce in its stead that of the one Supreme Being. Rammohan Roy is not a Christian, it is true, but the doctrine he inculcates differs very little from the Christian doctrine respecting the nature and the attributes of the Deity. If he can introduce it among his countrymen, it will be a great step taken towards advancing the cause of Christianity in the East.[54]

Yet Rammohan's apologetics were not a product merely of the colonial and evangelical encounter. As Brian Hatcher reminds us, Rammohan's early education and social world were steeped in the "discourse and culture of ethical formation that is known in Persian as *akhlaq*." Rammohan was therefore well versed, at least textually, in that older world of *bahas* and *munazara,* based on norms of shared civility and life experiences.[55] According to Hatcher, this *akhlaq* tradition was connected to an earlier, precolonial form of reform—that of "personal morality and public justice," which aimed to establish a sense of ethical consideration for the ennoblement of human beings and society.[56] Without considering this particular condition of Rammohan's mental make-up, both his non-Indian contemporaries and later commentators missed an important aspect of his engagement with the Christian Bible and with the Serampore missionaries. Rammohan's rapidly expanding international network of admirers perhaps did not realize the full extent of his reformist tendencies. They certainly took note of his radicalism as it related to the ethical rather than the miraculous content of the Bible, but beneath that was Rammohan's passionate desire to reform the Hindu religious system of his times and purge it completely of what he considered to be superstitious accretion of inhumane rituals. Rammohan was driven by an ideological commitment to transform Hinduism from an idolatrous, polytheistic religion into a rational, unitarian one. This reformist tendency had as much to do with his belief in Vedantic monotheism as it had to do with his conviction that conversion to

Christianity, especially in colonial India, was not driven by spiritual motives but by corrupted and base materialistic considerations.

In many ways, Rammohan was a pioneer in India of the study of comparative religious philosophies. His capacious mind used concepts that he found in other religious systems, including Islam and Christianity, to reinvent religious traditions like that of Vedic monotheism, which were to have a profound impact on the social, political, cultural, and religious history of India.[57] His first debates with the Serampore missionaries began after he had published his *Precepts of Jesus: The Guide to Peace and Happiness Extracted from the Books of the New Testament* in 1820.[58] In the introduction to the volume, in which he espoused a Unitarian view of Christian divinity, Rammohan explained that the *Precepts* emerged out of his conversations with many "teachers of Christianity." In examining the commentaries and writings of many authors on Christianity, he had found that belief in the Holy Trinity was seen as one of the fundamental tenets of Christian faith. He set out to question this belief. This famous series of apologetic debates emerged from the heated discussion between Rammohan and Joshua Marshman about Rammohan's decision to treat the Bible as a compendium of ethical messages rather than a divine message from God. In the eyes of the Serampore missionaries, Rammohan's emphasis on the ethical contents of the Bible verged decidedly on the agnostic. Rammohan disavowed the divinity of Christ and equating the importance of the Father and the Son in the Christian Holy Trinity.

In disagreeing with Marshman on Christ's divinity and the Trinitarian concept in the *Precepts of Jesus,* Rammohan used the tools of textual recordation—which the Serampore Baptists and other evangelicals had used to systematically devalue the cultural and religious beliefs of the colonized subjects—to brilliantly and decisively reject their premises.[59] In reply to Marshman, Rammohan used extensive quotations from the Hebrew and Greek New Testament to illustrate that there was no scriptural basis for Trinitarian belief. In 1823–1824, he published three *Appeals to the Christian Public in Defense of "The Precepts of Jesus."* Although the first two were printed by the Baptist Mission Press in Serampore, Carey and Marshman refused to print the third on the grounds that it was immoral and unchristian. Helped by Dwarkanath Tagore and Prosonnocoomar Tagore, Rammohan bought his own printing press, established it in Dharmatala in central Calcutta, and named it the Unitarian Press. He resumed both his journalism and his social and religious apologetics, publishing the third appeal from this press in 1823. This was the first printing press to be owned and managed entirely by an Indian.

As Rammohan perceptively pointed out, in matters of religious faith, people usually tended to adhere to their own beliefs due to prejudice or partiality. They were rarely amenable to opposing views, even if those views were more consistent with common sense, rationality, or even divine revelation.[60] The *Precepts* were exactly what Rammohan said they were: a compilation of the *moral precepts* found in the New Testament, parables and sayings of Jesus without the apostolic exegesis or an account of the miracles that could be attributed to the divinity of Christ. They were common-sense doctrines that would be useful in maintaining the peace and harmony of mankind, and which were incorruptible by metaphysical "perversions." Rammohan was preoccupied with the ethical content of the Bible:

> This simple code of religion and morality is so admirably calculated to elevate men's ideas to high and liberal notions of one God . . . and is also so well fitted *to regulate the conduct of the human race in the discharge of their various duties to God, to themselves, and to society,* that I cannot but hope the best effects from its promulgation in the present form.[61]

These precepts were supposed to be intelligible to learned and unlearned alike. Even from the short introduction, it is clear that Rammohan's preoccupation remained with rational and moral interpretation of religious faith, for the edification and uplift of society at large, rather than the advancement of narrow sectarian concerns.[62]

In a way, Rammohan was interpreting a sacred Christian text in order to find its applicability to the Indian way of life and to Indian Hindu society, in such a way that these ethics could be implemented in these life-worlds without the fear of conversion or evangelical interference. In his critical response, he parlayed the Christian scripture into sociopolitical ethics that Indian society should accept in order to project a particular image of itself to those who were not adherents of the same belief system:

> My view of Christianity is that, in representing all Mankind as the children of one Eternal Father, it enjoins them to love one another, without making any distinction of country, caste, color or creed; notwithstanding they may be justified in the sight of the Creator *in manifesting their respect towards each other,* according to the property of their actions and the reasonableness and the reasonableness of their religious opinions and observance.[63]

Such a rationalistic interpretation of faith in service to social reform was a new innovation in India, and the Baptist missionaries considered it to be a kind of Socinian (or Unitarian) heresy. Joshua Marshman was both horrified and enraged by what he saw as a perversion of both the Christian faith and the avowed goal of the evangelical enterprise in India.

One enduring form of the *akhlaq* tradition in which Rammohan was steeped was the syncretic accommodation of difference among communities of faith, which had been reflected even in the earlier forms of debate: the *tarkas* and *bahases* always followed certain norms of civility. We can see this assumption clearly in Rammohan's belief that Christianity and Christian apologetics, in their truest and sincerest form, engendered respect and civility among believers. He was to suffer a rude shock, as his innate training in *akhlaq* civilizational norms was challenged by the superior pose adopted by the Serampore Baptists, who went on a concerted and damaging attack against him. Marshman's answer was affixed to the Rev. Deocar Schmidt's refutation of the *Precepts* and published in the Baptist mouthpiece *The Friend of India*. Calling Rammohan an "intelligent Heathen *whose mind is as yet completely opposed* to the grand design of the Saviour's becoming incarnate," Marshman went on to say:

> In Britain and on the continent, there are many, who . . . will be *pleased beyond measure to find that by the testimony of an intelligent and unprejudiced Heathen, they have in Jesus Christ a Teacher who cannot search the heart.* Meanwhile the Deist and the Infidel will be no less delighted to find the miracles of Jesus Christ classed by a well-informed Hindoo with the Hindoo sage Agastya's drinking up the ocean in a fit of passion . . . and hence represented as being better suppressed though his precepts are excellent.[64]

Rammohan would, in one of his letters, note that the Serampore Baptists had called him "an injurer to the cause of Truth," an accusation that had obviously hurt him deeply.[65] It is clear from Marshman's tone that a civil and rational debate on the topic of faith within the colonial context was impossible. This was exactly what Rammohan had feared, and it required him to adapt his knowledge of the civilities of older Indian forms of apologetic disputation to a new colonial modernity. The main point of disagreement between Rammohan and Marshman was this: Marshman and his fellow missionaries believed that the divinity of Jesus lay at the root of his perception as the redeemer of lost souls, while Rammohan was completely uninterested in this idea of divinity. Instead, he sought a rational and monotheistic ideal of spirituality that could reform Indian Hindu society from the moribund superstitions he saw it encumbered with.

For a believer like Marshman, engaging with Christianity while refusing to embrace Christ's divinity or Christ's miracles was akin to heresy. In developing his system for the comparative study of religion, Rammohan had rationalized the theological and textual basis of the Holy Trinity. He hoped that this dialectic turn would prevent missionaries from elevating Christianity above Hinduism and Islam in their apologias and would therefore destabilize the racial hierarchy implicit in the civilizational rhetoric of the evangelical enterprise in India. If the Christian faith could be transmuted into mere moral precepts, to be followed by individuals and communities without any danger of conversion, the argument about the religious superiority of Christianity and the racial superiority of Europeans could not be upheld either. Marshman, by emphasizing that Rammohan was a *heathen,* made two retaliatory arguments: (1) that as an unbeliever he was excluded from a true understanding of Christ's message in the Bible and (2) that as a fallen soul he *could not be trusted* to truly understand the message of the Bible and give a correct interpretation of it. In fact, according to the Serampore Baptists, assuming that the Bible did not contain any divine messages that led to salvation, and instead only pointed human beings toward living a morally good life, was tantamount to blasphemy. Anyone who accepted Rammohan's thesis, that common sense and logic should dictate an understanding of the Bible as essentially a handbook on ethical living, was in danger of apostasy.

Rammohan made three separate answers to Marshman in his *Appeals to the Christian Public,* published from 1820 to 1823. It is in these appeals that the mood of the apologetics shifted, from theological debate to open confrontation of the methods of evangelization used by missionaries like the Serampore Baptists. Rammohan first objected to Marshman's use of the appellation "Heathen."[66] He called it "unchristian," arguing that his decision to separate the Bible's moral precepts from its stories of miracles was merely to safeguard the teachings of Christ against the "freethinkers and anti-Christians" who were a majority of the target demographic of the Christian missionaries in India. It was a clever and obviously provoking statement from Rammohan, who went on to make other more damaging accusations about the sincerity of native converts to Christianity. Specifically, he stated his sense of what "conversion" meant to the "natives" in the colonial Indian context, especially in Bengal.[67] For example, he wrote the following in 1824–1825:

> European missionary gentlemen and others for a period of upwards of twenty years, with a view to promote Christianity, distributing in vain amongst the natives, numberless copies of the complete Bible. . . . [Rammohan] saw a great number of Christian converts with a petition, which they intended to present to the highest ecclesiastical authority, stating that their teachers, through false promises of advancement, had induced them to give up their ancient religion.[68]

Rammohan was ill at ease at the insincerity of spiritual motive he thought he saw in the converts: "The Compiler felt indignant at their presumption, and suggested to the gentlemen as a friend, the propriety of not countenancing a set of men who, from their own declaration, seemed so unprincipled."[69] Rammohan first raised the issue of the abject failure of Christian missionaries in general, and the Serampore Baptists in particular, in their avowed goal of converting Bengalis. In a letter written to a correspondent in Baltimore in 1822, he stated, "I admire the zeal of the missionaries sent to this country but disapprove of the means they have adopted."[70] Rammohan pointedly said that he had resided for over twenty years in the same places as Christian missionaries and had observed them distributing countless bibles, pamphlets, and tracts on Christianity, in many vernacular languages, among Indians:

> During the last twenty years a body of English Gentlemen, who are called missionaries, have been publicly endeavoring in several ways to convert Hindus and Mussulmans of this country into Christianity. The first way is that of publishing and distributing among the natives various books, large and small, reviling both religions and abusing and ridiculing gods and saints of the former. The second way is that of standing in front of the doors of the natives or in public roads to preach the Excellency of their own religion and the debasedness of that of the others. The third way is that if any natives of low origin become Christians from the desire of gain, or from other motives, these gentlemen employ and maintain them as a necessary encouragement to others to follow their example.[71]

And yet this great evangelical bibliographic and linguistic enterprise had not made the slightest impression upon the minds of their intended converts. Indians, Rammohan insisted, were not prepared in the slightest to receive or understand the dogmas and mysteries of Christian theology. Rather, they used the pamphlets only for the paper they were printed on: "[Missionaries] have been so incautious and inconsiderate in their attempts to enlighten the natives of India. . . . The consequence has been that the natives in general instead of benefiting by the perusal of the Bible, copies of which they always receive gratuitously, exchange them very often for blank paper."[72] Thus, even though an enormous sum of money had been wasted in preparing these translations and in proselytization, the missionaries had in effect sabotaged their own mission. Rammohan said:

> Of the few hundred natives who have been nominally converted to Christianity, and who have been generally of the most ignorant class, there is grounds to suspect that the greater number have been allured to change their faith by other attractions, than by a conviction of the truth and reasonableness of those dogmas; as we find nearly all of them are employed or fed by their spiritual teachers, and in case of neglect are apt to manifest a rebellious spirit—a circumstance which is well known to the Compiler from several local facts.[73]

Rammohan's accusation that missionaries unethically used material means to save souls might have been influenced by an unfortunate encounter he had with Thomas Middleton, the first Anglican bishop of Calcutta.[74] This encounter was, at best, a tragicomic map of colonial misreading. At worst, it was a desperate and unsubtle effort by the official evangelical enterprise in India to gain a famous convert. The event was first mentioned in Sophia Dobson Collet's biography of Rammohan, which claimed his close friend and associate William Adam as the source. Adam, a well-known abolitionist, Harvard professor, and Unitarian minister in his later life, attributed his own conversion to Unitarianism to his collaboration with Rammohan Roy and William Yates on the translations of the New Testament into Bengali.[75] Mocked as the "Second Fallen Adam" by the evangelical establishment of both the Anglicans and the Baptists, Adam left behind some of the most important reminiscences of Rammohan's intellectual trajectory in the early years of his public career as a reformer and interlocutor between native Indians and the East India Company.

Bishop Middleton had arrived in India in 1814 under a cloud of uncertainty, since his patents did not clarify his position in relation to the East India Company and the various missionary groups operating in India. He believed that Indians were not ready for the Bible and that only a steady diffusion of arts and education would prepare the "oriental" mind to accept the gospel. Middleton had been acquainted with Rammohan since his arrival in Calcutta. His biographer mentions a letter of Middleton's to a friend at home in 1816, in which he mentions Rammohan, his admiration for Christianity, and his experiments with Unitarianism. Middleton obviously had high hopes of gaining Rammohan as a convert: "What will you say to me if he and his companions should be baptized at the cathedral by myself?!"[76] By April 1817, he knew better: "As to Rammohan Roy. . . . He seems, at present, to be as near a Deist as ever breathed. I see as little chance of his being a Christian, as of my becoming a Hindoo!"[77]

It is not inconceivable that he wanted to meet Rammohan one last time in 1820 or 1821, after the publication of the *Precepts,* since it clearly showed that Rammohan was still very interested in the ethical content of the Christian faith. According to William Adam, the meeting occurred in the summer of either 1820 or 1821. After his visit to Middleton, Rammohan arrived at Adam's home in a state of confusion in the afternoon and reported indignantly that Middleton had, rather unsubtly, pressed him to convert to Christianity. This unsolicited request and invitation to accept another faith and cement it through the public performance of a celebrated baptism was, for Rammohan, a breach of the etiquette of hospitality in itself. The very public nature of the baptism would serve to highlight the glories of a successful civilizing mission and celebrate Middleton as a saver of Indian souls. According to Adam's account as reported by Dobson Collet, Middleton compounded his errors by saying that such a change of faith would open the path of a great career to Rammohan: "He would be honored in life and lamented in death—honored in England as well as in India—his name would descend to posterity as that of the modern Apostle of India." Middleton may have meant this innocently enough, but to the redoubtable Rammohan, it seemed as if the bishop was trying to buy his conscience as well as his faith:

> "The sting of the offence was this," reports Mr. Adam: "he was asked to profess the Christian religion, not on the force of evidence, or for the love of truth, or for the satisfaction of his conscience, or for the benefit of his fellow-men, but for the sake of the honor and glory and fame it might bring him. This was utterly abhorrent to Rammohan's mind. It alienated, repelled, and disgusted him."[78]

It was around this time that Rammohan started publishing a short-lived periodical called the *Brahman Sevadhi* or the *Brahmanical Magazine: The Missionary and the Brahmin.* Aimed at religious polemics, as its name suggests, this periodical lasted for only four irregular issues between 1821 and 1822. At that point, Rammohan began publishing the much more famous *Sambad Kaumudi* (The Enlightenment Newspaper) under the early stewardship of his editor Bhabanicharan Bandopadhyay. The four issues of the *Brahman Sevadhi* were concerned mainly with contesting the letters of an unnamed *padri* or missionary from Serampore, quite possibly Marshman, who had printed a letter attacking what Rammohan termed the "supposed gross irrationalities and other faults present in all the Hindu Shastras" in the Baptist mouthpiece the *Samachar Darpan* (The Mirror Newspaper).[79]

This letter was printed on July 14, 1821. Rammohan expended considerable energy and eloquence in the *Sevadhi* not only refuting the charges but also attacking what he saw as the main irrational paradox behind Christian Trinitarianism: the old question of Jesus being both the Son of God and Son of Man and also God incarnate. However, it is the introduction to the four issues that merits examination here. This was a scathing criticism of both the missionary approach to conversion and British support—both official and unofficial—for missionaries, in far more vituperative language than he ever used in his English-language apologetic pamphlets. Rammohan pointed out that the first apostles all preached the faith of Christ in lands and empires where the state religion was not Christianity. As such, their activity had a core of true belief, which was tested in the face of real danger of retribution. Those who chose to convert to Christianity in those lands did so out of sincerity and as a result of true spiritual awakening. In India, the situation was completely different. India was ruled by the British, and the rulers were of the Christian faith. The missionaries, instead of belonging to a minority or being oppressed themselves, evangelized with the full knowledge and tacit consent of their countrymen, the British administrators: "In Bengal where the English are the sole rulers and where the mere name of Englishman is sufficient to frighten people; an encroachment upon the rights of her poor timid and humble inhabitants and upon their religion cannot be viewed in the eyes of God or the public as a justifiable act."[80] Since the power of the British was already absolute, Rammohan argued, the evangelical mission and conversion efforts were cruelly oppressive when it came to the already impoverished, weak, and terrified Bengali subjects. Rammohan's own grounding in the eighteenth-century Persianate *akhlaq* tradition meant that, to him, true faith had to bear markers of both reason and a sense of justice. Therefore the civilizing mission was neither in the spirit of true evangelism nor worthy of righteousness or praise, since actual or threatened violence could be used to induce Indians to accept the faith of the rulers. Indians could also be induced into converting to Christianity for the sake of material help promised by missionaries, which could alleviate their desperate poverty and hunger. In other words, Rammohan did not believe that there existed a discursive space for debating the merits of true Christian evangelism or conversion in Bengal.[81]

Taking a historical approach to the issue of religious tolerance and the old contentious dictum of *cuius regio, eius religio,* Rammohan condemned the unofficial sanction enjoyed by missionaries in British-Indian domains, which he felt emboldened them. The East India Company had allowed Indians to practice their faith undisturbed with leniency and toleration in the eighteenth century. Rammohan said that from Genghis Khan to the Arakanese pirates of eastern Bengal, invaders and conquerors had always oppressed their defeated subjects with regards to their religion and forced them to accept the religion of the rulers. It was to the credit of the East India Company that the British had not done so for the first half-century of their rule. For Rammohan, that earlier tolerant approach, when contrasted to the zealous evangelical efforts in Bengal since 1813, made their approbation of missionary activity even more offensive to their Indian subjects. The obloquy and calumny that missionaries directed against Indian religions, coupled with their inducements to material maintenance and advancement, attracted only the lowest, meanest, and poorest of Indians to the Christian missionaries. As a result, the entire community of native converts were themselves a great disgrace to the evangelical enterprise in India. The historical precedent of victors imposing their religious norms on a defeated and subjected people did not excuse the immorality and crudeness of the methods used to do so, especially for the British, who prided themselves on their civilizational mores and rule of law. He asked both the missionaries and the British administration to reflect on the fact that Truth and righteousness (*dharma*) might just as well reside in the poor cottage of a Brahmin as in the mansions and palaces of the foreign rulers of India. This salvo also clearly pointed to the close connection between religion and the changing nature of imperial governance of India.

A similar sense of disillusionment and distrust of converts and conversion is evident in Rammohan Roy's correspondence with Rev. Henry Ware, a renowned Unitarian minister and the fourth Hollis Professor of Divinity at Harvard, who was instrumental in establishing the Harvard Divinity School.[82] Ware sent letters to both William Adam and Rammohan Roy, inquiring after the possibilities of future success of Christian evangelism in India, and his letters to them were thereafter published in a pamphlet titled *Correspondence relative to the Prospects of Christianity and the Means of Promoting Its Reception in India* (1825).[83] A small notice affixed to the volume proclaims that the profits from its sale will be "wholly applied to the purpose of aiding the cause of Christianity in India." Ware's letter to Rammohan was dated April 24, 1823, and contained the same twenty questions that Ware had presented to William Adam.[84] A subset of the questions are as follows:

1. What is the real success of the great exertions which are now making for the conversion of the natives of India to Christianity?
2. What is the number and character of converts?
3. Are those Hindoos who profess Christianity respectable for their understanding, their morals, and their condition in life?
4. Of what caste are they generally? And what effect has their profession of Christianity upon their standing?
5. Are they Christians from inquiry and conviction, or from other motives?

Ware's letter to Rammohan reflects the popularity of the latter's apologetic theological tracts in both Britain and the United States—and the great success of apologetics parlayed through the medium of print, locally and globally. Ware mentioned that the aim of his missive was to inquire about the possibility of a Unitarian evangelical mission's success, if such a mission were to proceed from the United States to India. He was eager to know the opinions of "a native of India, bearing such marks of clear and enlightened views, and of extensive and accurate learning, as would do honor to the best educated European divine."[85] In a postscript, Ware asked one more question, to which Rammohan would pay close attention in his reply: "With the complete knowledge which you possess of the character both of the Hindoo and of the Christian Theology, and of their moral influence and tendency, do you think it desirable, that the inhabitants of India should be converted to Christianity; to what degree desirable, and for what reasons?"[86] This was an important question, since it seemed to offer the possibility of a reasoned dialogue on the inherent merit of Islam and Hinduism in the context of Indian culture and society, instead of insisting on the a priori theological superiority of Christianity and the necessity of conversion of Indians based on that metaphysical premise. In a letter dated February 2, 1824, Rammohan answered in thoughtful detail, "as my knowledge authorizes and conscience permits." His exasperation with the Serampore missionaries shines rather brightly in this letter, even at a remove of two centuries. Certain important facts also emerge from his answers. For one, even until 1824, the number of actual converts was very low. Rammohan claimed that there was a total of five converts in all of Bengal. Even if he underestimated, numbers were small enough to be insignificant, and backsliding was endemic. His letter also pointed out that Indian converts were generally not from the "respectable" classes—that is, there were no high-caste converts. On the question whether Indians converted due to inquiry and conviction, or other reasons, Rammohan answered wryly:

> A native embracing Christianity should be remunerated for his loss of caste by the gift of five hundred rupees, with a country born Christian woman as his wife; and while this report had any pretension to credit, several natives offered from time to time to become Christians. The hope of any such recompense being taken away, the old converts find now very few natives inclined to follow their example.[87]

He added that there were thousands of outcaste Indians who would change religious profession for "the smallest hope of worldly gain." If missionaries were willing to maintain the lowest of the low among the outcastes of India, he noted, then Hindu society at large would have no objection. Rammohan had apparently offered to send as many such men as desired to a missionary acquaintance, if he were willing to provide and keep these potential converts at a salary or stipend of no more than eight rupees a month. This was quite a large sum for the laboring poor, and though Rammohan was most likely being sarcastic, he was firm in his conviction that most Indian conversions occurred due to the temptations of financial respite offered by missionaries. Rammohan was equally clear that the failure of the evangelical conversion mission among the generally educated and financially well-off Hindus was *not* the same as a lack of desire to learn English. In fact, Rammohan surmised that two-thirds of the native population of Bengal "would be exceedingly glad to see their children educated in English learning."[88]

From his first *Appeal* to his reactions to Middleton's supposed offer of worldly renown and his response to Ware's letters, it is clear that Rammohan saw true conversion as based in a conviction in the superior merit of the religion one hoped to adopt. This conviction could only arise from a thorough study of scriptures, and an analysis of their respective merits. The poorer class of Indian converts would thus never count as true in their faith, since they presumably lacked the education or knowledge to make reasoned, logical, and rationalist inferences about the comparative merits of Christianity, Islam, and Hinduism. And Middleton's words, however innocently meant, probably convinced Rammohan that there was something hollow about the evangelical enterprise in India—the most important evidence of this insincerity being the offers of worldly gains to induce Indians to convert. Ultimately, he sensed an inherent tension between Christianity's moral merits as a code of ethics and the missionaries' "unchristian" interpretation of the message of evangelization.

This tension also appears in a number of Rammohan's other theological works. He continued to encourage the dissemination of the morals of the New Testament as a corrective to the idolatry and polytheism of Hindu Bengalis, and he positively aided missionaries like Adam and later Alexander Duff in establishing schools and creating a framework for English pedagogy in India.[89] But it was the means and methods of evangelism, and the missionaries' conversion efforts, that he found distasteful. In the process, his written apologetics embraced a discourse of profound suspicion about motives for conversion to Christianity.

In the nineteenth century, Bengali Hindus and Muslims understood conversion to Christianity above all as an acceptance of an alien belief system over all that was familiar. It was a sundering of social associations. And, ultimately, it was a refusal to uphold responsibilities to one's family and community of faith. It was perceived as an act of emotional and spiritual violence against both the family and the community at large. For natal communities that lost members through conversion, it seems that one of the only ways to reconcile or even attempt to understand such violence was to assign material rather than spiritual reasons to the act. To convert, according to this logic, would in some way erase the markers of race and ethnicity for Indians and open the doors of equal opportunities alongside the British.

This accusation, that native conversions were not sincere but motivated by the convert's desire for material gain, would permanently damage the credibility of both the missionaries and the native converts. Rammohan originated a series of stereotypes about Christian converts in his apologetic debates that were disseminated widely through the medium of print. These stereotypes would prove to be enduring and inescapable. Every native Indian convert thereafter, even high-caste ones, from Krishnamohan Banerjee in 1832 to Brahmabandhab Upadhyay in 1891, would face this charge of "unprincipled" insincerity. Each would also have to try and find their own place within the complicated sociocultural matrix of Indian communitarian networks. Rammohan's claim that native converts were profoundly and characteristically insincere, simply mimicking the colonial overlords for material gain, was one of the first Indian critiques of the evangelical project's efficacy—and it has informed misreading of the public act of conversion in India to this day. It continues to propel religious apologetics in the digital mediums of the twenty-first century, fueling widespread violence and derogatory slurs in India: those who choose to convert are often called "rice Christians" or simply "rice bags," referring to the money or food they might receive from the missionaries.[90]

CONVERSION, APOLOGETICS, AND THE IMPOSSIBILITY OF DIALOGUE

Rammohan's first public prominence in India and his earliest networks of communication in Britain, France, and the United States emerged out of the apologetic debates on Christianity and Hinduism, but the scholarship on Rammohan has usually focused on his reformist practices and his cosmopolitan and constitutionalist political ideologies. C. A. Bayly has argued that Rammohan Roy inaugurated a "progressive narrative of liberal constitutionalism" between 1822 and 1833 that went on to define the discourse on the constitutional history of India.[91] This liberal trajectory, Bayly argued, was characterized by Indians having equal access to colonial justice by serving on juries and through the operation of a free press in India that would lead to the emergence of an Indian public sphere.[92] Partha Chatterjee has criticized this account, rightly pointing out that this liberal moment was incredibly short-lived, not only due to the changing form of imperial governance in the two decades after Rammohan Roy but also because liberalism came to paradoxically allow for the coexistence of structures of democratic governance in the Western metropolis, while creating ideological justifications for repressive colonization abroad—as in India.[93] However, neither Bayly nor Chatterjee fully engaged with Rammohan's continued investment in the analysis of religious ideas and religious practices both in India and abroad—which ultimately, I argue, became a basis for his understanding of moral and political virtue.

In part, Rammohan was motivated by legal concerns as well, due to what he saw as undue preferment given to converts under the Anglo-Indian legal system. Rammohan's anxieties about the long-term effects of evangelism and conversion programs in India were exacerbated by the Jury Bill debates of 1826.[94] In his essay on the evolution of the Jury Bill, James Jaffe explains that one of the major problems that British lawmakers in India faced was the difficulty of ascertaining the veracity of testimonies presented before a juridical institution or arbitration court—akin to the disputation processes carried out before Indian *panchayats.* The problem, according to the British civilian Mark Wilks, was "the defective morals of the people." Veracity of testimonials could only be asserted if they were delivered under oath, and followers of Hinduism and Islam were, according to Wilks, significantly devoid of truthfulness anyway as these religions failed to "bind the consciences of men." Only oaths taken on the Bible could be a guarantee of true testimonials. According to Jaffe, oath-taking was therefore as much a religious issue as it was a legal one, and Wilks's report led to entrenched British prejudice against Indian participation in the legal system. Wilks had been educated for a career in the clergy and thus, we can assume, embraced evangelical attitudes about India even in his subsequent career as an administrator and civilian.[95] How did this concern about the religious character of oath-taking affect India? Jurors, like witnesses, had to take an oath. According to Wilks and those of his ilk, only jurors who could swear on the Bible could be trusted to be both truthful and dependable. This underlying bias in favor of Christianity meant that when Sir Williams Wynn, chairman of the East India Company's Board of Control, brought the Jury Bill to the floor of the British Parliament, a clause was inserted that only Christians were allowed to sit on juries in cases where the defendants were Christian. Therefore, while native convert Christians could serve on both grand and petty juries in India, regulations in Madras, Bombay, and Bengal made it impossible for Hindus or Muslims to serve. Further restrictions on eligibility to serve on juries centered on the construction of who constituted a proper "British subject." This meant that not only native Indian converts but also Anglo-Indians born of British mothers and Indian fathers were unfit to serve on juries.[96] This also narrowed the definition of colonized Indians to mere "subjects" rather than British subjects. But the damage had already been done in terms of Indian disaffection with what they perceived to be undue preferment of native Christians over Hindus and Muslims, even elite highborn ones.

Rammohan's correspondence with British civilian and ecclesiastical personages took up the creation of categories of colonial and legal difference based on religious criteria. His opposition to the use of colonial difference to disbar Indians, either Hindu or Muslim, from serving on juries rested on the idea that "introducing religious distinctions into the judicial system of the Country" would "stir up a spirit of religious intolerance." In an 1828 letter to J. Crawford, Rammohan clearly laid out his problems with the Jury Bill and his frustration with the elevation of native Christians above their Hindu or

Muslim fellow countrymen, based only on the superior merit of having converted to the religion of the British rulers:

> In his famous Jury Bill, Mr. Wynn, . . . has by introducing religious distinctions into the judicial system of this country, not only afforded just grounds for disaffection among the Natives in general, but has excited much alarm in the breast of everyone conversant with political principles. Any Natives, either Hindu or Mohammedan [Muslim] are rendered by this Bill subject to judicial trials by Christians, either European or Native, while Christians, including Native Converts are excluded from the degradation of being tried either by a Hindu or Musalman [Muslim] juror, however high he may stand in the estimation of society. This Bill also denies to both Hindus or Musalmans the honor of a seat in the Grand Jury even in the trials of fellow Hindus and Musalmans. This is the sum total of Mr. Wynn's late Jury Bill, of which we bitterly complain.[97]

Among Rammohan's objections to such religious discrimination was the fact that Hindus and Muslims of the highest social standing were still not considered fit to judge Christians. He objected that native converts, whom he considered to be both insincere and mendacious, were to be elevated above the elite Hindus and Muslims of India, from the *bhadralok* and *ashraf* gentry: "Christians, *including Native Converts,* are exempted from the degradation of being tried either by a Hindu or a Mussulman juror."[98] From the evidence that was available to him regarding the East India Company's policies in India, Rammohan was apprehensive that ideas of difference and discrimination between Indian religions under Anglo-Indian law, like the one presented in the Jury Bill, would bring about an internal split among the Indian body politic on the question of political citizenship. Though Wynn evidently changed his opinions, and by 1829 favored the admissibility of Hindus and Muslims to the upper ranks of the British administration "without distinction of blood and color," as a result of a petition by Rammohan and his supporters, the debate continued.[99] Even after Rammohan, the vexed question of which Indians could be allowed to serve on juries in the Anglo-Indian legal system—and whether distinctions ought to be made based on their religious affiliations—would continue, with the tabling of J. E. D. Bethune's so-called Black Act of 1849 and the infamous Ilbert Bill controversy of 1883. For Rammohan at least, the issue was clear: native Christian converts, for both moral and political reasons, could not be given legal or judicial rights over Hindus and Muslims, whom he considered to be India's more prominent and long-standing communities of faith, just on the basis of their adopted religion.

Partha Chatterjee is correct in asserting that the search for a linear narrative of nationalism and democratic political movements from Rammohan's liberal constitutionalism to the early twentieth century can "only seem foolhardy, or else even more ignobly, a fall from radical promises to shameful compromise."[100] Even within the broadly liberal contours of Rammohan Roy's religious and political beliefs, his opinions on conversion to Christianity and on evangelism in India show a surprisingly narrow and orthodox strain. His views on the supposed insincerity and mendacity of native Indian converts led to a rhetoric of suspicion and othering of India's Christians over the next two centuries and into the present day.

A narrative can be traced from Rammohan to the idea of Hindu nationalism in the twentieth century: the creation of categories of religious differences as the basis of political identity. By this, I do not mean to search for a prehistory of communalism, an effort that has been stringently critiqued by Ayesha Jalal. Rather, I mean to show that religious tensions surrounding conversion to Christianity began to flare in Bengal as early as the 1810s.[101] Nor do I mean to say that Rammohan created the politics of religious difference in South Asia. But the religious apologetics of the 1810s and 1820s do make clear that Rammohan and other Indians like him were aware that parlaying such religious differences into legal and judicial discriminations would lead to widespread disaffection among the East India Company's Indian subjects. Indian intellectuals suspected that this was especially true when the members of the religious group shown preferment by the British administration, in this case the native Indian converts, were supposedly little respected by their own countrymen—in particular, those countrymen who had prominent social and religious standing and collaborated closely with the Company. In other words, Rammohan's interactions with the evangelical enterprise in India demonstrate an early and growing awareness by Indians of the close connections between racial and religious difference—and the centrality of parlaying that difference in defining religious identities. This awareness, religious, social, and political, was the first impetus to the formation of an Indian public sphere: defending their own religion and their communitarian identities against the encroachment of Christian evangelical apologetics was possible within this public sphere, and Indians would go on to defend their faith robustly, raucously, passionately, in both vernacular languages and in English, for a century afterward. They would thereby create the discourse of suspicion and difference that would lead to greater and greater religious communal divisions within India's many faith communities.

The profound unease as well as the deep admiration that a figure like Rammohan evoked among Indian, British, and international audiences, and the sustained public sphere debates that originated from his efforts to create a dialogue on equal terms between Christian believers and Indians, were defeated in part by the racial superiority performed by his antagonistic missionary interlocutors but also because of his own contempt for Indians who converted. As a result, this early and somewhat forgotten episode of apologetics between Rammohan and the Serampore Baptist missionaries highlights how native Christian communities of faith in India were othered by their fellow countrymen, as well as by the evangelical and British colonial machinery. These debates, which occurred a decade before Rammohan's efforts to ban the practice of *sati* in 1829, actually created the apologetic politics of religion that would have an immense effect on the evolution of nationalism in India. I therefore argue that the Christian apologetic controversies prepared the ground for Rammohan's success in the public engagement in the debate on *sati*. It is not the ban on *sati* in 1829 but the moment of Rammohan's debates with the Serampore Baptists between 1815 and 1822 that should be accepted as the founding moment of the Indian public sphere in the historiography. The Christian conversion debates also set the ground for an enduring Indian socio-political tradition of an oppositional and negative definition of religious identity in both communitarian and personal terms. One was a Hindu or Muslim because one was not a Christian. If someone had converted to Christianity, the rupture of all communitarian bonds left that person bereft of defined legal, political, or religious personhood. This aspect of Rammohan's life and work needs to be better integrated into the historiography that seeks to posit him as the liberal founding father of modern India.

Apologetics in colonial India, from the very beginning, constituted a paradoxical genre. The early efforts at reasoned theological debate were unsuccessful, due to a lack of mutual racial and religious respect, which is clear from the tone of Marshman's replies to Rammohan's *Precepts*. The suspicions of bribery and insincerity on one hand and the fear of heathenish corruption and slyness on the other doomed the project to a fate of increasingly intolerant intersecting monologues. The problem in the conceptual categorization of an apologetic and partial modernity in colonial India is often due to a conflation of the two meanings of *apologia*, with more emphasis on the negative meaning than the rhetorically positive one. As the Rammohan Roy–Serampore Baptists controversy shows, apologetics—in and of itself a formal rational defense of one's own position regarding one's faith—became, in India, a contest of personal and racial vilification. This version of apologetic debate encouraged a debasement of the characters of chief personages of each religion. These apologetic contests ultimately created a template of communal tensions, suspicions, and othering of minority communities of faith, exemplified by the rhetoric used against native Indian converts.

A close study of the major Indian intellectuals of the early nineteenth century, including Rammohan, shows how deeply anxious some of these English-educated elite figures were to preserve their hereditary religious and cultural rituals and practices within the family and in the extended communitarian and kinship networks. Their reasoning, from Rammohan's orthodox Hindu nemesis Raja Radhakanta Dev onwards, was that if Hinduism had to be reformed, it had to come from within Hindu society. It had to be done with reasoned deliberation and debate that accounted for the traditional customs and scriptures, while conceding to British morals and ethics with performative grand gestures toward forms of Enlightenment rationality percolating into India.[102] Rammohan himself ascribed to this view. If we are to believe his biographer Sophia Dobson Collet and his interlocutor Alexander Duff, a missionary, this spirit of reformism from within was, paradoxically, inspired by a knowledge of the Protestant Reformation in the sixteenth century. Perhaps it is this event that has closer parallels to the events in nineteenth-century Bengal than the Italian Renaissance:

> Having read about the rise and progress of Christianity in apostolic times, and its corruptions in the succeeding ages, and then of the Christian Reformation which shook off these corruptions and restored it to its primitive purity, I began to think that something similar might have taken place in India, and similar results might follow here from a reformation of the popular idolatry.[103]

As we will see, such views had a long afterlife that included the aftermath of the Great Rebellion of 1857, when both Indian intellectuals like Sir Syed Ahmed Khan and hardened colonial administrators like Charles Trevelyan suspected overzealous Christian evangelizing by missionaries and colonial officials to be one of the major causes of the uprising.[104]

In critically analyzing Rammohan Roy's paradoxical admiration for Christianity as an ethical code of conduct, as opposed to his profound distaste for conversion efforts and native Indian converts, I do not intend to make a value judgment about the necessity of conversion over reformist tendencies within Hinduism. However, I do intend to argue that the language of reform used by the Bengali elite and intelligentsia, known as the *bhadralok*, beginning with Rammohan Roy, constantly obscured the oppression of and enmity toward members of their own communities who chose to convert to a different faith. The rhetoric of reform, if read against the grain, shows us the dark side of the mirror to the more widely known narrative of enlightenment and renaissance in nineteenth-century Bengal. It clearly shows that the language of positivism, liberalism, and enlightenment obscured the intolerance practiced against those who refused to conform, especially when they did so by embracing conversion to Christianity. The discourse of reform effectively created a genealogical pattern of oppression and exclusion of Indians who chose to leave their natal communities and convert to any religion other than the one into which they had been born.

Evangelism in Bengal would undergo a profound change in the late 1820s and early 1830s with the rise of English pedagogy. As demand grew for Indian administrators in the lower echelons of the English East India Company's government, educational institutions where English was the mode of instruction became the new site of contention between missionaries and Indian intellectuals. From the pages of printed pamphlets and periodicals, the battle for the souls of Indians would move into the public sphere and the law courts. The high-caste Bengali schoolboy (and sometimes his child bride) would become the new subject of debates about modernity, morality, and validity of conversions. The rhetoric of exclusion and threat of disinheritance would be used in novel ways to exercise tighter control over the community. It would also be used to justify the excesses of systemic and institutional hegemonic control over narratives of national belonging. Chapter 2 will discuss this second wave of Indian resistance to evangelism and the apologetic debates that developed around this alienation and antipathy.

CHAPTER TWO

The Contest over High-Caste Conversions

In his poem "Ingraji Nobo-Borsho" (English New Year), commemorating the beginning of 1852, Ishwar Chandra Gupta wrote:

> Look upon those red faces and pull closer the ham,
> Don't care for *Hinduani*—damn, damn, damn;
> Whatever my fate might be, I'll eat at the table,
> Drowning in Duff's tub, I'll go to the chapel.[1]

Ishwar Gupta (1812–1859) was a poet, author, rabid gossipmonger, and editor of the popular Bengali periodical *Sambad Prabhakar* (The Sun News).[2] His lifetime traversed the period between the renewal of the Charter of 1813 and the inclusion of the "Pious Clause" to the 1857 uprising that brought about the end of the Company Raj and the takeover of the Indian Empire by the British Crown. The rapid changes that occurred in India, and specifically in elite Bengali Hindu society in Calcutta, fascinated and troubled Ishwar Gupta in equal measure. He adopted the pose of a weary but attentive chronicler of these changes in the first half of the nineteenth century. Much of his poetry, comprising social satire and yellow journalism, focused on the decadence and corruption in Bengali Hindu society, especially among the elite *grihastha,* or householder middle-class families, and *abhijato,* or aristocratic upper-class families. Ishwar Gupta's poetry therefore is a historical record of the cultural and religious anxieties that plagued the aristocratic and educated Hindu elite of colonial Calcutta. His poetry is also an example of the kind of public religious apologetics that Indians, after Rammohan Roy, began to use to counter Christian missionary evangelism.

Ishwar Gupta reserved his harshest diatribes for the newfangled performance of a certain kind of Western modernity by the liberal and politically active Bengali Hindu elites who accommodated a number of British practices, particularly with regard to food and commensality, and insisted on incorporating British education, etiquette, and comportment in dress into their professional lives, while practicing a strongly orthodox Hindu lifestyle in their personal domains. Visions of lavish colonial balls, the consumption of alcohol and ritually prohibited food like beef and ham, and the companionate and open nature of social intercourse between British men and women—in short, the tangible glitter and pomp of British imperialism—promised a spiritually debased but incredibly tempting form of modernity.[3] The most obvious expressions of such problematic behavior involved breaking food taboos as well as violating commensality and purity rules through close contact with British men and women. Ishwar Gupta of course pointed out such daring and taboo behavior:

> Being gluttonous let's go to the hotel and shop
> We'll see what delight there is in the mutton chop
> Curry, eggs, fish and chips all on a dish
> I will eat all of it, how can I give it a miss?!
> When you see a red face, pull close the ham,
> Don't care for *Hinduani,* damn, damn, damn![4]

Hinduani, the social and cultural expressions of everyday practices of piety in colonial Calcutta's Hindu Bengali society, faced a dire threat in Ishwar Gupta's estimation. While some Bengalis imitated Western cultural expressions in the hope of social and financial advancement through employment in the British administration, others also believed that such mimicry might gradually pave the path for intellectual enlightenment as well as social and racial equality with the British. For example, Prosonnocoomar Tagore, one of the most important yet forgotten figures in nineteenth-century India, said in a speech at the Calcutta Town Hall on February 9, 1838:

> The day when the distinctions of color, caste, and religion, and the difference between conquerors, and conquered will be totally banished, is, I am happy to say, fast approaching. . . . *Education and allowing to the people of India the exercise of the political privileges regarding the English, as at home, is the surest way of establishing British rule in India on the firmest basis.*[5]

These hopes, together with the blandishments of colonial modernity, promised upward mobility for those Bengalis willing to become partners in the enterprise of empire. That promise proved hard to resist for many of the *madhyabitta bhadralok,* or the newly emergent and respectable middle class. For Ishwar Gupta and other conservatives like him, however, these rapid encroachments of colonial influence opened up Bengali Hindu society to a kind of anarchy and dissolution that was deeply disconcerting. One of the most insidious ways in which this dissolution spread, according to Gupta and his followers, was through the introduction of modern forms of occidental pedagogy in Calcutta. In the early nineteenth century, education in English had become an indispensable requirement for Indian boys in order to take part in the new colonial enterprise, as scholars like Rosinka Chaudhuri, Parna Sengupta, and Hayden Bellenoit have illustrated.[6] However, it soon became clear to Bengali conservatives that an English education—while necessary for social advancement and financial well-being—was fraught with danger for Indian subjects, especially if they attended schools that were run by Christian missions. Incidents of impressionable boys being converted to Christianity by their charismatic missionary preceptors, though extremely limited in number, created a panic among Bengali Hindu parents beginning in the early 1830s. Again, Ishwar Gupta spoke to this fear:

> Wherever boys' minds are laid astray
> You'll find the missionary having his way,
> They have spread their enchanting snares, they have captured
> the boys,
> Why would they let go of their prey, they rejoice in their
> successful ploys![7]

Therefore, one recurring target of Gupta's poison pen was the British missionaries operating in Calcutta and its hinterlands. None of them suffered more from his attacks than Rev. Alexander Duff (1806–1878), who came to Calcutta in 1830. He was a missionary of the Scottish Free Church, as well as a leading member of the Anglicist group who preferred the promulgation of Western modes of pedagogy and Christian proselytization in British-Indian domains. To marry these two objectives, shortly after his arrival in 1830, Duff founded the General Assembly's Institution in Calcutta, which soon became the school favored by most of Bengal's intellectual elite for the secondary-level English education of their sons.[8] According to Gupta, there were, "in every home, Duffy's boys with their AB learning."[9] Duff reappears again in Gupta's poem "Choddo-Missionary" (False missionary):

> On the pretense of education, the missionary Duff,
> Has installed an apostasy-tub,
> Because of his honeyed words of Love

These children acknowledge their savior to be Duff,
And falling in the exact opposite of love,
Immerse themselves in Duff's tub.[10]

The specter of Duff and his tub of love haunts Ishwar Gupta's verse, where it invites his audience, presumably the orthodox Hindu Bengalis of Calcutta, to feel an almost psychosexual shiver down their spines at the thought of "unnatural" forms of affection between young Bengali Hindu school boys and their missionary preceptors. These relationships, Gupta insinuated, "perverted" these boys away from the natural order of things: the love and obedience due to their parents, their families, and their natal communities of birth and faith. Ishwar Gupta's poems thus chronicle the decline of an ancient, idealized, and supposedly authentic Hindu way of life, now threatened with corruption by the Christian civilizing mission and the influences of British colonialism.[11] Ishwar Gupta obviously felt that the exposure of impressionable children to Christianity and British sociocultural influences in missionary-established pedagogical institutions would lead to the eventual decline and fall of *Hinduani*.

Ishwar Gupta was perhaps the most acerbic and entertaining critic of the new changes in Indian society under colonialism, but he was far from the only one: multiple members of the Bengali elite agreed with him and supported his views. Among those supporters and patrons were stalwarts like Raja Radhakanta Dev, Prosonnocoomar Tagore, and Debendranath Tagore. We will get to know them all in the course of this chapter. The targets of Ishwar Gupta's poison pen are also linked by a common thread: the necessity of creating a class of Indian subjects who knew the English language well, to serve as middlemen in the lower rungs of the British bureaucratic administration in India.

A contentious debate erupted in India in 1834 on this very issue. There were those British administrators and Indian elites, the Anglicists, who supported introducing Western models of pedagogy through the medium of instruction in English. The Anglicists favored establishing a pedagogy modeled on the British education system. Their opponents on the other hand preferred that students receive a thorough grounding in Indian languages and Indian classics of literature and law, most importantly in Persian and Sanskrit.[12] In 1835, Thomas Babington Macaulay, first law member of the Governor-General's Council in India, stepped into this debate with his infamous "Minute on Education," which was scathing about the inferiority of Orientalist pedagogy and literature.[13] He denounced as inferior all of the Indian epics, classical drama and poetry, and treatises on law, philosophy, and sciences—all of which had excited and enthralled British administrators like Warren Hastings and linguists like William Jones a generation ago. He famously said: "I am quite ready to take the oriental learning at the valuation of the Orientalists themselves. I have never found one among them who could deny that a single shelf of a good European library was worth the whole native literature of India and Arabia."[14]

Macaulay was adamant that an education system based on a study of these kinds of texts was not commensurate with the needs of the British administration. Macaulay's "Minute" effectively signaled the death of these old Indian modes of pedagogy in Sanskrit, Persian, and Arabic, and ushered in a new era—because the British administration decided to follow his advice.[15] Following his intervention, William Bentinck, the governor-general who had earlier gained renown by banning *sati* in 1829, passed the English Education Act of 1835. English not only became the primary medium of education in government-funded institutions but also the official language favored in administrative business, including in the civil and criminal courts of law, the Sadr Diwani Adalat (Revenue and Civil Matters Court) and the Faujdari Adalat (Criminal Affairs Court).[16] Macaulay, in spite of his family connections to the Clapham Sect, always stringently disavowed that Christian evangelism and religious conversion fell within the intended aims or duties of the British government in India.[17] Yet while he categorically refused to countenance any official administrative support to Christian missionaries, his description of Indian religions and culture borrowed strongly from the usual terms that early colonial ethnography used to systematically study and categorize Indian religions and cultures.[18] Much like Charles Grant, Macaulay argued in the "Minute" that communicating "Truth" to the Indian subjects was the primary goal. As we have seen, however, "Truth" was closely associated with Christianity. Macaulay asserts in the "Minute":

> Assuredly *it is the duty of the British Government in India to be not only tolerant, but neutral on all religious questions.* But to encourage the study of a literature, admitted to be of small intrinsic value, only because that literature inculcates the most serious errors on the most important subjects, is a course hardly reconcilable with reason, with morality. . . . *We are to teach it because it is fruitful of monstrous superstitions. We are to teach false history, false astronomy, false medicine, because we find them in Company with a false religion.*

The language that Macaulay used to describe Indian religions, toward which neutrality was to be sacredly observed, negated the very neutrality he seemingly championed.[19] To sum up, in order to make the imperial project a success, a pedagogy suitable to impart Truth and increase usefulness among Indian subjects had to be introduced. This meant that the indigenous education system, based on pedagogy imparted in Sanskrit, Persian, and Arabic, had to be superseded by English "occidental" education. Macaulay was convinced, in any case, of the superiority of English literature and culture. What his "Minute" went on to achieve is a central concern of this chapter: the creation of what I call the Macaulayan subject, the brown *sahib,* whom he infamously described as follows: "We must at present do our best to form a class who may be interpreters between us and the millions whom we govern, a class of persons Indian in blood and color, but English in tastes, in opinions, in morals and in intellect."[20] It was the project of educating and creating the Macaulayan subject that brought Bengali Hindus and the missionaries into headlong collision. The consequence of the Macaulayan moment of 1835 was the intimate exposure of Bengali schoolboys to missionary preceptors, which in turn opened the doors to conversion and led parents to panic about the future of their children and the survival of their communities. The contest not only took place in the public sphere but also stretched from the school to the courts of law in colonial Bengal. English education meant that the shadow of the missionary preceptor loomed large over Indian schoolboys, who received a thorough grounding in Christian religious instruction at missionary schools like Alexander Duff's General Assembly's Institution. Young boys who attended the Hindu College read Enlightenment classics by David Hume, Adam Smith, Thomas Paine, and others under the influence of their spirited and radically liberal Anglo-Indian teacher Henry Louis Vivian Derozio. They then began questioning the rituals and customs of their own religion, be it Hinduism or Islam, which seemed to them to be illiberal, superstitious, and often inhumane. And Bengali parents were faced with the existential choice of having to send their children to these new pedagogical institutions if they wanted them to succeed in the new colonial context but also thereby exposing their children to the dangers of Christian conversion. These Bengali parents and their communities fought back, decrying the excesses of colonial support for evangelism and asking for redress from the Anglo-Indian legal system. In order to have their children educated without the constant fear of losing them, they took to expressing their anger and concern through legal means, by using habeas corpus as a blunt instrument to defang the power and influence yielded by missionaries through their schools and make a case for their right to be judged according to Hindu legal customs and thereby retain their custodial rights over the persons and consciences of their minor offspring until they reached the age of maturity.

The conditions of the Company Raj meant that the necessity of learning English became inescapable, inexorably drawing the new generation of English-educated young men closer to the British administration and to middlemen like the missionaries in their varied roles as educators, preceptors, printers, and pamphleteers. The paranoia bred by this close and contaminating contact meant that the ideologically divided strands of the newly consolidated Bengali Hindu society banded together against what they saw as the threat of Christianity and conversion to the essence of Bengali Hindu identity. In the resultant discourse, the Christian missionary was marked as a disruptor of Hindu Bengali life-worlds and traditions—an agent of dark enchantment cast on the souls of the younger and more impressionable generation of Bengalis. With the closer interactions between Indian students and missionary preceptors, the creation and sustenance of a common ground, where a sophisticated debate on the theologies and philosophies of faith could be attempted, should have become easier.

Instead, particularly because the evangelical enterprise from the beginning contained within itself a hierarchical impulse based on both religious faith and race, such apologetics provoked a thorny response from the established order of Bengali cultural and political life. For elite Bengalis, the threat of evangelism was directed toward their identity—which was encapsulated by the idea of *Hinduani*—the state of being a good Hindu.

In the face of this aggressive battle to establish the hierarchies of saved souls and cultural norms, Calcutta's elite orthodox Bengali Hindu society faced off against missionaries and evangelically minded British administrators. The result was the evolution and emergence of a seemingly consolidated and unified Bengali Hindu society over the first half of the nineteenth century. Where previously there had only been caste-based ideological and factional strife, these decades saw Bengali Hindus uniting across caste, class, and various kinds of ideological associations to actively produce reformist narratives about their religion. The resultant apologetic dialogues focused on the need to safeguard younger members of their communities and also to preserve their religious customs and faith against the depredations by the colonial administration and the missionaries.

This chapter examines the contest between Bengali Hindus and Christian missionaries over the education and conversion of young boys, which occurred in three stages. The first involved the education of young Bengali Hindu boys at the newly established Hindu College between 1826 and 1831. There, the tutelage and mentorship of Derozio enabled a particular kind of radical liberalism and the development of a questioning spirit in the young students. The confrontational attitude that these students, known as the Young Bengal group, adopted toward the more conservative leaders of Hindu Bengali society, and the open challenge they levied at customary Hindu religious practices, ultimately led to an official showdown between the members of the Managing Committee of the Hindu College and Derozio, which ended in his expulsion in 1831. The actions of the students generated negative public sentiment toward liberal English education of the sort being provided at the college, in Calcutta. Bengali Hindus came to see these institutions as a threat to the established social and religious norms in Bengali Hindu society.

The contest was tripartite, involving the vanguard of Rammohan Roy's associates, who represented an older and more conservative form of liberal attitudes; Christian missionaries; and the newer generation of young men educated in English literature and philosophy, who wanted to overhaul systemic abuses in Hindu cultural practices. This is exemplified in the complicated relationship between Prosonnocoomar Tagore, a liberal Hindu associate of Rammohan Roy, and his nemesis Krishnamohan Banerjee, one of the earliest high-caste Christian converts, and perhaps the most well known and erudite. This encounter over their personal and religious differences, which began around 1830–1831, would continue until 1868 and ultimately spill over tragically into the lives of their children.

The tensions about the influence of missionary preceptors on young students would result in a series of high-profile legal cases from 1833 to 1863, where Bengali Hindu parents engaged in custodial battles with missionaries accused of abducting their young sons with the intent to convert them to Christianity. These custodial battles played out in the Anglo-Indian law courts, where aggrieved parents often brought habeas corpus writs demanding the restitution of custody over their offspring to them, with arguments made about Hindu customary practices that allowed fathers to have undisputed control over their children until age sixteen. Missionaries were well aware of the use of habeas corpus by parents: "The writ called Habeas Corpus, issued in the reign of Charles II to defend the liberty of the British subject, has in Indian been applied to secure the person of the youthful convert from his alleged detention by the missionary."[21] The parents' arguments hinged on two different but related issues: first, whether the boys who had converted were

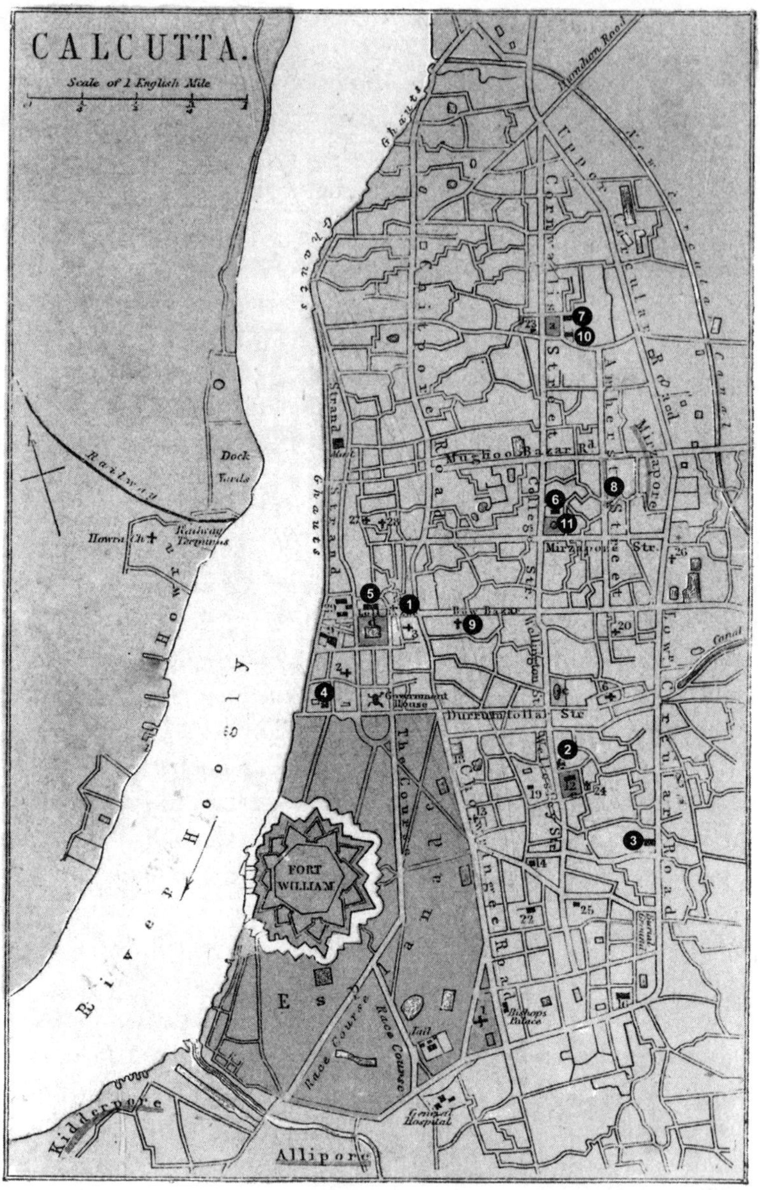

1 – Scottish Church
2 – Free Church of Scotland
3 – Baptist Chapel
4 – Supreme Court at Calcutta
5 – Fort William College
6 – Hindu College
7 – General Assembly's Institution, later the Scottish Church College
8 – Church Missionary Society Premises
9 – Baptist Chapel
10 – General Female School
11 – College Square

A map of Calcutta that shows most of the major mission churches and schools immediately after 1857.

Reproduced from *The Church Missionary Atlas*, 3rd ed. (London: Church Missionary Society, 1862).

minors in the eyes of both the law and Hindu customary practices, and second, whether the boys had the discretion, foresight, and intelligence to make a reasoned and conscientious choice about converting. In most cases, at least before 1857, the presiding judge determined on the basis of an interview whether the boy in question was fully cognizant of the life-changing nature of their decision to convert to Christianity. And as we will see, before 1857, in most cases the judgment favored the boy convert and the missionaries. After the events of 1857, when Indian opinion on the probable causes of the Mutiny became public, it was clear that the role of missionary preceptors in converting young boys was one of the chief grievances held by Indian subjects against the Company Raj.

As a result, judges became far more circumspect in cases of habeas corpus involving the conversion of minor boys. The schoolboys, their parents, their missionary interlocutors, and the British legal establishment faced off, using habeas corpus, to debate Hindu Indian versus British Christian interpretations of the limits of custodial right of parents over their children, and consequently, of the right of Indian children to self-determination—especially their right to conscientiously choose to convert to Christianity. The extraordinary paranoia about "missionaryism" that exercised Calcutta's elite, for example, first found expression through the deeply angry and hateful rhetoric aimed at missionaries by people like Ishwar Gupta, the Tagores of Jorasanko and Pathuriaghata, and the orthodox Dharma Sabha of Radhakanta Dev between 1820 and 1865. From theological discussion to rationalist debates about the imminent downfall of *Hinduani,* this phase of apologia transmuted from the public sphere to the realm of print in various newspapers, periodicals, and broadsheets, and the two sides dueled out their respective ideological positions passionately and virulently. The shift from the classroom to spirited public sphere duels in the print medium occurred especially when the erstwhile students of the Hindu College, the Derozians, put their dissatisfaction with the corruptions they saw hollowing out their own society and religion into print. In a number of periodicals and newspapers that they began to publish in Calcutta, they systematically critiqued what they perceived to be the superstitions and errors of their inherited religious, social, and cultural norms, under the influence of their teacher Derozio, between 1827 and 1832. In order to understand how apologetic debate spread from the classroom to the print medium and thereafter into the legal domain, we therefore have to lay the foundation by discussing Derozio and Derozians at the Hindu College in colonial Calcutta.

To sum up, therefore, this chapter focuses on the many different forms of apologetic dialogue that took shape in Bengal between 1830 and 1865. As this chapter will trace, religious apologetics functioned in three different contexts in three different ways. From the classroom, at the Hindu College, where the Bengali boys learned to question the ethics and customs of their own faith on a comparative basis under the tutelage of their teacher Derozio, the debates then moved into the Bengali public sphere, being performed through periodicals, newspapers, and journals that were the mouthpieces of different factions in Calcutta. Here, as we will see, the argumentation was much more concerned with the consequences that attended religious controversy and Christian conversions in Bengal. The discourse centered on the responsibilities and affiliations that were owed to one's natal community of birth and faith, and what conversion meant in terms of abrogation of these duties—for the community, the family, and the convert. And finally, these concerns spilled over into the domain of Anglo-Indian law courts, where parents, minor children, and their evangelically minded preceptors began to fight a complex legal battle to determine the right to personhood and freedom of conscientious religious decisions of the children in question.

CHRISTIANITY AND ENLIGHTENED PEDAGOGY AT THE HINDU COLLEGE

As a result of the entwined intellectual and religious ferment in Calcutta, the traditional caste-based hierarchical factions were reshaped into ideological ones. At this point in Calcutta, by the second decade of the nineteenth century, four major factions emerged, as S. N. Mukherjee has shown: the missionary faction, made up of Alexander Duff and his followers, the Church Missionary Society's members, and to a smaller extent the Serampore and Calcutta Baptists; the *Nastik* or atheistic / agnostic faction, consisting of the erstwhile students of Hindu College—most importantly those influenced by Derozio; the Brahmo faction, consisting of Debendranath Tagore and his followers; and last, the Dharma Sabha or orthodox faction, which counted Radhakanta Dev as its leader.[22] These factions engaged in fierce competition for control over the administrations and functions of pedagogical institutions such as the School Book Society, the School Society, and the Committee of Managers of the Hindu College. The Hindu College had been established in 1817 with the encouragement of both Indians and British administrative officers, including Rammohan Roy, the clockmaker and educationist David Hare, and

Sir Edward Hyde East, a justice of the Calcutta Supreme Court. Aimed at providing modern English-language education to Hindu Bengali boys of "respectable" backgrounds, the college shifted to its permanent premises in 1826. There, it saw one of the most bitter contests over the education of Bengali boys—which, as members of the four factions knew well, was as much a contest over the intellectual and cultural influences exercised upon these future "brown *sahibs*" as it was about their religious, political, and social affiliations.

The first occasion of conflict was the so-called Derozio affair, with which we are concerned in this section. In 1827, seventeen-year-old Henry Louis Vivian Derozio, of mixed Portuguese-Indian descent, joined Hindu College as a teacher and precipitated a social and intellectual revolution.[23] He was known among his students for being empathetic and principled, and for encouraging fierce independence of thought "to throw off the antiquated fetters of bigotry." His methods encouraged students to question the very foundations of their own society and identity and made him an intellectual role model to the "College boys." According to a contemporary source, "The teaching of Mr. Derozio, which sapped the very foundation of the religious beliefs of the students, in no time brought about an intellectual and moral revolution in Hindu society."[24] Following his example, these Derozians set about challenging the rituals and taboos governing Bengali Hindu society, most famously through their open and uninhibited consumption of beef and wine, which put them at loggerheads with elder members of their own communities.[25] Childish expressions of "modern" ways, intended to strike directly at Hindu superstitions, were rampant among the students of Hindu College. Entering Wilson's Hotel in Calcutta to eat beef, drinking wine and spirits at home, and breaking food taboos to the anguish of parents were common. Some went even further: when asked to perform the ritual worship of family deities, one young boy mockingly bowed in the English fashion to the idol and said, "Good day, Madam!" to the horror of his family. Madhav Chandra Mallik, one of Derozio's students, wrote in a contemporary broadsheet, "If there is anything that we hate from the bottom of our hearts, it is Hinduism."[26] Shibnath Shastri quotes a clerk in the Hindu College, Haramohan Chattopadhyay: "The principles and practices of Hindu religion were openly ridiculed and condemned, and angry disputes were held on moral subjects. . . . The Hindu religion was denounced as vile and corrupt and unworthy of the regard of rational beings. . . . It was then resolved that nothing but a liberal education could enfranchise the minds of the people."[27] And yet it was this same Haramohan Chattopadhyay who praised the genuine courage and integrity of the Young Bengal group in his reminiscences about the Brahmin reformer Ramtanu Lahiri: "Such and such a boy is incapable of falsehood, because he is a Hindu College boy."[28] Though Derozians were vilified for their critiques of the Hindu faith and of contemporary Bengali Hindu society, their fierce truthfulness and precocious intellectual brilliance also drew grudging respect. The childishness that governed these incidents of dissent against Hindu practices can be attributed to the extreme youth of both Derozio and his students. Given the riotous expressions of self-examination and resistance to the traditional social order by his students and other members of Young Bengal, Derozio soon became known as a deeply undesirable rabble-rouser to the conservative members of the Managing Committee of the Hindu College.

At the same time, Alexander Duff, who in June of 1830 settled in a house "nearly opposite the Hindu College," arranged for a series of lectures on "Natural and Revealed Religion," encouraged by the spirit of inquiry and the revulsion toward Hindu rituals among the "College boys." The lectures were to be delivered by well-known evangelicals in the city: Archdeacon Thomas Dealtry of the Calcutta Anglican establishment; John Adam, missionary in the service of the London Missionary Society; and James Hill, pastor of Union Chapel in Bow Bazar, Calcutta. The first lecture, by Hill, took place in August 1830, when "twenty of the foremost students of his own and of the Hindu College took their places in expectations of novel exposition. . . . Next morning the news flew like wildfire all over Calcutta. Students of the Hindu College had actually attended, in the house of a missionary, a lecture on Christianity! Soon the city was in uproar!"[29] The creation of Rammohan's Brahmo Sabha, the tensions simmering in Calcutta after Bentinck's promulgation of the ban on *sati,* and Alexander Duff's arrival and activities all added to this sense of a terrible crisis in Bengali Hindu society.[30] It was alleged that the activities of Derozio and the Young Bengal group had led to the withdrawal of 25 students from the Hindu College by their families. An additional 160 were allegedly absent, because their families suspected a rapidly spreading contagion of radical freethinking, beef-eating, and wine-drinking among good Hindu boys.

Retribution followed quickly. In late 1830, the Managing Committee of the Hindu College issued two circulars, one directed toward the students and one toward Derozio, criticizing their conduct as unbecoming and damaging to the Hindu College's reputation. The circulars were criticized immediately by Derozio, his students, and their supporters, as well as liberal

British administrators. According to Shibnath Shastri, "People everywhere were loud in their condemnations—this attempt to constrain freedom of thought and expression was unbearable to most."[31] Some of the criticism might have issued from Derozio himself, writing anonymously in the *India Gazette,* where an article called the situation "a tyrannical and absurd intermeddling with the right of private judgment on political and religious questions."[32] Rammohan, who personally favored openness to religious instruction, whether it was Christianity, Hinduism, or Islam, and had helped Alexander Duff set up his school in 1830, believed that it would strengthen the moral character of students. He too heard about the situation at the Hindu College. An acquaintance came to visit and said, "Have you heard, such and such a boy was a polytheist, and then a deist, and now he claims to be an atheist!" Rammohan reportedly laughed and replied, "Well, in the end, maybe he will be a beast."[33]

The rest of Calcutta's Bengali Hindu society did not exhibit the same restraint and sense of humor, instead holding the radical instruction provided at the Hindu College, especially by Derozio, to be the root of the uncontrollable heretical impulses in their offspring. Ramkamal Sen, one of the first Indian millionaires and a member of the Managing Committee of the Hindu College, drafted a censure, "Mr. Derozio Being the Root of All Evils and the Cause of Public Alarm."[34] Derozio ultimately became the sacrifice in the battle behind the two impulses that pulled Bengal in different directions: the desire to stabilize and preserve the *Hinduani* versus the desire for modernization and the stirrings of what has since been called the Bengal Renaissance. He was informed of the termination of his services and resigned from the Hindu College on April 25, 1831. In reply to a personal letter from Wilson, the vice president of the College Committee, Derozio also wrote a defense of himself. Something of his pedagogical model and the attitude of Young Bengal toward religion might be discerned in this letter. "If the religious opinions of the students have become unhinged in consequence of the course I have pursued," he said, "the fault is not mine. . . . If I am to be condemned for the Atheism of some, let me receive credit for the Theism of others."[35] Derozio encouraged a questioning of the religious and social mores of institutionalized religions, irrespective of whether it was Christianity or Hinduism. He wanted his students to make deliberate, rational choices about their lives and their faiths, without a blind belief in inherited superstitions. The infamy and cruel treatment Derozio received at the hands of the managers of the Hindu College broke his heart. He died of cholera in

December 1831, six months after his resignation from the Hindu College, at the age of twenty-two.[36]

Derozio's legacy to his students was that of sustained philosophical engagement with issues of dogmatic faith in the face of tremendous social and cultural backlash. He instilled in them an openness to other religious and political philosophies, which made possible both a closer engagement with Christianity and—in turn—an even more virulent backlash against Christian missionaries from Bengali Hindu leaders. Encouraged to challenge the superstitions and customs of Hinduism, some of his students became far more receptive to what they saw as the more rational, enlightened, and civilized religious and ethical system of Christianity. But unlike Rammohan, Derozio's students did not stop at admiring Christianity's ethical content. After his death, many of his students formed an intellectual and thereafter spiritual connection with Alexander Duff, who had by 1830 started giving lectures on Christianity and Christian ethics. Duff had developed a rational and critical explanation of the enlightenment potential of Christianity, which appealed to the young Derozians reeling from their teacher's death. They gravitated to Duff, and this closeness ultimately resulted in the first high-caste Christian conversions in Bengal.

FROM DEROZIANS TO CHRISTIANS

These conversions were in part a response to the spiritual and social isolation that the skeptical questioning of their own religion and culture had produced in these students of Derozio. They caused a sensation in Calcutta because such high-caste conversions had never before occurred, even at the height of the influence of the Serampore and Calcutta Baptists. The three boys who were baptized in the face of tremendous public opposition were Mohesh Chandra Ghose, Krishnamohan Banerjee, and Gopinath Nandy.[37] Mohesh Ghose was baptized on August 26, 1832, by Duff's associate, the Anglican Archdeacon Dealtry. He died a few years later in 1837, while preparing for ministry as a native preacher. Krishnamohan Banerjee was baptized by Duff on October 17, 1832, and would have a long and distinguished career as a pillar of Bengali Christian society. Gopinath Nandy was baptized by Duff on December 14, 1833, but ordained by American missionaries in the Northwest Provinces, and he would later manage a school at Fatehpur, where he and other native Christians would bear the brunt of Sepoy anger at the height of the Mutiny of 1857.[38]

Mohesh Ghose, whose baptism took place less than a year after Derozio's death, described his path to conversion thus: "A twelve month ago, I was an Atheist, a Materialist, a Physical Necessitarian; and what am I now? A baptized Christian! What a change! How has it been brought about? My progress was not that of earnest inquiry, but of earnest opposition. And to the last, my heart was opposed. In spite of myself, I became a Christian."[39] His words indicate that he felt a true spiritual calling. However, it is also important to recognize the profound crisis of spirit that Derozio's students must have experienced after his dismissal and untimely death. Alexander Duff and his associates—with their reasonable approach to Christian evangelism, and their ability to debate Enlightenment philosophy on equal grounds with these young men, teenagers really—proved an attractive intellectual refuge for many grieving members of the Young Bengal group. The missionaries also provided real refuge to those from the Young Bengal group who were ostracized by their own Bengali Hindu community as a result of their liberal, radical beliefs.

These high-caste conversions directly contradicted Rammohan Roy's assertion that only the mean and lowly classes gave in to the temptations of conversion, fooled by the promise of material gain—that conversion as such was not sincere but directed by worldly desires. This understanding of conversion, and the public performance of baptism, changed completely with the new wave of high-caste conversions from 1832 onwards. Motives of financial gain could no longer be ascribed to the young men, who mostly came from affluent, and sometimes aristocratic, families. In the two decades after Duff's first voyage to India in 1830, the *padri* or missionary in the role of a preceptor would become the main antagonist for Bengali Hindu society, because of their intellectual and spiritual control of young boys. These first high-caste Bengali conversions shook Calcutta's Hindu society to the core, especially since Duff had leveraged his pedagogical experience and his close ties to the colonial administration in order to ensure that unofficial colonial support would always be given to evangelism in Calcutta.[40] These tensions are clearly embodied in the debates between Krishnamohan Banerjee, who converted just a few months after Mohesh Chandra Ghose, and members of the prominent Tagore family. They first flared in the years leading up to Krishnamohan's conversion in 1832 and would extend for many years after his baptism, as we will see in Chapter 3. These debates, which played out in the pages of the newspapers and mouthpieces of Krishnamohan and the Tagores, followed a template. On one hand, there were learned and critical expositions on religious texts, both Hindu and Christian, and detailed analysis of the ethical context and the religious and philosophical content of these sacred textual traditions. On the other, there were personal and communal attacks, of various degrees of viciousness, aimed at each other's personal probity and morals, which were often found to be lacking. These apologetic debates, outside of the newspapers, found an active and long life among the various factions in Calcutta, channeled and distorted through a very well-developed rumor mill.

The centrality of one of India's most well-known families to these vicious early public apologetic debates on Christianity has largely been forgotten. The Tagore family held immense prestige and power in Bengal from the last half of the eighteenth century, when the British made Calcutta their center for trade, commerce, and political maneuverings. An 1880 article on the family in *The Oriental Miscellany* concluded, "Like the Rothschilds of Europe, the Tagores are a family noted for wealth and of great political distinction. But they surpass the Rothschilds in their devotion to literature and science, by means of which they will leave behind them an undying name, when their riches and political distinctions are forgotten."[41] Dwarkanath Tagore and Dwarkanath's grandson Rabindranath, the first Asian writer to win the Nobel Prize in Literature in 1913, were the most illustrious members of the Brahmo branch of this family, residing in the neighborhood of Jorasanko. Through their lives and times, these two giants neatly divided the Company and the Raj era of British colonial rule in India. Debendranath Tagore, son of Dwarkanath, was inveterate and unceasing in his opposition to Christian evangelism.[42]

The other, less remembered, if equally illustrious, family of Tagores came from the orthodox Hindu branch of the family residing in Pathuriaghata.[43] Prosonnocoomar Tagore was one of its most prominent members. Born in 1801 as the youngest of the six sons of the fabulously wealthy philanthropist Gopimohan Tagore, Prosonnocoomar began his public career as a Bengali landlord of means who invested primarily in indigo cultivation.[44] He incurred considerable losses in this venture due to frequent contestation and defeat in lawsuits in the Sudder courts, which adjudicated civil cases. Prosonnocoomar reasoned that these defeats owed to the unfamiliarity of Indians with British laws and judicial procedures. As a result, he determined to become a *vakil* or pleader in the Sudder Court in Calcutta and devoted his time to a comparative study of Hindu law systems and British legal procedures. His career as a lawyer was so successful that he was first appointed to the government pleadership at the Sudder court, a hitherto unimaginable preferment for a native

Indian subject in 1843. He held the post until 1854.[45] He then went on to become the clerk assistant to the Legislative Council of India under Lord Dalhousie and was instrumental in drafting the Indian Penal Code (IPC) of 1860. An article on Prosonnocoomar Tagore mentioned his contributions toward the codification of the IPC:

> The Committee of the Legislative Council . . . concluded their remarks with, "acknowledging the great assistance which they had derived from the extensive knowledge and experience of the Clerk Assistant to the Council, . . . and from his indefatigable exertions in carrying out their views." He assisted Sir Barnes Peacock and his colleagues in the final settlement of the Penal Code and revised the Vernacular Translation of the Code in conjunction with a few select Oriental Scholars.[46]

Thereafter, he became the first Indian to be offered a seat in the Viceroy's Legislative Council. In recognition of his efforts and services, he was awarded the Companionship of the Most Exalted Order of the Star of India on April 30, 1866. He was an acknowledged authority on Hindu jurisprudence concerning partition of joint families on questions of inheritance, and he prepared the seminal translation of the *Vivada Chintamani,* an authoritative compilation of customary Hindu opinions on various civil and criminal aspects of legislation from the Mithila School.[47] Prosonnocoomar Tagore was also the preeminent authority on the *Dayabhaga,* a twelfth-century Sanskrit commentary by Jimutavahana on Hindu inheritance procedure, which was accepted as the central authoritative text in British courts in Bengal in the nineteenth and early twentieth centuries.[48] In his multiple roles as an eminent landowner, elite intellectual, and legal expert, with connections to almost all the aristocratic families and factions (*dals*) in Calcutta, his mediation between the colonial administration and the Indian intelligentsia was indispensable for the East India Company, which sought to authenticate its rule of law in the Indian Empire.

In the late 1820s and 1830s, however, Prosonnocoomar was a successful landlord and a *vakil* in Calcutta, a theater enthusiast, and an avid journalist who produced and managed an important periodical called *The Reformer.* Dwarkanath and Prosonnocoomar, though second cousins, were also friends, tied by close kinship bonds in the way Indian extended families operated. Both supported Rammohan Roy's revolutionary ideas about political and religious reform, and both were members of the Atmiya Sabha that Rammohan established. In a Calcutta rife with factionalism, they were known to be important members of Rammohan's modernist *dal*.[49] They engaged in debate with the orthodox *dal* headed by Raja Sir Radhakanta Dev called the Dharma Sabha.[50] However, both Prosonnocoomar and Dwarkanath sided with the rival group of Radhakanta Dev on an important issue: they stood against evangelicalism and Christian conversion, seeing it as immensely threatening to the Hindu way of life.[51] Throughout the 1830s, followers of Rammohan Roy, like Prosonnocoomar Tagore, found themselves at loggerheads with the younger ultra-liberals of the Young Bengal group. Their opposing ideas on the nature and extent of reforms needed in social, legal, commercial, and public life created an intensely engaged yet deeply fractured public sphere in Bengal. The explosion of vernacular and English newspapers and periodicals, sustained by the emerging medium of print, played an important role in the dissemination of their debates, with each faction or *dal* having its own periodical as a mouthpiece.

Ishwar Gupta's poetry, as we have seen, deepened suspicion in Bengali Hindu society that the missionaries were especially good at enchanting the impressionable minds of Bengali boys who sought English pedagogy and thereby ensnaring these boys in the net of conversion. Once the conversion took place, the ruin of both the boys and their families was certain, and their loss of caste cemented forever. Ishwar Gupta's frenzied obsession with Duff and his "tub of love" embodies the fury and frustration of a society caught between the need to preserve its sociocultural identity and the need to provide English education to its young male members so that they could earn a handsome living—and, in turn, financially uphold the Bengali Hindu identity of their family through the practice of expensive rituals.

By 1831, Bengali Hindu leaders now turned their focus to how the depredations of "missionaryism" and the influence of *padris* could be contained.[52] One way was to attempt a reform of Hinduism from the inside, though perhaps not as radically as had been advocated by Rammohan Roy. The other way was to police the community, specifically the young men, who were most vulnerable to such dark influences, especially at institutions like Duff's General Assembly's Institution and the Hindu College. One correspondent, who only signed off as "A Hindu" (possibly Dwarkanath's brother Ramanath Tagore), wrote in the *Indian Gazette* on December 16, 1831:

> If merely for the sake of fashion, or other sinister motives a person will become a Christian, no dependence can be placed upon him, for should the fashion or any other motivate that may influence him after, he will not hesi-

> tate to change again. Therefore, observe my countrymen that conversion from one religion to another ought only to take place on the ground of conviction, and not by mere caprice of the moment. *If you think Hinduism contains any absurdity, pray reform it.*[53]

Playing on the idea of conversion as temporary imitation and mimicry, based on shallow motives of material gain, the author accused native Christian converts of being disloyal and fickle, and at the same time advocated reform within the Bengali Hindu community to ward off the tendency toward conversion to Christianity. In any event, the common goal of containing the menace of evangelical Christianity brought the Hindu and Brahmo aristocracy together, pitting them against the members of the Young Bengal group. Wishing for a complete reformation in religion and society, the Young Bengal group was not appeased by the conciliatory gestures of the older, generally more conservative liberals like Prosonnocoomar Tagore and his second cousin Debendranath Tagore.[54] Among the most well-known opponents of Prosonnocoomar's faction was Krishnamohan Banerjee. His mocking opinions about the older members of the conservative liberal faction and his association with Duff did not endear him to either Prosonnocoomar or Rammohan's followers such as Dwarkanath and later his son Debendranath Tagore.

Overtly, the major cause of friction between Prosonnocoomar Tagore and Banerjee was that Banerjee saw conversion as the only means of salvation for the Indians. The rise of the Indian vernacular press became instrumental in fomenting divisive debates about religion and identity between these two factions. Prosonnocoomar Tagore, as previously mentioned, edited and published *The Reformer,* a liberal journal in which he wrote progressive and erudite articles on education for women, freedom, and political equality for Indian subjects of the Company, all signed under the eponymous pseudonym. Banerjee published his own journal, *The Enquirer,* in which articles and letters repeatedly attacked Prosonnocoomar and other members of the Young Bengal group for what was perceived to be their halfhearted, half-enlightened reformist stance.[55] There was a generational gap between the two rivals, as Prosonnocoomar was about twelve years older than Krishnamohan. There was also a subtle class rivalry, given that Krishnamohan was a self-made man from a family of very humble means whereas Prosonnocoomar came from a preeminent aristocratic family with a huge personal fortune.

The immediate causes of the rivalry were tied to both personal conflict and journalistic principles. In 1831, a young scholar called Govindachandra Basak wrote a series of articles against Christianity, which Prosonnocoomar published in *The Reformer.* These were strongly refuted in *The Enquirer* by Krishnamohan and highly placed colonial administrators such as Ross Donelly Mangles, who was a member of the Council of India, and this exchange is one of the examples of apologetic debates being conducted through the editorials of dueling newspapers or periodicals, which served as mouthpieces for antagonistic factions in Calcutta.[56] Then, on September 12, 1831, in a widely read essay, "An Appeal to His Countrymen," Prosonnocoomar, professing his friendship with Rammohan Roy and championing Rammohan's radical ideas of religious reform, advocated the abolishment of idolatrous rituals and practices in *The Reformer.*[57] However, in spite of his public protestations against idol worship, Prosonnocoomar privately continued with the celebration of the Durga Puja in his home, with all the idolatrous pomp and ceremony associated with this great Bengali Hindu religious festival. This gave Krishnamohan and *The Enquirer* the opportunity to make direct personal attacks on Prosonnocoomar, sarcastically naming him the "Half-Reformer" and accusing him of inconstancy in personal principles and public action throughout the months of October and November of 1831. Krishnamohan expounded in scathing terms on the laxity of such a Hindu approach to reform of their moribund religion:

> The father meets his death, leaving the task of political improvement to the son; the son exerts not a thought upon it because his ancestors did not show him the way. Generations accordingly have passed in the miserable circumstances arising from weakness and moral imbecility. It is doubtful if the Hindu ever enjoyed what may be called political bliss, and whether he ever felt *the equality of men* in its strictest sense.[58]

As a member of the Young Bengal group, by 1831 Krishnamohan was at the heart of the conflict about the necessity of reforming Hindu society in Calcutta and well known for his views as the editor of *The Enquirer.* This finally led to his becoming a scapegoat in the tensions between the leaders of elite Bengali Hindu society and the radical younger dissenters. Shibnath Shastri recalls Krishnamohan's deeply troubled history as an unintended victim of the rivalries dividing native society in Calcutta:

> On the 23rd of August 1831, [Derozio's] favorite pupils got into a scrape. They used to meet in Krishnamohan's house. . . . Having feasted on loaves from a Muhammadan bakery, and on roast meat from the butcher, they threw the

> refuse of the dishes into the court of an adjoining house, and bawled, "This is beef, nothing but beef."
>
> The cry drew a crowd around Krishnamohan's house; and the offenders fled. The neighbours in a body then interviewed Krishnamohan's grandfather, and threatened to excommunicate him if he did not then and there expel his grandson from the house. This incident made him and his friends more unsparing in their criticisms on Hinduism.[59]

Shortly after his expulsion from his maternal grandfather's home in August 1831, Krishnamohan wrote a five-act play about the tensions over religion that were tearing apart Hindu families by bringing the older and younger generations into open conflict.[60] Called *The Persecuted*, it was a thinly veiled and dramatized account of his own experiences and that of other members of the Young Bengal group when they had tried to initiate apologetic debates about the merits of Hindu rituals with the more orthodox members of their own natal communities.[61] It was possibly the first play written in English by an Indian, and created a sensation on its publication in November 1831. In it, Krishnamohan made strident criticisms of the sanctimonious Hindu elite of Calcutta, laying bare their deceit and duplicity regarding their religious principles and rituals.[62] On December 3, 1831, the *Samachar Darpan* (The Mirror Newspaper) reported as follows:

> Notice on a play called *The Persecuted:* We have received a book written by Baboo Krishnamohan Bandyo. He has shown fine skill in composing the play. English is not the Baboo's mother-tongue, and if we keep this in mind, his writing is excellent. As for what the play is about, the people in Calcutta are so fractiously involved in factionalism (*daladali*), that it would be difficult for us to give a fair reading.
>
> He shows how the Hindu elite have left aside the dharmic rituals and remains addicted to libertinism. We do have to agree, even though the Baboo has been unnecessarily harsh with his criticisms, that he is not wrong.[63]

In the preface to the play, Krishnamohan laid out his reasons for writing and publishing it: "The inconsistencies and the blackness of the influential members of the Hindu community have been depicted before their eyes. They will now dearly perceive the wiles and the tricks of the Brahmins and thereby be able to guard themselves against them."[64] The play revolves around two main characters. The hero is Bany Lall, an elite Hindu Brahmin boy who is his orthodox Hindu father's only son and is also a member of the Young Bengal group. Bany Lall, like many real Young Bengal members, breaks the ritual taboo on eating beef and drinking liquor in his father's house—symbolic of his break with the inherent superstitions and unreason of his father's faith. It is a thinly disguised account of Krishnamohan and his friends. The villain is a Machiavellian newspaper owner named Lall Chand, who brings about Bany Lall's social ostracism through a public media campaign spreading lies and calumny about him in order to gain revenge for some imagined petty slight. The character was evidently based on a Calcutta aristocrat and legal expert who professed to be liberal and enlightened while being nothing of the sort. Since Krishnamohan and Prosonnocoomar had clashed continuously in the editorials and articles of their respective periodicals, there is a high probability that Lall Chand, the inveterate crook who wears a civilized mask, could be a veiled portrayal of Prosonnocoomar. Given Prosonnocoomar's role in establishing the first Indian theater in his garden house at Shurah and his enduring interest in plays, Krishnamohan might have written the drama with the idea that it would be quickly read and understood by Prosonnocoomar and his associates.

The scenes in *The Persecuted* between Bany Lall and his father, and between Lall Chand and his publicly upright and privately venal friends, show a rift growing in Bengali Hindu society, not merely between the older and younger generations in the public sphere but also within the deeply private domain of the *antahpur.* Some of Bany Lall's anguish results from his deep love for his father and his revulsion at his father's insincerely held but dogmatic superstitions. When Mahadeb, Bany Lall's father, learns that Bany Lall has been consuming beef and wine at home, both proscribed foods, he tells him, "I care not for the most dissolute life you may lead. But do preserve our caste." Bany Lall is disgusted by the fact that performing a mere show of allegiance to his father's Hindu faith would save him from ostracization and outcasting by his community, and that his integrity, questioning spirit, and adherence to truth in his personal and public life is seen as a major character flaw in the duplicitous world of his native community. Lall Chand, on the other hand, can get away with his conspiracies and vilification of Bany Lall and his friends by wearing a mask of enlightened civility, as the character himself confesses:

> *Lall Chand.* Why raise false reports against these fellows—exaggerate the least cause you may get-prejudice the people against them. Utter their names with the most abusive epithets. Do all these, nay more; I am resolved to summon all rich men to a common assembly, and laying these matters to

> their consideration pass an order to Mahadeb [Bany Lall's father] to turn his son out. That shall be my duty. While you cry out in the roads against them, abuse them at home; abuse them everywhere. Alarm the natives; let every street, every road, ring with invectives against them.[65]
>
> Ha! Ha! Ha! "my noble nature for the preservation of our religion!" what cannot Lall Chand do? My "noble nature" was once changed when I passed for a Christian. It may change again if necessary, and I may again be a "liberal" as they call it if circumstances turn out strangely.[66]

Bany Lall's insistence on the centrality of integrity and truth to his personal credo is deeply Derozian, and it highlights the rift that the Young Bengal group had exposed within their Bengali Hindu elite world:

> *Bany Lall.* Are these the effects of knowledge? Disagreement between father and son? What! Is knowledge to produce all these? Is a man by renouncing superstition to fall into such difficulties? Are we to set ourselves at defiance to all the calls of nature? A father versus Truth! Truth comes and hardens our feelings. Truth prevents us from yielding to a father's cries and a mother's solicitations. . . . A father's feelings are not more to be consulted than the dictates of TRUTH. A Kindred is not to trample upon Truth. I break down the chains, of filial duty for *Truth;* Witness this and do me justice.[67]

The shadow of duplicity, treachery, and profound corruption lies over the nineteen-year-old Krishnamohan's portrayal of contemporary Bengali Hindu society of the early nineteenth century. *The Persecuted* was never performed, and it does not seem to have been written for this purpose. Instead, it seems to be a manifesto and a rallying call for radical members of the Young Bengal group; as one of their most important members, Krishnamohan highlighted, through this play, which was entirely apologetic in nature, how the ethics of religious faith were intricately braided with both communitarian and political alliances in Bengal. It is also a poignant testimony to the loss of affective bonds and social kinship ties that frequently resulted from contestations over faith. *The Persecuted* clearly illustrates the ways in which the Young Bengal group's desire to articulate an independent personhood, and to realize the ideals of rational inquiry, political and civil liberty, and religious toleration, were repeatedly stymied by the apologetic defense mounted by the more orthodox members of Bengal's elite Hindu community. The play is a passionate invective and jeremiad against the lip service paid to ritual purity by Hindu society in Calcutta. It also chronicles the changing opinions of a new generation of young men as they encountered a delayed wave of rationalism and liberalism in the colonial pedagogical institutions of the early 1830s—and the uproar that resulted as they clashed with their families over questions of faith. *The Persecuted* upholds Christianity as the faith of reason and the only faith that promises salvation through an understanding of Truth.[68]

Krishnamohan, after his expulsion from his home, experienced complete ostracism from his community. He only found stable refuge and steady occupation with Duff, who offered him a place to stay at his own residence. Duff's generosity affected him deeply. He converted to Christianity a few months after his friend Mohesh Ghose in 1832 and was baptized by Duff. A later critic of Krishnamohan referred to the refuge he found with Duff after being expelled from his home in order to accuse him of converting for insincere reasons:

> The Rev. K. M. Banerjee may be the most pious Christian that we ever knew among the Hindu converts, and we will never venture to question the sincerity of his attachment to the Church. But the story, if true, throws one light on the subject that the baptism of Krishnamohan Banerjee was very probably under the influence of other circumstances than of honest conviction.[69]

Krishnamohan's wife, Bindubasini Devi, whom he married in 1828, was prevented by her family and in-laws from joining him after his conversion and spent close to three years living as a quasi-widow. It was only in 1835, when Krishnamohan won his suit for the restitution of conjugal rights with the help of the civil magistrate of Howrah, that he finally liberated his wife so she could live with him. Forced estrangement from one's wife (and infant children) as a result of conversion was a common experience for many Bengali Hindu (and Indian) converts. Krishnamohan would go on to become perhaps the most well-known of the native converts in Bengal. He was a brilliant orator and soon became an active participant in the evangelical effort to convert Hindu boys—which earned him the infamous epithet of *Ghar majano Kisto* or "Krishnamohan, the destroyer of homes."[70]

After Mohesh Ghose, Krishnamohan Banerjee, and Gopinath Nandy converted in the early 1830s, there were multiple cases of conversion of high-caste Bengali boys that we can find records of.[71] The conversion of Madhusudan Dutta, known as Michael Madhusudan after his baptism, caused tremendous controversy in Calcutta. Madhusudan was one of Hindu College's brightest students in the post–Young Bengal period, well known for his command of the English language and English literature and also for his precocious poetic talent. His friends included future luminaries like Bhudev Mukhopadhyay, the educationist; Raj Narayan Bose, the leader of the Brahmo Samaj and maternal grandfather of the revolutionary nationalist leader Aurobindo Ghose; and Gyanendramohan Tagore, the first Indian barrister and eventually a Christian convert himself. Madhusudan was deeply enamored of English literature, especially Shakespeare and Milton, and his poetic talents were nurtured by the principal of Hindu College, D. L. Richardson. Madhusudan himself later introduced the sonnet form to Bengali literature and wrote the epic *Meghnad-vadh Kavya* (The slaying of the demon-prince Meghanada), modeled on *Paradise Lost*.

When Madhusudan suddenly vanished in 1843, his friends—after much searching—learned that he was hiding in Fort William, awaiting baptism. His father Rajnarayan, a famous attorney with close links to the city's elite and powerful, and a very wealthy man in his own right, tried every means to retrieve Madhusudan—including having a band of men lie in wait to abduct him when he left the fort to go for his baptism. Madhusudan did not come back home. Krishnamohan Banerjee visited his father when he learned that Madhusudan's cousin was pondering legal means of gaining access to Madhusudan, who was being sheltered by the missionaries. Though his cousin wanted to file a writ petition of habeas corpus, Krishnamohan stressed that Madhusudan had legally attained the age of maturity and that there was very little to be gained in trying to forcefully stop his conversion.

Madhusudan, who had converted to Christianity mostly because of his attraction to English culture and literature, but also because he thought it would help him gain social advancement, found after the fact that he was an outcaste to both his own countrymen and the British. There are glimpses of the complicated regret he felt regarding his conversion evident in his poetic work, which has not received sufficient historical analysis, except in the work of Rosinka Chaudhuri.[72] The posthumous narratives regarding this conversion cast Archdeacon Dealtry and Krishnamohan Banerjee as the villainous *padris* who had lured him away by promising a voyage to Britain and a daughter in marriage, respectively. Both claims have been comprehensively refuted.[73] Michael Madhusudan Dutta spent his life battling the racial disadvantages of being an Indian, which his conversion to Christianity did not erase. Disinherited from his substantial familial wealth, he found it increasingly difficult to hold any occupation for very long and spiraled into destructive and ultimately fatal alcoholism. Much of his short life was spent, in fact, fighting fruitlessly to recover his patrimony. He failed and spent years submerged in poverty and debt before he died in complete penury.[74]

Therefore, we can see how the arrival of Alexander Duff in Calcutta in 1830 laid the ground for an open contest, with religious apologetics shifting from intellectual disputation to tangible social unrest that had a significant effect on individual lives, families, and communities, when minor schoolboys absconded from homes, converted, and found refuge with their teachers. These social tensions erupted in the Anglo-Indian courts, in legal contests between parents and missionaries over the custodial rights of minor children. There were many reasons for this change in the relationship between the Hindu Bengali middle-class and aristocratic families in Calcutta and the Christian evangelicals.[75] With the new demands for English education among Bengalis, young boys were increasingly exposed to occidental modes of pedagogy that prioritized a steady diet of English language, literature, and philosophy. The British administration hoped this would pave the way, in Macaulay's words, for a new group of "persons Indian in blood and color, but English in tastes, in opinions, in morals and in intellect."[76] With English as the language of transaction between the administration, the native bureaucracy, and British-Indian subjects, the path was paved for much closer contact between average Indians and their instructors, both missionaries and secularists, in new colonial institutions.

But conversion of school and college boys also brought to the forefront a related but important legal issue: the age of maturity of Hindu boys. Even if Hindu boys converted at the behest of their missionary or evangelically minded preceptors, were they of age to make these decisions regarding their conscience? Up to what age could parents of Bengali boys exercise unchallenged control over their offspring? These questions would be debated vigorously between 1833 and 1865, as Hindu families repeatedly faced off in custodial battles with missionaries in the Anglo-Indian court system.

HABEAS CORPUS AND THE LEGAL AGE OF MATURITY

While the earliest conversions of high-caste Bengali Hindu men to Christianity generated extreme controversy, the age of these converts precluded any debate about their capability to make the decision to be baptized. Krishnamohan Banerjee, born in 1813, was almost twenty and living independently at the time of his conversion.[77] Mohesh Ghose and Gopinath Nandy converted at similar ages. And Madhusudan, born in 1824, was nineteen years old at the time of his dramatic conversion. All four had clearly attained the legal age of maturity—at which point they were counted as adults capable of making decisions regarding their life on their own—which was sixteen according to accepted Hindu social and legal customary practices.

This section analyzes the ways in which tensions about the profound influence of missionary preceptors on young students, and the incidents of conversion of boys who had not yet reached the legal age of maturity, led to custodial battles between Bengali Hindu parents and missionaries. Paul Halliday, in his seminal study of habeas corpus, describes the mournful sighs of prisoners restrained illegally. According to Halliday, the common law writ of habeas corpus enables us to hear those sighs and, most importantly, to question the facts determining the legality of the restraint. In Halliday's words, "No other writ provided opportunities to think through the political threat posed by religious dissent."[78] In the Indian Empire, and especially in the cases regarding conversion of young school boys in Bengal, the judges in the courts listened both to the sighs of those boys who had embraced Christianity through conversion and to the sighs of the distressed parents who blamed the missionaries for leading their children astray. Such habeas corpus cases in colonial Bengal, with reference to schoolchildren, were concerned with the custodial rights of parents over their offspring. These custodial battles played out in the Anglo-Indian law courts, where aggrieved parents often brought habeas corpus writs demanding the restitution of their offspring's custody to them.

Whether the boy was a minor or not was difficult enough to prove at a time when no medical examinations existed that could establish without a shadow of a doubt the age of a person. Bengali Hindu parents often furnished a *janma-patrika* or astrological chart with calculations based on exact time and date of birth, but these often had very little veracity in the eyes of both missionaries and the judicial system. On the legal question regarding the conscientious choice of conversion, Anglo-Indian legal opinion gradually evolved over a period of thirty years. The consensus was that it was not the age of maturity but the age of discretion that was important to consider in cases of minor boys converting to Christianity. And in contrast to the accepted limit to the age of maturity for Hindu boys, sixteen, for the age of discretion it was legally established to be fourteen years, in line with British legal precedence.[79] I chart these contests and the evolution of legal opinion about conversion of Bengali Hindu schoolboys through a close examination of four habeas corpus cases with differing outcomes over a period of three decades.

The anger aroused in Calcutta society over the baptisms of Indians became far more intense when the converts were legally minors. Young students at missionary-administered pedagogical institutions, including Duff's own General Assembly's Institution, began to convert in the mid-1830s. These young boys, along with their child brides, received shelter and financial support from the missionaries and instructors at these institutions, who even helped them to leave their paternal homes and kept disconsolate parents from seeing their children before baptism, often with overt assistance from the colonial police force.[80] In almost all documented cases of such conversions, one of the most contentious aspects was the age of the child. These young future converts and their missionary preceptors invariably stressed that they had attained the age of legal maturity when they made the conscientious decision to be baptized. On the other hand, Indian parents relentlessly tried to use the habeas corpus writ to prevent these conversions. Furnishing as proof the astrological natal charts of the boys, cast at their birth, they claimed that the boys were below the age of maturity.

Two cases established precedence for the propriety of the habeas corpus writ in instances of the conversion of young schoolboys: *Rex v. Greenhill* in 1836 and *Reg. v. Maria Clarke in re Alicia Race* in 1856.[81] In both these cases, custodial rights as well as the education of minor children, especially the rights of parents to direct particular forms of religious instruction for children, became the locus of legal debate. Therefore, the judgments in both cases set the terms for proper custody of minors in case of disputes, especially when those in current custody of the minor child were charged with moral failings or in cases of disagreements regarding the religious education of the minor children. The minor status of the child and the moral fitness of the guardian decided custody in all instances, except in cases where the minor child was judged to be capable of using his discretion to choose where he wanted to reside. Both cases also established that habeas corpus could only proceed from the "illegal restraint" of the minor in question. There were multiple documented cases of conversion of young girls and boys in the Calcutta, Bombay, and Madras Presidencies between 1840 and 1860 in which the courts had honored the child's discretion and allowed them to convert unhindered by their guardian's or parents' objections. These included the cases of the boy Ragavaloo in *Queen v. Anderson* (Madras, 1846), the girl Mooniatta in *In re Mooniatta, Madras Native Herald for 1847* (Madras, 1847), the girl Sai in *Queen v. Wilson* (Bombay, 1852), and the boy Nagalingam in *Queen v. Anderson* (Madras, 1854). They also documented the case of the boy C. Narainswamy Chetty in *Queen v. Braidwood* (Madras, 1858), in which the decision actually went in favor of the boy's father.[82]

Between the mid-1830s and 1865, four custody cases in Bengal, all involving schoolboys, illustrated the evolution of legal consensus regarding the rights of parents over their minor children and significantly changed the terms of the debate. These four cases were documented in a far more expansive way than the elusive details we find of other instances of custodial battles over conversion of minor children. Therefore, these cases are useful in that they demonstrate how anti-missionary apologetics in this thirty-year period spread out from the antagonistic encounters documented in dueling newspapers in the public sphere and shifted to the Anglo-Indian legal domain through the use of the habeas corpus writ by Indians. All of these cases took place in Bengal and were adjudicated at the Calcutta Supreme Court (after 1857 the Calcutta High Court). Each one created considerable tension and public uproar in the city. The shifting political landscape in India, particularly the seismic changes wrought after 1857, also influenced the fate of such legal contests. The tumult of the 1857 Mutiny completely changed the tenor of legal disputes over the conversion of minor boys. In the aftermath, Indian intellectuals including Sir Syed Ahmed Khan asserted that missionary activity and the interference in the religious customs of the Indians—especially in seminaries and schools where children were indoctrinated—were two of the major causes for Indian disaffection that led to the Mutiny. After the events of 1857 and Queen Victoria's proclamation of noninterference in the religious rights of her Indian subjects, there were profound sociopolitical changes in India that affected the legal decisions in these conversion cases. Opinions such as those of Syed Ahmed Khan now had been accepted as official explanations for Indian disaffection as a result of the Queen's imprimatur. This encouraged judges within the Anglo-Indian court system to be more careful and deliberate in their considerations of custody cases between Hindu parents and missionaries.

The Case of Brijonath Ghose

The first case involving a minor Bengali boy converting to Christianity was that of Brijonath or Brojonath Ghose, whose name entered the legal archives in 1834.[83] He was educated at the Hindu College and then at the Mirzapur School of the Church Missionary Society at Amherst Street, supervised by

Krishnamohan Banerjee. According to reports in *The Asiatic Journal and Monthly Miscellany,* the boy was about fourteen or fifteen years old at this time and began talking about conversion with his schoolmates, having read the Bible. His father Rammohun Ghose had removed him from Hindu College in the fear that he would become an atheist under the spell of the members of Young Bengal. Brijonath's friends reported his desire for conversion to his parents, and his father now found himself in a quandary. Brijonath was confined at home, under strict watch.

Krishnamohan Banerjee inquired about the boy's absence at school and was informed of his confinement. At this point, the narrative diverges in contemporary sources. According to the account provided by *The Asiatic Journal and Monthly Miscellany,* Brijonath escaped on his own and, on reaching Mirzapur, asked for help from Krishnamohan, who secreted him away in the residence of Rev. Sandys.[84] But according to the biography of Daniel Wilson, the second Anglican bishop of Calcutta, Krishnamohan actually aided and abetted the boy in escaping his home and took him personally to the house of Rev. Sandys: "The boy communicated with the well-known Krishnamohan Banerjee, who was his friend, and on the plea that his life was endangered, was aided to escape."[85] Rammohun Ghose first went to the Dharma Sabha, the association of the orthodox faction in Calcutta headed by Radhakanta Dev, where he reported that his son was a minor and had been abducted forcibly from his home. This caused a furor, and Rammohun Ghose was advised to move to the national Supreme Court and file a habeas corpus plea for his son against Krishnamohan Banerjee. He appointed one of Calcutta's most well-known barristers, Longueville Clarke, as his advocate. Wilson, as bishop of Calcutta, ordered a short delay on the baptism of the boy while the case was in court.

Two questions were key to this case. Had Brijonath attained the age of maturity and thus achieved the freedom of conscience to choose his own faith? And had he been constrained by the missionaries? The missionaries argued that fourteen was an age at which young boys could make conscientious decisions, both under Hindu practice as it pertained to Bengal and in England, according to William Blackstone. Thus, Brijonath had every right to be converted. The judge Sir Edward Ryan disagreed that fourteen was an age at which a young Indian schoolboy could make such a momentous and permanent decision about the rest of his life: "The boy had been allured from his parents' home for the purpose of converting him to Christianity, contrary to the usages of the country. . . . I therefore say that to order him to be delivered to his father is a sound, proper and good decision."[86] Pathetic scenes followed in the courtroom after the verdict as Brijonath clung to his missionary preceptors and his father attempted to forcibly pull him away:

> In full court, the father advanced, and laid hands upon him. The lad cried bitterly, appealed to the judges, clung to the barristers' table, and was dragged away by force, amidst the shouts of the heathen, and the tears and remonstrance of Christians. The court sat silent, without a word of sympathy for the son, or caution to the father.[87]

The aftermath of the case involved a long and acrimonious series of letters between the barrister Longueville Clarke and Rev. Alexander Duff, since Clarke had called the missionaries' conduct "flagitious and dangerous," deeming the case "of great importance as the rights of Hindu parents were often invaded by the missionaries in Calcutta." Duff found the statements libelous when applied to missionaries in general, as it seemed Clarke had done. The missionaries also charged Brijonath's father with perjury: the forcible abduction that he described in his affidavit of habeas corpus had not happened, since Brijonath had gone with the missionaries of his own volition.[88] However, the most important insight into the case came from Duff, who opined:

> [If] the alleged right of fathers exists at all, it must be either natural or legal. Now I deny that there is any separate legal right. I am fully aware that the father is the guardian of his child as to all civil rights, till the latter be of age, but I question how far the law confers the right of religious instruction on the *father* alone. Rather I am prepared to deny that there is any such right conferred at all, else might the father prosecute the teacher of a religion different from his own for misdemeanor—an absurdity from which British law, with all its anomalies, is honorably exempt.[89]

Brijonath would return to be baptized when he was an adult, no longer legally or socially under his father's wardship. He became a teacher at the government school in Chaibasa, a tribal town in Singhbhum district (in present day Jharkhand).[90]

Duff made a momentous argument that flew in the face of all accepted social and legal norms pertaining to the rights of parents to custody of their children and the rights of parents to direct the religious instruction their child might receive, both in India and in England. Duff was essentially proposing that the right of Bengali Hindu fathers to their minor children was immaterial legally and spiritually, given that in the eyes of the evangelical establishment in

India, Hinduism was mere superstition and not a religion at all. So a child choosing to convert was making an enlightened decision and therefore should not be constrained by their parents. This question of the limits to parental rights was later to be reconsidered in three other cases involving minor boys, all of which caused immense social disturbance in Calcutta and across Bengal. Although eerily similar to the case of Brijonath Ghose, those involving Umesh Chandra Sarkar, Radhakanta Dutta, and Himanath Bose resulted in very different outcomes.

The Case of Umesh Chandra Sarkar

Dwarkanath Tagore (1794–1846), exhausted and unwell, wrote to his son and heir Debendranath from London in May 1845.[91] He had left this son in charge of his *zamindari* affairs, and reports from India were making him very anxious about the economic circumstances of the Jorasanko Tagore family. Debendranath, he realized with dismay, had things other than business on his mind:

> It is only a source of wonder to me that all my estates are not ruined. Your time I am sure being more taken up in writing for the newspapers and *in fighting with the missionaries* than in watching over and protecting the important matters which you leave in the hands of your favorite Amlas—instead of attending to them yourself most vigilantly. . . . I hear of nothing going right.[92]

Debendranath's preoccupation with missionaries was neither new nor unforeseen, as Dwarkanath's exasperated tone proves. His sustained opposition to Christian missionaries and to Christianity would endure over the next fifty-five years, and he would eventually play a key role in the expulsion of Christian Catholic convert and nationalist politician Brahmabandhab Upadhyay from his son's school at Santiniketan (see Chapter 6). In the 1830s and early 1840s, the relationship between the Christian missionaries and the Bengali intelligentsia had shifted away from the discourse of comparative merits and superiority of Hindu scripture and philosophical tracts in the newly emergent vernacular and indigenous print media. The apologetics shifted to legal questions concerning the right to self-determination of young Bengali boys (and girls).

As Brijonath's case demonstrates, the focus had also moved to vicious debates about parents' legal custodial rights to minor children who were influenced by Christian missionaries to convert. The next case of conversion of a minor boy to receive immense public notice was that of Umesh Chandra Sarkar and his child bride. It is the most well-known of these cases today, owing to the direct involvement of both Debendranath Tagore and Alexander Duff.[93] Importantly, this event also temporarily brought together the conservative faction of Radhakanta Dev and the liberal faction of Prosonnocoomar Tagore and his nephew Debendranath, since the case became something of a cause célèbre.[94] An 1845 article in *The Friend of India*, a publication sensitive to the moods and labyrinthine politics of the Calcutta elite, noted:

> In this crusade against Christianity we find men of all sects and parties meeting on common ground. The descendants of Gopimohan Peer Alee, the fallen, and of Gopimohan Deb, the prince of the orthodox, the Tagores and Debs—men who have faith in idols, and those who despise them—the Hindoo Pharisee, and the Hindoo libertine—Young Bengal and old Bengal—all are united in one general opposition to the truths of Christianity and in efforts to oppose its progress.[95]

The outcry was occasioned by Alexander Duff's conversion of fourteen-year-old Umesh and his eleven-year-old wife on April 27, 1845. Duff left behind his own recollections of this entire affair in a pamphlet he called *A Work of Grace at Calcutta: Being a Narrative of the Circumstances of the Recent Conversions There.*[96] The pamphlet consists of Duff's letters to his evangelical colleagues, primarily regarding Umesh's baptism, and also contains an excerpt of a letter supposedly from Umesh to his brother. According to Duff, Umesh's father and brother went to Duff's residence the same night that Umesh coaxed his young wife out of the family's carriage and then took refuge with the missionaries of the Scottish Church, in order to coax or threaten the young couple to come home. But Umesh appeared to be unmoved by their pleas. Duff and other members of the General Assembly's Institution prevented Umesh's father from forcibly removing him from Duff's home. It led to heartbreaking scenes, in Duff's account, with the father alternately cursing and pleading with his young son, who repeatedly spurned his efforts. Duff records the curses flung at Umesh by his father:

> "And you'll be smitten," said he, "with every disease, and overtaken by every calamity. You'll be deaf, and you'll be dumb, and you'll be blind, and you'll be a leper, and you'll pass through innumerable births of loathsome monsters and reptiles. Every pain and every misery will be yours. You will be an

eternal disgrace and reproach to your kindred and your country; all that hear of your name will load it with execrations; and the very depths of hell will everlastingly receive you."[97]

Umesh's family made several unsuccessful attempts to lodge a criminal complaint of coercion and kidnapping against Duff and other missionaries, including Krishnamohan Banerjee. The older Sarkar brother, Rajendra, was employed by Debendranath at their Jorasanko home. At this point, Rajendra decided to ask the Tagores for help. Debendranath Tagore used the incident of Umesh's flight to create a rallying cry for Calcutta's elite to band against the depredations of the missionaries. He wanted every Bengali Hindu (and Brahmo) to come together and put an end to the threat of conversion looming over boys who went to schools to learn English and instead turned into heretics to their natal communities.[98] The public outcry from some of Calcutta's most influential Bengali elite rejuvenated Umesh's family's attacks against the missionaries and strengthened their attempts to retrieve their son and daughter-in-law. In the pamphlet, Duff records Umesh's father and brother threatening both Umesh and Duff with legal action. These threats indicate that litigation, particularly in the form of applying for a writ of habeas corpus, was a well-known tactic for responding to the issue of missionaries taking or sheltering minor children with the intention of converting them to Christianity:

> They then dealt out the most formidable threats—declaring, moreover, that he was not of legal age—that they would apply forthwith for a writ of Habeas Corpus against me—that he and I would both be severely punished—and that have them [Umesh and his wife] rescued they would, by fair means or foul, though it should cost them lacs, or hundreds of thousands of rupees.[99]

The threat was actually carried out by Umesh's family with the support of their powerful backers from among the Bengali Hindu elite in Calcutta, including both the Tagore families of Jorasanko and Pathuriaghata, as well as the Mullick family of Pathuriaghata. According to Duff, multiple influential members of Calcutta's Hindu society tried to reason with Umesh about his decision to convert, including a young scion of the Sobhabazar Raj family, Raja Kalikrishna Dev.[100]

But just as his father's entreaties had fallen on deaf ears, Umesh was unmoved by the threats and persuasions of these leaders. Duff quotes from a letter that Umesh purportedly wrote to his elder brother on April 25, 1845, two days before his baptism, outlining his reasons for converting and attempting to justify his abandonment of his family and his community of birth:

> I received your kind note of yesterday morning and perused it with attention. I do not wonder, my dear brother, that you charge me with folly, inconsiderateness, rashness, and etc., in following the dictates of my conscience. . . . My present resolution to embrace Christianity is not a mere momentary impulse; it is the result of the calm, deliberate, and serious investigation of two years. . . . I left home of my own free will, and am now living at Dr. Duff's of my own free choice. I am under no restraint. . . . I am free to think and free to act.[101]

Duff mentions preventing the efforts of Umesh's family and their influential supporters to kidnap Umesh from his residence with the help of native *lathiyals* or staff-bearing militia. Two days later, Umesh and his wife were converted with great pomp by Duff, Krishnamohan Banerjee, and others. It was the first time in the history of Protestant missions in the Indian Empire that a man and his wife were both baptized publicly and together.

In his autobiography, Debendranath describes how the event drove him to terrible anger and roused his desire to make the strongest resistance against evangelism by uniting the factions of Calcutta society.[102] Ajit Kumar Chakrabarty reiterates this point in his biography of Debendranath, noting that Debendranath and his followers were at the forefront of the public opposition to Christian missionaries. Debendranath used his periodical, the *Tattwabodhini Patrika* (Theological Truth-Seekers' Periodical), to mount an apologetic challenge against missionaries, especially Duff and his faction.[103] Debendranath was probably one of the anonymous authors who in 1845 penned an apologia against Duff's relentless attacks on Vedantic Hindu philosophy in a widely circulated pamphlet called *Vaidantic Doctrines Vindicated.*[104] He was now also providing social, legal, and financial support to Umesh's family as the debate about religious and legal rights of Hindu parents and Hindu offspring shifted to the courts of law and the apologia took on the shape of legal discourse.

With the encouragement of their influential Bengali Hindu patrons, including the Tagores, Mullicks, and Devs, Umesh's family brought a case of habeas corpus against Duff—though interestingly, Umesh's young wife was not included in this suit. The public anger in Calcutta was aggravated by the fact that although both Umesh and his wife were minors, the Supreme Court ruled in Duff's favor. The bench, headed by Sir Laurence Peel, cousin of the conservative British prime minister Sir Robert Peel, refused to listen to Umesh's father's petition that the conversion was illegal because the boy was a minor and could not have assented to conversion without his permission as parent and guardian.[105] Instead, Peel reserved his judgment on the basis that no case of forcible restraint on the persons of Umesh and his wife could be made, since Umesh had taken his wife and gone to Duff's residence of his own accord.

The ruling negated the precedent of the Brijonath Ghose case, instead assigning a purely narrow construction on the use of habeas corpus involving minor children being sheltered or detained by missionaries with the intent to convert. Calcutta's Hindu society was distraught over the fact that the Supreme Court had removed the last option left to parents who wanted to prevent the conversion of their sons. They were also deeply resentful, suspecting that the colonial legal system had provided support to the missionaries in their program of conversion. Deeper anxieties were occasioned by the baptism of Umesh's wife: the missionary's shadow had fallen even upon the segregated inner domain or *antahpur,* into the private life of Hindus. Duff himself was profoundly aware of the negative impression that Umesh's flight and subsequent conversion created in the Bengali Hindu public sphere in Calcutta, where all of the elite leaders had put aside factional rivalries to combat the great threat of "missionaryism," made more threatening by what they saw as the complicity of the Anglo-Indian legal system. Duff wrote:

> Previously, the native community was split up and cantoned into various parties and sects, as hostile to each other as any one of them could well be towards the Christians; but the fearful cry which has been raised of common danger has for a time inspired them all with a wondrous spirit of coalescence and harmony—the whole mass of liberal Hindus. . . . All of these—the Pantheist and the Polytheist, the religious Conservative and the religious Radical, the metaphysical contemplator of the one supreme Brahma, and the groveling Idolater, the noisy Liberal, and the stern unbending Bigot—actuated by a new spirit of unanimity, have met as a sworn brotherhood.[106]

Debendranath Tagore's first reaction was to initiate written protest against missionaries' conduct, and he accordingly commissioned an article for the *Tattvabodhini Patrika.* Apocalyptic in tone, it was written by the rationalist Akshay Kumar Dutta at Debendranath's request. Dutta wrote of the wildfires of conversion activities that surrounded Hindu society and had the potential to burn every Bengali Hindu religious and cultural edifice to ashes. He asked Hindu parents to keep their boys away from the missionary institutions and requested that the aristocratic families of Calcutta band together and raise donations in order to promote schools and seminaries in line with Hindu principles. Dutta also wrote poignantly of the complete isolation that awaited the young Umesh and his wife after conversion:

> Now a child-bride in the *antahpur* has also left her own faith and embraced apostasy! What would a fourteen-year-old boy and an eleven-year-old girl even know about religion that they can take a reasoned decision to convert? In what way is it ethical conduct to take these children out of the fold and make them lose their religion? Now, they have been lost from their own true religion. . . . The only refuge left to them is Rev. Duff! . . . If you wish for the good of your families, keep missionaries away from your sons, stop sending your boys to schools run by missionaries!![107]

Immediately after the article was published, Debendranath personally visited the house of every aristocratic family in Calcutta, irrespective of their factional affiliation—from the orthodox "pope" of the "Vatican" Dharma Sabha, Radhakanta Dev, to the confirmed agnostic and old Derozian, Ram Gopal Ghosh. A meeting was called and attended by over one thousand people, and it was resolved that a free school called the Hindu-Hitarthi Vidyalay (Hindu Well-Wishers' School) would be opened immediately. The sons of the first Calcutta millionaire Ram Dulal Dev, Ashutosh and Pramathanath (or Latoo Baboo and Chatoo Baboo, as they were popularly known), promised Rs. 10,000 each. Other large donations followed, bringing in a total of more than Rs. 40,000 within the hour.[108] At least for a short time, this concentrated backlash against "missionaryism" led to profound difficulties for evangelical pedagogical efforts. On May 2, 1845, five days after Umesh's conversion, Duff recorded that the event had caused a panic among the Indian population:

> Doubts, suspicions, and alarms of every sort were widely and studiously propagated. Native society was considerably convulsed, and something like a panic seemed to seize all minds. Nor was the effect limited to Calcutta alone. From different and even distant parts of the country, urgent letters have been received, or messengers have arrived, to press the removal of pupils from an institution, in which, it was rumored, "all were to be forthwith converted to Christianity." Discussions and controversies were thus raised

in the native and English journals, as well as in most native families and social circles.[109]

By June 2, 1845, Duff had converted two other boys, Baikuntha Nath De and Harish Chandra Mitra. Following shortly after the spectacle of Umesh's conversion and the controversies roused by the case, these new conversions left Calcutta society completely convulsed. In a letter to a friend on June 18, 1845, Duff wrote:

> Never before, in this part of India, was the cry of "Hinduism in danger!" raised more wildly, vehemently, or universally . . . of a hue and cry, such as has never before been heard in Calcutta . . . yea, as if Hinduism itself was on the eve of being torn up by the roots and scattered. . . . The cry of "Down with Christianity! Down with the Missionaries!" . . . was heard to issue from every lip, resound through every street, and re-echo from every bazaar.[110]

Duff's description gives a feeling of the extraordinary anger, the sense of impending doom, and the panic that gripped Bengal over these conversions. The schools meant to educate a new generation of young Indians in the English language, and thereby bring about a new Enlightenment in India, were proving to be centers of apostasy and alienation.

In a later anti-Christian meeting convened on September 19, 1847, a harsher measure was proposed to contain the menace of "missionaryism": the loss of caste for those who sent their children to missionary schools. During these meetings, characterized by inflamed public opinions, some intemperate threats were also made against Alexander Duff by the aristocratic leaders of Bengali Hindu society, especially by Pramathanath Dev or Chatoo Baboo, who was, as we have seen, one of Debendranath's great supporters in the anti-missionary movement. These threats were reported back to Duff, who was incensed. He responded in a long series of letters, first written under the pseudonym Indophilus and then signed with his own name, which were published in the *Bengal Hurkaru* (The Bengal Mail-Runner) and the Baptist mouthpiece *The Friend of India*. The letters aimed to expose the violent, primitive, and irrational character of the Bengali Hindus of Calcutta, whom Duff called "the Voluptuous Baboos of the Metropolis."[111]

His descriptions show a society up in arms against a long-standing threat but also lay bare the deep tensions around the cultural, social, and political affiliations of Bengali Hindu society. The letters also illuminate the aristocratic faction heads' sense that they needed to control, surveil, and police the younger English-educated Bengalis who questioned the older generation without fear. The letters also make clear that Bengali Hindus were convinced that missionary-led pedagogy was a mere front for the greater objective of converting schoolboys to Christianity. To prevent more tragedies like Umesh's case, Calcutta's elite leaders were determined to ostracize parents who knew of the dangers of "missionaryism" and still sent their children to missionary-run schools to learn English. On the other hand, as Duff reasoned, in the new age of British imperial control, preventing young Bengali boys from learning English would prove detrimental to Bengali society's efforts to become partners and middlemen in the daily functioning of the British-Indian Empire. Duff indignantly wrote:

> The great object of the Association is to inflict the penalty of the loss of caste on all who shall allow their children, or their wards, to attend Missionary seminaries; but how can those who have themselves exhibited a most courageous and laudable disregard of the Hindu shastras, and who live after the more rational and convenient fashion of Europeans, pronounce expulsion from caste . . . ? They are working against the tendencies of the age.[112]

After the scandal of his supposed "abduction" and conversion to Christianity, Duff provided for Umesh's care, continuing education, and future occupation—and later that of Umesh's wife. According to the list of converts from government and missionary schools published in 1852, Umesh held a job with the Treasury and posted at Danapur, in Bihar.[113] He went there with his wife but died soon thereafter of consumption (tuberculosis). His widow returned to Calcutta with their baby son in 1856–1857 and found refuge with Duff's friend Rev. David Ewart, first pastor of the Bengali Church. Umesh's wife, whose given name cannot be found in the archives, later became an instructor at the native girls' school—the Duff Girls' School, which was run by the General Assembly of the Scottish Church in Calcutta.[114] Mrs. Sarkar received a princely salary of three pounds or thirty rupees per month, with free board and lodging for her and her son. She probably remarried at some later date and is referred to as Mrs. Chatterjee in subsequent records.

It is worth noting that this kind of self-sufficiency and employment would not have been available to her if she and Umesh had not converted. No Hindu widow in the first half of the nineteenth century would have had her degree of education or been allowed to hold a job outside the home. The fact that she could remarry also owed to her conversion. Despite the passage of the Hindu Widows' Remarriage Act of 1856 (the result of the labors of another great Bengali social reformer, Ishwarchandra Vidyasagar), remarriage was almost unheard of for "respectable" Hindu widows until the next century.[115] Her and Umesh's son was educated at the General Assembly's institution and probably became a native preacher.[116]

It is evident that at least in the erstwhile Mrs. Sarkar's case there were some material benefits to her conversion. This might encourage us to assume that her conversion was indeed insincere. But those benefits must also be weighed against her complete severance from her natal community and her familial and kinship matrix, as well as the loss of the social and moral capital and the stability, support, and safety of those relationships. We must also remember that at the time of her conversion, she was barely eleven years old. It would be hard to believe that she would have had material gain in mind when she converted, given that she was a child at the time. Ultimately, any material gain by Mrs. Umesh Sarkar as a consequence of her conversion must be weighed against the deep violence of exclusion and disinheritance that she and her first husband faced, and then the uncertainty of her life as a widowed mother who had no familial connections to depend upon.

The joint conversion of Umesh and his wife was important for two reasons. First, *zenana* conversions had been a cherished goal of British evangelicals from the time of William Carey and the Serampore Baptists. Umesh's wife was one of the first successful examples of how the influence of missionary pedagogy and preaching could percolate through the young husbands who attended missionary schools to their segregated and impressionable young wives within the private inner domains of Bengali households. Second, joint baptisms of this sort, enabled by the flight of both husband and wife to a sympathetic missionary's residence, made it possible for the couple to continue their conjugal relationship, without forcible separation from each other, often for very long periods of time. In most cases, when only a young boy converted, his deracination and spiritual death in the eyes of his communities of birth and faith meant that his wife was bound to the austere and lonely penances of Hindu widowhood.[117] This was enforced by her maternal and marital families, the latter of which perhaps vented their grief and frustrations about the decisions of their son on their innocent daughter-in-law. Similarly, the young husbands suffered—both because their baptism irreparably separated them from their families and their social matrix, and also because the loss of their young spouses, and sometimes children, compounded their grief and loneliness. The wives of converts generally had two choices. If they did not want to or could not join their husbands, they had to suffer a lonely life of neglect with their in-laws, shut away from the world in the *antahpur*, or remarry where such customs were prevalent, as among the Parsis. Alternatively, they could take the extremely risky path of converting and joining their apostate husbands. This was only possible when their husbands undertook legal action, including filing the writ of habeas corpus in courts.[118]

As we have seen, Krishnamohan Banerjee's wife Bindubasini Devi could only join him after legal action compelled his family to hand her over. And she had to convert so that she would not be pressured to leave him and return to her in-laws with her children. There were multiple cases of such forced separations, where the wife's future also became completely uncertain when their converted husbands were compelled to sever all ties or remarried and abandoned them to forced widowhood, or sued to take custody of the children and alienate them from their mother forever.[119] If a first wife rejoined her husband after his second marriage, she had to contend with a *shotin* or co-wife in the household. Such a situation, amounting to bigamy, was also very irregular for the Christian missionaries who abhorred these incidences and wanted to prevent them from happening—going so far as to oppose government policy that would legalize such marriages. The Indian Marriages Act of 1865 made bigamy a crime for married Indian Christian converts. However, also in 1865, Krishnamohan Banerjee wrote a petition opposing the British administration's attempt to allow converted men to abandon their unconverted spouses and remarry—he wanted to stop the passage of the act and highlight the potential difficulties it would cause for converts who were estranged from their spouses.[120]

Krishnamohan was certain, both from his own personal experience of forced estrangement from his wife after his conversion in 1832 and from counseling many separated couples over his decades as a native pastor, that "the tendency of the Bill is to hinder rather than to facilitate reconciliations of husband and wife, and . . . it repels the unbelieving wife or husband from embracing Christianity." His criticisms were noted but ultimately did not stop the passage of the Native Converts' Marriage Dissolution Act of 1866.[121] The estrangement of young converts from their wives was a distressingly common situation among Christian converts in nineteenth-century Bengal, as can be seen from a poem written by one of the members of the famous Rambagan Dutt family, whose senior branch had been converted by the missionaries of the Scottish Church including Rev. Ewart and Rev. Lal Behari Day, both close associates of Duff.[122] Govin Chunder Dutt, father of the famous poet sisters Toru and Aru, wrote a poem about the plight of husbands who had converted as true believers while their wives had converted because there was no other way to cohabit with their husbands and children securely.[123] George Smith's biography of Duff contains a letter written to him by Rev. W. S. Mackay, which mentions the Rambagan Dutt spouses: "We found that all the brothers and most of their sons were so far believers in Christianity that they were making preparations in their families, getting their affairs in order, and conversing with their wives. The wives were willing to remain with their husbands but are still firm idolaters."[124] Govin's poem, "A Hindu Convert to His Wife," printed in a collection titled *The Dutt Family Album,* is obviously autobiographical in nature. It describes the pathos and loneliness of husbands estranged from their wives as a result of conversion to Christianity:

> Nay, part not so—one moment stay,
> Repel me not with scorn.
> Like others, wilt thou turn away,
> And leave me quite forlorn?
> Wilt thou too join the scoffing crowd,
> The cold, the heartless, and the proud,
> Who curse the hallowed morn,
> When daring idols to disown,
> I knelt before the Savior's throne?[125]

The separation of married couples when one of them, usually the husband, converted was one of the tragic consequences that embittered converts. In such situations, missionaries pointed to Umesh and his wife as exemplars: ideal partners united in their faith, their enlightenment, their resolve, and finally in baptism.

The Macaulayan subject was supposed to be an interlocutor between the British administration, the ruling white class, and their Indian subjects. Instead, these young Indians, influenced by English pedagogy and its promise of liberal subjecthood, as well as the encouragement of their missionary preceptors, hoped to erase markers of imperial, racial, and social hierarchies through conversion to Christianity. In the process, alienated from the true aim of the British civilizing mission—creating middlemen at the lower rungs of the colonial bureaucracy—and from their native communities of birth and faith, these Indian converts became stranded in the irreconcilable gap between British policy and Indian social reality.

The Case of Radhakanta Dutta

Two years later, in 1847, the case of Radhakanta Dutta came before the Anglo-Indian court system. The boy's father, Ramchand Dutta, alleged that James Ogilvie, a missionary of the Scottish Church General Assembly, was holding his son forcibly with the intent to convert him to Christianity. It seems that the unwritten Indian precedent for this case was that of Umesh Chandra Sarkar. Just as in Umesh's case, the defendants here were the General Assembly's Institution and its preceptors; the judge was again Sir Lawrence Peel. The decision was also similar. Although he was barely fifteen years old (not eighteen, as the missionary sources, including Duff, insisted), the boy was judged to be mature enough to conscientiously choose to convert to Christianity. Yet again, the Anglo-Indian legal system waved away the possibility of missionaries' culpability in influencing the boy's decision.

In the habeas corpus writ that Ramchand Dutta filed on July 8, 1847, the boy's age was given as fourteen years, eleven months, and nine days, which was below the Hindu religious and legal age of maturity of sixteen years. Radhakanta was a student at Queen's College in Cornwallis Square in the Simlah neighborhood of north Calcutta, where Ogilvie was superintendent and resident instructor. The Queen's College, going by Ogilvie's testimony, appeared to be affiliated in some manner with the General Assembly's Institution, and Radhakanta was a day scholar at the school. In his reply to the habeas corpus writ, filed on August 20, 1847, Ogilvie also said that Radhakanta had represented himself as being seventeen years old and that he was not under restraint by Ogilvie but free to go wherever he wished. Ogilvie added that although he could not compel Radhakanta to do anything, he had tried to persuade the boy to appear before the Calcutta Supreme Court.

Sir Laurence Peel, who had also refused to issue a writ for habeas corpus in Umesh Chandra Sarkar's case, adamantly refused to listen to the advocate for Ramchand Dutta, Longueville Clarke, when he argued that the Brijonath Ghose case had set a precedent. Peel instead agreed with the defense lawyers Thomas Charles Morton and Theodore Dickens that the 1835 case of *Rex v. Greenhill* was the true precedent in cases of habeas corpus brought with regards to infant children: if the child were of an age to freely exercise his conscientious choice, the court should "set him at liberty to go where he pleases, and, if necessary, give him the protection of an officer in going."[126] Peel and the bench concluded that the case was governed and limited only to the extent of the writ of habeas corpus and could not deal with the question of a

Hindu father's natural right over his children, the religious usages of the country, or the question of forcible abduction with intent to convert the infant to Christianity, as had happened in the Brijonath case a decade ago: "But if a child, though a minor, were neither actually nor constructively under any restraint whatever at the time of issuing the writ, the writ could not be directed against himself [the child] when actually at liberty, and practically a free agent, to assert the father's alleged right to the possession of the person of such child."[127]

Peel added that missionary preceptors were actually third parties in habeas corpus cases between children who converted and their distraught parents—if a child went to their missionary preceptor with the intent to convert, the missionary could not be held responsible for his decision or accused of kidnapping the child: "It is important to keep the writ to its proper use, to prevent third persons, who are neither constructively nor actually guilty of any restraint on the person of the child, from being involved in such distressing disputes between parent and child, and from being needlessly exposed to litigation."[128] In fact, Peel opined, "That the writ of Habeas Corpus is not the mode to assert such a right, if it exists, is abundantly clear." Radhakanta was called to court and questioned by the chief justice:

> *By the Court:* Where do you wish to go—you are at liberty to go where you please, to your father's or Mr. Ogilvie's?
>
> *Radhakanta:* I do not wish to go to my father's house but would rather return to Mr. Ogilvie's.
>
> *The Court:* For what reasons do you not wish to go to your father's house?
>
> *Radhakanta:* Because I think I should not get salvation and for no other reason.

The court found no reason to doubt his capacity, ordering him to be protected to the place from whence he came, and Radhakanta was returned with the protection of a police officer to Ogilvie's school.[129] The court lauded the bar for its restraint in refusing to discuss religious questions in this particular case and not asking Radhakanta any question with the intention to judge his religious opinions past or present. In characterizing the incident essentially as a secular and private dispute between parent and child, and by assigning third-party status to missionaries, this case made an important intervention in the narrative of missionaries as kidnappers who forcibly converted Bengali boys to Christianity—Peel exonerated missionary preceptors of any direct responsibility in the decision their students might or might not make regarding conversion to Christianity. This decision made it difficult for Indian parents to hold missionaries legally culpable for their children going out of the fold and also gave missionaries protection from litigation. Peel's reasoning in this case thereby overturned the precedent of the Brijonath Ghose case, which had favored Indian fathers over missionary preceptors in matters of personal faith and religious instruction of infant children. Effectively, Peel made Indian parents and their children direct antagonists to each other and excluded missionary culpability from legal consideration of a child's right to convert.

The Case of Himanath Bose

The tides of Indian opinion, already anguished and enraged on the subject of conversion of minor boys, took a decisive turn with the most infamous and egregious example—that of the young heir to the defeated Sikh Empire, Maharaja Duleep Singh. After the Sikh Empire fell in 1849, the heir presumptive, Duleep, was exiled and sent to the care of Dr. John Login in Fatehgarh in Northern India.[130] With the encouragement of Login and the support of Dalhousie, Duleep was converted by his retainer, Bhajan Lal, in 1853 when he was less than fifteen years old, was separated from his mother, and was then taken to England in 1854. This event was profoundly controversial, as Duleep was a minor and his ability to conscientiously and consciously choose baptism was questioned in both India and Britain. There were political as well as social criticisms of Dalhousie's open approval of the conversion, not only because of Duleep's age but also because of his status as a ward of the British Empire as a prince of a ceded and defeated princely domain. One important British commentator, Lord Monteagle, comptroller general of the English Exchequer, was scathing in his opinion: "His conversion to Christianity will scarcely be looked upon as an act of the Maharajah's own free will. He has evidently been made the victim of that 'Missionary fanaticism,' under which several Hindu youths of this country, hardly out of teens, were converted into the children of Jesus."[131] John Clarke Marshman, the son of the Serampore Baptist and Rammohan's adversary Joshua Marshman, opined in the Baptist mouthpiece *The Friend of India,* "It will of course be observed, particularly in England, that it would have been more advisable to postpone this irrevocable renunciation of [Sikhism] until matured age should give to the young Maharajah the knowledge and experience necessary to make a permanent decision."[132]

Duleep's case continued to make conscientious British administrators like Monteagle wary of the rising animosity of Indians toward missionary "fanaticism" all over India.[133] Anger and panic over Duleep's case continued to add oil to the fire of dissatisfaction over conversion of minors and cemented in the minds of the Indian people a belief in the treacherousness of the missionary preceptors in schools, a significant catalyst of the conflagration of 1857. As we have already seen, the events of 1857 completely changed the British attitude to evangelical conversion programs, especially when it concerned minor children.

The 1863 case of Himanath or Hemanauth Bose illustrates how far public and legal discourse in India had shifted in the aftermath of 1857 and how the judges in Indian courts were more concerned with the injured sentiments of Indian parents on the topic of conversions of minor children. Of all the cases that I have found in Bengal of minors seeking to be converted and parents intervening with a writ of habeas corpus, Himanath's case aroused immense interest, both among the Indian public and the missionary establishments. The case came before the controversial judge of the Calcutta High Court, Sir Mordaunt Wells. The habeas corpus writ asked for a direction to Alexander Duff and Lalbehari Dey to produce Himanath, fifteen years old at the time, and to deliver him to his father, Kaliprasanna Bose. The facts of the case were these: The boy had left his home for school on June 16 and had not returned home thereafter. Kaliprasanna had found through inquiry that Himanath was preparing for baptism at the mission house of the Free Church in Cornwallis Square. By the precedents set in the Radhakanta Dutta case, this should have been a case easily dismissed, leaving Himanath free to be baptized. Yet this case, unfolding in the aftermath of the Mutiny, had a very different outcome.

Mr. Bell, the defense counsel, urged Mordaunt Wells to only consider the limits of the habeas corpus writ and to follow the precedent set by *Queen v. Ogilvie in re Radacaunt Dutt.* Yet Wells refused, arguing that Sir Laurence Peel had put too narrow a construction on the limits of habeas corpus. He asserted that no such precedent, compromising so severely a father's right to the religious education of his minor children, could be found anywhere in English law. In fact, he relied on *Queen v. Maria Clarke in re Alicia Race* to challenge the construction put on the Radhakanta Dutta case.[134] Wells contended that since Hindu law fixed the age of maturity at sixteen, no earlier age needed to be considered as the threshold for attainment of discretion, especially in such ponderous issues as religion. He asked Duff and Lalbehari

Dey to think about the dangers of encouraging their students to convert at a young age in haste, as many often later regretted their choice due to the isolation from their home, loved ones, and social networks. Such conversions could only increase the chances of converts backsliding into superstition, bringing infamy to the baptizers themselves. Wells was also deeply moved by Himanath's father's counsel, Mr. Newmarch, who reflected on the loneliness of a young boy who converted, thereby estranging himself from his community and his relatives. Newmarch's words eerily echo those of Akshay Kumar Dutta in Umesh's case:

> For the system of Hinduism and the tyranny of caste are such that a convert must isolate himself from kith and kin and cast off at once and for ever all family ties. When a Hindu child takes up the Christian religion, it takes up this penalty with it, and becomes an outcast, so far at least as its own people, its own country, its own family, are concerned.[135]

Wells was just as adamant that he, as a Christian judge, was not fit to question the boy on religious principles in any way that would appease the Hindu subjects to whom he was supposed to be impartial—just as a Hindu judge could not, to any satisfaction of Christian missionaries, ever interrogate one of their own on religious principles. He also considered the reverse of the situation in which Kaliprasanna found himself: no Christian missionary would suffer to hand over their minor children, even if the children wished it, to a Brahmin priest in order to imbibe the philosophies of the Hindus. Wells reportedly stated, "A mother's claim is ten thousand times as great as the rights of Missionaries: the rights of Missionaries are insignificant as compared with a mother's rights."[136] Any Indian Hindu parent would expect the court to order the custody of a child lured away by missionaries back to their father. Every Hindu had that same right. In fact, Wells voiced one of the fears that had haunted the British administration since the Mutiny of 1857—that the conversion programs of missionaries had been one of the catalysts for the apocalyptic events that had unfolded and almost led to the end of the empire in India:

> If Dr. Duff were to ask him here to deliver up a child of his own in the custody of the Brahmins, could anyone suppose that he would hesitate for a moment to take that child from the Brahmin, and deliver it up to Dr. Duff? Has not the Hindu then the same right as the Christian to the custody of his child?

> If it were not so, where was the line to be drawn? *We should have a system of forcible conversions carried on in India, the consequences of which would be lamentable indeed.*[137]

Wells was of course referring to the Mutiny and the Indian anger regarding missionary interference and conversion of boys. In doing so, he strikingly and publicly held missionaries of long-standing repute in Bengal, like Alexander Duff, responsible for potentially destabilizing the newly settled Crown Raj through their continuing and controversial efforts at conversion of minor children. This was an incendiary move, and Wells's rebuke from the bench of the Calcutta High Court sent shockwaves through the missionary communities not only in Bengal but across India. He reversed the precedent of the Radhakanta Dutta case on the merits of the *Alicia Race* verdict and ordered for Himanath to be given up to his father, which was done. His critique of missionary culpability in the conversion of Indian minors against the wishes (and legal rights) of their parents drew great opprobrium from both the missionaries and the wider white population of Bengal. The judgment sent alarm bells ringing in the evangelical community in both India and Britain, and the missionaries were deeply concerned about the consequences of the case on the evangelical program of conversion in India. Duff, who had spent thirty-three years in India at this point and was at the forefront of missionary successes in converting high-caste boys in Bengal, fell ill when he heard Wells's judgment. Shortly thereafter, he retired to Britain. The end of his fabled career in India was taken by his compatriots and colleagues as an omen about the future of the civilizing mission. They were swift to condemn Wells, and the fallout was a public denunciation of his character and service and a lamentation about the weakening political, social, and legal position of evangelism in the Indian Empire.

Wells had previously enraged the Indian public sphere in 1845 by accusing Raja Radhakanta Dev and Raja Kalikrishna Dev, who were at the forefront of the public outcry in the case of Umesh's conversion, of immorality. Again, in 1861, Wells had been contemptuous regarding the morality of native Indians during the controversial and celebrated *Nil Darpan* (Indigo Mirror) case. He had, to the horror of Bengali society, called India "a nation of forgers and perjurers" from the bench of the Calcutta High Court.[138] His reputation as a curmudgeon did not improve when he sentenced the much-admired missionary, educationist, book historian, and ethnographer Rev. James Long to hard labor and imprisonment from July to August, 1861, which alienated both

Indians and the evangelical establishment.[139] However, Wells's stand in favor of the Hindu father's absolute rights over his minor children redeemed him somewhat in the eyes of Calcutta's Bengali Hindu elite. The judgment also earned him the profound displeasure of both missionaries and his other countrymen in India, from evangelically inclined members of the British administration to journalists, businessmen, and planters. A pamphlet published right before his retirement and return to England gathered some of the criticism levied at him by the press in India. The Himanath Bose case featured as a centerpiece that was supposed to demonstrate his capricious pronouncements as a judge. For example, the pamphlet included this critique from *The Indian Reformer* of July 24, 1863:

> But it will be asked, has not Sir Mordaunt given satisfaction to the Native community by his judgment in the recent case of Himanath Bose? It would be affectation to deny that that decision has given satisfaction to the majority of the Hindu community. But is that decision, looking at it from a Hindu point of view, to be regarded as a national benefit?[140]

Similarly, *The Ryot's Friend,* on September 9, 1863, was scathing:

> Our readers need not be told that we allude to the . . . Himanath Bose case. It was a despicable attack on the philanthropic missionaries who have crossed seas and oceans to diffuse the light of knowledge and Christianity in this benighted land.
>
> Our readers may be aware it was this savage onslaught of Sir Mordaunt which brought about the last illness of the Revd. Dr. Duff,—an illness which had well-nigh proved fatal, and which will soon compel the Revd. Gentleman to close his philanthropic labors in the cause of our regeneration.[141]

The criticisms of Mordaunt Wells by missionaries and their supporters did not end here. The Calcutta Missionary Conference released a bitterly critical statement on his conduct and judgment in the Himanath Bose case.[142] The statement noted that before 1845, a period that included Brijonath Ghose's case, the Anglo-Indian courts generally sided with the parent or guardian in such cases. Between 1845 and the Indian Mutiny, the period of the Umesh and Radhakanta cases, the courts generally favored missionary endeavors. After 1857, the outcomes of habeas corpus cases that parents lodged to prevent their children from converting depended on the particular context of the region and the temperament of the judge presiding.[143] In order to show that the judgment in the Himanath Bose case was both arbitrary and damaging to the evangelical enterprise, the Calcutta Missionary Society documented multiple cases of conversion of minors between 1840 and 1860.

The point was to demonstrate that, after 1845, cases of habeas corpus instituted to prevent conversion of Indian boys and girls very rarely went against the missionaries. But as the cases of Himanath Bose and C. Narainswamy Chetty illustrate, after 1857, the judges in Indian courts were also far more cautious in deciding such habeas corpus cases. The landscape was changing along with the change from Company to Crown rule. In the period between 1830 and 1851, Christian evangelism was at its peak in India. Missionaries achieved significant success in their conversion endeavors during this period, and elite conversions were openly aided by devout British administrators in an unofficial capacity. Bengal's Hindu society hoped that Wells's judgment in the Himanath Bose case would firmly and uniformly establish sixteen as the legal age of maturity of Hindus in India, so that a father had an undoubted right to the custody of his children prior to this age. This was not what happened. In December 1864, the *Missionary Herald* reported on the case in an article titled "Youthful Converts in India." The article mentions prominently that habeas corpus was commonly used by Indian parents whose children had decided to convert to Christianity without their blessing. It also dwells on what it characterizes as Wells's preoccupation with the fact that Himanath had not attained the legal age of maturity at the moment of his supposed conversion. The judgment, pronounced with "indecent haste" according to the *Herald,* also clearly established that a minor like Himanath, no matter his intellectual acuity, did not have a "right to independent action." This legal opinion, that parental rights over a minor superseded the minor's conscientious choices, completely overruled previous rulings. The *Missionary Herald* charged Wells with "contempt for Christian missionaries and native converts" and argued that "a decision like this was calculated to throw many obstacles in the way of the great work of evangelizing India."[144]

At the same time, a similar conversion case in the Bombay Presidency, that of a boy called Witta Dhummu, showed a small silver lining for the missionaries. When Dhummu's parents brought a habeas corpus case, the judge, Sir Joseph Arnould, set the boy at liberty to choose where he would reside—with his missionary preceptor and future baptizer, Rev. Forbes, or with his parents. When the boy chose Forbes, the court directed that he was free to act as he chose. This exceptional development was due to Arnould's ruminations on age of maturity versus age of discretion for Indian boys, which influenced his decision to let Dhummu go with his missionary preceptor, in contravention of the commonplace precedents set by legal decisions since 1857, where, as we have seen, the judges were usually biased in favor of the Indian father's custodial rights over his children. Arnould pointed out that while the age of maturity was sixteen, age of responsibility for criminal conduct was twelve, "the law thus recognizing the greater precocity of Indian youths." Arnould said he would not go so far as to argue that the age of responsibility for criminal conduct should also be the age of conscientious decision regarding conversion to Christianity. He put a respectable face on his conviction that Indian Hindu, Muslim, and Parsi boys should be allowed to convert at will, even if they had not attained the age of maturity, by saying "that the period of life at which discretionary rights commenced should not be fixed at a more advanced age than in England." He therefore took fourteen, the age of discretion in England, as also applicable in India.

Of course, the evangelical community in India was far more pleased with Arnould's decision than with Wells's judgment. It preserved their rights to proselytize to young schoolboys, which would have been completely shattered if Wells's decision was considered the only legal precedent. Arnould was therefore hailed as a hero, since his judgment preserved hope for the Indian evangelical establishment that "heathen fathers will be compelled to respect the rights of conscience in their children, and those cruel persecutions be averted, which in so many cases in the years gone by, have destroyed the blossoming hope of the Christian Church in Hindostan."[145] The ripple effect of cases involving the conversion of minor boys continued to be observed well into the future. The Himanath Bose case was discussed at length by Ernest John Trevelyan in his Tagore Law Lectures of 1877, named for and funded by Prosonnocoomar Tagore in his will, on "The Law Relating to Minors in the Presidency of Bengal."[146] Trevelyan judged that the precedent followed in the Brijonath and Radhakanta cases, that of *Rex v. Greenhill,* applied equally to Himanath's case:

> When the infant is brought before the court by Habeas Corpus, if he be of an age to exercise the choice, the Court leaves him to elect where he will go. If he be not of that age, and a want of discretion would only expose him to dangers or seductions, the Court must make an order for his being placed in the proper custody.[147]

Trevelyan also felt that Wells had put a very narrow construction on what the age of maturity was. He concluded that Arnould's judgment was more balanced in this regard. Trevelyan also concluded that Wells's construction of the limits of habeas corpus in the Himanath Bose case depended on the charge of supposed "abduction" levied by Bose's father against the missionaries. Such a charge, of course, accompanied almost every habeas corpus writ relating to the detention of minor boys by missionaries with the object of conversion to Christianity. Under the Indian Penal Code, the definition of kidnapping depended on the age of discretion for both boys and girls, and not on their age of maturity:

> Whoever takes or entices any minor under fourteen years of age if a male, or under sixteen years of age if a female, or any person of an unsound mind, out of the keeping of the lawful guardian of such minor or person of unsound mind, without the consent of such guardian, is said to kidnap such minor or person from lawful guardianship.[148]

Since kidnapping was a criminal charge independent of the ability of the minor to consent, Wells used this provision to reverse the precedent of the Radhakanta Dutta case. Wells had thereby limited the power of the missionaries to save the souls of their pupils and also tried to establish the complete control of a Hindu father over his minor children below the age of sixteen. But by fixing the age of discretion for Indian boys at fourteen, the Anglo-Indian law thereafter established that Hindu fathers had undisputed legal control over their children below that age. But it was also true that the age of discretion, fixed at fourteen, limited paternal authority over a child's right to make conscientious decisions regarding the state of his soul—when it came to converting to Christianity.[149]

The issue of conversion therefore allowed the legal contestation over the age of discretion under Hindu personal law, which had varied according to customary usages in different Indian provinces. There emerged from this contestation an understanding that, although sixteen was unequivocally the age limit of legal maturity under Hindu law, in cases of conscientious choice of baptism the Anglo-Indian courts would adhere to the age of discretion in line with British legal precedence. Thus for Bengali Hindu parents, the age of danger was between fourteen and sixteen, precisely the age at which they hoped their children would become proficient in English language, literature, and civilizational attitudes. The fear of this looming crisis led to increased surveillance of young boys, while the public panic caused by these cases of conversion and the ensuing legal contestation cast a long shadow over the relationship between India's Hindu communities and native Christians that would extend through to the twentieth century. This issue about legally deciding the age of maturity for Indian boys (and girls) would lead to the promulgation of the Indian Majority Act (Act IX) of 1875.[150]

CONCLUSION

The complicated way in which Bengal was slowly modernized in the first half of the nineteenth century was always a socially as well as a racially vitiated issue. Imperially conditioned evangelism and the civilizing mission, intended to educate and enlighten Indians into being good subjects of imperial rule, brought forth a backlash from Bengali society, including deeply adversarial apologetics in the public sphere, as well as legal contestation on the conversion of young schoolboys. This backlash, as we have seen, took place in two stages. The first stage involved the interaction of Rammohan Roy with the Serampore Baptists in the 1810s, which was briefly revived during Roy's correspondence with the Boston Unitarians and Henry Ware in 1823–1824. The second stage began in 1830, with Duff's arrival in Calcutta. Duff fundamentally shifted the target of conversion efforts from the subaltern milieu of the poorer castes and communities to the high-caste elite and intelligentsia of Bengal. His apologetic methods, including the use of open letters to the nascent Indian press and lectures to the students of Hindu College, brought forth an immediate and antagonistic response from Bengalis. When young boys began converting to Christianity, sometimes with their child brides, Bengali Hindu parents felt a lack of control that fanned the fires of paranoia—and sometimes descended into violence against both missionaries and children who had gone astray. This contest ultimately spilled over into the Anglo-Indian courts, as we have seen.

To engage in rational and undistorted communication, the parties involved must share the same language as well as "the same cognitive, the same normative, and the same objective and subjective worlds."[151] This was impossible to achieve between Indian intellectuals and British evangelical missionaries in the sociopolitical sphere of the early nineteenth century, not only because they lacked a shared social world or norms but also because dialogue itself was marked by power dynamics. When Rammohan Roy's language of rationality and logic met the missionary interlocutors' language of religious convictions, there could be no true dialogue: Rammohan's reduction of the Bible to a worldly compendium of ethical norms of behavior was antithetical to the missionaries' convictions of true belief in the divinity and miraculous powers of Christ. Similarly, dialogue between a missionary and his converts was also always marked by disparities of power and race in the colonial Indian context. The apologetic content of the missionary's conversation was to proclaim the sovereignty of both Christianity and British imperialism. The apologia developed by Indians like Rammohan Roy and others like him was to contest this superiority and protect their own religious and communitarian identity, and, if necessary, to reform their communities of faith from within. The ungovernable Indian subject of reform, paradoxically, was formed by the very tools of liberal humanistic education. English pedagogy was supposed to turn Indians into useful middlemen and subjects of the ruling *sahibs,* but instead created Calibans: "You taught me language, and my profit on it/Is I know how to curse."[152]

In the second phase of apologetic encounters, Bengalis—especially newly educated young men like the Derozians of Hindu College—learned how to use the analytical tools of Western philosophical discourse and turned their discerning eyes on the superstructure of Hindu religious idolatry and rituals. In dismantling the cultural and ritual norms that grounded daily pieties of Bengali Hindu society, they paradoxically paved the path for Christian missionaries to step in with religious and ethical instruction, leading to highly publicized high-caste conversions. The use of litigation, and particularly habeas corpus, to engage missionaries in a battle for the control of the younger members of Bengali Hindu society was a response to missionaries' increasing penetration into both the private and public domains of the Bengali intelligentsia. The varying responses to these cases, both legally and in the public sphere, show the changing perceptions of the role of religion and the evangelical mission in British India over a thirty-year period. Before 1830, the highly stratified and regimented hierarchies of caste-based social interactions and exchanges had played a part in creating social and political identities and affiliations. By 1845, a growing opposition to the evangelical Christian mission had unified Bengali Hindus around a common sense of identity and purpose. To those who staunchly identified with their religious faith as orthodox Hindus or pious Muslims, native Christian converts—both from the respectable classes and the so-called lower classes—always appeared insincere, driven by ulterior motives such as material gain or sociopolitical advancement. It is not an accident that when high-caste converts could no longer be easily accused of selling their souls for money or maintenance they were accused instead of converting due to their social ambitions for racial advancement. Seen as the cause of corruption and isolation, conversion also became a catalyst for self-examination in Bengali Hindu communities, which came together to protect themselves against this supposed threat.

In fact, I would argue that this sense of a cohesive Hindu society did not emerge with the social movement to ban *sati* in 1829, which actually divided Bengali Hindus even further on religious lines. Instead, it was conversion to Christianity that effectively forged what could be called, in some sense, the modern Bengali Hindu ecumene. The threat of conversion also enabled creative ways of combating evangelical influence, including the legal use of habeas corpus writs and increased surveillance of younger members of the society. What emerged from this process was a fractured and fractious, but highly self-aware and self-protective, colonial modernity, contending with the new apologetic discourses required to define its own identity.

One of the consequences of converting to Christianity, young Bengali boys would soon realize, was disinheritance—at the most obvious level, they lost any rights to their patrimony. But implicated in the loss was also any social or moral capital that might have been their birthright as a result of familial and communitarian networks, which would have provided both security and access to support that was lost irretrievably as a result of their conversions. Conversion began to slowly mean an inheritance of violent loss and unmooring of not merely low-caste or poorer converts but hitherto socially and economically privileged high-caste converts as well. Their missionary preceptors would begin to lobby the British administration to rectify what they saw as a terrible wrong being perpetrated against their enlightened students and deterring others from conversion. The grieving parents, who had lost their children and faced loss of face and ostracism in their communities as a result of their child's actions, began to use the Anglo-Indian legal system to ensure that converts would not inherit any of their ancestral or patrimonial possessions. We will see how that contest developed in the next chapter.

CHAPTER THREE

The Great Tagore Will Case

In his 1862 volume *Hutom Pyancha'r Naksha* (Surveys of the hooting owl), social commentator and satirist Kaliprasanna Singha (1841–1870) reflected on one of the most prominent Christian conversions of the last decade. The epitome of the liberal Calcutta aristocrat, Singha was well known for his translation of the *Mahabharata* into Bengali from the original Sanskrit version. Under his pseudonym *Hutom Pyancha*, or the Hooting Owl, he also diligently chronicled the life and times of the new imperial city of Calcutta. Among the targets of his acerbic pen were the vagaries and fashions that swayed public opinion in Bengal, including the *Khristiani hujoog*, or the "conversion to Christianity craze":

> There was a new craze that everyone seemed affected by! We have heard that some of the Brahmin Thakurs of Bhatpara will convert next. But instead of the people from Bhatpara, it was Babu Prosonnocoomar Thakur's son Gyanendramohan who went outside the fold! Krishnamohan Bandyopadhyay offered up his daughter to this new coreligionist. . . .
>
> The situation was such that Enlightenment spread and light broke free from the holes in people's roofs; some were disinherited, some repented and fell into real hard times. The *Khristiani hujoog* was like a lantern held up by a stranger at night—it illuminated the path for a while, but in its passing, left behind a deeper darkness![1]

Singha, hereafter referred to as Hutom, was alluding to the highly public fallout between two of the most influential members of a colonial Bengali aristocratic elite family: Babu Prosonnocoomar Tagore or Thakur (1801–1868) and his only son and heir Gyanendramohan (1826–1890). Prosonnocoomar, who had dueled in print with Krishnamohan Banerjee in the 1830s, had by the early 1840s risen to become an eminent legal scholar and lawyer—and in 1854 the first Indian member of the governor-general's Legislative Council. Under the guidance of his father's old nemesis Krishnamohan Banerjee, Gyanendramohan converted to Christianity in 1851 and married Krishnamohan's daughter amid enormous public scandal. In response, Prosonnocoomar disinherited his son and willed his ancestral properties to his nephew Maharaja Jatindramohan Tagore instead.[2] Gyanendramohan contested his father's will in a legal case that would come to be known as the Great Tagore Will Case. Moving from the civil court in Calcutta to the Privy Council in London, where it was finally resolved in 1872, the case pitted two of the most influential members of the Tagore family against one another and involved properties valued at hundreds of thousands of pounds sterling. The events

Oil portrait of Prosonnocoomar Tagore, Companion of the Most Exalted Order of the Star of India, legal scholar, landowner, and intellectual.
Rabindra Bharati Museum, Jorasanko.

that precipitated it illuminate a tangled web of debates over converts' legal rights to their inheritance, the conversion of Hindu boys to Christianity, and the spiritual roles of husbands and wives in sustaining the orthodox Hindu family structure. The outcome of the case in turn catalyzed important legal precedents regarding the rights of Christian converts to inherit ancestral property.

Since the early 1800s, the Anglo-Indian legal system had been adapting to the peculiar circumstances of colonial rule, further complicated by the existence of innumerable local customary laws and practices. These laws and practices often conflicted with British lawmakers' understanding of the legal landscape—which relied on precedence, rigid codification, and a sense that laws were fixed as written. Indeed, British lawmakers favored the dharmashastras and especially the *Manusmriti*—thereby mistranslating a commentary on social morals and their legal applications into a code of positive Hindu law. The facts of the Great Tagore Will Case proceed from the complications that surrounded inheritance in India after the passage of the controversial Lex Loci Act in 1850. This law confirmed that converts to Christianity in India could not be disinherited by their fathers from ancestral and paternal property. The Lex Loci Act was a joint effort between missionaries like Alexander Duff and British administrators sympathetic to evangelism in India. From the 1830s, Duff and other missionaries campaigned relentlessly to prevent converts from suffering economic losses through disinheritance.[3] When the draft of the law was published in 1845, many Indians saw it as a direct religious assault on Hindu identity.[4] It had evolved from the Bengal Code Regulation VII of 1832, which first promised a modicum of legal safeguard for converts with regards to their inheritance. The Lex Loci Act, ratified as the Caste Disabilities Removal Act XXI, thereby contravened customary practices of inheritance rules in Bengal and comprehensively provided (or seemed to provide) ironclad assurances to converts that legally they could not be excluded from inheriting their ancestral and patrimonial properties just because of their conversion. Conversion, in other words, no longer posed a disqualification from inheritance, and the Lex Loci Act seemingly took away the power of Bengali patriarchs to dispose of their estates as they wished.[5] This was its essence:

> So much of any law or usage now in force within the territories subject to the Government of the East India Company as inflicts to any person forfeiture of rights or property, or may be held in any way to impair or affect

> any right of inheritance, by reason of his or her renouncing, or having been excluded from the communion of, any religion, or being deprived of caste, shall cease to be enforced as law in the Courts of the East India Company, and in the Courts established by Royal Charter within the said territories.[6]

The Great Tagore Will Case played an important role in establishing the primacy of Hindu laws of inheritance in disputes between family members, especially in cases of conversion to Christianity by male heirs. Although the colonial government protested that it was justified on grounds of enlightenment and toleration, the native feeling of persecution by "missionaryism" led to an outpouring of anger and a consolidation among the various *dals* or sections of Hindu and Muslim elites in Calcutta and Madras.[7] Indians had long suspected the British were privileging the rights of converts above those of Hindus and Muslims. The Lex Loci Act only stoked these suspicions, and many feared that it might be used as a tool to require mass conversions in the future.

The Hindu inhabitants of Bengal, Bihar, and Orissa raised an immediate challenge to the law in the form of a petition containing 8,401 signatures. This petition, which sought a repeal of the Lex Loci Act, was eventually presented by Lord Monteagle in the British Parliament on May 26, 1853. Its language and construction closely resemble those of Prosonnocoomar Tagore's essays on inheritance and his will. It is very likely that Prosonnocoomar drafted this petition or perhaps consulted on the language of the draft. The petition was supported by Sir Herbert Maddock, the ex-governor-general of India Lord Ellenborough, and the Earl of Granville.[8] Lord Ellenborough, when he spoke in favor of repealing the act, noted that Indians were justifiably alarmed by its passage:

> The number of converts, *pseudo-converts,* to Christianity was at the present time so infinitely small, that there were very few cases indeed in which the Act could be called into operation. Let the House observe what immoral motives the existing Act suggested to the native population of India. It was not to be wondered at that such a law excited the remonstrances of the natives of India. They were entitled to look upon this as only the first indication of an intention on the part of the Government to interfere with their religion.[9]

As his reference to "pseudo-converts" indicates, the suspicion that Indian converts were insincere and motivated by material gain—which had been evolving in the Indian public sphere since Rammohan Roy—was shared by many British civilians as well.

The 1853 petition also articulated one of the most important objections to Christian converts inheriting ancestral property: the fact that these converts could no longer fulfill the religious obligations required of Hindu sons who inherited ancestral property from their fathers. As the petition said:

> By the ancient Hindu law, a man's right of inheritance to ancestral property is made to depend on his capacity for the performance of certain religious duties towards his ancestors, a disqualification for which, either by reason of loss of caste, physical deformity, or moral degradation, subjects him to forfeiture of that right to property which he derived from his "beneficial acts."[10]

Inheritance under the prevalent customary usage in Bengal—based on the *Dayabhaga,* a treatise written by Jimutvahana—also made clear that performing these customary religious duties was mandatory for a son hoping to inherit his patrimony.[11] In most cases, a son's conversion meant that he was deracinated—and therefore no longer fit to perform the last rites of his parents or the Hindu rituals of *sraddha.* This meant, in turn, that the gates of heaven were forever barred to the unfortunate parents. The petition pointed out why a son's conversion was a disaster on a cosmological scale, why deracination and disinheritance had to happen as a consequence, and ultimately why the Lex Loci Act was a terrible intervention by the Anglo-Indian legal system into Hindu customs:

> A religious Hindu having an only son looks to that son as his assurance, that those religious rites will be duly performed, on which he believes his salvation and that of his immediate ancestors to depend. If the son becomes a Christian, or from any other cause is deprived of caste, the father is entitled by Hindu law to adopt another son, who would by the same law take the inheritance. The Act in question by severing the inheritance from the adoption, and securing it to the original son, virtually and practically annuls the Hindu right of adoption.[12]

Gyanendramohan's conversion to Christianity in 1851 and the desperate grief it brought to his father Prosonnocoomar and the Tagore family seem to be the hidden subtext to this petition. Gyanendramohan's subsequent second marriage to Kamala, Krishnamohan Banerjee's daughter, meanwhile proved to be the final impediment to any reconciliation with his own father. For Calcutta's elite Hindu society, this incident became the most important illustration of how the British administration had used the Lex Loci Act to legally protect and encourage Christian conversion. To be sure, Gyanendramohan was one in a long line of elite young Bengalis who had converted since the early 1830s, many under the influence of Duff. Yet he was also the only son and heir of the Pathuriaghata branch of the Tagore family, one of the most illustrious of Calcutta's affluent families.[13] Because of the circumstances of his birth and upbringing, Gyanendramohan—even more so than previous young Bengali converts—incited an uproar when he was baptized in 1851. According to the mouthpiece of the Serampore Baptists *The Friend of India*, "There have been many converts from the upper ranks of Hindoo society, but this is the first instance, we believe, in which sacerdotal rank has been combined with wealth, and it has created a proportionate sensation."[14]

Gyanendramohan's case illustrates the legal complications that arose when the question of inheritance of Indian Christian converts came into consideration under the Anglo-Indian legal system. Customs of Hindu and Bengali inheritance laws were unequivocal regarding the power of Hindu fathers to alienate their property away from a son who had been disqualified as a result of their character or conduct, until the Lex Loci Act of 1850. The Lex Loci Act ran counter to that long-accepted regional legal interpretation and brought Anglo-Indian legal reformism in favor of converts into direct and open conflict with the religious and legal rights of Hindus in colonial India. In the cases of habeas corpus that we discussed in Chapter 2, the young schoolboys remained with their missionary preceptors and refused to return home or abjure their conversion, lost their patrimony, and had to rely on their new evangelical Christian connections to eke out a living. One important example of this, as we have seen, was the poet Michael Madhusudan Dutta, who was reduced to penury in later life as a result of his disinheritance. The Great Tagore Will Case illustrates the ways in which Christian converts fought back against their disinheritance, holding out hope that the Lex Loci Act provided them legal security against such financial violence. The social prominence of the parties to the Great Tagore Will Case, the enormous bequest that was being contested, and ultimately the legal question about right and security to property that Prosonnocoomar's will brought to the fore as a result of him entailing his estates on his nephews make this case an exemplar of the tangled web of religious, social, economic, and financial losses that were the fate of Christian converts. The Great Tagore Will Case further illustrates the ways in which contests over inheritance in the Anglo-Indian legal arena constituted an important way for apologetics regarding faith and belonging to be performed in colonial Bengal. By staking certain kinds of legal rights, both the Hindu father and the Christian son were making claims of security to practice their religion of birth or choice, without interference, and claiming protection under Anglo-Indian law. The result of the Great Tagore Will Case, as we will see, established the primacy of the Hindu father's rights over any claims of the Christian convert child and paved the way for further social, legal, and economic marginalization of India's converts.

When Prosonnocoomar disinherited his son, he directly refuted the provisions of the Lex Loci Act. Indeed, Gyanendramohan's suit proceeded from his belief that the law protected his right to inherit. The outcome proved otherwise. Like the custody case of Himanath Bose, *Tagore v. Tagore* was decided in the aftermath of the 1857 Mutiny—when British administrators and lawmakers were far more cautious about their intrusions on Indian religious rights, including the influence of the Lex Loci Act. The Indian intellectual Syed Ahmed Khan had even called the Lex Loci Act the second major cause of disaffection among Indian subjects that led to the rebellion.[15] Little more than a decade after the rebellion, *Tagore v. Tagore* essentially nullified the power of the Lex Loci Act to guarantee legal and financial inheritance to Christian converts. Moreover, it would be accepted as a precedent in similar cases until the Hindu Inheritance (Removal of Disabilities) Act of 1928.[16] The result of the Great Tagore Will Case, in other words, was the defanging of the Lex Loci Act: Prosonnocoomar's actions provided a path for any Hindu father who wished to disinherit a misbehaving son.

Just as importantly, the fallout from Gyanendramohan's disinheritance illuminates the forms of material and social rupture experienced by both converts and their families. Hutom's satirical account of the Tagore family controversy acknowledges the difficulties faced by Indian converts, who found themselves at once excommunicated from their natal communities and unable to join Anglo-Indian society as a result of racial discrimination.[17] What his account does not fully reflect, however, is the devastating sense of rupture that conversion inspired in both anti-conversion intellectuals and the converts themselves. His treatment of conversion as a fad belies the intense fears among Hindus and Muslims that mass conversions would overtake Bengal—as well as the intense pain and sense of misunderstanding felt by both Indian converts and their families.

Gyanendramohan Tagore's inheritance case provides a particularly rich insight into the inheritance of losses that Indian converts and their families endured. In colonial India, as the cases of the 1830s and 1840s showed, baptisms were publicly performed spectacles: they were held in public settings, usually churches, with much celebratory fanfare organized by the missionaries and British administrators. Through baptism, the imperial power could demonstrate to its subjects the success of the civilizing mission, which touched not only the colonized subject's body but also their very soul. The fallout from Gyanendramohan's conversion sheds light on the painful ways in which Indian converts lost their social and moral capital within their natal communities—and were, in many cases, erased from family history. Indeed, the case offers an especially vivid window into the social and emotional fabric of the debates around evangelism in Bengal. It shows us the ways in which relationships between the older Bengali liberals of the Rammohan Roy generation and the new English-educated radicals were reshaped in the fire of Christian evangelism and conversion programs, as illustrated in the wrenching relationship between father and son, Prosonnocoomar and Gyanendramohan, in this chapter. Gyanendramohan's highly affecting relationships with his first and second wives, Bala Sundari and Kamala Banerjee, are also particularly traceable in the archive of missionary pamphlets on successful Indian conversions, especially *zenana* or female conversions. For this reason, his case also reflects the complicated place of *zenana* conversion in upper-class Hindu families.[18] Such conversions were rare within the highly surveilled *antahpur* or inner domains of elite households. But Bala and Kamala became, for missionaries, two important and exemplary cases of successful women converts. In contemporary missionary accounts, Bala figured as the catalyst for Gyanendramohan's own conversion: it is her death that precipitated his spiritual crisis, followed by his formal baptism and conversion. While Bala's assertive and self-realized conversion was seen as a model to be emulated, Kamala's own demure piety and faith was seen as a reflection of her father Krishnamohan's deep commitment to Christianity and a proof of the moral improvement that could be brought about in generations of young Hindu Bengali women through the civilizing effects of a Christian education for Indian women converts. While missionary narratives of idealized Indian Christian women were far from reality, the ways in which Bala and Kamala are depicted in missionary pamphlets illustrate the agency that missionaries wished to see in women who could drive conversions through their effects on their husbands and as pious partners to future converts.

INTIMATE LOSSES

On his return from his first trip to Britain, Prince Dwarkanath Tagore—the eminent Bengali entrepreneur, proprietor, and banker—brought the well-known Scottish abolitionist George Thompson to India. Thompson had been active in England, the United States, and the West Indies. He was notable for his brilliant oratory and had a strong interest in the Indian Empire, especially in the British colonial administration's treatment of Indian subjects. In India, where he arrived in January 1843, he proceeded to give a series of public lectures that aroused admiration from the Indian intelligentsia and disaffection among white Europeans (he was called "the grievance-monger"). Among the eminent Indians who invited Thompson to share his views on the political future of Indians under the East India Company's rule was Rev. Krishnamohan Banerjee, at whose home Thompson gave a speech.[19] Thompson asked the educated young Bengali men to discharge the duties of enlightened citizens and agitate for their due political and legal rights through meetings, political activism, and petitions. He also urged them to ask for amelioration of their grievances through legislative reform, famously saying, "The battleground of freedom for the world is on the plains of Hindostan."[20] One major outcome of his visit was the establishment of the Bengal British India Society. Founded on April 20, 1843, this was the first long-lived protopolitical association in India concerned with Indian interests and Indian stakes in the British Empire.[21] During this visit, Thompson was a guest at Prosonnocoomar Tagore's palatial home in Pathuriaghata. When he returned to Calcutta in 1856, he once again stayed with the Pathuriaghata Tagores. He noted with interest that this afforded him a uniquely close view of a Hindu family's inner domains and wrote detailed letters back home to his younger daughter Amelia, describing the rituals and daily practices of the household as well as members of the Tagore family, including Gyanendramohan.[22] This is the first—as well as the most detailed and intimate—portrayal of young Gyanendramohan and his wife Bala that survives today.

In an almost thirty-seven-page letter to Amelia, written from Calcutta and dated March 23, 1856, Thompson detailed the history and genealogy of the Tagore family and their present circumstances.[23] According to him, Prosonnocoomar was the wealthiest living member of either of the two Tagore houses of Pathuriaghata and Jorasanko. He owned extensive landed properties in the Rangpur, Dinajpur, 24 Parganas, and Bogura districts of Bengal and in Munger in Bihar, with over 300,000 tenants. He also owned a large number of shares in the indigo management business in Calcutta and an oil mill. By Prosonnocoomar's own account, as reported by Thompson, his income from all sources exceeded £40,000 per annum.[24] This income had been even higher when he practiced, because his earnings from the bar alone were close to £10,000–£12,000. After he left active practice and took on the honorary position on the Viceroy's Legislative Council, his consultation fees still brought him £2,000 per annum. He supported about 200 people on this income, both family members and employees. His philanthropic donations were renowned throughout Bengal, as was his staunch belief in certain Hindu orthodox practices, like his support and upkeep of the family deity's temple and *debottar* lands at the Mulajore Kalibari and the family's annual Durga Puja celebrations.[25] Prosonnocoomar's library was a wonder of colonial Calcutta, holding close to 5,000 books. It was fully cataloged and overseen by a full-time librarian. This was the affluent world into which Gyanendramohan was born on January 24, 1826. His birth was celebrated with great pomp and munificent philanthropic donations by Prosonnocoomar, who was reportedly overjoyed at the arrival of the long-awaited heir (Prosonnocoomar had two daughters, both older than Gyanendramohan, who lived in their father's house with their husbands and children). Gyanendramohan was the only son and heir, and because of his conversion and subsequent disinheritance, a source of great curiosity for Thompson.

At the beginning of his letter to Amelia, Thompson said that the suffix "Mohan" was added to the names of those who were beloved. He proceeded to call his daughter Amelia Mohan throughout the letter. Assuming this knowledge came from his host Prosonnocoomar, it may speak to the affection that he still felt for his prodigal son. Thompson alternated between calling the young scion of the Pathuriaghata Tagore family Gyanendranath and Gyanendramohan, and noted that he had first met him as a boy of fourteen or fifteen years old in 1843.[26] It seems at that time Thompson was impressed by the fragile and gentle boy's "quick intelligent mind and . . . insatiable thirst for knowledge." He became good friends with him, and they spent time exchanging their views on English manners and Hindu customs. Thompson was also present during Gyanendramohan's first wedding in 1843 and inspected the lavish *joutuk* or bride gift of jewels, worth £10,000, that Prosonnocoomar gave to his daughter-in-law.

What Thompson did not know was that complicated lineage rituals came into play in the choice of brides for both the Hindu Pathuriaghata and the Brahmo Jorasanko branches of the family. The Tagores had cemented their position in Bengali society through their own abilities, their entrepreneurship and official connections with the English and French East India Companies, their munificence and charities, and their role as cultural ambassadors of the Indian Renaissance since the eighteenth century. But their caste status was uncertain in the extremely caste-conscious and tightly knit aristocratic Hindu community of Calcutta. It was weakened by the so-called Pirali taint, a result of the forced conversion to Islam of two ancestors in the sixteenth century, which had also led to a concomitant fall from their previous pristine *kulin* Brahmin caste status and a reduction of their social prestige for the nonconverted Hindu members of the extended Tagore family. This dark spot in their elite lineage loomed over the family and weakened their position in the complicated caste matrix of nineteenth-century elite Hindu Bengali society. The Tagores had long been hyperaware of this tainted legacy and had performed grandiose public acts of devotion to increase their social prestige as devout Hindus. For example, Gyanendramohan's grandfather Gopimohan Tagore had directed his most famous act of charity toward a religious institution: the Kalighat temple.[27] Nevertheless, most elite caste Hindu families did not intermarry with the Tagores. The Tagore brides, for generations, had usually been chosen from the same Pirali caste, usually from Jessore, the Tagores' ancestral home, now in Bangladesh.

However, the choice of Gyanendramohan's bride was a social and religious coup for Prosonnocoomar. The girl was Bala Sundari Chakrabarty, from a spotless kulin Brahmin subcaste, marking her as much more highborn than Gyanendramohan's own aristocratic lineage.[28] She was the daughter of a priest devoted to the worship of the goddess Kali. Bala's maternal family were very poor and certainly no competition for the so-called Rothschilds of Calcutta. The family deity of the Pathuriaghata Tagores, in whose honor they consecrated a temple at Mulajore, was Kali as well, which may be one of the reasons why they chose a bride from a family devoted to the goddess's worship. But in this case, Prosonnocoomar may have aimed to gain respect and cement his position among the Hindu Bengali elite of Calcutta by choosing a girl with a spotless caste lineage, albeit from a much poorer background. In other words, the gossip would have us believe, Prosonnocoomar had purchased at low cost the high price of social prestige in Calcutta by choosing Bala for Gyanendramohan. Following the complicated rules of elevating one's social standing in a deeply religious and caste-conscious community, such a marriage could only enhance the prestige of the Pathuriaghata Tagores and lessen the blot on their caste purity.

Gyanendramohan, by all accounts, fell in love with his young wife and devoted his time and attention to educating her in accordance with the progressive ideals of female emancipation championed by Raja Radhakanta Dev, by his own father, and by his older cousin Debendranath Tagore of the Jorasanko Brahmo branch of the family.[29] Gyanadanandini Devi, wife of the first Indian Indian Civil Service (ICS) officer Satyendranath Tagore (the second son of Debendranath Tagore, and Gyanendramohan's second cousin), wrote the following in her memoir, *Puratani* (Those old days):

> Gyanendramohan was very fair and short of stature. He was the apple of his father's eye, which is why Prosonnocoomar arranged a marriage for him with the most beautiful girl he could find from Jessore. Gyanendramohan fell in love and became devoted to her—he would remain with her always, going to the extent of fanning her while she slept. When this wife died, Gyanendramohan was grief-struck and taking advantage of his disturbed mind, a Christian *padri* called Krishna Bandyo converted him to Christianity in the guise of consoling him.

Gyanadanandini was a guest of Gyanendramohan Tagore during her visit to England in 1877, and in any case would have heard of the family scandal because the Pathuriaghata and Jorasanko families maintained close social ties. In her retelling of the scandal, Rev. Krishnamohan Banerjee was entirely to blame for Gyanendramohan's conversion. Perhaps this version of the story circulated in the wider Tagore family to console the heartbroken Prosonnocoomar Tagore.[30]

Thompson's letter, meanwhile, narrated this episode as a remarkably detailed bildungsroman. He detailed the growth of understanding and enlightenment in the unlettered Bengali bride as her husband assiduously shared his own English learning with her. According to Thompson, Bala Sundari progressed so far in reasoned debate and understanding that she was convinced of the ultimate truth residing in the Bible. Thompson asserts, "On the subject of religion, <u>she determined</u>, were it possible, <u>to know the truth</u>."[31] Something curious happened, however, with this lovely shy bride of nine who entered the Tagores' palatial Pathuriaghata mansion and emerged as an exemplar of converted women with her death. She was immortalized in contemporary evangelical Christian hagiographies as the ideal model for native *zenana* converts. Bala Sundari, with her death, passed into evangelical Christian lore—a highly improbable fate for an orthodox Hindu woman from her social milieu.

Thompson's depiction of Gyanendramohan and Bala's love is a narrative of romantic bibliophilia. Their story has strong parallels to Alexander Duff's account of the way in which Umesh Chandra Sarkar and his wife became convinced of the superior merits of Christianity. Both couples joined pedagogy, theological research, and romantic conjugality in their private lives: reading religious tracts and debating the merits of Hinduism and Christianity led to spiritual and intellectual closeness and appear to have been an act of making love in both cases. One missionary account I will discuss a little later, by Edward Storrow, pointed out that Gyanendramohan and Bala read together every night—the only time of the day when the young couple were allowed to be intimately together. Similarly, missionary accounts portray both Umesh's wife and Bala as more resolute in their Christian faith than their husbands. According to Duff, it was Umesh's wife who urged him to resist his family's entreaties and hold fast to their mutual desire to be baptized.[32] Similarly, Gyanendramohan and Bala read theology together, questioning the foundations of their own identities as Hindus when faced with Christian apologetics such as *The Pilgrim's Progress,* which was on their reading list. So was Richard Baxter, the nonconformist and great Reformation-era Protestant theologian, whose highly controversial *Call to the Unconverted* (1658) became a Methodist favorite in late eighteenth-century Britain and later circulated in India. Bala Tagore also read the New Testament in Bengali, possibly the 1839 translation by William Yates of the Calcutta Baptist Society. From Thompson's letters and later missionary narratives, it appears that Bala had a spiritual conversion first, while her husband still hesitated. For Gyanendramohan, speculations on theology were perhaps more a philosophical exercise than a path to salvation. He was torn between the differing theological debates concerning unitarian precepts of Hinduism, which were championed by Rammohan Roy and then his cousin Debendranath, and the Trinitarianism professed by most Calcutta churches of any denomination.[33] Storrow corroborated this account of his conflicted feelings, presenting them as directly spoken by Gyanendramohan:

> "My wife," said Gyanendramohan Tagore, "often told me that as I taught her this new religion, it was but just that I should put her in a position to learn it perfectly and profess it freely. But I was in a predicament for I was a Unitarian, and did not know what Church to join, for all the Churches in Calcutta are Trinitarian. . . . While affairs were going on in this way, the work of Dr Pye Smith on the Messiah fell into my hands, and fortunately for both me and my wife my views began to take a Trinitarian turn."[34]

To learn the English language and English deportment, Bala Sundari was placed in the care of an English governess, Mrs. Sidley, a practice quite common in liberal aristocratic families in colonial Calcutta.[35] The presence of English books in the apartments of the young couple and their discussions of religious precepts seemed to indicate to the visitors the triumph of the colonial civilizing mission, a sign that it had had permeated even the most intimate realm of the Indian family's inner domains.

Bala proved to be an indefatigable student and her religious education ensured that she steadily gained strength in her faith. Learning English opened a wider world of Christian theology to her, and she no longer had to rely on her husband's translations. At length, she renounced the wealth, jewels, and rich attire befitting a woman of her station. Her in-laws, suspicious of her attitude and actions, asked her to perform the daily rituals of the worship of household deities, which she refused to do, even when entreated by her mother-in-law. Yet Gyanendramohan's mother, who had asked Bala to worship the Shivalinga (thereby evoking theatrical horror from the missionary chroniclers of Bala's life), reconciled with her only son and his wife before her own death in 1847. She bequeathed to them her not inconsiderable *stridhana* or private property.

Edward Storrow depicted Bala rebuking her husband for his weakness in not renouncing his timidity and embracing Christianity. In this narrative, Bala made the full journey from the daughter of a priest of "the dark and terrible" Kali to an ideal convert, educating herself into enlightenment and salvation.[36] Storrow's account was matched by Thompson's description of Bala as a strong-willed young woman whose belief in Christianity was so profound that she asked Gyanendramohan to renounce his family and take her away so they could freely practice their faith:

> She would urge him to fling away his fears—to renounce his doctrines of expediency—would insist upon following the dictates of conscience, and would say, "Better, dear Gyanendramohan, to be poor, and in our poverty to be free to make an open avowal of our conviction, and to live as we believe God requires, than to be rich, and to conceal our real opinions on the all-important subject of religion."[37]

Bala then contracted what Thompson called "rapid consumption," perhaps, as he suggested, due to the mental anguish she underwent. Realizing that she was dying, she urged Gyanendramohan to "take courage and face the consequences of a public renunciation." She also wished to be baptized before death. The inner domains of the aristocratic families were closely guarded in colonial

Calcutta. As a result, according to Thompson, there were "insuperable difficulties" in granting her last wishes, though her husband declared that he had dearly wished to fulfill her request. On June 18, 1851, she advised her husband from her deathbed: "Hear my last words, when you may, do justice to the memory of the wife whom you have been instrumental of leading out of the darkness of idolatry into the light—I die a Christian."[38] Bala's adamant desire to live out their conversion publicly is striking and singularly important. Her insistence makes it clear that she knew conversion to Christianity in India had to be lived and performed publicly.[39]

Bala's deathbed scene is echoed in missionary accounts of women converts. Several such deathbed accounts of converts can be found in a pamphlet printed by the Baptist Mission Press in 1880. Each narrative in the pamphlet, which was titled *Shantishojja*, (Peaceful deathbed) included the convert's avowal of Jesus Christ as her savior just before death. This pattern makes clear that public avowal on one's deathbed was considered necessary to be counted as a Christian in life, irrespective of whether formal conversion and baptism had taken place. Whether Bala actually avowed her Christian faith before dying or not, the pamphlets depicting her life clearly followed a predetermined script in asserting that she had done so. Bala's conversion fits the Protestant model of epiphany and spiritual awakening rather poorly. Because she never made a public renunciation of Hinduism and a public avowal of Christianity, her life as narrated by Thompson and her other missionary hagiographers never quite fits into the neat narrative of credible and sincere conversion—a fact that is perhaps exacerbated by the idealized nature of her portrayal. Exhortations to Gyanendramohan to gather courage to publicly renounce Hinduism, attributed repeatedly to Bala in these narratives, strongly hint at Gyanendramohan's own ambiguity about his spiritual leanings and his hesitation in committing fully to the public performance of baptism. The narratives establish Bala both as a cipher of the ideal converted Hindu woman and—perhaps even more importantly—as Gyanendramohan's alter ego, his more enlightened mirror.

Bala's sudden illness and death set the stage for Gyanendramohan's spiritual agon. He was baptized shortly thereafter with much fanfare by Rev. Krishnamohan Banerjee, his preceptor at Bishop's College and his father's inveterate enemy. Despite the testimony of Thompson and the later sources on Bala and Gyanendramohan's life, who all attribute Gyanendramohan's conversion to an attempt to honor his beloved wife's deathbed wishes, it is certainly possible that Gyanendramohan's astute future father-in-law timed the baptism for after the passing of the Caste Disabilities Removal Act in 1850 so that Gyanendramohan would be less likely to lose his regal patrimony. Thompson, trying to present a balanced account of these events, includes an account of the social effects of Gyanendramohan's conversion on Prosonnocoomar. Before ending his letter, he cautioned his daughter Amelia, "Pronounce no judgment on the father, till you have all the facts before you. Prossono, who little dreams I have been writing about his Christian daughter-in-law, has promised me some additional information regarding the Thakur [Tagore] family."[40] In a subsequent letter, Thompson mentioned that he had seen Gyanendramohan at Bishop's College, and the meeting left him shocked at the changes in his erstwhile friend:

> From what he said in company . . . his mind appeared to be alienated from his countrymen at large, and . . . he had become a staunch advocate of the Company's rule in India and was in a state of mind regarding his father by no means such as I could approve. . . . I shall be very much grieved if I am confirmed in the belief that his feelings towards his father are of an unchristian nature.[41]

Both Hindu and Muslim Indians felt constant anxiety that conversion was not only mimicry of British faith and morality in order to supersede racial and colonial discriminations but also a harbinger of the psychological ills that derived from colonialism itself. Conversion itself was understood to be fostered by a kind of self-hatred: no one who loved one's faith and one's community and was truly dedicated could ever contemplate conversion. Gyanendramohan's departure from the professed patriotism of the Tagore families at Jorasanko and Pathuriaghata, for which they were justly praised in the Bengali public sphere, and his avowal of support for Company rule played on another common anxiety Indians felt about their countrymen who converted to Christianity: disloyalty to their communities of origin and loyalty to the alien British.[42]

It seems improbable, if not outright unbelievable, that a young couple, the only heir to an aristocratic joint family and his wife, could discuss Christian theological doctrines and even practice Christianity without sparking complete uproar in their families and social networks. The Pathuriaghata Tagore family consisted of almost 200 members at the time of Gyanendramohan's conversion. The absence of backlash is even more improbable given Prosonnocoomar's eminence in native society and prominent association with the colonial British administration. Yet Thompson's letters do not suggest that the young couple faced any reproach or punishment for their activities, other than the fact that Gyanendramohan's mother Umatara urged her daughter-in-law to perform the daily rituals of worshipping the family deities. This urging may not even have been related to Bala's suspected Christian tendencies but rather a routine part of the required training she would undergo to assume the reins of the inner domains of the Pathuriaghata Tagore mansion when her husband would inherit the position of head of the family from his father. Thompson may have been motivated by feelings of delicacy because of his friendship with Prosonnocoomar, but given the otherwise frank nature of the letter, and the fact that it was a private missive to his daughter, this seems unlikely.

Most missionary accounts describe the harsh response Indian converts faced from their communities of birth, faith, and kinship, which they renounced on conversion.[43] But Thompson's letter to Amelia also preserves a rare glimpse into the psychological effects that the conversion of a child, especially the only son and heir, could have on a parent. According to Thompson, when he asked Prosonnocoomar about his son's conduct, he said only this in reply:

> "Before my son left me," he said, "I was happy in my profession, which brought me Rs. 80000 (£8000 sterling) a year. But when he left home, I at once quitted the Bar forever and started on a journey to Kashmir. I was absent nearly a year. On my return, Lord Dalhousie sent for me, and pressed upon me the acceptance of the situation of Clerk Assistant to the Legislative Council of India in 1854. . . . He gave me a high position and opened to me a path in which I might be of service to my country. *But I shall never be myself again, having lost my only son.*"[44]

Gyanendramohan's symbolic act of renouncing his community starkly contrasts with his father's actual renunciation and self-imposed exile because of his son's perceived shameful act, which struck against the family's honor and position in society. The implicit reason for Prosonnocoomar's acceptance of Dalhousie's offer was that it gave him a way to reestablish his preeminence among the Calcutta *bhadralok* elite. But when Gyanendramohan was erased from the records of the Pathuriaghata Tagore family, his father lost his own sense of self through the irreparable loss of the son. Prosonnocoomar and Gyanendramohan never met again, even though Prosonnocoomar did not die until 1868, seventeen years after Gyanendramohan's conversion. Prosonnocoomar Tagore's last will and testament refers to his beloved son only once: "I have already made such provisions for my son Gyanendramohan Tagore as I consider sufficient, and he will take nothing whatever under this my will."[45] These provisions were the *joutuk* or marriage gift bestowed upon Gyanendramohan and Bala of an estate with an annual rent of Rs. 7,000 and the monthly allowance he gave his son.[46]

Gyanendramohan attempted to reconcile with Prosonnocoomar when he was on his deathbed. He tried to visit his dying father, but Jatindramohan, his cousin and the beneficiary of Prosonnocoomar's will, barred Gyanendramohan from entering the house. Jatindramohan was fearful, the gossip went, that Prosonnocoomar, driven by paternal affection, would reconcile and change his will back in favor of his estranged son. There are varying accounts of what happened next. By one account, Prosonnocoomar heard what had happened and cursed his nephew with infertility, saying, "as I have been deprived from seeing my son one last time, so shall you and your descendants never have any male heirs." The curse was a potent one: the Pathuriaghata Tagore family survived through adoptions of male heirs through the next four generations.[47] By another account, Gyanendramohan heartbrokenly cast the imprecation that would haunt Jatindramohan's line for decades to come: "He who prevented the dying father from seeing his son—he too will die without a son!"[48] The slamming of the door to his father's house in Gyanendramohan's face aptly embodies the violent severance of relationships between converts and their natal families and communities of origin. When Prosonnocoomar passed away, it was Jatindramohan who performed the ritual of *mukhagni* or lighting of the funeral pyre at his *antyesti* or cremation—a sacred ritual usually reserved for the firstborn son. It was also Jatindramohan who carried out the *sraddha* or sacred homage rituals for Prosonnocoomar. Gyanendramohan, as a Christian convert, was disqualified from performing these last rites for his father and was not allowed to attend the magnificent funeral.

Bala Sundari Tagore as the Ideal Zenana *Convert*

Besides Thompson, three other sources describe the life and marriage of Bala and Gyanendramohan—though it appears that Thompson was the source for all three. The earliest description of Bala Tagore's "conversion" was Rev. Edward Storrow's *The Eastern Lily Gathered: A Memoir of Bala Sundari Tagore,* published in 1852. Storrow was a London Missionary Society member who was sent to Calcutta in 1848, where he lived with Hannah Mullens and her husband Dr. Joseph Mullens.[49] Hannah Mullens seems to have invented the template for Indian missionary narratives about *zenana* conversions and ideal Indian women converts. She is often acknowledged as the writer of the first Bengali novel, called *Phoolmani and Karuna: A Book for Native Christian Women,* which is a moral tale about two Indian women. Phoolmani is an ideal native convert, with a harmonious and pious family, while Karuna is the lazy, lying, scandalous Hindu woman, who is finally saved from her life of moral turpitude through Phoolmani's influence.[50] Mullens's work was published in 1852, almost at the same time as Storrow's pamphlet. A clear line of influence can be traced between her fictional depiction of Phoolmani and Storrow's reflections on Bala—Mullens's template for a good woman convert is quite evident in Storrow's descriptions of Bala's ideal qualities. Both are prototypes of the idealized female native convert, who can function as pedagogical inspiration for and validation of missionary activism targeting the native *zenana.* This is clearly articulated in the subtitle of Storrow's hagio/biography: "With observations on the position and prospects of Hindoo Female Society."[51]

In this genre, the path to conversion was also the path of great trials. The problem with Bala Tagore's history, or rather the version of Bala Tagore's history that could effectively be held up as an ideal to be imitated by native converts, is that recognizable patterns of trials of the soul are simply not present. Gyanendramohan and Bala led a very comfortable and privileged life together. Gyanendramohan himself said of his father, "*My father at this time was a liberal in religion***.** Being a man of considerable influence, he had joined the party who thought that some changes might advantageously be made in the form of Hinduism."[52] Therefore, Bala's achievements speak just as highly of the liberal opinions of her father-in-law and her husband, regarding the education of women, as they do of her own desire to seek the truth of the Christian faith. The family's reactions toward her possible apostasy were fairly mild, and even indulgent, just as they were toward her husband. It seems the family believed that these much-adored children would never actually leave the faith of their ancestors, and that their interest was fueled by a momentary flirtation with evangelism, in a somewhat extravagant response to the liberal reformatory spirit championed by the Tagores at this time. Of course, this was a tragic misconception, and the fallout seems to have taken every family member by complete surprise.

The historical circumstances surrounding the publication of Storrow's account tell us why Gyanendramohan's baptism caused a furor—there had been multiple baptisms of young schoolboys in Calcutta in the previous six months, and public anger was already great. Gyanendramohan's conversion was preceded by the conversion of six pupils from Bhowanipore Educational Institution, under the guidance of Mullens and Storrow, in June. According to Storrow's account, Bala died after a short illness in 1851, and Gyanendramohan converted a few weeks afterward. These events must have occurred rather quickly, since Joseph Mullens wrote to the *Evangelical Magazine and Missionary Chronicle* in July, describing the occasion as a sign of God's favor on missionary activity: "The Lord seems to be carrying on his work with special power in sight of his enemies in this city."[53] Gyanendramohan converted in 1851, under the auspices of the Church Missionary Society, an event that understandably amazed native opinion in India given his family and social standing. Together, this sequence of events convulsed Hindu society in Calcutta.[54]

After Bala's death, Gyanendra's remarriage to Kamala Banerjee, and Prosonnocoomar's public disowning of his son, the Pathuriaghata Tagores sought to obliterate Gyanendramohan from the family's history. George Thompson hinted at this catastrophic event, noting that Gyanendramohan's name was erased from the Tagore family's genealogical charts.[55] The provisions of the will exacerbated the bitterness of his relationship with his family and with the cousin who inherited his father's estate. Thereafter, almost no official biographies of the Tagore family mention Gyanendramohan—and the few that do merely offer a terse sentence stating that he converted to Christianity. In the eyes of Hindu society, his apostasy meant that he was spiritually dead.[56] This erasure also unmoored the convert from his social matrix, intended as it was to obliterate his identity as a member of the community.

In Storrow's account, Gyanendramohan, reminiscing about the circumstances that led to his disinheritance, later said this of his father's attitude toward him: "My father, however, kept himself peculiarly quiet and passive, feeling that though my views were very different to his own, yet that it became him as a parent, to treat us with respect, and to afford us that protection which, as the head of our house, we had a right to expect at his hands."[57]

The *Evangelical Magazine and Missionary Chronicle* hinted that Prosonnocoomar had heard of Gyanendramohan's plans to convert and had tried to prevent the public humiliation he knew awaited the Tagore family as a result of his son's decision. He offered to settle on his son an income of £12,000, and an allowance of £2,000 / month immediately, if Gyanendramohan would only refuse a public baptism by Krishnamohan Banerjee, regardless of his private beliefs.[58] Even after being disowned, when Gyanendramohan moved to Bishop's College, Prosonnocoomar still arranged to give his son an allowance of Rs. 1,000 a month, or about £1,200 a year. This was an extremely comfortable income, even in England. In India it was a princely sum, though a fraction of what Prosonnocoomar possessed and what his son would have expected to inherit had he not converted.

The second narrative of Bala's life, an 1856 pamphlet titled *The History of a Converted Hindoo Lady,* published by the Society for Promoting Female Education in the East, offers disturbing new details about the treatment of Gyanendramohan and Bala. The sensationalized account is difficult to believe: "The offence of the Cross was great in [Prosonnocoomar]'s eyes. . . . He rendered his son a prisoner at home, rigorously excluding him from intercourse with all Europeans, and forbidding him to go beyond the limits of his own grounds. For ten years[!] the youthful pair lived in this domestic captivity."[59] This was outright slander, for many reasons. Prosonnocoomar was well known for being one of the only aristocrats who extended his munificence liberally to everyone who came to him in need, irrespective of their religious identity: "In his charities he was at once liberal and discriminating. . . . The number of private recipients of his bounty, whether in the shape of annual allowances, or of occasional help in the hour of need, was legion, and included many poor Christians as well as Natives."[60] Also, given that Gyanendramohan's first marriage lasted from 1843 to 1851, the ten years of captivity already sounds like an exaggeration for sensational effect. Given the Tagore family's liberal stance on matters of religious reform, their wide network among Europeans and elite Indians, and their vocal detractors, it seems hardly credible that Prosonnocoomar could have virtually imprisoned his son for ten years without incurring gossip. Moreover, Gyanendramohan clearly was not housebound during this period: he attended Hindu College and then Bishop's College, where he made friends like Rajnarayan Bose, Shibnath Shastri, and Bhudev Mukherjee, all of whom mention him in their autobiographies.[61]

The third narrative of Bala and Gyanendramohan's life can be found in Rev. Edward Jewitt Robinson's *Daughters of India,* published in 1860. It largely rehashes the two earlier narratives and adds more dialogue for Bala to demonstrate her fearless total commitment to the Christian faith. Jewitt also includes a glorious paean to the ideal *zenana* convert:

> Only eighteen years of age, affectionate, sincere, highly intelligent, a friend to the poor, on the point, against her nation's opinions, and against the prejudices of the majority of her relatives, of receiving the sacrament of baptism, baptized, like Cornelius and his friends, ere the outward sign could be

administered, by the Holy Spirit of God, a Christian heroine, a perfect wife, the beautiful Bala laid her earthly loveliness aside for her fairer form in Paradise.[62]

Bala's case has been analyzed in detail by two scholars before me, Anna Johnston and Deepra Dandekar. Both of these important studies focus on the missionary narratives of Bala's life, analyzing the tropes of salvation from superstition through conversion. Yet they also elide the importance of Bala's background as not only a high-caste Hindu woman but also the wife of Gyanendramohan and daughter-in-law of Prosonnocoomar Tagore. In establishing Bala as an exemplar of women's conversion in Bengal, the missionary pamphlets repeatedly stress her agency.[63] Yet at the same time, all of these pamphlets rely on the firsthand testimony of her husband—it is Gyanendramohan's reminiscences of Bala and her spiritual turn to Christianity that remained the most important evidence for her depiction as an ideal high-caste woman convert and cemented her posthumous fate as the exemplar for *zenana* and self-driven, self-realized Christian conversion. Bala's atypical background for a converted woman is highly important: despite the formal narrative route that missionary pamphlets take on Bala's life, conversion, and death, the fact remains that their source is often her husband Gyanendramohan. It is evident from the pamphlets that he determined which details of her life and death were to be immortalized in their pages. Furthermore, his own spiritual journey is projected onto his much beloved first wife: in every retelling of Bala's life and conversion, Gyanendramohan seems to seek a psychological resolution to his own life's choices.

In this sense, these missionary pamphlets highlight the urgency Christian missions in India felt for successful converts within the inner *antahpur* of orthodox Hindu households. But these pamphlets also seem to tell a story about Gyanendramohan's deferred agency in his own Christian conversion. His ambivalence about taking the public step toward conversion through a spectacular baptism knowing it would bring about excommunication from his family and community, his realization of his spiritual duty to be true to his inner convictions regarding the merits of Christianity, and ultimately his desire to fulfill his wife's deathbed wish of living freely as a Christian are retold and reshaped as a response to Bala's urging and his reaction to her exhortations. Gyanendramohan seemingly cloaked his own hesitations with Bala's supposed strengths in these reminiscences of his wife and his old life to these missionary chroniclers, to an extent that one wonders if he wanted to offset his own feelings of guilt about his Christian sympathies onto his wife. In some sense, perhaps he was absolving himself from owning up to the responsibility for the misfortune that he suffered as a result of his widely publicized conversion. It was perhaps also a way to explain to his relatives, friends, and social circle the circumstances behind his decision to convert.

Gyanendramohan also cultivated a long association with Krishnamohan Banerjee, later to be his converter and subsequently his father-in-law. He was very close to Banerjee's family as well. But the missionary narratives elide these facts in order to present a recognizable discourse on the heathen cruelty of Gyanendramohan's relatives and Bala's suffering and miraculous spiritual awakening into true Christian faith. Even within *The History of a Converted Hindoo Lady*'s narrative, the story of imprisonment and isolation faced by Gyanendramohan and Bala is challenged: it records a certain Mrs. Ellerton's frequent visits to Bala, introduced to her by Bala's governess Mrs. Sidley. It also describes Bala attired as befitting the wife of the family's only heir. She is described as looking like a goddess, "a beautiful young woman, most superbly and modestly dressed, and loaded with jewels, some of which I never saw the like of, heretofore . . . studded with diamonds, rubies and emeralds. Her nose ring had three pearls, the center one very large. Bala . . . replied to our questions in English."[64]

Gyanendramohan married Kamala, the daughter of Krishnamohan Banerjee, on April 15, 1852, at almost exactly the same time as *The Eastern Lily Gathered*, Bala's great eulogy, was published. Kamala must have been aware of the enormous consequences her husband faced in choosing to convert and in marrying her. She was well known in the native Christian society in Calcutta for her beauty, her education, and her quiet nature. Gyanendramohan married her when she was fifteen years old, in St. Paul's Cathedral in Calcutta.[65] She contracted consumption or tuberculosis quite early in her marriage and spent over a decade suffering from this dreadful illness and from multiple pregnancies, miscarriages, and stillbirths. All the while, her husband repeatedly traveled to England and back again—not only to gain some distance from his social network, which had excommunicated and shunned him, but also to find a cure for his wife. They had three surviving children together: two daughters, Bhavendrabala and Satyendrabala, and a son, Prossonnomohan. Gyanendramohan named his son after both his grandfathers, perhaps in hope of a reconciliation that was never to happen. His daughters, interestingly, retain in their own names that of their father's first wife. Of his daughters, only Satyendrabala outlived her parents.[66]

Kamala Tagore (née Banerjee) had no hagiographic pamphlets written about her. In archival records, she appears only in conjunction with stray references to her husband. During Gyanendramohan's first sojourn in Britain, she accompanied him on his many visits to "Schools, Reformatories and Hospitals." In the 1856 pamphlet *The History of a Converted Hindoo Lady*, we find the spouses visiting Calmel Gray's Yard Ragged School in oriental costume. There, Gyanendramohan made a speech to the children and told them they were fortunate to be born in a Christian land.[67] We only have one record of Kamala speaking, in 1856, when the Tagores entertained several missionary friends and Indian students at their Kensington Street home in London. Rakhaldas Haldar, a young student who kept a journal of his visit, spoke about the eager gladness with which Mrs. Tagore conversed in Bengali with him—a poignant reminder of her loneliness in Britain. In the few fragmentary narratives of her life, she is depicted as the perfectly submissive and quiet Christian wife—a stark contrast to Bala Sundari Tagore's assertiveness, confidence, and intellectual curiosity. Kamala's identity seems to be submerged in and an extension of her husband's religious and social convictions. In the first tumultuous days after her marriage and her husband's sensational disinheritance, which must have affected her immensely, Kamala found solace in friendship with her husband's cousin, a young widow called Maheshwari. Maheshwari had grown up with Gyanendramohan's first wife Bala and had also converted to Christianity, after a daring escape from her widow's exile in the holy city of Banaras, "Siberia of the poor widowed Hindu," perhaps encouraged by Gyanendramohan himself.[68] Kamala returned to Calcutta with Gyanendramohan in 1859, when her tuberculosis became terminal, and was cared for by her parents and Maheshwari in her last days. She was buried in Park Street Cemetery. Her grave is untraceable, though Gyanendramohan made provisions for the upkeep of her mausoleum in his will.[69] In any case, Kamala Tagore remains a haunting, ghostly presence in the story of Gyanendramohan's life. Her world, like Bala's, can only be reconstructed through the words of the men in her life.

Filial Relationships and Christian Conversion

Prosonnocoomar Tagore was a complicated man. He was often mocked as the "Half-Reformer" by the members of the Young Bengal group, who pointed to the contrast between his public reformism and his staunchly held private conservatism. Yet by the standard of his times, when converted children were regularly threatened not only with loss of their inheritance or homes but also with assault and murder, Prosonnocoomar's actions speak not only to his affection for his son but also to his liberal and progressive attitude.[70] His complicated attitude toward reformism and suspicious hostility toward Christianity was common in both branches of the Tagore family, as indicated by Debendranath Tagore's outraged commentary on the affair and on Gyanendramohan's conduct toward his father. From Debendranath Tagore's reminiscences, it is clear that Gyanendramohan had fought bitterly with his father over the continuance of his allowance, which had hitherto allowed Gyanendramohan to live a life befitting his status as the only heir to an immensely rich aristocratic family.

Debendranath's relationship with his cousin Gyanendramohan was tense, and they often clashed on questions of religion and ritual observance. The first public rift occurred in 1846, during the celebration of the funerary or *sraddha* services of Prince Dwarkanath Tagore, Debendranath's father. Debendranath had performed the services with the strictest Vedantic rituals, commensurate with his belief in Brahmoism. Raja Radhakanta Dev of Sovabazar and Prosonnocoomar, both associates of Dwarkanath and otherwise fond of Debendranath, strongly rebuked him for deviating from the accepted orthodox Hindu funerary services. Gyanendramohan poured oil on the fire when he wrote to *The Englishman* periodical under the pseudonym Justicia, criticizing Debendranath's management of the affair. He charged his cousin with hypocrisy, since Debendranath had—according to established Hindu social norms—provided alms to the Brahmins and the destitute who gathered on the occasion of the *sraddha,* although the event itself had been held strictly according to pure Vedantic norms.[71] Debendranath would later go on to scorn the sincerity of Gyanendramohan's conversion. In a letter written to his close friend Rajnarayan Bose during the monsoon months of 1851, Debendranath reported sarcastically:

> Gyanendra Babu has begun quarreling with his father since his wife died and has compelled Prosonnocoomar to write him a hand-note worth a hundred thousand rupees and is now staying in a separate house. Krishnamohan Bandopadhyay now possesses his heart entirely. He will probably convert, but right now it is impossible to say. Anyone possessing the slightest bit of righteousness cannot behave as Gyanendramohan has done—is there a greater sin than hurting a most loving father intimately?

In a follow-up letter, Debendranath confirmed Gyanendramohan's conversion: "Gyanendra Babu is a convert Christian; perhaps now his desire to give speeches in English will be fulfilled!"[72]

The Pathuriaghata Tagores had felt very insecure in their public status as an orthodox elite Hindu family after Debendranath accepted Rammohan Roy's radical Vedantist monotheism and the junior cadet branch of the Jorasanko Tagore family converted to Brahmoism. For the Pathuriaghata Tagores, these developments meant that a stronger public performance of their staunch orthodox Hindu Brahmin beliefs was required. Gyanendramohan's public baptism undermined Prosonnocoomar exactly at the point when he was most liable to face social ridicule. Ram Gopal Sanyal, contemporary chronicler of the salacious details of the lives of illustrious Indian men, recorded that one of the first to shame Prosonnocoomar in public was Krishnamohan Banerjee, by loudly exclaiming on their relationship as in-laws in order to insult the proud Brahmin aristocrat.[73] He did so, Sanyal records, in the public space of the new railway station at Howrah Junction: on seeing his nemesis there, Krishnamohan declared that Gyanendramohan had indeed married his daughter Kamala, making Prosonnocoomar a close relative. This public spectacle was calculated to cement Prosonnocoomar and the Pathuriaghata Tagores' fall from grace in Calcutta's closely knit aristocratic Hindu community:

> On one occasion, Babu Prosonnocoomar arrived at the Howrah Railway Station with his wife to go to his summer retreat at Pirpahar in Monghyr and accidentally, at the very same time Rev. K. M. Banerji and his wife came there in order to go to a place by the same train. When he saw Prosonnocoomar, he said in a loud tone to Mrs. Banerji, "Look, look, our *Beyayi* [bridegroom's father] is going there." On hearing this, Prosonnocoomar became ashamed, and with a quicker motion he tried to evade his presence. But the Reverend K. M. Banerji was irrepressible. He, with a still louder voice, called out, "*Beyayi, Beyayi*! O bridegroom's father!! Come, come, let us travel in the same compartment with our *Beyayin* [bridegroom's mother]." Thus insulted, Prosonnocoomar abandoned the idea of travelling with him in the same train, lest he should insult him more, and returned home on that day.[74]

Around the same time as Gyanendramohan's baptism, Radhakanta Deb chaired the second anti-Christian meeting in Calcutta. In this meeting, unlike the previous one in 1847, the objective was to find either some way to definitively prevent conversions, or to agree to some *shastric vyavastha* or textual evidence to support the return of converts into the fold after the performance of appropriate penances.[75] Although measures were proposed, there were doubts as to the efficacy of implementing them, or even of their acceptability by Brahmin *pandits* outside Bengal. The meeting reinforced the atmosphere of panic and virulent anti-Christian sentiments among the leaders of Bengali society, for whom the fact that one of their own had committed apostasy was unforgivable. Some of this Hindu anger was vividly parodied by Krishnamohan Banerjee in a satirical pamphlet under the nom de guerre Sanjaya Redivivus.[76] There he called Raja Radhakanta Dev, the leader of the orthodox Hindu party, Rashavakanta or Gadhakanta (lord of the asses). For Krishnamohan, elite Hindu Bengalis like Radhakanta and Prosonnocoomar did not have a leg to stand on in their demands for upholding the sanctity of Hindu religion against Christianity or the repeal of the Lex Loci Act. They had themselves violated Hindu norms of caste purity and deviated from orthodoxy by choosing a Kayastha like Radhakanta Dev as the head of society or *samajpati,* thus elevating him above Brahmins, which was a grievous sin.[77]

Strikingly, in 1854, Prosonnocoomar attempted to bring his younger cousin Chandramohan Tagore back into the fold of orthodox Hinduism. Chandramohan belonged to a cadet branch of the family and had converted to Christianity through a hasty baptism after a quarrel with his father. Chandramohan's reconversion was initiated through the performance of an elaborate ritual of *prayaschitta* or repentance, at the cost of thousands of rupees. Prosonnocoomar was helped in this novel enterprise by his cousins Ramanath and Girindramohan Tagore.[78] He also had the implicit support of the Raja Radhakanta Dev and his Dharma Sabha. Through these public acts of sponsoring reconversion, Prosonnocoomar sought to offset the damage that Gyanendramohan's conversion and remarriage had done to the Pathuriaghata Tagores' social standing. Of the Tagore family members, only Prosonnocoomar and his supporters attended Chandramohan's repentance ritual. The other members of the extended Tagore family did not attend, which is a hint that they did not think this reconversion was admissible. Chandramohan spent much of his life in Orissa, far from Calcutta and from home, and then his last days away from his family, in the Calcutta suburb of Baranagar. His case shows that even if reconversions were attempted at immense expense, they were often not acceptable to the wider familial network. If Gyanendramohan had hoped for a reconciliation, Prosonnocoomar knew from his experience with Chandramohan that he could never publicly agree to it. Even if Gyanendramohan showed public remorse and underwent the elaborate Hindu rituals of repentance, he would never be accepted wholeheartedly back into the fold, and the Pathuriaghata Tagores would face even more social opprobrium for reaccepting him.

Yet Gyanendramohan himself had also already taken steps that made such reconciliation impossible. The missionary pamphlets that glorified Bala and Gyanendramohan, while vilifying the Pathuriaghata Tagores, must have been excruciating to Prosonnocoomar and the extended family—especially since Gyanendramohan was the source of these unflattering reports on their orthodox behavior. But given George Thompson's shock at the change in Gyanendramohan's opinions about his father, it seems likely that it was his marriage to Krishnamohan Banerjee's daughter Kamala—even more than the conversion itself—that finally severed his relationship with his father. The marriage reinforced the estrangement (and disregard) of his father and his family that had been established by the public performance of Gyanendramohan's conversion. Therefore, the preservation of his father's social position depended on a public disavowal of the wayward son's beliefs.

THE GREAT TAGORE WILL CASE

Once Gyanendramohan had performed the widely advertised and public act of conversion through baptism after Bala's death, he immediately became a social and religious outcaste. He was disinherited by his devastated father. The problem created by Prosonnocoomar's will was this: Gyanendramohan had presumed that under the Lex Loci Act he could not legally be disinherited from his father's property. As I said earlier, he and his father-in-law, Krishnamohan Banerjee, possibly timed his 1851 conversion and second marriage for after the passage of the Lex Loci Act in 1850, so as to prevent the possibility of disinheritance. Yet Prosonnocoomar found a way to subvert the Lex Loci Act using his knowledge of the Hindu laws on inheritance. He was the foremost scholar on the *Mitakshara* treatise, which laid out the legal circumstances of inheritance outside Bengal, and he had translated into English the most important Sanskrit commentary on the *Mitakshara*.[79] Prosonnocoomar had even greater expertise on the *Dayabhaga,* the treatise originally written by Jimutvahana, which was the prevalent textual authority on inheritance laws in Bengal. British administrators and legal scholars had discussed this treatise extensively since the early days of Company rule in Bengal during the eighteenth century. It was first translated by the polymath and Calcutta Supreme Court judge Henry Thomas Colebrooke in 1810, after which numerous English commentaries were written on it.[80] Prosonnocoomar Tagore devised a table of succession based on the treatise, clearly laying out the order in which inheritance passed from the father or male head of a Hindu family to various other members through relationality of degrees of consanguinity. He also laid out under what circumstances this order could be interrupted or alienated away from a potential successor or inheritor.[81] This table was widely used in deciding inheritance cases in Bengal by 1860.

Unlike the *Mitakshara*, the *Dayabhaga* specifically prescribed that the father had absolute rights to his own as well as inherited ancestral property and could alienate or gift this property to whomsoever he wished in his own lifetime. In other words, the son's rights to property emerged from the father and passed to the son only at the father's death (or disqualification). They were not inalienable rights bequeathed on a son when he was born.[82] It is this particular interpretation of *Dayabhaga* that Prosonnocoomar elucidated in his collection of legal essays on property rights in Bengal.[83] And it is this interpretation that he used to circumvent the provisions of the Lex Loci Act, which would otherwise have allowed his son to inherit his estates, both ancestral and personal. Under this understanding of the *Dayabhaga*, he bestowed his property upon his nephews and grandnephews: Jatindramohan Tagore (1831–1908), Woopendramohan Tagore, Ramanath Tagore, and Durgaprasad Mukherjee. They were to hold the estate in trust, pay off all debts accrued to Prosonnocoomar during his lifetime, make provisions for the worship of the family's Kali idol at the ancestral Mulajore temple, and fund the legacies and bequests that Prosonnocoomar had made in his will. After these affairs were settled, they could enjoy the rent and proceeds of the estates. Of the four inheritors, Jatindramohan alone was to enjoy all of Prosonnocoomar's real estate (personalty). After Jatindramohan died, the enjoyment of the personalty was to pass onto the natural male heirs of his line, generationally through primogeniture, and for the rest of the estate similarly in tail in the male line for the other three inheritors. The interests from the estate amounted to Rs. 2,500 a month, in Jatindramohan's share. Prosonnocoomar's estates were entailed on his heirs through the creation of successive life interests for them. This meant that under Prosonnocoomar's will his beneficiaries, including Jatindramohan, would enjoy his estates during their lifetimes.[84] This proviso was based on the English entail, which would, regardless of the Lex Loci Act, prevent Gyanendramohan from inheriting any part of his father's estates during Gyanendramohan's lifetime. This extraordinary legal measure, which circumvented and therefore nullified the provisions of the Lex Loci Act, created an unprecedented crisis in colonial British interpretations of Hindu rights of inheritance. The result was the infamous Great Tagore Will Case (1868–1872), wherein Gyanendramohan contested his father's will in successive courts until the case was legally resolved in the Privy Council in England.[85]

Gyanendramohan contested the will on the grounds that Prosonnocoomar had in effect nullified Hindu customary legal usages by creating what amounted to an alternative trust on his properties, in his bequest to the four beneficiaries whom he designated as trustees, and an estate tail by devising a succession through the line of male nephews and grandnephews. He hired a strong team of lawyers to represent his interests at the Calcutta High Court, including Michael Madhusudan Dutta as legal adviser—who had himself contested his own disinheritance on the grounds of conversion to Christianity barely half a decade earlier. Gyanendramohan faced a drawn-out, exhausting, and difficult legal battle that would bring into question the very fabric of accepted legal norms of Hindu inheritance laws in the Bengal Province and the extent to which the Anglo-Indian legal system could interfere in or reform these norms. As Justice Phear, puisne judge at the Calcutta High Court, acknowledged, "The testator has for the first time in the history of litigation in this Presidency made a show of creating an estate tail and this suit is the legitimate consequence of this novel attempt." Gyanendramohan also objected to the administration of the estate by these trustees, who he alleged were laying his father's properties to ruin. The judgment on the case, given by Justice Phear on April 1, 1869, immediately dismissed Gyanendramohan's allegations of waste. But the first problem, that trusts were not usual in Hindu inheritance customs in Bengal, was legally important to resolve. Phear concluded that trusts were a common feature in customary usage in Hindu inheritance laws and reconfirmed the father's right, in Bengal, to alienate his property away from his male heirs.[86] Phear ruled that Gyanendramohan's suit to declare his father's will invalid, and therefore to conclude that Prosonnocoomar had died intestate, had failed materially from a legal point of view. However, for Phear, the key legal question was whether—by creating successive life interests of Jatindramohan and his natural heirs in the property—Prosonnocoomar had created an anomalous situation of uncertainty in the cases where an inheritor died before the next heir in line was born, since to render an inheritance valid "a person taking under a will must be a person in existence in fact or in contemplation of law at the death of the testator."[87]

The principle of inter vivos applied to Hindu laws of inheritance in cases where a will existed. In the case of Prosonnocoomar's will, Phear declared that the settlement of lifetime interests on "unborn generations" of his beneficiaries' heirs was primarily why the intended entail failed. This opinion was upheld both in the Calcutta High Court and in the Privy Council.[88]

The case went on appeal in the *ijlas* of Sir Barnes Peacock, chief justice of the Calcutta High Court, who had worked closely with Prosonnocoomar when they were both members of the Legislative Council.[89] Peacock knew Gyanendramohan well too, since Peacock was already the chief justice of the newly created Calcutta High Court when Gyanendramohan was entered into the rolls of the court as barrister in 1865.[90] Peacock wholly opposed Phear's legal reasoning. First and foremost, according to Peacock and the bench, "it follows, that a private individual who attempts by gift or Will to make property inheritable otherwise than the law directs, is assuming to legislate, and that the gift must fail, and the inheritance take place as the law directs." Peacock reiterated that creation of estate entails for alienation of properties away from male heirs directly contravened Hindu law:

> The testator had no powers to create estates entail and certainly not estates tail descendible as he intended to the heirs male of the body according to the rule of primogeniture. The right of inheritance according to Hindu law is regulated with reference to the spiritual benefits to be conferred on the deceased proprietor. No such estate as an estate tail is known to that law.[91]

Peacock pointed out that inheritance by rule of primogeniture was unknown in Hindu law and in India and therefore completely contradicted the law of the land, even if estate entail was a common feature of English law. He ruled that Prosonnocoomar's mere inclusion of the words "and he will take nothing whatever under this my will" was not enough to legally disinherit Gyanendramohan, who would "take by descent and his right to inheritance whatever is not validly disposed of by the Will and given to some other person."[92] Peacock decreed that the entail created on the male heirs of the elder line of Jatindramohan was null and void, that Prosonnocoomar had indeed died intestate under the law for the portions of his will pertaining to his personalty, and that only the life interest that Jatindramohan was promised under Prosonnocoomar's will remained valid. Therefore, the property would revert back to Gyanendramohan if and when Jatindramohan predeceased him. For his lifetime, however, Jatindramohan was entitled to the full enjoyment and usage of the material movable and immoveable properties that Prosonnocoomar had willed to him.[93]

When the case finally moved to the Privy Council in 1872, their lordships the members of the council first observed that Prosonnocoomar had not, in his lifetime, initiated or attempted any legal or ritual "proceedings of exclusion or degradation" for his convert son. This was the Hindu ritual that amounted to the exclusion and outcasting of a son from the family and community—the act of making a son *tyajja putra.*[94] But the Privy Council also observed that "the Act XXI of 1850 appears to their Lordships to be conclusive to show that Gyanendramohan's change of religion did not affect his right of inheritance or suit." The question, therefore, according to the Privy Council, was whether Prosonnocoomar's will was valid. This question had to be "dealt with and decided according to the Hindu law prevailing in Bengal, to which alone the property in question is subject." The Council concurred in the opinion of Sir Barnes Peacock. They pointed out that "an estate in tail male, such as that which the testator has attempted to create in each series of limitations, is not authorized by Hindu law. It could not exist, with the terms of non-alienation attempted to be annexed to it, even in England." The Privy Council went on to say that the will,

> clearly as language can speak without express words, declares that it was not the intention of the testator that any person should have the estate of inheritance defined by the ordinary law. Their Lordships are, thus, of the opinion that a life interest has been created in Jatindramohan Tagore and that the estates of inheritance and subsequent estates or interests attempted to be created by the will have failed.[95]

Lord Justice Willes of the Privy Council, echoing Peacock, further argued that Gyanendramohan could not inherit because he was unable—as a Christian—to perform "spiritual benefits" for the deceased that would result from the rituals of cremation and *sraddha* performed by a Hindu son for his father, which would allow the father's soul to reach heaven. This was an argument also posed by Jatindramohan's legal counsel. (Recall that the petition of 1853 had also made this exact point to explain why it was against Hindu customary and legal precepts for a Christian convert to inherit.) These benefits were directly connected to the inheritors' fitness to perform the religious duties as proper to descendants: "In the Hindu Law of Inheritance, the heir or heirs are selected who are most capable of exercising those religious rites which are considered to be beneficial to the deceased." This was an interpretation of the condition of being *sapinda,* of consanguinity, with the deceased in order to be eligible for inheritance. But being *sapinda* also meant that the inheritor had to fulfill funerary obligations for the deceased, which of course a converted son could not do. This interpretation of eligibility to inherit depending on "spiritual benefit" was first pointed out by the Indian legal scholar Justice Dwarkanath Mitra. Ludo Rocher, in his authoritative translation of the *Dayabhaga,* quotes Mitra: "The whole theory of inheritance is founded upon the principle of spiritual benefit, and . . . it is by this principle, and this principle alone, that every question relating to it must be determined."[96] This was also supported by the great legal scholar Krishnakamal Bhattacharya and was generally accepted as an important interpretation of the rules that governed inheritance in Bengal. Lord Justice Willes, following Justice Dwarkanath Mitra, added:

> The law of inheritance amongst the Hindus is generally regulated by the performance of funeral oblations, in this sense that the duty of performing the obsequies and subsequent rites being regarded as of paramount importance, the determination of the person on whom it devolves and the nature of the ceremonies to be celebrated settles incidentally who in sequence are entitled to the estate. . . . A rigid regulation of the right to succession by funeral oblations is, however, peculiar to Bengal.[97]

The implication here is that Gyanendramohan's apostasy from the Hindu faith and conversion to Christianity had led to deracination and thus left him incapable of performing either his father's last rites (*sraddha*) or the upkeep of the family deity at Mulajore.[98] The descendants of Jatindramohan Tagore to this day hold Gyanendramohan's spiritual death and inability to perform these duties as the real reason for his exclusion from Prosonnocoomar's will. The current head of the Pathuriaghata family, Mr. Sreejit Tagore, confirmed in personal correspondence that Gyanendramohan was disinherited because of his deracination and therefore his inability to perform the worship of the family deity.[99]

It is clear that Prosonnocoomar did consider his only son and heir to be spiritually and legally dead. In his table of succession according to *Dayabhaga,* under Hindu law, he says that when a man dies without a male heir his property devolves first on his brothers, and on event of their predeceasing him, passes to his nephews: "Respecting the nephew's right of succession, he, who was associated with the owner, is, on his death, first entitled to his estate."[100] This is also why Prosonnocoomar willed his estates primarily to Jatindramohan

Tagore, his most loved nephew but most importantly the eldest son of his generation in both the Pathuriaghata and Jorasanko branches of the family and a person fit to carry out the rituals appropriate to the family *lares* and *penates* (roman household gods).[101]

The precedent of *Soorjeemoney Dossee v. Denabondhu Mullick,* decided in July 1857, also held great import for the resolution of the *Tagore v. Tagore* case. This case arose from the question over whether a legal bequest by a father to his sons might increase in value between the father's death and that of one of the sons, and in that case how the increased valuation of the bequest was to be divided among the inheritors and in which order of succession. In the course of deliberation, the judges debated what a will under Hindu law might mean. According to them in this case:

> The value [of the bequest] must depend wholly on the construction of the will. In determining that construction, what we must look to, is the intention of the Testator. The Hindu law, no less than the English law, points to the intention as the element by which we are to be guided in determining the effect of a testamentary disposition. Primarily the words of the will are to be considered. They convey the expression of the Testator's wishes; but the meaning to be attached to them may be affected by surrounding circumstances, and where this is the case those circumstances no doubt must be regarded.[102]

The two key factors in the construction of the will as a legal instrument were the intentions of the testator and the law and customary usages prevalent in the country. Following this precedent, the members of the Privy Council opined in the *Tagore v. Tagore* case, "A man cannot create a new form of estate or alter the line of succession allowed by law, for the purpose of carrying out his own wishes or views of policy." The Privy Council mostly upheld the rulings of Sir Barnes Peacock, confirming that for the purposes of the law—despite what the Lex Loci Act might promise—the Bengali father had the same power of disposition over ancestral as over self-acquired property, even to the prejudice of the son. But since it was illegal to create an entail by willing life estates to the beneficiaries, and then to their unborn heirs in perpetuity (such a gift had to be made between sentient beings), Prosonnocoomar had indeed died intestate. Gyanendramohan was his heir-at-law and was heir-in-reversion to his estates, which—assuming he outlived his cousin—would revert to him and his heirs on Jatindramohan's death.[103] The Privy Council's judgment allowed Jatindramohan to enjoy life rights in his uncle's estate, meaning that he was "beneficially entitled for his life to use and enjoy the library, carriages, horses, farmyard, furniture, jewels, gold and silver plate, and other articles belonging to the testator," Prosonnocoomar Tagore.[104] This was a pyrrhic victory for Gyanendramohan in many ways. The long judicial process, including the appeals to the Privy Council, drained his finances, while Jatindramohan had substantial resources at his disposal, both his inheritance from his father Harakumar Tagore and his uncle Prosonnocoomar's vast estates. Gyanendramohan could not enjoy any of his hard-won inheritance while Jatindramohan was still alive.[105] Gyanendramohan died in 1890, leaving only one surviving daughter, who died in 1905. Jatindramohan outlived his unfortunate cousin by almost twenty years and his cousin's daughter by almost three years. Prosonnocoomar's will remained established in its essence, and the estates passed to Jatindramohan's descendants.[106]

The Privy Council's judgment in this case is extraordinary in hindsight. The novelty of the case had been in Prosonnocoomar's creation of an entail in the English manner upon his nephews and his nephews' natural male heirs, to the exclusion of his deracinated son. The judgment and its aftermath are important to our understanding of the ways in which the Anglo-Indian legal system thought about conversion, for four major reasons. First, when the Lex Loci Act was passed in 1850, Indian converts, missionaries, and British administrators saw it as an infallible safeguard against disinheritance for those who wished to convert. This jubilatory mood vanished after the Indian uprising of 1857, because Indian commentators and British administrators alike believed that evangelical missionary interference in the religious customs of Indians—as exemplified in the Lex Loci Act—had been a major reason for the rebellion. The Anglo-Indian judicial-legal establishment evidently took this idea quite seriously, shifting away from older prevalent attitudes of paternalist reform, especially in cases of conversion to Christianity. The effects of this shift included a fundamental change to the hierarchies between Indian fathers and sons, allowing fathers to hold the power of disinheritance over their children. As Mitra Sharafi reminds us in her magisterial study of Parsi legal culture in India, "The English law of testamentary disposition shifted the architecture of family life not only among Parsis, but among Hindus and Muslims, too. English law (and its influence) gave testators the unfettered freedom to write a will in favour of anyone."[107] The decision in *Tagore v. Tagore* provided security to Hindu laws of inheritance in Bengal, including the father's right to disinherit a son who converted to Christianity.

Second, in deciding *Tagore v. Tagore,* the judges of the Calcutta High Court and then the lords of the Privy Council depended on legal commentary on the *Dayabhaga*-based Hindu inheritance laws in Bengal. As the most popular commentary on the *Dayabhaga* was by Prosonnocoomar Tagore, the judges specifically depended on his interpretation of inheritance laws and customs in Bengal. Strangely, in this case, it was Prosonnocoomar's own will that was under contestation. The British administration in Bengal and the Anglo-Indian legal institutions regarded Prosonnocoomar as the foremost authority on interpretations of Indian legal traditions. Their respect for, and dependence on, his interpretation of the *Dayabhaga* predisposed the judges of the Calcutta High Court and the members of the Privy Council toward his legal opinion. They held as unassailable his view that the *Dayabhaga* ensured a Bengali Hindu father's absolute right to dispose of his property in whatever manner he wished.

A court case is, by nature, time-consuming and tedious. It lacks the immediacy of a brilliant baptismal ceremony like the one that had made Gyanendramohan a cause célèbre in 1851. Yet the memory of his conversion and disinheritance had been controversial enough that it endured in public memory for the next two decades. Public interest in the *Tagore v. Tagore* case remained quite fervid from 1868 to the end of the nineteenth century, also because of Jatindramohan's subsequent political and philanthropic stature in Bengali society. Jatindramohan inherited Prosonnocoomar's political importance and influential legacy, becoming a member of the Legislative Council of Bengal and honorary secretary of the British Landowners' Association after his uncle's death.[108] The judgment that the orthodox and pious Hindu Jatindramohan would enjoy the life interests in his uncle's estate over his unfilial, Christian, disinherited, and therefore publicly detested cousin Gyanendramohan was received with joy in Calcutta.

Third, the Great Tagore Will Case was most important to the Calcutta High Court judges, as well as the Privy Council members, in order to define the legal conditions under which a Hindu will could function as an instrument of transfer of estates. The legality of Gyanendramohan's disinheritance was *not* under legal debate. Yes, the judges had averred that Prosonnocoomar should not have alienated his ancestral properties away from his son in a prejudicial manner. But Prosonnocoomar knew through his studies of the *Dayabhaga* and its commentaries that "in Bengal it was discovered that although Sanskrit texts accepted as legal authorities prohibited certain transfers of property, the medieval commentators, or some of them, interpreted the prohibitions as applying only in conscience, the breach of them leading in appropriate cases to censure and outcasteing, while the legal transaction would remain valid."[109] This was the principle of *factum valet* applied to Hindu law: "What ought not to have been done, is [often] valid when done," because to accept the validity is in favor of equity, justice, and good conscience.[110]

Instead, the concomitant issue was whether British constructions of inheritance, such as entail, could be allowed under customary Hindu law. The question about the legality of Prosonnocoomar's will was entirely related to his devise of successive life interests of his nephews and their male heirs in his estate, which went against the inter vivos principle. The Lex Loci Act might have promised Gyanendramohan that he could not be disinherited as a result of his conversion. The judges of the Calcutta High Court and the members of Privy Council in London were, however, convinced that the Lex Loci Act did not contravene the Bengali Hindu father's right to alienate his ancestral and personal property to the exclusion of his male heirs, as long as it did not go against the customary practices of the country. The proviso of customary Hindu inheritance practices trumped the legal safeguards of the Lex Loci Act. In effect, Prosonnocoomar's disingenuous will had rendered the Lex Loci Act completely impotent.[111] Within a period of twenty years, the outcome of *Tagore v. Tagore* essentially proved that the right of disinheritance still lay in the hands of the Hindu father, and that the Christian convert son had no place of legal safety.

Finally, it is important to recognize that Gyanendramohan's Christian convert identity was completely elided in the deliberations around his suit. His legal position regarding inheritance was entirely tied to his identity as the firstborn and only Hindu son to a devout Hindu man. He was disqualified under Hindu succession law because his conversion had resulted in his deracination and therefore his inability to provide funerary services for his deceased father or the upkeep and ritual worship of the family's deity and *debottar* properties. On the question of inheritance, then, his change of faith itself was immaterial in the eyes of Anglo-Indian law. Rather, his failure as a Hindu son was the crux of the disinheritance suit. In the course of the lawsuit, it became increasingly clear that his father's absolute right to alienate his properties was an established fact to the Anglo-Indian legal system as a matter of custom in Bengal under the *Dayabhaga*. The failure of Prosonnocoomar's bequest owed only to his imposition of particular limitations on the inheritance, which were all unknown in Hindu law: his creation of the entail; his vesting of rights to the estate in perpetuity on the male line of his nephews, favoring primogeniture and disregarding the principle of inter vivos gifts; and finally, his exclusion of his daughters and their descendants from the estate. The Anglo-Indian legal system viewed these conditions as repugnant to Hindu law and to the customs of the country—and that is what led to a failure of the will as a whole, beyond the life interest created in Jatindramohan Tagore. Even in England, where entails in the male line were fairly common and of customary usage, this particular construction by Prosonnocoomar in his intentions regarding his estates would not be admissible except in very rare cases: "This clause shows an intention that each tenant though of inheritance should be prohibited from alienation, a restriction which in England could only be imposed by Act of Parliament, as in the case of the settled Abergavenny estates, and some others settled upon families ennobled and endowed for public services."[112]

Gyanendramohan was only declared heir-in-reversion to his father's estates because the Anglo-Indian legal system deemed that Prosonnocoomar's will had failed in its essence, beyond the life estate to be enjoyed by Jatindramohan. Since Prosonnocoomar had legally died intestate, Gyanendramohan as his natural heir would inherit the immoveable properties if Jatindramohan predeceased him.

After the Privy Council decree in his favor as heir-in-reversion, Gyanendramohan tried to institute a forfeiture suit against Jatindramohan in the Calcutta High Court for not having occupied Prosonnocoomar's *baithak-khana* and then for having used his personalty to repair the house. But Gyanendramohan was told he was debarred from doing so under the doctrine of laches, since any such suit should have been brought within twelve months of Prosonnocoomar's death. Moreover, it was pointed out, Jatindramohan could not have taken possession of his uncle's house because of the ongoing lawsuit. Gyanendramohan had not filed suit sooner because he had been hoping for a quick resolution of the inheritance dispute under the protections of the Lex Loci Act. When he argued that only the Privy Council's decree had given him legal locus standi to challenge his cousin's life interest in a forfeiture suit, he was told that he could not sue under the legal maxim of *quod approbo non reprobo:* since he had legally benefited from the settlement of his father's will, he could not also deny his cousin's valid life interest in his father's estates, which Jatindramohan had been unable to claim for four years due to Gyanendramohan's lawsuit! In a decree by the Calcutta High Court dated May 31, 1873, Gyanendramohan's forfeiture plea was found to have no merit: "The plaintiff has failed in every part of his contention," Judges Macpherson and Pontifex stated. His suit was summarily dismissed. The Great Tagore Will Case had finally come to an end, quietly, and in tremendous disappointment for Gyanendramohan.[113] In the process, the Lex Loci Act had been thoroughly dissected and lost any semblance of authority to safeguard the inheritance rights of converts in India.

The Posthumous Life of Disinheritance

Why did Gyanendramohan hold fast to his Christian faith and identity, even through these storms of misfortunes? Was it because his conversion actually had been sincere, contrary to the speculations of everyone around him? Or was it that he had to hold steadfast to his faith of choice because there was no way to return and the point was moot anyway after his father's death? There is no way to know. However, there is a pervasive sense of profound sadness in Gyanendramohan's life after the final resolution of the case. He spent the rest of his life trying to reclaim the part of his identity that was stripped from him by the conventions and customs of Hindu society. After the Privy Council determined that the property would revert to him on Jatindramohan's death, he would sign his name as "Gyanendramohan Tagore, Esq., Heir in Reversion to Prosonnocoomar Tagore"—an attempt, it seems, to remain connected to the family and the father who had abandoned him.[114] Years later, as the professor of Bengali and Hindu law at the University of London, he would give a lecture on the position and prospects of religion in India. Referring to himself as a Brahmin Christian, he dedicated the lecture to the native Christians of India. He said, "Religion is more than a sentiment, it is the realization of the moral life of a nation in a corporate form; and in that corporate form, it becomes the source of nationality and patriotism, and also of all the good deeds of which a nation is capable in its national character."[115]

In Gyanendramohan's own last testament and will, an extraordinary fourteen-page document, he would speak of what he considered his father's unjust actions: "My late father made ample provisions for all his relations other than myself, whom he disinherited."[116] Gyanendramohan was steadfast in his conviction that his conversion to Christianity had led to his disinheritance. The will also documents his bitterness toward his Indian relatives: "I consider myself to be under no moral obligation to provide in any way for any of my relations other than my surviving daughter Satyendrabala Tagore because I have been for many years estranged from them in consequence of my reception in the year 1851 into the Protestant Church."[117] The will is also a record of Gyanendramohan's obsessive interest in recovering his patrimony from Jatindramohan. Instructions for his solicitors in the event of the deaths of Jatindramohan and his younger brother Sourindramohan Tagore take up almost eight densely packed pages of the will. Even the most cursory reading of Gyanendramohan's will makes it clear that he was haunted by his lost patrimony and his unrealized future as Prosonnocoomar's only son and heir. Despite its formal rhetoric, the will cannot conceal that he felt something very close to hate for the cousin who had seemingly supplanted him in his father's affections. The dry legal language also cannot quite conceal the painfulness of the memory of desolation and betrayal that Gyanendramohan attributed to his father's act of disinheriting him.

Rakhaldas Haldar, who documented Kamala Tagore's quiet presence in London in his diary, recorded that he met Gyanendramohan many more times. He astutely observed that the family's privileged lifestyle could not be supported merely by the meager salary Gyanendramohan earned as a professor. Even after their estrangement, Gyanendramohan depended on the stipend that his father paid to him monthly. In a later meeting, he also surprised Haldar by saying that missionaries ought not to have anything to do with education in India. Haldar recorded that Gyanendramohan laughed when he said this and offered to find an English wife for him in the next breath. Although seemingly said in jest, it is a startling comment, especially coming from someone like Gyanendramohan, who had been held up as a shining example of what missionary evangelism could achieve in India.[118]

Although Gyanendramohan had legitimate cause for grievance, he never lost his sense of connection to his motherland or his identity as a Bengali Brahmin convert to Christianity. A few years before his death in 1890, he was honored in a gathering of expatriate Indians who lived in London. His speech on the occasion testifies to the tensions of being both an Indian convert to Christianity and a Bengali. He said:

> It is the sincere request of this old man to all of you, but especially to those of you who have embraced Christ and converted—wherever you find yourself, and in whatever condition you find yourself, in whatsoever environment, even if you have accepted an alien religion—never ever forget that you are Bengalis, that it is the blood of Bengalis that flows through your veins, this mortal body of yours was nurtured by the crops and the waters of Bengal.[119]

Even after almost twenty years of self-imposed exile and a series of personal disasters, Gyanendramohan's sense of patriotism was still strong. His characterization of Christianity as "an alien religion" is startling—but he had always been a complicated and contradictory man, just like his father. Considering the long years of exile in England, the constant encounters and negotiations with his identity as a racially disadvantaged British colonial subject, as a disappointed and disgraced son, and as a father and husband who faced one bereavement after another without the consolations or support of family and community, in a place very far away from his home in Calcutta, it is perhaps easy to understand Gyanendramohan's desolation. And it is perhaps easy to understand that he might have sometimes considered that moment of conversion to Christianity, which had fatefully and terminally estranged him from his father, his relations, and his society, as a harbinger of disaster, though he remained dedicated to his religion of choice. From his sensational conversion in 1851 and his staunch support of British rule in India to this moment in the late 1880s when he proclaimed his love for his country and defined Christianity as an imposed, foreign religion, Gyanendramohan's life encapsulates both the career of Christian evangelism in India and the losses, tensions, and irresolvable contradictions of being an Indian convert. It seems that he never resolved these tensions in his identity. It is also certainly true that his bitterness was exacerbated by the loss of his father's affection, his patrimony, the deaths of his wives and children, and finally his exile from his country.

The only child to survive Gyanendramohan was his daughter Satyendrabala. Ties with family in India had been almost completely severed, except for rare visits by her Jorasanko Tagore family cousins Satyendranath and Rabindranath, who were not connected to her disputed Pathuriaghata patrimony. Of a visit in the late 1890s, Rabindranath wrote, "I saw Satu—she is so lonely, and I was deeply saddened." A letter preserved in the British Royal Archives, from the lonely Satyendrabala to Queen Victoria, gives a desolate picture of her isolation in London after her father's death:

> I am quite alone here, of all my race and family the last in England—my father, sister and brother having all died since we came to this country. I have gone through much sorrow and trouble and have suffered deep private wrongs. In the present position of my affairs, it is of the greatest consequence to me not to lose the prestige which Your Imperial Majesty's gracious countenance will give me in the eyes of my Indian relations; from

> whom I am separated by difference of religion, yet to whom I must look for friendly cooperation in regard of my estate and affairs. . . . I also venture to ask that my name may stand with our own Brahmin title affixed to it of Sreemutty, by which the ladies of our House and Castes are known in my own country.[120]

Here, Satyendrabala begs the Queen to extend her favors again, so that the sign of royal grace will make her Indian relations offer cooperation regarding her father's properties in India. She also insists on being recognized as a Brahmin, perhaps even more than as a Christian—an identity that connected her, however tenuously, with her father's country, community, and family.

Satyendrabala came to Calcutta at some point between 1891 and 1900 and negotiated with Jatindramohan Tagore to sign away her patrimony. Perhaps she knew that this was mere formality, as her uncle had already held these estates in reality (if not legally) for at least thirty years. Contesting him in a court of law would require financial and legal acumen and sociopolitical support in India, which she lacked. Maharaja Jatindramohan Tagore, Knight Commander of the Most Exalted Order of the Star of India, was in fact doing her a financial favor by initiating a legal handover through purchase of her share of Prosonnocoomar's estates. All we know of Satyendrabala after this episode is that she suffered from suspected breast cancer, for which she was treated by Dr. Umadas Bandopadhyay during her Calcutta visit. She died in London at the age of fifty, sometime in or before 1905, three years before Jatindramohan himself passed away.

Disinheritance and the Convert's Identity

The losses that Gyanendramohan experienced would deeply affect his younger cousin Rabindranath, who went on to produce an extraordinary analysis of the distinction between communitarian social ties and personal religious faith. In a 1912 essay titled *Atmaparichay* (Self-Recognition), published in the *Tattvabodhini Patrika* (Theological Truth-Seekers' Periodical), in Baishakh, Rabindranath would say:[121]

> We are not bound by any rules to listen to what some Hindus say, but it is also evidently true that Kalicharan Banerjee was a Hindu-Christian, and before him Gyanendramohan Tagore was a Hindu-Christian, and before him, Krishnamohan Banerjee was a Hindu-Christian as well. That is, they were Hindus in a communitarian sense but Christian by their religion.[122]

The problem of conversion, especially elite conversion in Bengal during the nineteenth century, was that it did not signify just a spiritual change in faith. It also meant a profoundly disturbing severance from communitarian identity as well as social and economic losses for those who converted. It was a civil death. A convert's erasure from his family's genealogical charts and history was intricately linked to the erasure of his identity as a member of his community—which is why it is so difficult to recover the voices of converted Indians from the archives.

If we compare the Great Tagore Will Case with the other inheritance suit that became similarly infamous in colonial India and caused a public sensation—that of *Abraham v. Abraham,* which began in 1854 and went up to the Privy Council in 1863—it becomes even clearer to what extent the Lex Loci law faced a challenge and was rendered ineffective by the conflict over Prosonnocoomar's will. *Abraham v. Abraham* was also a complicated inheritance lawsuit, between two brothers who were Indian Christian converts, and hinged on the question whether the law needed to consider the question of their identity as Christians in deciding the suit. In Chandra Mallampalli's pioneering analysis of *Abraham v. Abraham,* he points to Lord Kingsdown's discussion of "converts to the Christian religion" in the deliberations over the case in the Privy Council. Kingsdown averred that a convert is "at once severed from the family and regarded by them as an outcast. The tie which bound the family together is, so far as he is concerned, not only loosened, but dissolved." But this process of changing faith, Mallampalli observes, for Kingsdown, opened up new arenas for Christian converts to assert their agency. Kingsdown believed that that conversion afforded a kind of fluidity for converts, in defining their identities, and this fluidity was a marker of free will in such a way that could encompass "change and choice." This choice, of a new religion, a new lifestyle, a new propensity to multiple and complex identities, also meant for Kingsdown, that a more dynamic framework of law needed to be developed, which would enable the Anglo-Indian legal system to deal with the multilayered problems regarding legal rights of converts. For example, inheritance, within the parameters of *factum valet,* by privileging "justice, equity and good conscience" could be ensured through laws like the Lex Loci Act. The convert's freedom of conscientious choice and security of inheritance was Kingsdown's legal project as a reformist jurist, Mallampalli infers, as evidenced in the Privy Council's 1863 verdict in *Abraham v. Abraham.*[123]

But in the eyes of the Privy Council, barely half a decade after *Abraham v. Abraham,* Gyanendramohan's identity and legal rights—in spite of the Lex

Loci Act—remained tied to his abandoned religion and his inability to perform the ritualistic Hindu obligations to his birth family and community. His identity as a Christian convert ultimately could only be legally defined, in a negative sense, through his deracination as a Hindu son and heir. In some ways, this kind of rigidity in defining personal identity on the basis of unitary religious faith would be enshrined officially by the British Administration in India's decennial censuses. Beginning in 1872, the Indian census was an enormously complicated legal, administrative, and statistical undertaking. It would gradually fix the legal identity of a person to a singular religious faith in a permanent manner, such that religious identity would translate in vicious ways into political claim-making during the late nineteenth and early twentieth centuries.

Despite the existence of colonial legal safeguards, the moral and material capital of Christian converts in India was imperiled by the act of conversion itself. And ultimately, the loss of property and loss of moral capital cannot be meaningfully disentangled for those who were disinherited in colonial India. For even the wealthiest converts, economic losses resulting from conversion compounded the emotional losses. And we have already seen how many native intellectuals, both Hindu and Muslim, attributed conversions to mercenary aims rather than spiritual awakening. Converts remained in constant search of creative ways to express these losses, repair their mutilated sense of self, and inscribe their experiences. Gyanendramohan, for example, sought legal recourse to the wrong that he felt his father, and in a more general sense, his natal community had inflicted upon him as a result of his conversion. And in the legal arena, despite a prolonged court case, he was ultimately unable to claim his patrimony as his father's son and as a convert. His disinheritance was marked into law as a result of his father's legal maneuvering. For both Prosonnocoomar and Gyanendramohan, encounters with Anglo-Indian law became an apologia: a defense of their individual personal beliefs about the importance of religious faith in determining social and communitarian identity as well as personal legal rights such as inheritance. In fact, it seems that entangling converts in long legal battles, which they often fought without access to financial resources while their relatives enjoyed the benefits of the estates they hoped to inherit, was a way to censure them for their lack of filial or communitarian piety. Prosonnocoomar, when he disinherited his son, would almost certainly be aware that Gyanendramohan would contest the terms of the will and that it would require considerable financial resources for the inheritance suit to be decided. The long legal process was a punishment, as

Prosonnocoomar very well might have intended for Gyanendra. There is a poignant irony to the father using a colonial device to disinherit a son for getting too close to colonial influence.

Gyanendramohan and others like him—such as his friend, adviser, and legal colleague, the great Bengali poet Michael Madhusudan Dutta—fought convoluted legal battles and suffered impoverishment to gain back what they perceived as their just shares in ancestral properties. It was not merely the loss of patrimony but a belief that the colonial state had promised Indian Christian converts certain safeguards that propelled them to fight these legal battles. After 1857, the Anglo-Indian legal system itself became cautious about paternalistic judicial interventions into Indian personal law, which depended on religious customs and traditional customary practices. These inheritance cases had complicated effects on the genealogies of personal law reform in India, especially in the changed sociopolitical landscape after 1857 and the beginning of the Crown Raj.[124] If enlightenment through conversion to Christianity was also a severance from all inherited social and moral capital, the figure of the convert bears within itself the true paradox of the British civilizing mission in India.

CHAPTER FOUR

Conversion and the Politics of Land Ownership in Colonial Bengal

Of the many complex reasons for the 1857 Rebellion detailed in its aftermath by British historians and Indian interlocutors alike, intelligence failures topped the list—especially the failure of British officials to respond to fears of forced mass conversions to Christianity among the Indian population.[1] The proximate catalyst was universally recognized to be immense Indian anger due to Christian evangelical and proselytization efforts.[2] Bengal, where the 1857 Rebellion began, was no exception to the building anger and resentment over the spread of evangelization across India. British commentators noted the influence of Radhakanta Dev's orthodox Hindu association, the Dharma Sabha, on social reactions to proselytization. The historian Sir John Kaye, for example, quoted John Hearsey, one of the officers stationed at Barrackpore where the uprising began: "A report has been spread by some designing persons, most likely Brahmins, or agents of the religious Hindu party in Calcutta (I believe it is called the *Dharma Sabha*), that the *Sipahis* [Indian soldiers] are to be forced to embrace Christianity."[3]

After the brutal suppression of the revolt by soldiers at Barrackpore cantonment, Calcutta had turned its face away from the Rebellion of 1857. Yet this did not mean a peaceful Bengal Presidency, which saw widespread localized disturbances, primarily over the right to land and the questions of ownership and belonging attached to that land. The Blue or Indigo Mutiny of 1861, an outpouring of anger by Indian peasants coerced into cultivating the unprofitable indigo crop by British planters, was described in contemporary records by both British administrators and Indian journalists and intellectuals as one of the many law and order infractions that occurred in the Lower Bengal Presidency—from the Santhal Hool in Chota Nagpur to the stirrings of the Indigo Mutiny in the districts of Bakarganj, Murshidabad, Pabna, Khulna, and Narail in east Bengal.[4] In 1861, the Church Missionary Society's Rev. James Long was tried on charges of libel and accused of sedition for his part in translating and publishing the play *Nil Darpan* (The indigo mirror), composed by the playwright Dinabandhu Mitra. Long had merely edited the play, which fictionalized the atrocities being perpetrated by white planters on the Indian cultivators recalcitrant about planting indigo. It had been anonymously translated by Bengal's most famous Christian convert, Michael Madhusudan Dutta, whom we met previously. The controversy intensified because 500 copies of the play were published and distributed under official seal by W. S. Seton-Karr, the secretary to the lieutenant governor of Bengal. Indian society in Calcutta seethed in anger over the Long case, and public anger was heightened by the damning reports of planter and British civilian collusions, which were documented by young pioneers of Indian investigative journalism in periodicals like the *Hindoo Patriot.* Sisir Kumar Ghose, editor of the *Amritabazar Patrika* (Periodical of the Market of Immortality), was one of them.[5]

In fact, Indian scrutiny of planter repression of the impoverished Indian peasantry and miscarriages of justice had begun much earlier, in 1848, with the rabble-rousing against J. E. D. Bethune's proposal of the so-called Black Acts, which would "place British-born subjects under the criminal jurisdiction of the ordinary courts—courts which were often presided over by Indian judges."[6] The white planters had agitated against the Black Acts since they felt that the protection they received from a jury of their fellow white peers in the Anglo-Indian courts would be compromised by the presence of Indians on the juries who would naturally be more sympathetic to the Indian peasants that the planters exploited and terrorized. Similar issues regarding what this planter class felt was its due from the British administration would convulse India again in 1883 with the vicious racial controversies surrounding the "Ilbert Bill."[7] Therefore, caste and economic tensions in rural Bengal in the decade before the Indigo Mutiny, exacerbated by evangelical conversion programs, led to almost thirty years of peasant uprisings. As *Nil Darpan* had poignantly pointed out, the Bengali peasants, especially those who had converted to Christianity, suffered in this tussle of interests between the planters, the missionaries, the high-caste Indian landlords and the British administrators:

> *Jaate malle Padri dhore:* Your caste is robbed by the Missionaries,
>
> *Bhaate malle Nil Bandore:* Your rice is robbed by the indigo monkeys [indigo planters]![8]

This chapter examines an incident called the Baropakhya Case, which occurred in Bakarganj, later one of the centers of the Indigo Mutiny, in 1861. In

1855, an English planter named Brown and his Hindu officials violently dispossessed Christian peasants of their land at Baropakhya because of their conversion. The Baropakhya Case is a now forgotten but important microhistory that illustrates exactly the kinds of caste- and conversion-related tensions around land possession and indigo cultivation that led to profound violence against peasants by planters. Baropakhya was widely discussed in the public sphere, both in India and in Britain, and the major topic of debate was the corruption of British governance in Bengal that had led to the kind of violence in this small rural village. The concern around Baropakhya was not about the victims, as we will see, but about how the British administration could be redeemed in the public eye. In this case study, ultimately, the central debate was about the promise of upward social and racial mobility provided (or not) by conversion to Christianity. The actors in the Baropakhya Case were the Bengali peasantry, the nonofficial white population, which showed a distinct split between its evangelical and planter components, and last but most importantly, the British administration and legal system. Records of such court cases help historians to closely reconstruct the subaltern strata of discourses on subjecthood, rights, and the ramifications of religiously influenced acts of social oppression. This can be done, as the Baropakhya Case illustrates, through a reading of public sphere perceptions of colonial justice, which had to navigate issues of land, rights, religion, and belonging, traversing multiple shifts of colonial and Indian alliances at several levels. As I will show in this chapter, the issue at the heart of this case was not merely British evangelization or Indian disaffection with Christian conversion efforts. It was a multidimensional problem of disrupted public law and order. There was the lack of religious toleration and the intentional disruption of the right of missionaries to evangelize by white planters and Hindu landowners. The right of converts to be secure in their property after conversion was completely disregarded. And finally, there was open collusion between white planters, Hindu *zamindars*, and the British administrators to pervert the course of justice and to politely whitewash the tyrannical reign of white planters in Bengal.

The role of missionaries in facilitating conversions of the peasants and *ryots*, especially in Bengal, created a complex relationship between the British administration, the nonofficial white planter population, the missionaries, and the converted Indians themselves.[9] In many cases, converts saw access to the missionaries as a way to find counsel on nonreligious issues such as land proprietorship, which was the most important consideration for India's peasant population as their livelihood depended on agriculture. The complexities of plantation labor and the profoundly unequal relationship between the planters and the *ryots* involved in indigo cultivation in Bengal created both systemic and actual, tangible violence in the lives of *ryots*. After conversion, *ryots* often turned to the *padris* (missionaries) for mediation and mitigation of their wretched condition both legally and socially. Christian conversions then remained not only in the realm of the theological but also had profound political, administrative, legal, and social repercussions.

The events of the Baropakhya Case exposed these fault lines at the heart of British colonial rule in Bengal, opening them up to scrutiny in both the colonial metropole of Calcutta and Britain as well. The case was mediated through the white missionaries and subaltern converted Christians, whose faith, morals, and sociopolitical alliances were all perceived to be nebulous by both the official and nonofficial white population in India. The British population in India, barring those with evangelical beliefs, generally believed that Christian converts possessed suspect and low characters, as did Hindu and Muslim Indians. The fallout from the case was damaging to the British administration's rule of law. Evangelical Indian Christian missions took the events of this case as a sign that the colonial administration had chosen to side with the nonofficial white planters against the missionaries. The white planters felt exactly the opposite, especially after the interference of the lieutenant governor of Bengal, Sir Frederick Halliday, who censured the sitting judge in the case for overturning the decision of a lower court that had found the planter culpable in the kidnap and torture of converted Christian peasantry. All stakeholders continued to entertain this general feeling of unjust bias until 1861, when the simmering conflict burst into open conflagration amid the Indigo or Blue Mutiny (1859–1862).[10]

"Feelings are not property, it is true, but much of the enjoyable value of property depends upon them," said William Theobald in 1857, in his summation of the demands of the nonofficial white population in deltaic Bengal regarding judicial constraints applicable to their own class. Largely planters trading in indigo, like Mr. Brown of Baropakhya, who perpetrated the outrages against his Christian convert peasant tenants, these British men and women wanted only juries of British Christian peers and an exemption from prosecution and public appearances in the *mofussil* or lower courts, whose magistrates and judges, they alleged, were sometimes Indian, and even when they thankfully were not native, often betrayed evangelical sympathies. Such dangerous sentiments made them more prone to listening to missionaries and native converts in issues related to rent and landed property.[11] Theobald sympathized entirely with this British planter class but acknowledged in his report that the close ties between land, belonging, and rent were a problem haunted by class and religious affiliation. At all levels of society, there remained fraught questions about what a convert could materially own, how his spiritual affiliation impacted ownership of land, and where he belonged in Bengal's urban centers and rural society. These questions had even more complicated implications for an extremely caste-conscious and hierarchical rural milieu like that of Baropakhya, where power resided in the hands of the Hindu *zamindar* and the white planter. The presence of converts and their reliance on white missionaries was an unwelcome change in this stratified world. The British official and nonofficial population were suspicious of conversions among Indians precisely because they suspected that it would help the converts to bypass colonial hierarchies in collusion with missionaries. The missionaries of Baropakhya—and later colonial officials like Charles Trevelyan—argued that native Christian converts became the subject of nonofficial white violence precisely because their conversion allowed them to evade the waiting room of history altogether. In other words, they claimed that the enlightened maturity that was supposedly conferred on low-caste Indian converts automatically as a result of their conversion to Christianity would help to erase the racial handicaps they would otherwise face. It would also supposedly allow the converts to resist the unjust and immoral practices of governance by indigo planters, Hindu *zamindars,* and corrupt British administrators. Of course, such an interpretation faced deep resistance from both the colonial administration and the planters of Bengal because the act of governance, materially or ideologically, legally and illegally, presumed racial and civilizational superiority, and mere conversion to Christianity could not be seen to erase that difference in status.

THE OPPRESION OF CHRISTIAN CONVERTS BY *ZAMINDARS* AND INDIGO PLANTERS

Bakarganj, as the British *Imperial Gazetteers* point out, was bounded by the Rivers Meghna and Shahabazpur on the east, by the Baleswar River on its west (also referred to as the Madhumati in its northern reaches), and by the Bay of Bengal in the south. More than one-fourth of the total area of the district was covered by these rivers, their tributaries, and the Meghna estuary, rendering the land deeply difficult to navigate without intimate personal knowledge of the topography.[12] The low-lying flat land, usually at an elevation below that of the high tide, meant that for three months during the monsoon season flooding would submerge the area, and even when the water subsided, these regions formed great, nearly impassable marshlands—the *beels.* This topography made it difficult to police crimes, great or small, a problem compounded by the fact that the district was so remote and lacked communications infrastructure. Between 1880 and 1900, Bakarganj had the largest number of annual murders registered in South Asia and paralleled only Peshawar (in Northwestern British India, and now in present day Pakistan) in the numbers of violent crimes.[13] It was in this remote, unhospitable, and violent district that one of the most important instances of the fallout from conversion to Christianity occurred.

There were precedents for what happened at Baropakhya. In a previous case that occurred in Bahirgachi village in Nadia in 1841, an armed conflict between the landlord's militia and Christian converts resulted in the death of one of the native Christians. The judge at Krishnanagar, Hon. J. C. Brown, refused to punish the offenders on the plea that "as the person killed was a native Christian, and the witnesses brought forward were also converts, their testimonies were not deserving of credit."[14] On that occasion *The Friend of India,* the mouthpiece of the Serampore Baptists, had commented ruefully, "To reject an evidence because it was uniform and came from Christians, was to degrade the character of our tribunals, wantonly to depreciate the character of Christianity itself, and unjustly to obstruct its progress by teaching the heathen that they may oppress the native converts with impunity."[15] The situation had not changed very much in the intervening decade, since justice was still inaccessible to Christian converts and their rectitude viewed with suspicion.

Baropakhya pointed to the wide fault line between the goals of civilization and enlightenment at the heart of the Indian evangelical enterprise and the political, social, and economic consequences for India's converted Christian population. As we will see, they were barred from inhabiting even the land that rightfully belonged to them. They were truly disinherited from the Indian colonial matrix, from their own natal communities, and from the ranks of the official and nonofficial white population in India, who considered themselves racially superior to Indians who only nominally shared their faith. Of the two and a half million inhabitants of Bakarganj, barely 6,500 were Christians and the majority of them, close to 4,000, were Baptist Protestants, largely due to the outreach efforts of the Serampore Baptist Mission. By Henry Beveridge's estimate, there were more Indian Christian converts in Bakarganj than in any other district in the Bengal province, except Nadia and the 24 Parganas.[16] The converts were mostly from the Chandal and Namasudra communities—untouchables in the caste-based hierarchies, known as *Dalits* today. The relationship of Bakarganj's Hindu and Muslim inhabitants with that of their lower caste neighbors was already one of deep tension and violent repression. When these neighbors converted to Christianity and became more vocal about their rights, supported by the white missionaries, the situation became intolerable for their high-caste neighbors and their white planter landlords. Christian converts upset long-standing caste-based hierarchical relations in Barisal, their presence caused constant tension regarding land ownership, and evangelical efforts on their behalf were perceived as deeply threatening to the settled way of life in the region.[17] Baropakhya, Gaurnadi, and surrounding areas were demographically Hindu majority areas, and the lower caste status of converts added layers of complexity to the enmity between them and their upper-caste Hindu neighbors and *zamindars.* J. C. Jack, the district gazetteer for Bakarganj, commented that the conversions in Gaurnadi and neighboring areas such as Baropakhya had occurred "largely in a spirit of revolt against caste bondage and zamindari oppression."[18]

The events of the Baropakhya Case unfolded in the month of July in 1855, when the early torrential monsoon season had flooded rivers, tributaries, and lakes and rendered significant parts of the southern tip of the Gangetic delta in eastern Bengal impassable. Barisal was notoriously remote and difficult to access, as expressed in a local proverb: "Aaite sal, jaite sal, tar naam Barisal"—a year to go and a year to return, that's Barisal. According to Henry Beveridge, the gazetteer, "During the rains, most of the country is a swamp, and the rice fields do not dry up till January or February. There are also extensive depressions in which the water remains all the year round and which are generally known by the name of *beels.*"[19] Two missionaries of the Baptist Mission Society, Rev. J. C. Page and Rev. John Robinson, were making slow, damp, and muddy progress by boat from Barisal to Lashkarpore, in Bakarganj district (now in Bangladesh), to preach in the bazaar there.[20] They had reason to be happy, even in their labors in the midst of a swamp, because in the preceding six months they had experienced remarkable success in their conversion efforts. Out of the 300 families of Hindus and Muslims who lived in the villages of Baropakhya, Goila, and Mullahpara, about 35 people had started inquiring about Christianity at the beginning of the year. Some had broken caste by worshipping with the native Christians of Chabikarpar, another village about two to three miles from Baropakhya, and had been baptized formally by the missionaries. Most were residents of Baropakhya village. The missionaries had hopes of more converts, but at the moment their attentions were focused on establishing a chapel for their new congregation. The villages of Baropakhya, Goila, and Mullahpara formed a part of the *taluk* or estate of the British planter Edward Brown. Adjoining lands were administered by two Hindu landowners, Mohan and Nandakumar Munshi of Goila. The Munshi brothers and Brown were on fairly cordial terms, and the Munshis also acted as Brown's *gomasthas*—they were his agents in collecting taxes and making sure that each peasant tenant produced their designated quota of indigo.

When Rev. Page asked Brown, as a good Christian landlord, to provide some land to erect a chapel, the planter proved recalcitrant. It is evident from the papers submitted for consideration in the sessions court that Brown simply evaded the request in his direct communications with the missionaries, saying he had to make detailed inquiries about the location of suitable land for the chapel. He said that the Hindu *ryots* of his estate were prejudiced against the

Grihasther Jishu Khrista (Jesus Christ of the Bengali householder), by A. D. Miller. Reproduced in *Prabasi,* April 1935 (Bengali year Baisakh 1342).
Mukul Dey Archives.

Christians and that he was unwilling to take any step that might be disagreeable to the majority of his tenantry. Brown also asked that a chapel not be erected until he permitted such a construction expressly.[21] This reluctance on Brown's part, and the reasons he offered to the missionaries for it, would prove important in the gross miscarriage of justice that would later befall Baropakhya's converts. When months had elapsed with no response from Brown to the missionaries, a young convert named Ramakrishna offered his own land to them—a vacant plot of raised land called a *bhita*. There the Baptist Mission erected a residence for its native preacher Kenoram and gathered some construction material for the long-awaited chapel.

The happy hopes of Page and Robinson for their new converts, however, were soon to suffer a devastating blow. On the way to Lashkarpore, on July 3, 1855, they received a note from the native preacher Shoron at Chabikarpar saying that the Christians at Baropakhya had been assaulted violently, their houses had been plundered and damaged, and some of them had been forcibly carried away. The organized attack had occurred on the night of July 1, 1855. Two days had already passed before news could be sent to the *padri sahibs*. In the following months, efforts to establish exactly what had happened during that night and who was responsible for the attack culminated in a stand-off between the missionaries and the planters on one hand and the judiciary and executive branches of the British colonial administration on the other. This case attracted widespread attention as it illuminated the violence—torture, abduction, and in extreme cases murder—enacted by white planters and Indian *zamindars* to keep their wayward tenants or *ryots* in line.[22] Iftikhar-ul-Awwal refers to the opinions of J. C. Jack and Henry Beveridge, the district gazetteers of Bakarganj and Barisal, who recognized landownership as the most proximate cause of violence and murders in Bakarganj:

> Land was another fruitful source of violence in the district. Besides riots occurring among different categories of landowners over the possession of land (the adage that "Possession is nine-tenths of the law" being well appreciated), there were also perennial disputes between landlords and ryots over issues such as the enhancement of rent and eviction from holdings.[23]

The Baropakhya Case squarely pitted missionaries, native converts, and planters against each other and pointed to widespread collusion between the local judicial, executive, and landholding classes, subverting the course of justice in an orchestrated fashion. The case also raised grim speculations about the ways in which political connections and authority were overruled by religious sentiments and relationships born out of evangelical solidarity between civilian officers and the missionaries, thereby enabling abuse of official power from the metropolitan center of Calcutta to openly influence local issues. In India, the Baropakhya Case necessitated the intervention of the lieutenant governor Sir Frederick Halliday, who was then remonstrated against by Indians and planters for his close relationship to the Baptist Mission. In Britain, meanwhile, speeches in Parliament were made by Hon. Arthur Kinnaird, the Scottish banker and Whig Parliamentarian, highlighting the abuses that had come to light at Baropakhya.[24] In one speech, Kinnaird also detailed other horrific attacks on Christian converts by *zamindars,* citing a letter from an unnamed deputy magistrate as proof that Baropakhya was not an aberration but a common, if extremely violent, example of the norm:

> The persecutions of the Christians are this year more fearful and unheard of than ever before. Dismissing and fining the Christians, and robbing, plundering, beating them, is the order of the day in all the Christian villages. Sometimes it happens that in one day Christians of three or four villages are coming to us, lamenting that their houses, threshing floors, or fields, were plundered. Meanwhile these shameless plunderers put lawsuits in the Court, stating that the Christians have plundered their fields, and against as many Christians as they possibly can at once, that no witnesses may remain to give evidence against their statements. Tuesday last, the threshing floor of a Christian was plundered, and he so much beaten, that he fell down for dead. He had a severe stroke over the forehead, two teeth broken, and was so much beaten and trampled upon, that he was not able to stand. We hear that the zamindars, who have caused this cruelty, and have plundered our brethren, came into the Cutcherry (Court house) yesterday, saying, "There may come a Christian of our village complaining that we have beaten him, this is a lie. He was drunk, fell, or injured himself, and therefore we beg that his complaint against us may not be accepted."[25]

Both native Indian landlords and British planters used conversion to Christianity as a pretext to expropriate renters' properties, a fact corroborated by a number of contemporary sources, including a manuscript written by a Bengali Christian convert called John Sarkar. His "Beel Churchgulir Itihas" (A history of the *beel* churches) was a history of the Bakarganj churches that described the spread of conversion efforts in Barisal.[26] Sarkar was initiated as a native preacher by the founding members of the Baptist Mission of Serampore: William Carey, Joshua Marshman, Leach (first name unknown), and

John Mack. After a first few years in Cherapunji and in the Khasi and Jaintia Hills in India's northeast, he returned to eastern Bengal and spent the rest of his life in Jessore and Barisal.[27] There had been sporadic violence against converts by planters and *zamindar* since 1845, when Sarkar first went to Jessore. As Sarkar notes, "The zamindars and talookdars at this time united, their object being to uproot the Christian sects from the *beels.*" He enumerated a few of these incidents in his manuscript. In Dighaliya, after the missionaries and native preachers encouraged widow remarriage, nineteen widows had converted to Christianity and married in a mass ceremony on the same day. Afterward, converts' houses were looted by the landlord's *lathiyals*—a private militia bearing batons, clubs, and maces. The converts had to leave their homes in a predominantly Hindu village and seek refuge with the Muslims of Sitaikundu. A man named Dulai was beaten and thrown into a cesspit. In a separate incident, the *zamindar* Ramratan Roy of Narail had two convert families abducted, assaulted, starved, and confined in his *cutcherry* (estate office) by his *lathiyals.* There, he tried to make them recant their new faith. When they refused, he had the families released but made it impossible for them to live on his estate. These converts relocated elsewhere, with the help of the missionaries.[28] The *zamindars'* and planters' concerted effort to oppress native converts continued unabated in Nadia, Jessore, and Barisal, forcing Rev. J. C. Page to write to the Baptist Mission Society of England in 1850 that "injustice and downright oppression" kept the native Christians of Barisal "continually unsettled and in fear."[29] In another report of 1854, Page stated that the *zamindars* and planters of Barisal had held several meetings "to make a united and daring attempt to rid the *zillah* [district] of the odious Christians."[30]

The reasons for such oppression were complex and manifold, although prominent among them was *zamindar* and planter anxiety about how conversion would destabilize the rural social hierarchy on which much of their power rested. For most of rural Bengal, the *zamindar* and the planter were the only authorities who dealt with the tenants, providing administration, justice, employment, and opportunities for commerce. Recourse to the British administration was rare, and as a missionary from Jessore said in 1855, "government officials were known more by name and dread, than as paternal rulers and protectors of the oppressed."[31] However, the fact that native converts often turned to the white missionaries in cases of injustice regarding landownership or rent disputes created the specter of two parallel centers of racial and religious hierarchy. The networks of executive, legal, and judicial influence wielded in rural Bengal by white planters and native landowners competed directly with the moral, religious, and righteous influence nominally yielded by the missionaries. The power struggle, actual or anxiously imagined, in such cases threatened the established right of landowners to extract profit from the land and the *ryots*. In the Baropakhya Case, such anxieties of influence created a legal and political impasse, visible in the way the controversy reached the upper echelons of the British administration in Calcutta.

The events at Baropakhya unfolded on the monsoon night of Sunday, July 1, 1855. The day had passed quietly. Most of the Baropakhya Christians had spent it worshipping at the chapel in the neighboring village of Chabikarpar, returning to Baropakhya after the evening service. There had been no hint of any disturbance or disaffection from either their Hindu or Muslim neighbors or from Brown and the Munshis. The calm was shattered that night, about six hours before the morning, when the houses of converted Christians at Baropakhya were attacked by a mob of heavily armed men, anywhere between one to two hundred strong. Asleep when the attack came, the converts could offer almost no resistance as a scene of total confusion and violence unfolded in all their houses simultaneously. The details of this case are mostly gathered from a pamphlet by the Baptist missionary Edward Underhill, who was also the secretary of the Baptist Missionary Society in India from 1849 onwards.[32] He had collected information from both Page and Robinson, as well as from John Sarkar, who was the most senior Indian missionary in Barisal at the time of the attacks on the Baropakhya converts.[33]

Underhill's pamphlet appends the eyewitness statements of the victims, and their recollections of the events are terrifying. The attackers carried shields (*dhal*), javelins (*sarki*), sticks (*lathi*), and clubs (*mugur*), all familiar weapons of the trained militia (referred to earlier as the *lathiyals*, for the bamboo sticks they carried to lethal effect) of *zamindars* and planters in Bengal. Ledoo, a wealthy peasant who was known in Baropakhya and the surrounding villages as the first and most devout convert, received the worst of the attack. He was beaten badly, his hands were tied with ropes, and he was stripped naked and made to stand and witness the assault on his friends and family. His pregnant wife Roso was dragged out of the house, her gold nose ring and silver necklace were snatched from her, and she was kicked to the ground twice while she tried to resist. She too was stripped naked and assaulted in front of her husband and neighbors, then bound hand and foot and made to stand nude and witness the mayhem.[34] Ledoo and Roso, in their statements before the magistrate, said Ledoo had been roused by the *lathiyals* calling his name loudly and that when he answered they said, "Mr. Brown and Nandakumar Munshi have ordered you to go, and you must go."[35]

The attacks on the houses of the other Christian converts were just as ferocious. Janoo, his wife Gouri, and their four-year old son Hridoy had been asleep on the floor on the eastern room of their hut when a javelin struck through the mat-and-mud wall and pierced the child on his arm, drawing blood. His wails awakened his parents, and when Janoo took the boy in his arms to shield him from the javelin thrusts, he was hit in the hand as well. By the time he had transferred his wounded and crying son to his wife, the walls of his hut had broken down under the assault. Janoo was thrown to the floor, stretched out, and beaten black and blue with a stick. The attackers also pierced the heel of his left foot with a javelin, hobbling him, so he could not escape. Gouri, his wife, and Ledee, his sister-in-law, were then assaulted before his eyes, stripped naked and bound, as was the child, Hridoy.[36] Ramakrishna, the young convert who had offered the use of his own *bhita* for the purpose of erecting the chapel, was assaulted next. He and his two brothers Nobo and Harakrishna were beaten, as was their mother Monee and grandmother Malancha, and were bound with ropes. All the houses were plundered, the cattle led away, any brass and stone plate seized, and the stored granaries emptied out. Some of the converts succeeded in fleeing, but fourteen people were captured and taken away, either by boat or on foot. Of the fourteen individuals missing, five were men, two were boys of twelve and fourteen years of age (Ramakrishna's brothers), and six were women, one very old and infirm (Malancha, Ramakrishna's grandmother) and one in an advanced state of pregnancy (Roso, Ledoo's wife), together with one child around four years old (Hridoy, Janoo's son).[37]

The treatment of the women at the hands of Brown and Munshi's *lathiyals* is couched in careful terms by both Underhill and John Sarkar. Sarkar says the following, for example: "Moved by Satan, Mr. Brown and Mohan Munshi began persecuting the Christians and gave them unspeakable dishonor and distress. . . . They behaved in such base manner toward the Christians at this time that it would be shameful to even bring it to one's lips." The detail that stands out starkly in the reports by Underhill and Sarkar is this—the women had all been stripped naked, assaulted violently in front of family and friends, and then bound and made to witness the torture of their kin. And while there are descriptions of the wounds suffered by the men in the assault, there is a stark silence regarding the wounds that the women might have suffered—as if there was not any language available to describe their trauma.

This lacuna, this silence, hints at terrible sexual violence. As Elizabeth Kolsky has shown, rape could be discussed in multiple ways within the social and legal constraints specific to South Asia: the terms *assault* and *carried away* were ubiquitous in judicial records documenting cases of rape.[38] Though the Baropakhya survivors gave their testimony in front of the police and the judges in the local courts, the ambiguity and silence around what had happened to the women was maintained, presumably to allow for the barest cover of honor for survivors of gang rape and their families. The terrible truth was this: on that dark monsoon night, not only were the Christian converts of Baropakhya assaulted and kidnapped but the women were also subjected to sexual assault and rape in front of the male members of their families, in fact in front of what constituted the entire Christian community in their village. They were violated by the trained militia of a white Christian British planter and his orthodox Hindu associates, stripped literally and figuratively of their dignity and their sense of safety, while their male relatives were tortured and deprived of their possession of land. This kind of spectacular public brutality was one of the ways—still prevalent today—in which an entire minority community in South Asia could be shorn of social standing and honor.[39]

The captives were taken first to the *cutcherry* or office of Mr. Brown at Mullahpara. At the directions of his *naib* (chief of staff), Bhairabchandra Guha, who was shocked at the state of the women, they were then removed to the house of Mohan Munshi in Goila. There, the men and women were separated, with the men being imprisoned in the outhouse or the barn and the women taken to the inner quarters of Mohan Munshi's wife and mother, presumably to prevent another instance of sexual violence. The men, including Ramakrishna's young brothers, who were minors, and Hridoy, Janoo's infant son, were bound with ropes. Details about the torture of the converts emerge from the evidence of Ramakrishna. Ledoo, who was suspected as the ringleader of the Christians because he had been the first to convert, was placed in iron fetters. The next morning, and for a week afterward, he was routinely beaten, his legs were twisted so that the left one swelled up hideously, sticks and iron bars were passed through his fingers and toes, and the *lathiyals* took turns standing on his hands so that his fingers were crushed. He was also shut up in a dark pit dug into the floor of the barn for hours at a time. The *lathiyals* tried to take Janoo out to torture him next, but Hridoy clung to his father and cried so loudly that they had to abandon their plan for fear of discovery.[40] When Brown's attorney, Ishanchandra Sen, asked Ramakrishna if Brown had ever before oppressed the converts settled on his estate, Ramakrishna said the attack was premeditated: "From before this, he was angry and said he would not keep the Christians on the *bhitas* this year; the cause of his greater anger is this that the *Padri Saheb* put up a house on an empty *bhita* of mine. On that great anger resulted!"[41] The men were confined in stocks and routinely beaten wherever they were confined. The women were safe only as long as they remained in the inner quarters at Goila, under the protection of Mohan Munshi's mother and wife. There, perhaps out of pity for the violence they had already suffered, the women received far kinder treatment: they were given clothes to cover up, and they received rice to eat and betel nut to chew. However, they faced regular threats of rape and assault from the *lathiyals* of Brown and the Munshis, who, in spite of the protection offered to the converts by the *andarmahal* (inner quarters, for girls and women of a family, and sacrosanct), continued to terrorize them. From the testimony of Janoo's wife Gouri we know that during the month-long period when the converts were ferried from one place to another to conceal them from the police's attentions there was at least one incident, when the threat of rape seemed to be very real and imminent:

> Then the servant . . . came and was about to dishonor the wives of Ledoo and Bhairab, when I called aloud and began to appeal to the authorities. On this, Ramdayal, hearing my voice came and said, "You shall not dishonor these persons while they remain in my house; take them away!" After that they imprisoned us four days there and using four boats brought us near the house of Taransen.[42]

By this time, there was an outcry in the district. The Baptist missionaries Page and Robinson had learned of the assault on July 3, 1855, and had complained the next day to the district magistrate H. A. R. Alexander. In their complaint, Page and Robinson made the following allegations, echoing John Sarkar's language:

> We beg to remark further that for some time past there has been quite a league formed among the Zamindárs and Talookdārs of all the villages where Christians reside, to put them down or drive them out, and thus prevent the spread of their religion. . . . To involve our people in a series of lawsuits, obtain for them a bad character in the opinion of the authorities, and then to attack and plunder them, and expel them from their estates, is the object the landlords are endeavoring unitedly and perseveringly to prosecute.[43]

Previous attempts at intimidation of the Christians had already been brought to the notice of the deputy magistrate, an Indian gentleman named Babu Gurucharan Das. The accounts of the plunder and abductions at Baropakhya strengthened the missionaries' fear that the converts were in grave danger, which they communicated to Alexander, who took immediate cognizance of their complaint and asked Das to proceed to Baropakhya for immediate investigation. With the deputy magistrate's assurances, Rev. Page and Rev. Martin proceeded to Baropakhya, where they were joined by Gurucharan Das on July 13, 1855. Das questioned eyewitnesses and went to survey the houses of the converts to confirm the reports of plunder and appropriation of land. He found the houses had been razed to the ground and the earth turned over, plowed, and sowed with plantain and betel nut. From the state of the roots of a few plants that Das pulled up, it was clear that the planting had happened very recently, only a day or two ago. Das ordered the *daroga* or police officer in charge of the nearest police station at Gaurnadi to proceed to Goila to release the captives. When a team of police officers went to Mohan Munshi's house, they said they found no trace of the abducted converts.

The news of the deputy magistrate's visit spread, and from the later testimonies of the abducted converts it is clear they were ferried from place to place by boat and kept at a number of hideouts belonging to Brown and the Munshi brothers. The converts were further split into five groups and carried to a number of different places, all within the borders of Brown's estates. They were transported by boat using the Madhupasha River—from Mullahpara to Goila (Mohan Munshi's house), to Arabunya, Gelabad, Kadamtola, Jagooah, and Taransen. The river was entirely bordered by mangrove forests, the natural habitat of crocodiles, poisonous snakes, and tigers, making it impossible for the converts to attempt escape and making it clear to them that their tormentors could easily murder and dispose of their bodies if the need arose.[44] The specific destinations and the order in which they were taken there differed for the five groups, but all of the converts identified them as places where they had been confined. In the meantime, Rev. Page reported to the deputy magistrate Gurucharan Das that the *daroga* named Salmonihac, of Gaurnadi, and his second-in-command were both financially beholden to Madan Mohan Das, one of the chief perpetrators of the assault and a close associate of the Munshi brothers. As a result, neither the *daroga* nor his *muhuri* were in any way investigating the main suspects or trying to find the converts, who had reportedly been sighted at this time by several people in the villages where they had been confined.

Further substantiating the missionaries' suspicions of police collusion, the *daroga* and *muhuri* of Gaurnadi now presented the deputy magistrate Das with two different pieces of "proof" that the native Christian converts of Barisal had staged the assault on their Baropakhya brethren to shield them from countercharges of plunder and assault on the houses of their Hindu neighbors. The *daroga* Salmonihac presented three witnesses, a twelve-year old boy and his mother and grandmother, who alleged that it was Ledoo, Janoo, and other Christians who had attacked and plundered the houses of their Hindu neighbors, Kashinath, Bolai, Tapasayaram, and Jagannath Kirtaniya. In this assault, the three witnesses alleged, they had been kidnapped by the Christians and rowed by boat to be hidden away in Chabikarpar village with a view to coercing them to convert. When asked how they were released and came to depose, they replied that the police had found them while patrolling and that their captors had fled in another boat. The charges and countercharges continued, while the local police contravened every order of the deputy magistrate and professed themselves unable to find the abducted converts, even as daily reports of sightings of the missing converts grew increasingly strident.[45] Compounding the difficulties of the Baropakhya converts and the Baptist missionaries, no lawyer or pleader in Bakarganj was willing to take up the case because, as John Sarkar sorrowfully explained, all the other planters and *zamindars* had joined the cause of Brown and his Munshis and had suborned the *vakeels* (lawyers) and *muktears* (revenue agents).[46]

Finally, after repeated instructions from both the deputy magistrate Gurucharan Das and the magistrate Alexander, the *daroga* reported that he had information that the converts were hiding in the outhouse of another convert, Madhav Christian of Ghorijongol (a village near Chabikarpar and not very far from Baropakhya). Proceeding there on the night of August 9, a month and a half after the assault on the converts at Baropakhya, he reportedly found five of the abducted men and women, including Ramakrishna and his mother and grandmother. On the night of August 13, the *daroga* claimed to have found Ledoo, Janoo, and Harakrishna, Ramakrishna's brother, roaming around disoriented in Jagooah. He also claimed that he had information about the rest of the converts hiding in a predominantly Christian village, Ashkor. Salmonihac, beholden financially to Brown and the Munshis and clearly in league with the accused, pretended that he was afraid to go to Ashkor to retrieve the converts, as he anticipated assault by Ashkor's Christian residents. This was all part of the plan to demonstrate that it was the Christian converts who were malicious and lawless, not the planter and his accomplices.

But he had information about a boat carrying some of the converts from Ashkor to Chabikarpar. On August 14, he presented Ledoo's wife Roso, Janoo's wife Gouri and son Hridoy, and Ramakrishna's brother Nobo to the magistrate, Mr. Alexander. He claimed he had intercepted them on their way to Chabikarpar after a wild boat chase in which these converts tried to elude the arm of law and escape over the *beel* under the cover of darkness. However, in a comic turn of events in this tragic case, a ledger was found in this boat containing details of monetary advances made by the planter Brown to his officer Madan Mohan Das, for buying gunpowder and shot and for advancing money to *lathiyals* who were subsequently identified by the converts as those who had assaulted, abducted, and tortured them.[47]

The converts claimed the reports of Salmonihac, the *daroga*, were completely fictitious and that the rescue was prearranged and staged precisely to allow the real perpetrators to escape. They deposed that they had been forcibly taken to the houses and villages of native Christians, abandoned there by Brown's hired goons, and found by the *daroga* lying in wait, obviously with prior information from Brown and his associates. In fact, the *lathiyals* had left in plain sight of the police force, and Salmonihac had made no efforts to prevent their escape. They rightly suspected that this was done to delegitimize the claims of the *padri sahibs* and to render the conduct of the convert Christians of Bakarganj and Barisal criminal in the eyes of the British administration. This was a conspiracy, the Baropakhya converts asserted, to make it easy for Brown and the Munshi brothers to illegally usurp the lands and goods of their convert Christian tenants. In fact, before they were "rescued" and delivered to the magistrate, they had been taken to Goila in the dead of the night, to Mohan Munshi's house, where efforts were made to beguile them into accusing the missionaries Page, Martin, and Robinson for their abduction. They were promised that their land and property would be restored to them if they acted as instructed. For example, Ramakrishna said that Mohan Munshi's brother-in-law tried to coach him to say that Rev. Page had confined all the converts in native chapels scattered all over Bakarganj. One of Mohan Munshi's officers, Kirti Ganguly, threatened the converts that only on giving evidence favorable to Brown and the Munshis would they receive back their land and property; otherwise they would be driven out of Brown's estates. Gauri, Janoo's wife, reported that the female converts were threatened in a comparable manner by one of the *lathiyals,* Krishna Singh, employed at the Mullahpara *cutcherry* by Brown. Singh reportedly said, "If you do not speak in favor of the Saheb Mr. Brown and the munshis, we will cut up your husband and Ledoo into pieces and throw them into the river, or we will break their bones and throw them into some Christian's house. I can kill and I can save."[48]

While being questioned by the magistrate, between August 9 and October 13, 1855, the converts were all asked variations on one question: "What is the reason of Mr. E. Brown and Mohan Munshi's people committing this outrage upon you?" The answer invariably was "They have committed the above outrage on account of our embracing the Christian religion."[49] This clear articulation of the motives behind the violent outrages perpetrated against them leaves no doubt that the converts were certain that their religious faith made them dangerous to their landlord, and it is precisely because they were Christians that they were targeted and deprived of their rightful possession of their lands and goods. The supposed paternalistic relationship between a landowner and tenant could not be sustained when the converts could easily find another source of support in the figure of the white missionary, who could and did stand as an alternate source of racial and political power against the planter, in the hierarchy of relationships between Indians and the nonofficial white population of rural Bengal.

The magistrate, H. A. R. Alexander, was confronted with the remarkably consistent testimony of the adults among the abducted Christians, which was counteracted at every turn by the reports prepared by the *daroga.* The only discrepancy was in the account provided by a man named Sagar Seal. The converts claimed that he had gone mad because of the torture and because he had been drugged. Subsequent reports that the converts were being forcibly removed from their houses and lands even if they held the *pattahs* (title deeds to property) resulted in a personal visit to Baropakhya by Alexander himself. During this visit on October 9, 1855, he found the converts ejected from their homes, which were resettled by Hindu *ryots.* Alexander's report clearly states that the converts were oppressed by Brown and the Munshis:

> We having ourselves proceeded to the premises of Ledoo Christian in Baropakhya, it was seen that the house on the premises had been built but a few days, and a person named Ramakrishna settled there. He says that the *Pattahs* of the *Bhita* were received from the *Maliks* (owners) Mr. Brown and Mohan Munshi. On the same day, we went on to Ramakrishna Christian's premises, which were also looked at; but in those premises a man named Bhasaram was settled, who stated that he had received the *Pattahs* of the said Maliks. Looking at the state of the house, it did not appear to have

> been finished even a week. For these reasons, there can be no doubt that the houses were [previously] occupied by the Christians.[50]

The magistrate passed an order on November 28, 1855, convicting five men, including Madan Mohan Das and Kirti Ganguly, directly identified by the fourteen Baropakhya victims. Most of these men worked as *naibs* or *gomasthas* of Brown and the Munshis.[51] On charges of "aggravated assault, plunder, and forcible and illegal confinement of the Christians of Baropakhya," each of the five accused were sentenced to imprisonment and hard labor for up to six months, to be commuted on the payment of fifty rupees as a fine.[52] In effect, the sentence was a decree upholding the impunity with which the assault had been perpetrated. Nevertheless, it exhibited at least a surface concern for the rule of law in Bakarganj and satisfied the missionaries as well as the Baropakhya victims that, however nominally, justice had been served. There was sufficient circumstantial evidence against Mr. Brown and the Munshis for having ordered the assault in the first place, for forcibly dispossessing the converts of their homes and lands, and later for coercively harvesting the rice crop on their fields and taking it away, leaving the converts without a source of sustenance. The names of Brown and the Munshis did not even feature in the charge sheets.[53] H. A. R. Alexander's judgment was immediately appealed, and the accused were let out on bail. The case was up for review in the court of Hon. F. B. Kemp, who pronounced his judgment on January 6, 1856, six months after the events at Baropakhya.

The judgment by Kemp thoroughly reversed Alexander's verdict. Alexander had stated his belief in Rev. Page's character and judgment and had relied heavily on his collection of eyewitness accounts of the assault to corroborate the events at Baropakhya on July 1, 1855, and the month-long imprisonment of the converts. Kemp, however, seemed suspicious from the very beginning about the missionaries' involvement with the case. Alexander had written in his opinion, "Were this a false case got up for the purpose stated by the defendants, I cannot believe that Mr. Page would knowingly take any part in the prosecution of innocent parties."[54] For Kemp, the close relationship between Rev. Page and his converts in Baropakhya in particular, and in Bakarganj in general, was indicative of a cynical attempt by the missionaries and the native converts to interfere in the relationship between a landlord and his tenants and to besmirch the reputation of an honest man like Mr. Brown out of petty financial motives regarding land ownership and rent. Nor was the judge's skepticism about the converts' testimonies unusual—in general, conversion was supposed to be deeply insincere and attempted only for material gain by people with ulterior motives and low morals. The idea that converts were "rascals" was "universal in India," said the *Dacca News,* reporting on the strange turn that the Baropakhya Case had taken under Kemp.[55] As we have seen, there was precedent for the judge's cynical view of the testimonies by the Christian converts.

Kemp accused Page and Robinson of disregarding Brown's extreme and repeated reluctance to build a chapel at Baropakhya, which Brown maintained was on account of the disaffection of Hindu tenants of his estate. He also hinted at improprieties in recording the first information reports about the assault—Kemp stated Page had written a private note to H. A. R. Alexander, hinting at collusion and exercise of improper influence by the missionary on the civilian. However, it was clear from the documentation that the first report by the family members of the abducted converts to the *daroga* Salmonihac had been disregarded, which forced Page, Martin, and Robinson to lodge a formal complaint with the magistrate, *not* as a private letter but in the form of a signed notification. The names of the abducted converts were missing from this notification, since neither of the missionaries had yet visited Baropakhya, but Kemp inferred that this was another sign of the missionaries colluding to arrange an abduction of their own flock.

The misreading of evidence, which is presented in tabular form in Underhill's pamphlet, is staggering—even considering the caveat that the most detailed records of the case are to be found in a pamphlet written by a missionary belonging to the same evangelical group as Page, Martin, and Robinson, who were in the eye of a legal storm and were being tarred as conspirators and perjurers. Judge Kemp prioritized the evidence of the three witnesses produced by the *daroga* Salmonihac, who claimed that it was the Baropakhya Christians who had plundered their Hindu neighbors' homes and thus were in hiding. Kemp disregarded the testimonies of the Baropakhya converts. In his opinion, ten adult confessions, similar in their account of their illegal confinement and transportation from place to place, were rendered doubtful by Sagar Seal's testimony—even though the other Baropakhya converts reported that Seal had gone mad as a result of being tortured and poisoned. Kemp said:

> There are very gross and material discrepancies in the evidence of the remaining alleged captives. The Magistrate observes in his decision that the discrepancy between the evidence of this man [Sagar Seal] and that of the

> other Christians is quite unaccountable. *I account for it by supposing nay believing that Sagar Seal is the only one amongst the Christians who has spoken anything approaching to truth.*[56]

From the record of Kemp's judgment, it is not clear why he thought only Seal had been truthful out of the fourteen converts. But one can hazard certain guesses. The very consistency of the evidence of the Baropakhya converts that had sealed the primary convictions of the officers and *lathiyals* of Brown and the Munshis was read by Kemp as *far too* consistent. In other words, he suspected that they had all been coached to give similar details to the questions posed by the magistrate during his interrogations. The fact that the police had found all the abducted converts near Christian villages, or at the houses of fellow Christian converts, cemented his opinion that this was a case of false accusations. Kemp disregarded the repeated testimonies that the converts had purposely been taken and left near the villages and houses of other native Christians and that at every spot they found the police waiting for them, as if they knew that they would find the hapless and disoriented men and women there.

Kemp dismissed the belief, shared by the converts and Page, that the presence of the police proved that the officers of the law were in cahoots with Brown and the Munshi brothers. He sensationally dismissed the ledger with records of monetary advances made to *lathiyals* by Brown for their services during the Baropakhya outrage, asserting that it had been planted on the boat by a prostitute called Padma—whom Kemp also accused of enjoying Page's protection, as she was his attorney's lover.[57] This was a direct attack on Page's own moral character. One of Kemp's remarks in this judgment, or miscarriage thereof, illustrates the fraught relationship between personal faith, religious identity, and sociocultural belonging. These were aspects of daily lived life and impinged in a material way upon the converts' right to property:

> *Now without entering into the question whether a Landholder has the power to eject tenants who are obnoxious to the majority owing to their apostasy,* I would observe that if the determination of the Talukdars had been such as it is stated to have been, they might easily have carried off the native catechist Kenoram; this step would have effectually checked the spread of Christianity in their estate.[58]

By not entering into the question, Kemp brought the question to the forefront. It was because the Baropakhya converts had committed apostasy, and thus deviated from being model tenants for Brown and the Munshis, that they were assaulted, cruelly tortured, and dispossessed of their land.[59] By converting, and thereby choosing to trust a different authority in the person of the white missionary, the Baropakhya victims lost the protection, however meager, of their landlords and the support of their Hindu and Muslim neighbors. And finally, though they nominally shared the same religion as their proprietor Mr. Brown, the immense racial and social differences between the Indian converts and the white planter were impregnable to appeals of either justice or mercy. The position of the convert tenants was lowly enough that repudiating these coreligionists on the basis of commercial gain was an easy way for Brown, the Munshis, and other landlords in general to assert mastery over their *ryots* belonging to other religions.

The publication of Underhill's pamphlet on June 28, 1856, created an uproar in both London and Calcutta among the evangelical institutions, as well as among politicians and administrators who were sympathetic to the cause of missionaries in India and to the secondary aim of British imperialism in India: the success of the civilizing mission, which could only be advanced through conversion of India's heathen subjects. The Baropakhya Case was even more troubling to the British administration at Calcutta, since evangelism, at least on Brown's plantation in Bakarganj, had led to a very visible and therefore incredibly disturbing exhibition of a loss of public law and order. Equally troubling was the fact that the East India Company's covenanted servants were seen to be profoundly implicated in this breakdown. The reasons of state had come to open confrontation with a particular community based on their change in religion. The confrontation had made visible the fracture in imperial ideology regarding the Christian civilizing mission within the colonial government with regards to the white population it administered to, in addition to its millions of Indian subjects. Such fractures were dangerous for the cohesive image of a rational and paternalistic British administration. The criticisms of Kemp's judgment, therefore, were severe.

In the conclusion of the Baropakhya pamphlet, Underhill wrote: "[The Baropakhya converts] are told that the laws of India can give no remedy for that wrong. They are therefore constrained to appeal to that sense of right which must be supposed to exist in the minds of the community."[60] By community, Underhill meant that of their fellow Christians, administrators, civilians, and the audience in Britain, since appealing to fellow native converts, just as poor and helpless as Baropakhya's oppressed men and women, could do very little. This community found, in the social and legal outrage committed at

Baropakhya, a vindication of their long-held suspicion that the East India Company was content to let heathenism flourish and would gladly impede missionary activity as long as commercial profit and a thin veneer of political and social control over the Indian subjects existed.

The earliest criticisms of *ryot* suppression by landlords can be found in material from a conference of Baptist missionaries in Bengal held on September 4–7, 1855. In two papers submitted by missionaries working in Jessore and Bakarganj, similar charges were leveled at landlords by Rev. Schurr and by Rev. Page (of Baropakhya fame) himself. The primary charge was the old and recognized one: missionary activity made *zamindars* and planters anxious about infringement on their absolute right to extort tenants for personal gain and to coerce them into planting the unprofitable crop of indigo through a storm of terror, usually unchecked by the local administration. Schurr criticized the caste system for deadening every vestige of compassion and solidarity among the *ryots* themselves, and for the unchecked cupidity of native landowners and their corrupt officials. Some of the planters, Schurr magnanimously allowed, were good Christian men, but they were at the mercy of their venal and unscrupulous native agents and officials. However, most European planters and their families lived dissolute lives: in his words, the planters "look upon the natives with disdain and call them 'niggers' not remembering that they are living upon these very 'niggers.'"[61] Page, freshly bruised from his experience in Baropakhya, was even more stern in his censure. He concentrated on the question of the power that the landlords held over the lives of tenants. Page strongly believed that violence against peasants was exacerbated by the perception of the planters that missionary interference and the introduction of evangelism and conversion to Christianity among their *ryots* made the peasantry defiant and no longer amenable to coercion. Page pointed out that the peasants in turn saw the Christian teacher, that is, the white missionary, as someone with equal power to the landlords. Converts respected and followed missionaries, he noted, in large part due to the belief that missionaries could intervene and save them from the coercions of the planters, and that missionaries could thereby aid the *ryots* in resisting oppression.

Converts also were better educated, through the pedagogical efforts of evangelical missions, than their Hindu or Muslim counterparts. In addition, they were more aware of legal remedies and ways to enforce the power of legal relief in case of distraint under the *haftam* laws, regularly used by landlords and planters to dispossess tenants of rightfully held leases.[62] Christian converts also usually refused to pay the customary taxes and gifts, called *abwabs,* demanded for religious festivals, births, deaths, and marriages in the home of Hindu *zamindars,* as well as costs related to the functioning of the *cutcherry* and payment of gifts to police officials and native administrators allied to white planters. Page suggested that a defense league of missionaries and native preachers needed to be created, with careful written descriptions of every encounter with landlords and their officials, so that legal protection could be sought on well-substantiated grounds. He also made a startling proposal: the *pattahs* or lease documents of converts needed to be examined carefully, and recorded by missionaries, so that the planters and *zamindars* could not illegally coerce them out of their property.[63]

The most important and influential criticism of Kemp's conduct and the resolution of the Baropakhya Case came from Charles Trevelyan, brother-in-law of Thomas Babington Macaulay, who wrote a small pamphlet under his well-known pseudonym, Indophilus. The pamphlet, titled *The Baropakhya Christians and Judge Kemp's Unrighteous Decision,* was published in September 1856. Trevelyan, himself an experienced colonial administrator who had previously served in Bengal, was convinced by his perusal of Underhill's account of the case and reflected on the unholy confluence of "zamindary violence, police chicanery and judicial wrong." He saw this as evidence of the blighted conduct of both the *unchristian zamindar,* the planter Brown, and Judge Kemp, whose conduct he termed a "prostitution of the judicial office."[64] In analyzing the severe repression of conversion in eastern Bengal by both Indian landlords and white planters, Trevelyan drew a clear connection between enlightenment of Indians and conversion to Christianity. He went on to analyze the reasons for the oppression of Christian converts by landlords and the failure of justice in the rural context, where decree by the landlord superseded the law administered by the colonial civil servants and judicial officials. Calling Christianity "*an Enlightenment, in the highest sense, and in every sense,*" Trevelyan described conversion as a stimulant toward the realization of even Indians that they were *men* and not children administered to by despotic landlords.

This realization of intellectual and moral maturity led to an understanding among the converts of themselves possessing, "as British subjects . . . sundry legal rights and privileges, of which it was a felony to rob them," invested in them by supreme legislature.[65] Trevelyan imagined a kind of incipient social revolution, which could be heralded by mass conversions to Christianity among the rural peasantry. This imagined revolution was almost proto-Marxist in nature and deeply ironic considering it emerged from one of the most conservative of colonial British civilians. It supposedly would ultimately lead to the overthrow of the lawless *zamindars* and dissolute white planters by the *ryots*—both those already converted and thus enlightened and, following their example, the soon-to-be converted heathens. Calling the events of the case a national disgrace and an unimaginable occurrence in the long-settled British province of Bengal, Trevelyan excoriated officials like Kemp, whose conduct was a "Crimson stain on the cause of Justice in India" and was more becoming of a "Chinese Mandarin, a Turkish Pasha or a South Carolina slaveholder" than a person bearing the credentials of a British magistrate.[66]

The defect in Kemp's conduct, Trevelyan asserted, was that even if Christian converts were indeed religiously and morally "worthless," under Anglo-Indian law, their religious identity or deficient moral character was still not sufficient grounds for prejudicial interpretations of the liberal right to property and ownership of material goods. Kemp's personal biases against the missionaries and the native converts led to an improper and unrighteous application of the law, which *visibly exhibited* preferential treatment to a particular class of British subjects over another, and even more horrifically, these two classes of subjects shared the same religion. H. A. R. Alexander, on the other hand, maintained the illusion of justice, though his sentence was light to the point of exculpation of the accused in the case. Colonial law could not visibly exhibit the entrenched biases inherent in it, both doctrinally and embodied through those who administered it. Thus, according to Trevelyan, Alexander's conduct was righteous, whereas Kemp's was manifestly unrighteous. Trevelyan, in effect questioning the lieutenant governor Frederick Halliday's ability to reform an administrative and legal system so riddled with corruption, recommended an oversight committee in the form of a royal commission that could investigate cases of "complex iniquity" like the outrage at Baropakhya. Arthur Kinnaird would later reiterate Trevelyan's demand during his speech in Parliament on the Baropakhya issue. Trevelyan also pointed out that the inherent racial bias that led to a characterization of native Christian converts as the lowest and meanest class of British subjects, immoral and unworthy of preference, was a missed opportunity to cultivate a class of uniquely loyal subjects sharing in the same enlightened religious views as the white British population in India. Converts, Trevelyan argued, could be a bulwark against the adherents of Hinduism, a religion he called "the vilest quagmire of moral slime and filth under the sun."[67]

Evangelical missions in India condemned the Baropakhya incident as well. The Free Church of Scotland, which flourished in Calcutta and had made a decided mark for itself under the guidance of Alexander Duff, in this particular instance took the side of the Baptist Mission and recorded their indignation at the indignities being borne by missionaries and their native convert flock. In an article titled "Persecution of Native Christians in India," published on December 1, 1856, *The Home and Foreign Record* took up the Baropakhya Case.[68] Having read both Underhill's pamphlet and Trevelyan's interventions, the author of the article concurred: embracing Christianity was the precursor to the understanding and enjoyment of natural rights pertaining to life, liberty, and property. India's native Christian converts thus presented a grave challenge to the supralegal excesses of its landlord and planter class. It was the duty of a liberal and civilized colonial power to guarantee the security of those inalienable rights of its subjects. Baropakhya was a failure of colonial governmentality, and the agent of that failure, Judge Kemp, had to be strongly censured.

Underhill had submitted a copy of his pamphlet to the government of India on August 22, 1856. As a result, the Bengal administration was directed to take necessary action. Faced with growing criticisms of Kemp's conduct, and veiled insinuations that he was failing in his duties as the first lieutenant governor of Bengal, Sir Frederick James Halliday acted. On Halliday's instructions, the Sadar Nizamat Adaulat at Calcutta, the Supreme Court of criminal justice, called for a review of the Baropakhya Case. The bench, consisting of Judges Colvin, Raikes, and Patton, after examining the evidence on October 31, unanimously decided that Kemp's judgment was not in accordance with the facts of the case and that he should, at the minimum, have upheld H. A. R. Alexander's sentence on the accused. Halliday censured Kemp but, on the instructions of the government of India, did not give in to the demands of the missionaries that he be transferred out of his posting at Bakarganj, which would have confirmed the imputation of partiality and would reflect very poorly on the colonial administration.[69] Kemp's career stalled for a while, but he subsequently gained reputation as a particularly dispassionate and unbiased judge.

Ram Gopal Sanyal, contemporary chronicler of the lives of illustrious British administrators and aristocratic Indian men and an inveterate gossipmonger, wrote admiringly about Hon. Justice Francis Baring Kemp in 1894. In this retrospective tribute, written thirty years after the cataclysmic events of the 1857 Rebellion that had entrenched the fear of Christian evangelism in the minds of the British administration, the Baropakhya Case became an event in which Kemp was the victim of the missionaries and their machinations: "As usual, the missionaries raised a long howl." It was Frederick Halliday, in this account, who emerged as unrighteous and partial to the evangelical cause, due to his close friendship with John Clarke Marshman, son of the Serampore Baptist Joshua Marshman and editor of the "rabble-rousing" *Friend of India.* In Sanyal's description, Kemp was "gentle, generous and just, all had equal confidence in him."[70]

No memory or record remains of the poor Bakarganj victims or their subsequent fate. They mostly disappear from the archives after their forcible ejection from their *bhitas* in consequence of Kemp's judgment. Underhill, after his return to England, mentioned in a brief report to the Baptist Missionary Society that, having been deprived of their homes, their land, and even their share of the crops they had planted, some of the Baropakhya converts resorted to visiting the Sunderban mangroves to cut wood and sell it for fuel—dangerous and poorly remunerative work in forests and marshes populated, as noted earlier, by tigers, snakes, and crocodiles. The torture visited upon them, compounded by the hard labor of gathering wood, led to about three or four of the men contracting malarial fevers and dying within a year.[71] Outrages against Christian converts continued in Nadia, Jessore, and Bakarganj, especially in and around Barisal, for many years, and judicial redress was always uncertain. According to John Sarkar, the Baropakhya culprits, having been released from prison, resumed their harassment of Christian converts at the behest of Brown and his Munshis in 1859. That year, they raided the house of the native preacher of Patighar, Madan Kusali, kidnapped him, raped his wife and paraded her naked in the neighborhood, "looted Madan's house, seized him and carried him and did not shrink even from taking his wife's clothes. The loot of Madan's house, his capture, the treatment of his wife!"[72] This was an exact reenactment of their violence against the Baropakhya converts in 1855.

This time, the converts of Bakarganj did not take the route of seeking legal redress but took the law into their own hands: they surrounded the house, the *Gupta Bari,* where Madan and his wife had been restrained, freed the couple, and engaged in looting and arson. The reprisal from the police and the law was swift and brutal. The missionary Mr. Page, who had been at the forefront of trying to get justice for the Baropakhya converts and had thus offended both the official and nonofficial white population in Bakarganj and

Calcutta, was named in the charge sheet along with John Sarkar and the main instigators of the loot of the *Gupta Bari.* Justice Kemp sentenced the Indian converts to five years of hard labor at the sessions court, though Page and Sarkar were let off with a stern warning. The *sahib daroga* of Patighar went to Dighaliya and arrested a number of convert women whose relatives had been judged guilty for the *Gupta Bari* incident. They "spoke very abusively and insulted them exceedingly," another account of the threat or actual act of sexual violence visited upon converted Christian women to further humiliate and terrorize their male kinsmen. When Sarkar and the converts complained, the deputy magistrate of Khulna, a fiery young man named Bankimchandra Chatterjee, was sent to investigate the repressions. Chatterjee would later become the pioneer of the novel form in the Bengali language, the intellectual source of a particular right-wing interpretation of Hindu nationalism, and would engage in debates on the merits of Christianity with British missionaries. Bankimchandra went to Dighaliya personally to take stock of affairs. He found that the converts were being harassed by Brown and the Munshis, as well as the *zamindars* of Kotalipara, and censured the planters and the landlords.[73] However, the oppression of Christians continued in Bakarganj for many years thereafter.

The Baropakhya missionaries had assumed that conversion to Christianity granted superiority to Indian converts—or indeed, to any Indian willing to trust in the missionary's morality over the planter's excess. The events of 1855 proved this assumption to be disastrously incorrect. When peasants and *ryots* demanded equitable treatment from the British administration and the British-Indian legal system in the face of planter repression, the faith of the converts and the presence of the missionaries as witnesses and mediators created a complication where unspoken but institutionalized racial hierarchies could no longer be unquestionably enforced in the pursuit of and meting out of justice. The Indian Christian converts, even when they were not a member of the elite urban intelligentsia, still created disruptions to the entrenched worldview of the British administrators and the nonofficial white planters, that they were unquestionably superior in the established hierarchy of colonial Indian society. As a result, the faith of the Indian converts, and the effects of conversion on their morals, became the grounds on which the British administrative and legal establishment contested the idea that change of religion also meant upward mobilization in terms of racial affiliations. The apologia provided by Indian peasants and *ryots* of their Christian faith, with support from the missionaries, in front of planters and landlords, as well as in courtrooms, became a metaphor for the limited efficacy of the civilizing mission in India, as well as a testament to the ruptured and interrupted success of the enlightenment project within the Indian experiment.

The Baropakhya Case illustrates the kinds of tensions that led to the Indigo Mutiny and the decades-long peasant unrest in eastern rural Bengal thereafter. It demonstrates that the locus of tensions between planters, *zamindars,* and peasants was not singularly about the rural economy, or about certain kinds of patriarchal relationships mediated by local control that were disrupted by Christian conversions and the increased meddling of missionaries in preexisting power structures. What it does illustrate for us is that all the vaunted claims of civilizational enlightenment that Christian conversion was supposed to bring ultimately did not matter at all when it came down the specificities of lived worlds in these areas. Baropakhya proved conclusively that Indian converts would insuperably be condemned by the act of their conversion, to be disinherited, to be exiles, both spiritually and materially, from both their natal communities as well as the community of the *sahibs* that they aspired to belong to.

CHAPTER FIVE

The World of Munshi Meherullah

On June 7, 1907, a Muslim tailor named Munshi Meherullah, forty-five years of age, died of complications arising from pneumonia in a small village called Chatiantala, on the banks of the Bhairab River, in Jessore. Jessore was, as L. S. S. O'Malley put it, a "land of moribund rivers and obstructed drainage, notoriously unhealthy, with fever silently and relentlessly at work, destroying many, and sapping the vitality of the survivors and reducing their fecundity."[1] It was the middle of the monsoon season and the weather was cloudy, with high winds. In the wet, humid, and marshy environs of riverine eastern Bengal, such deaths were not uncommon, hastened often by the unavailability of trained doctors or medications so far away from the metropoles of both Calcutta and Dhaka. After he lay in bed untreated for a month, Meherullah's associate and *murid* Jamiruddin arranged at personal cost to have a Muslim doctor from Calcutta come and attend Meherullah.[2] By then, however, it was too late.

What can the life of a forgotten tailor and his bygone milieu illuminate for us about the politics of religion, belonging, and identity in late nineteenth-century Bengal? As Anne Blackburn posits in her account of Hikkaduwe Sumangala, the great Sri Lankan Buddhist theologian, the study of local "habits of thought and modes of affiliation" help us to analyze better the "intellectual creativity of lives fashioned in the context of colonialism."[3] In the small, unremarkable tragedies of rural peasant life, Meherullah's death could have been an ordinary chapter, the loss of the tailor felt deeply only by a very close and tight-knit circle of family and friends and his memory quickly forgotten. It would certainly have been lost to the archives of history. The extraordinary qualities of Meherullah and his unlikely influence on Bengali Muslim society make this story slightly more complicated. The ripples of dismay at Meherullah's demise spread from Jessore to Dhaka and even to the colonial capital city. The premier Bengali Muslim weekly *Mihir-o-Sudhakar* (The Sun and the Moon Periodical), published from 42 Metcalf Street in Bowbazar, Calcutta, by Sheikh Abdur Rahim, led the chorus of grief-stricken obituaries. A few days after Meherullah's death, the periodical printed a notice of death that in fact amounted to a dirge about the fate of the subaltern Muslim society of Bengal, particularly east Bengal:

> The political and religious world of Bengali Muslims is shrouded in great darkness. During this sorrowful time, the person . . . who for the last eighteen years had dedicated his life to the uplift and reform of religion and society and infused a new life in the lives of Bengali Muslims, that greatest of orators and preacher of the true values of Islam, Munshi Mohammad Meherullah, alas, is no more.
>
> The Christian *padris* shook in fear when they heard him defend Islam. His advice brought many Christian converts back into the fold. The effect of his burning speeches wrought a new sense of living religion in the lifeless Muslims of Bengal. Bengali Muslim Brethren! You have lost a true friend today.[4]

Other important Bengali Muslim periodicals and newspapers echoed the *Mihir-o-Sudhakar*. The *Soltan* (Sultan) said, "All hope of reforming a fallen society and religion has seemingly ended! The sleeping Bengali Muslims are surrounded by profound darkness." The *Islam Pracharak* (Evangelists of Islam), published by a few members of the Sudhakar group, and the *Moslem Suhrid* (Friend of Muslims) emphasized the social loss Meherullah's death had caused.[5] Three issues are fairly evident from the tone and content of the obituaries, even in their surviving truncated and excerpted forms. First, the tailor Munshi Meherullah had transcended his humble origins to occupy the role of reformer and social conscience for a large section of Bengali Muslims. His influence crossed the spectrum of class and sectarian differences, from *atrap* to *ashraf* and from those following the Tariqah-i-Muhammadiya to the Fara'idis and the members of the traditionalist Hanafi school, which were the most prominent among the different sects of Muslims in Bengal.[6] In his self-appointed role as an arbiter of Muslim identity in rural Bengal, Meherullah's acceptability as a spokesman for the religious, political, and social aspirations and duties of Bengali Muslims was acknowledged in the print medium by the centers of high intellectual exchange in Dhaka and Calcutta.[7] These patrons included, for example, the Sudhakar group, who also acted as his publicists. These central nodes of exchange of information also aided in the dissemination of his opinions and views, especially to the educated *ashraf* or elite aristocratic Muslims of both Dhaka and Calcutta, as they allowed him the space to contest Christian evangelical polemics in the pages of their widely subscribed periodicals and pamphlets. His oratorical powers were obviously exceptional since they are mentioned in every obituary. The power of the spoken word, and his ability to wield it precisely for an intended audience, helped him to appeal to the many illiterate or literacy-aware peasant Muslim communities spread through the remote rural areas of deltaic Bengal. These men and women also gathered by the thousands to hear him give speeches at the *waz-mahfils* or to see him engage Christian missionaries in debate in deeply antagonistic but entertaining *bahases*.[8]

This form of apologetics, religious in tone but social in content and purpose, part written and part oral, is characteristic of what C. A. Bayly called the Indian ecumene. In this case, it was a distinct Bengali Muslim ecumene, one rarely mentioned in the predominant Hindu-Brahmo elite intellectual discourse that flourished in and around the metropole of Calcutta.[9] Few pamphlets written by Meherullah survive today, and those that have survived often seem to be elaborations on his public speeches. These were printed in very low numbers (copies are rare) and were usually cheap. The limited print run did not affect his popularity, because in erstwhile rural Bengal, even if the rate of literacy was low, it required only one literate person who could read the text to a community of avid listeners, who would then orally circulate the message and argument of the text to a wider community. Thus, exchange of information and religious politics would find a much larger audience than could be numerically verified by tallying literacy rates in colonial Bengal. The language of the pamphlets is uniformly idiomatic, aphoristic, rustic, and playful. Meherullah's rhetoric is indebted to genres like poems, folk songs, folktales, and parables, and is in general easy to memorize and recite.

Second, all the obituaries made liberal use of metaphors involving death, darkness, and sleep. Across the spectrum of Bengali Muslim society, there was a clear sense that social, religious, and political stagnation from within and without had rendered Bengali Muslims particularly wretched. The *Islam Pracharak* of August 1891 proclaimed, "The Christian preachers have rendered the situation in Jessore utterly chaotic; many uninformed Musalmans [Muslims] have been unnecessarily enchanted by them—in the districts of Nadia and Jessore innumerable illiterate poor peasants have converted to Christianity."[10] Poverty and illiteracy made the Muslim peasantry particularly vulnerable to the malicious influences of both fake religious preceptors and conversion programs by Christian missionaries, who sometimes used extremely critical language against Islam and Prophet Muhammad. In such a situation, Meherullah reminded Bengali Muslims of the duties enjoined by their professed faith and guided them away from sacrilegious practices, which were often seen to be an unhealthy syncretic admixture of Hindu rituals in Muslim rites and customary social usages.

One such example was the prohibition on widow remarriage in *ashraf* families, especially those purporting to be Sayyids, Sheikhs, and Khondkars, which Meherullah and other reformers saw as un-Islamic and an import from high-caste Hindu practices.[11] When elite Muslims reproached Meherullah for his advocacy of Muslim widow remarriage, telling him that the customary practices of highborn members of the *ashraf* class could not be interfered with, Meherullah shot back by saying even the Prophet had taken a widow for his first wife. He asked, "Who among us is more learned than the Prophet?"[12] Maulana Hafez Ahmed, writing in the same vein in the June 1891 edition of the *Islam Pracharak,* was critical of the admixture of un-Islamic practices and pseudo-Hindu ritualism in the devotional practices of rural Bengali Muslims: "Before the arrival of Hazrat Maulana Karamat Ali Marhum, most of the Muslims of Bengal had fallen into the grievous sin of idol worship. They discarded the practices of *namaz* and *roza,* and entirely busied themselves in the rituals of Manasa-puja, Shitala-puja, Satya-Pir'er puja, animal sacrifice during the worship of Kali, and so on."[13]

There was no significant change in this syncretic situation thirty years later. The eminent Bengali poet Ismail Hossein Shiraji wrote in complete exasperation in the *Soltan* of September 1923,

> The effects of Hindu ritualism are very strong on every class of Bengali Muslims barring the Karikars. In many places Muslims vow sacrifices to Kali on the fulfillment of their wishes. On the day of Lakshmi-puja, most Muslim women conduct all rituals except that of direct idol worship. In Nadia, Jessore, and Pabna, the Muslims pretending to be the *neda'r faquirs* are nothing but Baishnabs of the Kartabhaja and Sahajiya sects.[14]

In such a situation, where all the forms of Bengali Islam seemed to be inundated with religious ritualism borrowed from Hinduism, preachers like Meherullah worried about the souls and identities of Bengali Muslims, especially in the rural areas where such apostasies and heresies were far more common. He asked Bengalis to become better Muslims by being more attentive to the true faith and therefore transforming into stronger, more pious, and more conservative *deendars.* He attacked detractors like *pirs, faquirs,* and Christian *padris* using the same polemical, theological, and apologetic rhetorical tools that were being used by them against Islam.

Third, the obituaries all mention Meherullah's investment in the issue of charity and the form that charity should take to benefit the oppressed rural Muslim peasantry—which seems to have been an object of intense debate. The Bengali Muslim peasantry or *atrap* were devoted to him, while the elite *ashraf* seemed to have accepted Meherullah's many philanthropies—which were made possible through wider communitarian collaborations—as an ideal model for future endeavors. However, there was also a popular recognition that the tailor-evangelist's charismatic personality had made many of his achievements possible. Duplicating such success was perceived to be almost impossible, thereby adding another layer to the despair engendered by Meherullah's sudden and untimely death. Meherullah seemed to have made the dissemination of education and debt freedom his most important agendas, since these measures were vital for the uplift of a perpetually debt-ridden and illiterate rural peasant population. The grinding poverty was often compounded by a lack of medical care, access to education, or gainful employment apart from the often unprofitable business of agriculture at the mercy of moneylenders and erratic weather. His relentless apologetics against Christian evangelism seemed to stem from the recognition that in many cases it was the wretched conditions of existence in rural Bengal that made it easier for the missionaries to influence people and save souls by offering the promise of material benefits. The missionaries did this most visibly through their humanitarian efforts in setting up educational institutions and hospitals. Meherullah recognized and was deeply conscious of the material conditions of performing faith. He was also aware that these conditions could be exploited to serve his preferred form of social activism and religious reform better.

From the obituaries, it is clear that for Meherullah and the Bengali Muslim intelligentsia at large it was this understanding of the materiality of religious faith and religious identity that determined their stance on Bengali Muslims, especially the non-elite Muslim peasantry of east Bengal. This understanding led to the belief that political and social rights could only be asserted when these fundamental problems that beset Muslim society could be radically solved. As the *Mihir-o-Sudhakar,* the *Soltan,* and other such periodicals stated, Meherullah had taken a step toward comprehensive social reform by using his own meager earnings from his lecture tours and using both his social and moral capital to elicit donations from the Muslim and Hindu landed gentry and elites to set up *madrassas, maktabs, pathshalas,* and schools.[15] He personally took financial responsibility for the education of many young students and encouraged young educated Muslims to make their voices and political opinions known by writing in periodicals and newspapers.[16] Since there were no other figures in Bengal who could appeal across the spectrum to both the elite and the poor subaltern sections of the Muslim population (with the exception, to a much lesser degree, of Meherullah's disciple Jamiruddin), these obituaries expressed a justified fear: that Meherullah's philanthropic projects would remain unrealized for lack of an inspiring charismatic leader who could exhibit similar pragmatism in his approach to social, political, and religious reform and uplift of Bengali Muslims.

Meherullah anchors a forgotten episode of Muslim reformism in Bengal against Christian evangelism in the period between 1886 and 1908. This chapter is also in conversation with historiography on liberalism and empire, which privileges a materialist understanding of liberalism based on right to property and a Bengali Muslim politics of peasant independence deriving and evolving out of that right. Andrew Sartori's analysis of proprietary rights to land held customarily by the *ryots* paints a partial picture of Muslim peasant political agitation.[17] From the peasant revolutionary Titu Mir in the early nineteenth century to the Fara'idis, we can trace a line of Bengali peasant politics where agitation for land rights by the peasants was deeply imbued with a sense of religious fervor and played an important role in defining the Muslim self. With Meherullah, this story gains a new dimension. It was just as important to be a good Muslim, as Meherullah's story shows, as it was to be a good cultivator.[18] Defining the parameters of being a good and true Muslim demarked the lines of political and social agitation, where religion and right to property were interwoven, proximate, and omnipresent strands. The conditions of faith in rural Bengal were riven with tensions between the peasantry and Christian missionaries proselytizing through use of material modes of provision of medical and educational services. Such tensions were effectively expressed intracommunally as well, in an effort to completely expunge the space of the syncretism that allowed accommodation of other religious and cultural practices within Bengali Islam.

The commonly accepted secular historiography of Bengal has always focused on the emergence of communal tensions between Hindus and Muslims. Meherullah's life and his milieu challenge the high-caste Hindu-Brahmo understanding of the poor Muslim peasant as a blank slate onto which the politics of *swadeshi* or "own country" could be easily mapped. The sustained rarity of Muslim characters in the works of Bengal's Hindu / Brahmo writers, who otherwise evocatively described the landscape of rural east Bengal, reflects a kind of nationalist *darshan* (vision) of Mother Bengal. In other words, these texts elide the pluralistic religious complexities and political differences of a large section of Bengal's Muslim population. As Dipesh Chakrabarty says in a different context, this was an act of aesthetically reducing the political and removing it from historical time. Bengali Muslim reformists like Meherullah protested these erasures of their selves from the land they inhabited.[19] If we study figures like Meherullah against this normative narrative, we find that a hidden story emerges, that of a rural Bengali Muslim milieu that was shaping itself in reaction to Christian evangelism and the inchoate threat of Christian conversions. This narrative complicates the binary of Hindu-Muslim contestations in Bengal and India and adds nuance to the history of marginalization of minority communities of faith in colonial India. Meherullah's story, then, offers a window into the transformation of subaltern communities in colonial India during the late nineteenth century. Importantly, it is a story that resists the dangerous narrative of communalism and separatism so prevalent in the historiography of Indian colonialism, with its overdetermined origin in 1857 and telos in 1947. Through Meherullah, we can see how non-elite, nonmetropolitan Muslim milieus began the process of defining self and sovereignty against the looming specter of intrusive British classification processes that labeled the Muslim as the exception to the Hindu norm. Meherullah reimagined the relationship between religious faith, political identity, and subalternity to foreground the ways in which the rural Muslim peasantry of Bengal was redefining its commitment to *swadesh* and *swajati*—one's own land and one's own community. Saidiya Hartman's poignant use of the concept of *waywardness,* which she deploys with explosive effect to speak of "intimate histories of social upheaval," is a useful heuristic for contextualizing Meherullah's life. Marginal lives, Hartman shows us, are theorized and historicized within negative paradigms and are often erased and silenced. And yet, she points out, they can be read against the archival grain as "beautiful experiments" in how to live. As Meherullah's narrative shows, Bengali Muslim subaltern lives reflect such *waywardness,* claiming "the right to opacity" and thereby resisting easy classification.[20]

It is worth considering that there is already a refiguration of the limits of Muslim identity as it pertains to religious faith and political affiliation that emerged in the last three decades of the nineteenth century.[21] It is important, in my consideration, to look beyond cultural and economic contingencies and squarely place the question of the religious as both the social and the political, at the heart of the historiographical debates about this newly emergent Muslim identity. Apologia, as a spirited defense of one's own faith and consequently one's understanding of one's own social network and moral capital, appears in this period as neither partial nor luxurious.[22] It defined the ideal Bengali Muslim subject as operating beyond the limits of the conciliatory approaches that had been central to the interactions between an older generation of Muslim intellectuals and their Christian missionary counterparts. The understanding and definition of religion and religious action shifted from syncretic, private, everyday piety to textually approved performances of prayers and rituals. This reconfiguration of religious faith and political identity focused on the performance of social and cultural practices in the domain of the political. It is this performance of religious sensibility, dependent on strict exegesis of the Quran, that begins to define a good Muslim in rural Bengal. This was a particular form of reenchantment of the world, a return of the numinous to the space of the nomos, where religious and faith-based practices formed the basis of political identity as well as social action and resistance. It was deeply intimate and intimately divisive in its desire for homogeneity and religious purity within the community. In centering a particular understanding of the religious as inextricable from the political, this intellectual Muslim narrative broke with past syncretic accretion of pluralistic religious practices and conciliatory accommodations. It led subaltern Muslims in rural Bengal, like Meherullah and his followers and students, toward voicing their own possibilities of other ways of belonging in the world. This was, ultimately, a refusal of erasure of Bengali Muslim voices from the emergent narratives of Indian nationalism.

CHRISTIAN CONVERSIONS DURING FAMINES IN BENGAL

Between 1866 and 1896, the regions of Jessore and the adjacent district of Nadia (Meherpur, the home of Meherullah's adversary turned disciple or *murid*, Jamiruddin, was a subdivision of colonial Nadia) suffered from a series of natural calamities. The relief operations and appeals to the government for help had been spearheaded by the Church Missionary Society's Rev. T. J. Lincke, who said, "If I were to tell the instances of how long many must go without food, and what sort of materials they contrive to convert into food, you could not believe it." His colleague Rev. F. Schurr of Kapasdanga was bleak in his observations: "They will be forced to eat the rind of trees, grass, etc. I have never witnessed such misery in my life."[23] There was terrible flooding in Nadia and Meherpur in 1871, 1885, and 1890. According to the Nadia *District Gazetteer*, the population had decreased by more than 1 percent in 1891 due to the distress and suffering caused by the flooding. Malaria was endemic. The hospital in Meherpur (attended by 8,120 outpatients and 59 inpatients), a dispensary in Shikarpur (attended by 5,644 outpatients), and a dispensary for women and children in Ratnapur were maintained by the Church of England Zenana Mission Society, aided by the District Board.[24] A dispensary in Ranaghat was established by a retired Bengal civilian, James Monroe, and maintained by the Church Missionary Society.[25] Though the ratio of Muslims to Hindus was six to four in 1891, the ratio of Muslim boys to Hindu boys in school was only one to two.[26]

Abul Ahsan Chaudhuri, the biographer of Sheikh Jamiruddin (who before his reconversion to Islam was known as Rev. John Jamiruddin), points out that the decades-long vicious cycle of epidemics, flooding, and famines and the unsettled agricultural ecosystem in the aftermath of the indigo troubles led to not only a population decline but also a partial breakdown of socioeconomic infrastructure in Nadia, Jessore, and surrounding areas.[27] The lack of education, a tattered rural economy, and repeated natural calamities, combined with the zealous charitable efforts of Christian missions and evangelically minded colonial administrators, meant that this region became one of the only places in Bengal other than the 24 Parganas to evince some success in non-elite Christian conversions.[28] In 1872, Hindus made up 45.3 percent of the population, Muslims constituted 54.3 percent, and the rest was made up of Baishnabs, Hadis, Namashudras, and other sects. As the *District Gazetteer* notes, by the 1901 census the total number of Christians was 8,091, compared to 676,391 Hindus (40.56 percent) and 982,987 Muslims (58.95 percent).[29] The increase of Christian converts was absolutely nominal, up 794 from 1891 and 1,669 from 1881 (for example, Meherpur had 11 Christians in 1901). The Church of England had the lion's share of converts, 5,836 in number, while the Roman Catholic Church had 2,172 adherents.[30] Jessore, home to Meherullah, presents a similar demographic picture to its neighboring district. Jessore town was small, with a total population of only 8,911 inhabitants. Jessore district had a population of 1,272 Christians in 1911, up from 912 in 1900. The number of native Christians was 1,220 in 1911, up from 867. This means the total number of official and nonofficial whites in Jessore was 52 in 1911, up from 45 in 1900. Of the total number of Christians, Baptists made up 307 and Roman Catholics 902.

Why did the Bengali Muslim populace feel so deeply threatened by Christian evangelism in the district, especially when they made up 62 percent of the population and numbered 1,087,554 in 1911?[31] Rafiuddin Ahmed attributes this partially to the hurt sentiments and collective pride of the community when even one member was lost to Christian apostasy.[32] The reality seems to have been slightly more complicated. There was a historical tension between white Europeans and the peasantry of Jessore. Since the Jessore market drew large rural crowds, it was also central to displays of disaffection between the local European indigo planters and the aggrieved peasantry who found it economically untenable to cultivate the crop, making Jessore a flashpoint of trouble during the Blue Mutiny in 1860. Disturbances continued in a muted fashion until 1890, when an arbitration board headed by Alexander Smith, the district commissioner, raised the price of indigo crops by 50 percent. The raise eroded the profit margin for planters completely and brought an end to indigo cultivation.[33]

James Wise, civil surgeon and ethnographer, also made a series of observations about the relationship between Muslims and native Christian converts. Like high-caste Hindus, Muslims of east Bengal practiced rituals of untouchability with regards to Christians. On inadvertently coming in close contact with the person, clothing, or food of the native converts, they would bathe. And if a convert entered their home, they would throw away all cooked food and drinking water. They did not practice similar rituals of taboo with low-caste Hindu neighbors, except for *Wahhabis,* who treated both native Christian converts and Hindus with "equal repugnance."[34] Educated middle-class Muslims would not sit at the same table as Christians, even with British officials.[35] Wise's observations are borne out by the descriptions Kazi Nazrul Islam left of the so-called low-caste Muslims and the "Oman-Kathlee" (Roman Catholic) inhabitants of Ranaghat and Krishnanagar in his 1930 novel *Mrityu-Khuda* (Hunger for death). The novel opens with a confrontation between a Muslim woman and a Christian one when their daughters, who are good friends, manage to contaminate the drinking water pitchers by brushing inadvertently against each other at the village pond. The Muslim woman, described as *gajal* (thin and sharp as a nail), screams at her plump Christian neighbor: "*Haram-khor* Christian from God knows where! It's because you partake of the forbidden meat [pork], that you put on fat like a wild swine, right?"[36] Her neighbor returns with equal salty passion, "Oh you dried piece of fish! Of course, you'll say this, won't you? After all, the shine on your face comes from the money your son makes by cooking the same *haram* meat at the house of the British Judge Sahib!"[37] One of the spectators to this feud, a certain malaria-eaten woman called Pnuter Ma (Pnute's mother), can't help interjecting, "Gajal! Remember, the Judge Sahib is from our race—we are the race of kings, understand?!" There is a profound tragic irony in this assertion of moral superiority by Pnuter Ma, who draws a dubious link between the lowest of the poor Indians and the most exalted of the white British colonial administrators, through a barely shared religious identity. Later, the protagonist of the novel, Mejo-Bou (second wife), converts to Christianity because the Roman Catholic missionaries are her only source of assistance during the illness of her family members and in supporting her desire to be educated. Mejo-Bou's conversion has tragic consequences. She is excommunicated by her community and has to leave her two children behind. When one of the children dies, Mejo-Bou is only allowed to fulfill the last rites of her baby son Khoka on doing *tauba* (repentance) and reconverting back to Islam.

In such a society, the visibility of Christian missions, the implicit racial hierarchies practiced by the white missionaries and colonial officials, and the explicitly insulting nature of Christian apologetics, especially about the Prophet, created an impression in the Bengali Muslim ecumene of a much larger threat of Christianity to the true faith. The prehistory of economic coercion regarding indigo plantation remained a vivid memory. The private but influential support of colonial officials was also a visible threat. So was the diffusion of pamphlets and periodicals virulently attacking the falsity of Islam as a religion. The *Islam Pracharak* of September 1891 complained:

> The primary enemies of our religion are the Christians. They spend hundreds of thousands of rupees each year, both women and men disguising themselves in many ways in order to further their efforts, their convictions are unshakable, and they rain money like water in propagating their religion. And then, when there are famines, they lure the wretched sufferers of those regions with promises of aid. It is in this way that nearly all peasants of some villages near Krishnanagar in Nadia have accepted the *Isa'i Din.*[38]

The *Anjuman'e Ettefaq'e Islam* (Association for Islamic Unity) concurred: "Many of [the peasants] sought sanctuary with the missionaries during the last terrible famine. If the Muslims had money or education that enlightened them to the true glories of Islam, they'd never ever convert to Christianity by falling victim to the lure of the *padris,* even if their lives were mortally imperiled by the ache of hunger."

And an unknown folk singer sang:

নদীয়া জেলার আজি বেরাদর'গন।	Look, brothers from Nadia,
যত কেরেস্তান লোগ কর দরশন।	Look at all these Christian people!
বাপদাদা তাহাদের আকালের বারে।	Their forefathers, during the famine,
পেটের দায়েতে মজে যীশু মন্তরে।	Compelled by hunger sang Jesus's praise!
দেলজান হতে তারা যীশু না ভজিল।	But they never prayed to Jesus from their heart,
আফসোসে আখের সবে পরান ত্যাজিল।।[39]	They die with profound regrets.

During the period of Meherullah's ascendency, the cultural spaces of Muslim-Christian apologetics in eastern Bengal were informed by two important factors. The first was the immediate historical context. Naya Miya, Dudu Miya's son and inheritor of the Fara'idi movement, died at the age of thirty-two while on a pilgrimage to Mecca in 1884. Naya Miyan had led the last successful charge, politically, economically, and ideologically, against the twin forces of Hindu *zamindari* extortion of Muslim peasantry and the rapid rise of the Ta'aiyunis (followers of Karamat Ali Jaunpuri) after 1857 in east Bengal.[40] The Bengali poet Nabin Chandra Sen wrote in detail about Naya Miyan's dealings with the *zamindars* of Faridpur and later in Palang, which ended in the sensational kidnap and murder of the agents and factors (*gomasthas* and *piyadahs*) of the Chakrabartis, the *zamindars* of Palang. When Sen, as the deputy magistrate of Madaripur, made inquiries, the Muslim peasants said sarcastically that the men had been carried away by *Allah'r Chil* or the Kite of Allah—a well-known Fara'idi codeword for murder and consequent immersion of the corpses and the evidence in the watery grave of the Meghna River. Sen also reported on one of the largest *bahases* or debates between the Fara'idis and the Ta'aiyunis held at Madaripur between Jaunpuri's son Mawlawi Hafiz Ahmad and Naya Miyan, and named it the battle of the Ju'mah, or *Ju'mah'r Yuddha.* Naya Miyan, according to Sen's testimony, held his own against the learned and theologically acute salvos of Hafiz Ahmad and his followers.[41] Naya Miyan's death weakened the Fara'idi movement considerably, and left a vacuum in the rural Bengali Muslim ecumene in the sphere of Islamic reform and theological debate. Meherullah would come to fill this vacuum and take on the position of an undisputed leader of this milieu.

The second factor was the passage of the Bengal Tenancy Act of 1885, which wrought significant social and economic changes. After a series of rent strikes, the depositions of the landlords, who were largely high-caste Hindus, failed to convince the colonial administration of the wisdom of noninterference in the relationship between *ryot* and *zamindar*. The Bengal Tenancy Act invested the *ryots* with "right to the land with substance and security."[42] One of the major aims of the Fara'idi movement had been precisely to secure these rights for cultivators of the land, immortalized by the slogan *Langal jar, jomi tar* (He who owns the plow owns the land). With the Bengal Tenancy Act, and a corresponding withering of *zamindari* rights to land, the Muslim peasantry experienced new economic and social stability. In other words, 1885 represented the final closure of a kind of political and economic possibility for the Hindu landlords, and the opportunity for new articulations of rights and reforms for the Muslim peasantry. This shift, in turn, would impact the flowering of subaltern discourses on religion, culture, social hierarchies, and resistance against the suspected depredations of evangelical Christian missionary activity.

After receiving the legal right of the individual to property, Bengali Muslims turned their attentions toward better defining themselves as subjects and citizens. The category of reform most intimately accessible to them, which also offered the most visible potential for resistance, was religion. In this, three major religions had to be considered. The first was their own faith, a uniquely Bengali Islam (or South Asian Islam), which the reformers saw as hopelessly syncretic and muddled. The second was the Hinduism of their neighbors. There was an increasing concern in the Bengal Muslim milieu that ritual practices and customary sages borrowed from Hinduism had led to pollution of their own social rites and customs. As such, Hinduism was the excess, the interiorized impurity, which had to be exorcised in order to be better Muslims. The third, and most externally threatening, religion was the faith of the colonial imperial state. Christianity was viewed with profound suspicion as a tool of erasure of their identities as Muslims, which could be yielded by the missionaries with blunt force, aided by the soft power of the colonial state. In an atmosphere of rapid change, compounded by ecological disaster and socioreligious disarray, with increasing intrusion of the colonial state, both officially and unofficially, into the lives of Bengali Muslims, this made for deep unease and tension. It is not surprising that Munshi Meherullah and his followers, who were born and raised in this society, recognized these fault lines and began their work of social reform and defending Islam against Christian evangelicalism in unsettled rural Bengal during this period.

THE LIFE-WORLD OF MUNSHI MEHERULLAH

Meherullah's *murid* Jamiruddin wrote a short biographical essay about his master and guide after Meherullah's untimely death, parts of which were published in 1909 in the *Islam Pracharak.* Called *Meher Charit* (The life of Meherullah), the biography is the earliest and most authentic contemporary record of Meherullah's life and labors and acted as the source material for two subsequent biographies of Meherullah, written by Asiruddin Pradhan of Jalpaiguri and Habibur Rahman.[43] These quasi-hagiographic and clearly partisan literary works are our main source of knowledge about Meherullah, the elusiveness of his character, and the hypnotic thrall in which he held his audience, offering up a portrait of the common man reimagined as folk hero. Meherullah thus becomes more than what he was, not only a charismatic self-taught tailor who assumed the role of spokesman for Bengali Muslims but also an ideologically inscribed cipher holding the key to the Bengali Muslim *mofussil* milieu and mentality.[44]

Meherullah, who through his writing "defanged the poisonous Christian missionaries and *padris,*" was born on Poush 10, 1268, or December 24, 1861, at the home of his maternal uncles in a village called Ghope, in Jessore district.[45] His mother went back to her husband's village with her son when he was six months old, as was the custom for a woman's first pregnancy and childbirth. The sparsely populated village where Meherullah grew up, which would remain his base for most of his adult life, was Chatiantala, located on the edges of a dense forest. Meherullah's father Warisuddin was a pious Muslim, but in order to educate his son he had Meherullah admitted to a Hindu *pathshala* at the age of five years, where he finished *Barna Parichay* (Introduction to the Bengali alphabet), parts 1 and 2, and started on the Bengali reader *Bodhoday* (Reading comprehension). Written by the great Bengali reformer and educationist Ishwarchandra Vidyasagar, these primary textbooks were essential reading for most Bengali boys (and a few Bengali girls as well).[46] However, before the young boy could finish *Bodhoday,* his father passed away, impoverishing the family and leading to a temporary break in his education. This was the extent of his formal education in Bengali. After his maternal uncles took on part of the financial responsibility for him and his three younger sisters, Meherullah's mother encouraged him to begin on a course of religious Islamic studies, hoping that would result in a profitable livelihood. Meherullah went to be educated by the Moulavi Ismail sahib in Karchhia village, where he learned Arabic and Persian and memorized the Quran and selections from the *Golestan* (flower garden) and *Bustan* (orchard) of Sa'adi.

He also picked up a smattering of Urdu from another teacher, Munshi Moshabuddin of Kayalkhali.[47]

Meherullah's eclectic and seemingly patchwork education was interesting precisely because of the preeminence it gave him among the rural Bengali Muslims. First, knowledge of Arabic and therefore of the Quran in the original was limited to only those Bengalis who received a strictly Islamic education in *madrassas* or belonged to the elite *ashraf* class. This elite *ashraf* intelligentsia had closer ties to the vibrant courtly Muslim culture of Northern India and also greater access to the refined graces of Persian literature and Arabic theology, of the *akhlaq* and *adab* genres.[48] Such training would also have been available to middle-class educated Hindu Bengalis born before 1835, as evinced in the autobiographies of Debendranath Tagore and Dewan Kartikeya Chandra Roy, reminiscing about their childhoods.[49] For someone of Meherullah's socioeconomic status, though, such training was very rare, and it was a formative influence on his charismatic oratory and writing. His erudition, in his milieu of mostly illiterate Bengali Muslim peasantry who relied on this literate and personable man to translate their religion and their world to them in a language they understood, naturally translated into his prominence as an arbiter of Muslim piety and Muslim belonging in rural eastern Bengal.

The Quran had been translated by the Brahmo preacher Bhai Girish Sen, who worked tirelessly from 1881 to 1886 to publish the Bengali version. Mohammad Akram Khan, eminent journalist and founder of the Dhaka newspaper *Azad* (Free), called this feat an "extraordinary and wonderful achievement" and "one of the eight wonders of the world."[50] However, even the Bengali translation was not available to most Bengali Muslims, and Islam as a religion and the tenets of Islam circulated through *puthi* literature, folk literature, and even novels, from Syed Sultan's *Nabi Vamsa* (on the family and descendants of the Nabi, Prophet Muhammad) in the sixteenth century,[51] to Mir Mosharraf Hosain's novel, *Bishad Sindhu* (The ocean of sorrows), published in three volumes in 1885, 1887, and 1891, parts of which were often memorized and then sung in the form of *Jari-Gaan*.[52] As James Wise wrote in his seminal work, such knowledge of Persian and Arabic along with a rigorous grounding in the Quran as Meherullah gained was rare in his immediate social world, in which

> the vast majority of Bengali Muhammadans are ignorant and simple peasants, who of late years have been casting off the Hindu tinsel which has so long disfigured their religion. They are now taught that to be good

> Mussulmans nothing more is necessary than the repetition, at stated intervals, of certain prayers in a language they cannot pronounce, still less understand.[53]

As mentioned earlier, Meherullah's academic and religious training made him an authority in his immediate social community, while also giving him the means to connect to elite intellectuals from the metropolises of Calcutta and Dhaka. He would use his linguistic and literary abilities to travel between rural and urban intellectual networks to brilliant effect in his programs of aggressive apologetics aimed against Christian evangelism, as well as in his efforts at social reform in rural east Bengal. At the same time, he remained attuned to the habits and dispositions of the subaltern rural peasant milieu he belonged to. His future written work used the *puthi* form and the dialect of *dobashi* Bengali to bring sophisticated commentary on Islam and duties of Muslims to this particular subsection of Bengali Muslims. In his speeches, providing entertainment and education to large audiences, he liberally used verses and couplets from Sa'adi and Hafez in the original Persian, immediately translating them into Bengali, and quotes from the Quran in Arabic.[54] After his student Jamiruddin reconverted to Islam as a result of Meherullah's influential debate with him on the nature of the Quran, Meherullah's speeches began to contain references to English *tafsir* or exegesis, a powerful pamphlet genre of missionary Christian commentary on the corrupt nature of Islam and the degeneracy of Muslims, since Jamiruddin had learned English to a good level during his time at a seminary in Allahabad.[55]

This was an astonishingly effective performance of authenticity that strengthened his status as a uniquely powerful expositor on religious and cultural matters pertaining to Bengali Muslims. Mixed with folktales and parables in *dobashi* Bengali, this effortless journey between genres and idioms of religion, literature, and culture rendered Meherullah's oratory forceful and poignant at the same time. He cajoled and entreated Muslims to remember what made them great, what separated them from Hindus or Christians, and requested their cooperation in the reform of their religious and social practices. All three biographers of Meherullah remembered, even decades after his death, the power of his spoken words and his ability to deploy them with devastating effect on both the educated elites and illiterate rural audiences. Asiruddin Pradhan described Meherullah speaking at one such meeting in Baisakh in 1895. Held at Noakhali at the town hall and presided over by the district magistrate, it was attended by elite Hindus and Muslims as well as colonial officials and Christian missionaries. According to Pradhan, "The power and courage of his speech was almost supernatural in its effect, certainly beyond the ability of a human being to describe adequately. People listened to him spellbound, in complete silence and with rapt attention, only to periodically interrupt with cries of 'bravo,' '*marhabba*' and the thunderous sound of applause."[56] Meherullah's fame as a speaker grew enough that he was mentioned by the district magistrate of Bogra in the 1901 census of India: "In November last, a Muhammadan reformer, Munshi Meherullah of Jessore, was invited by the Hanafis to deliver lectures. . . . Excellent lectures on the necessity for reform for the Musalman community."[57]

Habibur Rahman was even more effusive in his recollections. According to him, in a speech that was four to five hours long, Meherullah never repeated himself, and he enlivened his narrative with mellifluous recitations from Farsi poetry, folk parables, and stories from the Quran. The effect, even on the poorest and meanest of his audience, was one almost of intoxication. The sincerity of his advice, combined with the authenticity performed and enacted through his intelligent interjection of Arabic and Farsi quotes, made even his detractors take him seriously and reconsider their previous positions. He had, Rahman would have us believe, the ability to affect the deepest emotions and principles of men and women—the reason he was such an effective orator and reformer:

> Those who heard him were never able to forget him or his words. This is the reason that even after almost two decades since his passing, hundreds and thousands of Bengalis have kept hold of his memory in the deepest sanctums of their hearts, tended to his remembrance as they would for someone who was the dearest of family members, someone who was one of their own. He enchanted Bengal in an incomparable way that had not been seen before or since.[58]

It was not merely his immediate communitarian affiliations or education that influenced Meherullah's intellectual and social commitments. Direct contact with the forces of colonialism and Christian apologetic evangelicalism sharpened his sense of identity and his understanding of his roots. The phase of his life immediately after the formal end of his education in religion and theology, and his future debate with John Jamiruddin, were decisive moments in the construction of Meherullah's philosophical, theological, and social reform program. According to Rahman, at the end of his Urdu education, Meherullah left Chatiantala and moved to Jessore town in search of a vocation.

He trained as a tailor, an occupation that was largely served by Muslims in Bengal, and became apprenticed to a well-known local sewing master called Jahan Baksh Mriddha, who had gained renown due to his appointment as the family tailor to a *sahib-bari* (residence of the British officer). Being the private supplier of clothing to a *sahib-bari* meant that Mriddha had close connections to the white European residents of Jessore town—including colonial officials and their families, as well as planters and missionaries. All of them were addressed, in Bengali, as *sahibs* and *mems* (madams). As Mriddha's apprentice, Meherullah entered this network of primarily service-class Indians who were employed by the colonial administration and therefore had ample chances to observe the colonial masters at close quarters. Meherullah saw, firsthand, the ways in which Christian evangelism worked in the towns and villages of rural Bengal.[59]

Asiruddin Pradhan writes of the frenetic evangelical activity in Jessore during the last two decades of the nineteenth century. Meherullah had, by this time, finished his apprenticeship. He had also gained enough of a clientele—including the favors of the district magistrate, if his hagiographers are to be believed—to be able to afford his own shop in the market of Jessore town.[60] A market is, in most societies, a place for the transaction of both goods and information, engendering both economic and intellectual commerce. Missionaries had always found marketplaces particularly efficient for large and diverse gatherings of people to whom they could preach. Missionaries also supplied apologetic pamphlets, which were objects of curiosity to the general populace. Pradhan says that Christian missionaries were usually very energetic and that to gain converts they relied on a combination of persuading the audience and disparaging the Quran and the Prophet. The activities of the missionaries touched Meherullah personally:

> Many of the *Karigar* Muslims took refuge in Christianity. Even Munshi Meherullah's very close friend, Shri Dhanai Biswas, was enchanted by the glittering untruths uttered by the missionaries, and abandoned Islam to be baptized as a Christian. Their persuasion and their emphasis that Islam was false created a storm of unrest in Meherullah's mind, and he almost took the fatal step toward baptism. He was very influenced by the *padri* Ananda Babu's speeches and by reading the many pamphlets that the missionaries distributed.[61]

Meherullah was saved from this misstep and spurred onto his path as a defendant of Islam through his reading of two apologetic pamphlets that contested the claims of the missionaries. These were *Khristian dharm'er bhrastata* (Falsehood of Christianity) by Hafiz Niamutullah Ahmed from Calcutta and *Injil'e Hajrat Mohammad'er Khabar Achhhe* (The gospel contains news of Hazrat Muhammad, the Prophet) by Rev. Babu Ishan Chandra Mondal (alias Maulavi Ehsanullah Sahib), a Hindu who had converted first to Christianity and then to Islam. As the personal tailor to the district magistrate, Meherullah also made the summer trip to Darjeeling, where he came across the *Mansur'e Muhammadi* (Favored by the Prophet), a short-lived Islamic periodical published in Mysore, as well as a greater selection of both Christian evangelical pamphlets. These included North Indian Urdu and Hindustani Muslim apologetic pamphlets refuting the evangelical claims.[62] Meherullah was convinced that the only way to stop the depredations of Christian evangelism would be to beat the missionaries at their own game. He began by preaching in the market of Jessore town where his shop was located.

This created a sensation, according to Habibur Rahman. The spectacle of the Christian *padri* denouncing Islam and the Prophet on one side of the open marketplace and a young Bengali Muslim man in worn-out clothes refuting the missionary on the other was met with astonishment by the market's buyers, sellers, and loiterers, who carried the tale to their villages and homes. Meherullah had gained a certain amount of fame among his countrymen, and he used this notoriety not only to launch his passionate anti-Christian apologetic propaganda program but also to make his presence felt in the many *waz-mahfils* and *milads* that were held as communitarian meetings. In these *mahfils,* Meherullah spoke about the Prophet, his life, and his philosophy—the knowledge of which was the only way to gain and practice true faith or *iman.* And increasingly, Meherullah spoke of his own conviction that *Deen* (Islamic faith) and *Duniya* (the world) could not be considered separately. A reform of Bengali Muslim society was necessary to combat not only Christianity but also the rot that had set in from within and left rural Muslims backward, both in politics and culture.[63]

In 1886, Meherullah wrote his first pamphlet, about sixteen quarto pages, called *Khristiya Dharm'er Asarata* (The worthlessness of Christianity). There is some indication that this small sally caused a great deal of irritation to the Baptist Mission in Jessore for some years. Rev. T. W. Norledge, writing of the mission's work in Jessore, spoke of his bewilderment when one of his converts, a certain Khater Mian, took to pamphlets and books to justify his decision to convert. When Khater remained absent from two subsequent Sunday prayer sessions, Norledge set out to see him in his village, along with Dhanai

Babu (who was quite possibly Meherullah's close friend who converted) and Elmesh Babu, the native preachers. The new convert was surrounded by friends and neighbors, some of whom refused to share Khater's hookah. They appeared to be discussing religious matters. The arguments were being substantiated with the help of a Bible missing several pages and a tiny pamphlet called *Christianity Worthless,* which apparently made "objections to the doctrine of the Trinity." One can only imagine the emotions of Dhanai Biswas on seeing his erstwhile friend's work in the hands of his new, possibly backsliding convert![64]

It was during this early stage of his life as a social reformer and apologetist that Meherullah gathered around him a group of like-minded Muslim men, such as Munshi Mohammad Kasem of Ghurulia and Munshi Mohammad Ibrahim from his birthplace Ghope, who began to work with him in trying to openly confront evangelism in Jessore district. They managed, in a short period, to attract attention from the Bengali Muslim press in Calcutta and the intellectuals associated with the Bengali Muslim ecumene. The *Islam Pracharak,* one of the first newspapers to notice the activities of Meherullah and his associates, wrote, "In Jessore district, the Christian preachers had created a great ruckus—many Muslims, unconscious of their false blandishments, almost chose the path of falsehood. Preachers like Munshi Meherullah, Munshi Mohammad Kasem and others have, through rigorous endeavors, put an end to their efforts."[65]

The influential *pir* of Furfura Sharif, Abu Bakr, who was a follower of Karamat Ali Jaunpuri, took interest in Meherullah's activities and influenced his opinion that the politics of the Hindus could not be the politics of the poor Muslim peasantry.[66] The third and most important addition to his network of communicators, intellectual patrons, and supporters was the members of the Sudhakar group of Calcutta. The editors of *Mihir-o-Sudhakar* and later the *Soltan,* Mohammed Riazuddin Ahmad and Abdur Rahim; the editor of *Islam Pracharak;* contributors like Pandit Riaz-al-Din Ahmad Mashahdi and Sheikh Abdul Rahim; and other leading lights of the Bengali Muslim intelligentsia came to know of Meherullah through his efforts on behalf of the *Islam Dharmottejika Anjuman* (Association for the propagation of Islam), which organized conferences to debate the state of Muslims in Bengal, roughly around 1886.[67]

Meherullah embarked on his career of reform as a contributor to and correspondent of the *Sudhakar,* reporting on the open debates or *bahases* between Christian missionaries and Muslim apologists. This included a famous confrontation he had with the Baptist missionary Robert Spurgeon and Ishan Mondal, mentioned earlier, whose pamphlet Meherullah had read, on October 7, 1891, in Pirojpur in Barisal. Reports of the confrontation belie the urgency and tension of the event, presenting it as somehow juvenile and banal. The debate was not one that could be described as theologically acute or intellectually stimulating. For example, Spurgeon asked Meherullah about the nature of Prophet Muhammad's relationship with Allah:

> *Spurgeon and his associates:* Muslims consider the Nabi Hazrat Muhammad as the Friend of Allah—now, friendship is truly tested during times of danger and sorrow. If Hazrat Muhammad was indeed a friend of Allah, why was his immediate family, indeed his dearest grandsons Hassan and Hussein, made to suffer such abjection, such inglorious death in the great battle of Karbala? Answer if you can!
>
> *Munshi Meherullah:* The compassion and sympathy shown by the *padri* toward the family of our Prophet is truly worth our gratitude and thanks. But we say the missionaries have been paying such attention to the goings-on in the house of others that they've let the affairs of their own household slip from their minds! When the Rasul went to speak to Allah of the premonition of terrible tragedies that were to befall his family, Allah said sadly, "*Dost,* here you are weeping for your grandchildren, but see, those Christians have crucified my dear Isa (who they say is my son)! What can I do, the *padris* have stolen all my powers!"[68]

The sly humor that Meherullah used to combat the assertion of the Christian missionaries is striking, as is his subtle accusation that the *padris'* false statements about both Allah and his Prophet were issues of grievous insult and injury to the psyche of rural Bengali Muslims. This was not a complicated theological debate on the minutiae of the Quran or the Bible in their respective portrayals of Muhammad and Jesus. Rather, it was a quick-witted spontaneous repartee that would disarm and silence Meherullah's interlocutors and provide entertainment to his audience.

This impertinent use of laughter derailed the fundamental seriousness of the missionary endeavor of creating a religious hierarchy based on a comparative truth-value of greatness assigned to the chief personages of each religion. But this laughter, and the resultant discomfiture of the missionaries, is also a moment of disruption of the unofficial colonial civilizing mission, which was to be achieved through displays of both power and piety. It could also have been a gesture emphasizing the fruitlessness of such encounters: a true Muslim who knew the Quran would never be swayed by such questions from Christian evangelicals. The *Islam Pracharak,* in its first published issue, reported in detail on the Pirojpur debate meeting, claiming that it attracted close to 400 people. It also claimed, somewhat surprisingly, that five Hindu *pandits* from well-known families had acted as judges and moderators of the debate.[69]

A similar *bahas* was later held in Ranaghat in March 1897. The local Muslims complained to Meherullah that the town was one of the main seats of missionary power. Both Hindu and Muslim residents accused Rev. Monroe, the director of the Ranaghat Medical Mission, of misleading people into converting to Christianity in order to save their souls when all they wanted was material help from the Ranaghat Dispensary to save their bodies. Monroe had also offended the Muslims on previous occasions by writing or distributing pamphlets that suggested, in short, that Hazrat Muhammad Rasulullah was a fraud, a cheater, and a licentious person, while also saying that "Islam was not a religion of men but of pigs."[70] Meherullah arrived to a gathering of thousands of local Muslims and Hindus, with a substantial police force having been deployed to keep the peace. The atmosphere was tense with anticipation. Though the meeting was held in a mango orchard a few hundred feet from the Ranaghat Dispensary, Monroe and his associates failed to turn up. It was possible they did not want the tense event to tip over into violence during the argumentation. Or perhaps, knowing by then how Meherullah handled theological debates with Christian missionaries, they just did not want to be made fools of in public. Whatever the reason for their absence, the audience was deeply disappointed. Mozammel Haq, the poet, wrote with displeasure, "It's a matter of great astonishment and regret, that those who can make forays into the deepest interior of our villages tirelessly to spread the love of Christ could not manage to attend this meeting in front of their own doorstep!"[71] Meherullah soothed his fractious listeners by giving a seven-hour speech, and his associate Jamiruddin spoke for three hours, thereby turning the *bahas* into a *waz-mahfil.* This event was the last open *bahas* between Christian missionaries and Muslim apologetists in Bengal, though the argument continued in periodicals and pamphlets.

Meherullah's characteristic apologetics against Christian evangelism translated into the print medium with vibrancy and humor. His *Jawabunnesara* (Answers), providing answers to major theological questions that the missionaries used to critique Islam, written in 1898, took the form of a dialogue between a Christian missionary and himself.[72] One of the questions pointed out that there were no easily available Bengali translations of the Quran. As such, was it not fruitless to read the words of Allah by rote, in a language of which the *namazi* (one who offers the *namaz*) had no knowledge and could not hope to comprehend? The question reflected a deeply Protestant Christian concern about the comprehensibility of the Holy Word but also served as a direct attack on the nature of Muslim piety in Bengal. Meherullah answered using the same rhetoric of practical common sense: if, in riverine eastern Bengal, many hundreds of men and women could buy tickets printed in English for boats and steamers, not knowing the language or what it meant for their journey, and still have faith that they would be taken care of and reach their destinations, wasn't it evident that Allah and the *alims* (scholars of Islamic theology) would steer the devout Muslims on the path of piety even if they couldn't read the Quran in Arabic?[73]

On one hand, Meherullah leveraged his charisma in the name of reformist social and religious activism by relying on forms and rhetorical instruments of the "economy of enchantments" common to practitioners of customary Islam in rural eastern Bengal. On the other hand, the content of his lectures and speeches prohibitively proscribed any belief in miracles or saintly intercession in the lives of the Muslim peasantry. Depending on a strict interpretative understanding of the Quran and the role of religion in creating ideal Bengali Muslims, Meherullah in his subtle way made fun of the missionaries when they tried to use Jesus's ability to perform miracles to argue for the superiority of Christianity over Islam.[74]

Meherullah's *Radde Kristian o Dalilol Islam* (The truth of Islam returned to the Christians), an 1888 tract that was essentially an improved version of his *Khristiya Dharm'er Asarata* from 1886, brought him even more fame. It made a point of criticizing not only Christian evangelism but also the listlessness of Bengali Muslims involved in intrasectarian debates. Meherullah stringently criticized the moribund nature of Muslim social life in Bengal, which was bereft of any desire for progress. He contrasted this state of affairs with the way the Quran and Islam were finding new proponents in both Britain and the United States, through the enlightened conversion of true believers like Abdullah Quilliam of Liverpool and Alexander Russell Webb of the United States.[75] The *Radde* proves that Meherullah was in tune with many of the debates about Islam taking place in the wider world, even from within his rural sphere of influence. He wanted the light of the Truth contained within Islam to spread across all layers of Bengali society and thereby restrict the influence—spiritual or material—exercised by missionaries. He often compared missionaries and converted Muslims to bats: creatures of the night, blind to Islam. On the fundamental issue of a Trinitarian understanding of Christian Godhead and the nature of Jesus's divinity, Meherullah took a different position, once again inflected not by theological intricacy but by blunt common sense. He said:

> Jesus called on God as Father through his devotion, and in this devotion saw everyone else, including his disciples, as a brotherhood, united in a common faith. A simple, discerning reader can comprehend immediately that this was not a paternal bond made on claims of inheritance. We Muslims only legally accept that bond as paternal which is one of blood.... Such faith, devotion or courtesy does not imply a right of inheritance either of blood or of spiritual and worldly riches.... As such, we cannot accept the missionary contention that Jesus was, in essence, divine as the truly begotten Son of God.[76]

At every stage of his career, Meherullah maintained this rhetorical stance of approaching religion as a part of lived life, inflected by the daily practices of piety of the simple rural Bengali Muslim community—even though his theological acuity can be gauged by the sophisticated elision of finer points of theological debate, in which the Christian missionaries were used to participating.

In 1893, the *Sudhakar* published Meherullah's first salvo against John Jamiruddin on the questions of the authenticity of the Quran and external apocryphal additions to the Hadith and the Sunnahs. This exchange established Meherullah's reputation as the most successful interlocutor between elite *ashraf* Muslims and the rural *atrap* peasantry. The debate shifted slowly and exclusively to the print medium, which also offered a greater and more serious attempt at textual analysis and exegesis. The language used in these apologetics is also indicative of the slowly emerging Bengali Muslim public sphere, its primary concerns, and in some ways, its social and political identity.

Language of Truth, Language of Belonging

All available sources on Meherullah's life and times stress the pivotal importance of his debate with Rev. John Jamiruddin, who reconverted to Islam as a result and was thereafter known as Meherullah's associate Sheikh Jamiruddin

Vidyabinod. Jamiruddin was the obverse image of Meherullah in many ways and represented a cautionary tale on the effects of Christian evangelical glamour cast on hapless Muslims. The narrative of Jamiruddin's life, managed carefully by Jamiruddin himself, reads much like a sentimental novel of prodigality: the protagonist goes astray, comes into contact with a heroic figure who challenges his sinful waywardness, deeply introspects on his life and choices, has a moment of epiphany and a divinely directed anagnorisis, and finally returns to the straight and narrow path of religious fidelity. At that point, the prodigal son is joyously accepted back into the fold.

Unlike Meherullah, Jamiruddin was born into a prosperous middle-class Muslim family, one of seven brothers. His father Amiruddin was an orthodox and strict man given to performing all religious rituals with close attention to detail and expecting the same from his sons and wife. He was a *jotedar*, a landowning peasant, with substantial holdings in the ancestral village of Gnaradob-Bahadurpur in the Meherpur district. He also ran a bookshop called Amiruddin Library at 433 Upper Chitpore Road in Calcutta. Chitpore was famous for its trade in cheap mass-market chapbooks, pamphlets, and periodicals, called *Bat-tala* books, as well as for the trade in Bengali theater or *Jatra* pamphlets. Amiruddin admitted his son to a *maktab*, instead of a *pathshala*, where the young Jamiruddin went through a rigorous grounding in Islamic theology, learned to read the Quran in Arabic, and imbibed the forms and rituals of reading *namaz* prayers and keeping the *roza*. After a short stint of learning Bengali, and then English at Amjhupi Christian School, he was sent to Krishnanagar to study at the Normal School there in 1885.

It was during his stay at Krishnanagar that Jamiruddin came into contact with Christian missionaries, especially Rev. E. T. Butler, the principal of the school, and Rev. Jani (Johnny) Ali, a Cambridge-educated Muslim convert to Christianity. Jamiruddin's description of his own conversion clearly reflects the devastation it caused to his immediate family members. His first attempt at baptism failed in 1885, when his parents learned of his intentions and his father and elder brothers brought him home from school. However, this was only a temporary delay, as Jamiruddin "thought and conferred endlessly, read all the theological works on Christianity that I could find, and finally, causing my parents and brothers unimaginable sorrow, was baptized on the afternoon of 25th December 1887, by Padri Sullivan Sahib, and entered the community of Christians."[77] Through the encouragement of Butler, Sullivan, and Ali, Jamiruddin developed an interest in becoming a native preacher, and he was sent to train at St. Paul's Divinity College in Allahabad. He performed very well at the seminary and received a thorough grounding in Hebrew, Greek, Sanskrit, and Christian theology, as well as what were called "Mohammedan controversies" (exegesis on the Quran by Orientalists like Carl Pfander, William Muir, and W. W. Hunter).[78] He also came into contact with Nilkantha Nehemiah Goreh, who had gained fame as one of the most influential syncretist Christian theological philosophers in India.[79] So roughly at the same time that Meherullah was coming into his own as a defendant of Islam against Christianity, Jamiruddin was embarking on his career as a native convert missionary.

Jamiruddin and Meherullah's paths finally crossed, metaphorically, in 1892, when Jamiruddin was still a student at St. Paul's in Allahabad. He wrote an essay in the Bengali periodical *Khristian Bandhab* (Friend of Christians), the mouthpiece of the Church Missionary Society. The article, titled "Asal Koran Kothai?" (Where is the real Quran?), restated the popular apologetic evangelical argument that the Quran was a corrupted form of divine revelation and that the Bible was the only authentic source of God's Word. Meherullah answered Jamiruddin's criticisms in passionate, almost vitriolic fashion in a series of five articles published in the *Sudhakar* periodical in 1892. The first essay, a direct answer to Jamiruddin, was titled "Sarbattrai Asal Koran" (The true Quran is everywhere: Revealing the Isai or Christian fraud"). The argument turned on the authenticity of the words in the Quran and the possibility of apocryphal additions or deletions in later times that might be suspected to have distorted the message of the Prophet. In that case, Christian missionaries like Jamiruddin contended, the Quran was liable to charges of corruption—a lesser version of the true words of God that could be found incorruptible in the Bible. This was not a new argument. The people of the Book or *Ahl-e-Kitab* were said to have received grace through divine revelation, but Christian missionaries in India, beginning with Carl Pfander onwards, had stressed that there were degrees of authenticity in the reception of the revelations. To theological hairsplitters like Pfander and his ilk, the issue of Prophet Muhammad's illiteracy, the mistakes or elisions that might have been made by the many *hafiz* in noting down the Prophet's words, and the alterations made to the Quran and the Hadith due to the Muslim sectarian split between the Shi'as and the Sunnis created insuperable difficulties in ascertaining the truth-value of Islamic Revelation. According to missionaries, this immediately gave hierarchical supremacy to the truth-value of the Bible over the Quran.[80]

Meherullah was having none of this old stale argument. His article begins with a direct personal attack on Jamiruddin, laying bare his intellectual debts and antecedents and his scholarly pretensions. Meherullah's language in the articles was *sadhu Bangla,* or the chaste Bengali used for writing by the Calcutta elite, a departure from the *dobashi* Bengali he used in his pamphlets for wider dissemination in rural eastern Bengal. Yet the pointed insults were very much in the vein of his speeches: he called Jamiruddin's attack pointless, a regurgitation of previous work by Pfander, Rev. Amanuddin, and Rev. Jacob Kanti Nath, and an attempt to gain the favor and approbation of his white masters in Tyangra (the site of the Church Missionary Society's mission in Calcutta). Meherullah stressed that Jamiruddin's work bore all the marks of inattentive scholarship by a senseless boy. What is extraordinary in his answer to Jamiruddin is Meherullah's knowledge of the Muslim apologetic movement of Northern India. Meherullah seemed to know by heart the apologias penned against the depredations of Christian missionaries by writers from Kanpur, Lucknow, Aligarh, and Delhi. He reminded Jamiruddin that just as there was nothing new in his misguided assertions about the corruptibility of the Quran, he was also wasting the time of Meherullah and other faithful *alims.* All the objections that could be raised against Jamiruddin's reasoning had already been pointed out by Maulana Rahmatullah Kairanawi in his *Izhar ul-Haq* (The truth revealed), which was a thorough refutation of Pfander's *Mizan-ul-Haq* (The balance of truth).[81] Meherullah also pointed out that the work of Rev. Amanuddin, whom Jamiruddin had extensively quoted, had also already been refuted by the Kanpur Maulavi, Mohammad Ali Sahib, in his *Sirat-ul-Eikin* (The path of belief).

Meherullah adopted a pose of weary disgust and passionate disapproval of the attempt of a fellow Bengali ex-Muslim to bring the sanctity of the Quran into disrepute. He said, "It is the cowardice and slothful lethargy of Bengali Muslims that results in such unbearable audacity going unpunished, and the numerous refutations of such blind willfulness, already available in Urdu and Farsi, being untranslated and unpublished."[82] He called Jamiruddin a blind bat, saying that it was not the fault of the sun that the bat could not open its eyes to the light of truth. This, as we have seen, was his favorite metaphor to connote willful spiritual myopia on the part of Christian missionaries and Muslim converts to Christianity. He also hotly contested Jamiruddin's assertion that any of the Shi'a exegesis used the ugly word *Kafir,* or unbeliever, to describe the third Sunni Rashidun Khalif Usman—who, according to

Jamiruddin, had burned the original Quran, which resulted in the destruction of an entire sura. However, a sarcastic Meherullah expressed his suspicion that Jamiruddin might have heard the word being used by a lumpen miscreant who was Shi'a by chance, and being but a boy had misguidedly thought it was textually corroborated:

> If such a thing has happened, I ask my brother to remember the honeyed words used by the Roman Catholics to describe the Protestant cleric Luther. I am sure if he asks Roman Catholics and Protestants in Calcutta, they will agree that there are profound differences in the opinions of the two groups regarding the accepted text of the Bible.

And on the incendiary charge of the Prophet Muhammad's illiteracy, Meherullah was scathing:

> True, in our ordinary understanding, Hazrat Muhammad was illiterate. And yet, he was illuminated by God-given *Nabuwat.* As soon as he received the Ayats of the Quran, he made a thousand *Sahabis* memorize them instantly. . . . Two or four of the *hafiz* could make mistakes, not all of them at once! And if the Prophet found any such mistake, he corrected them at once, since he was the greatest *hafiz* of them all. . . . There has been no corruption in the Quran. . . . Only the Quran will remain, eternal and true.[83]

Jamiruddin had no answer to this eloquent defense of the Quran, and Meherullah's sharp reprimands created a tumult in his heart. However, it still took him almost three more years to renounce Christianity. The path he followed is illuminative of the extraordinary religious ferment in Bengal during the last two decades of the nineteenth century. His study of the Bengali Quran, translated by Bhai Girish Sen, during his stay at Madhugadi village created the firm impression in his mind that it was the Gospels—not the Quran—that had undergone change. It came to him like an epiphany ("A voice spoke in my ear," he says in his autobiography) that the Christians had intentionally removed from the Bible the comment by Isa (Jesus) that the Prophet to follow him would be called Ahmad.[84] He was disturbed, and his faith in Christianity suffered a further devastating blow. He turned for a while to the study of Brahmo theology and concentrated on books written by Raja Rammohan Roy and Keshabchandra Sen. He also went to Calcutta hoping to be converted to Brahmoism.

It was there that he heard a lecture by the Brahmo preacher Nagendranath Mitra, who spoke in Albert Hall on "Muhammad and His Religion."

Mitra refuted the false charges of licentiousness cast on the Prophet by Christian missionaries and, in a very Thomas Carlyle–inspired manner, called Muhammad a true hero. The lecture deeply affected Jamiruddin, who returned to Meherpur abandoning his plans of Brahmo conversion. He read deeply on Islamic apologetic works in Bengali, including Meherullah's *Radde Kristian o Dalilol Islam* (Refutation of Christianity and evidence of Islam) and the *Eslam Tattva* (The essence of Islam), written by two members of the Sudhakar group, Mohammed Riazuddin Ahmad and Sheikh Abdur Rahim, who were also Meherullah's associates. He finally resigned his missionary work, returned home, and reconverted in front of his joyous family. However, his neighbors and villagers were not quite as ready to believe that he had had a change of heart, or to forgive his previous transgression of having committed apostasy. As a result, he was made *Ek-ghore,* meaning he was cast out from his community for ritual infractions, and ran up a huge debt. It was at this time that he reached out to Meherullah. For Meherullah, Jamiruddin's reconversion was both a personal and political landmark in his efforts to curb the influence of Christian missionaries and Christianity in eastern Bengal, an event that further raised public estimation of the effectiveness of his social reform program and his own personal charisma. Meherullah was happy to hear of Jamiruddin's return to the fold and immediately took him under his wing and paid off his debts.[85] Jamiruddin spent the rest of Meherullah's life as his chosen student, the greatest victory Meherullah obtained in his battle against Christian evangelism, his *murid* and in many ways the bearer of his intellectual and social legacy.

THE DEFINITION OF THE SELF AND THE COMMUNITY

Why did Meherullah affect a clear disinterest in open debate with his missionary interlocutors in *bahas* meetings, deferring their theological inquiries with a joke, a folktale, a recitation from a Persian poem? And why did he take it upon himself to write with a rich vein of irony, albeit very lucidly, while engaging with a young converted member of his own social milieu? Meherullah's actions cannot be adequately examined within the rigid analytical categories of Islamic reform, colonial modernity, or appeasement of Hindu sensibilities. He charted a new path ahead for *atrap* Bengali Muslims through his anti-conversion apologetics. The very act of engagement with the colonially and racially inflected and predetermined theological debate between Christian missionaries and Muslim *alims* was, Meherullah understood, merely a performance of social, racial, and theological superiority. The outcome of such debates was always undecided and indefinitely deferred, because apparent victory for any one side was completely unacceptable to the other side, placing their very identities in peril. Meherullah cut through the dense minutiae of the arid scriptural thicket and made the contest merely about demonstrations of superior wit before a deeply partisan audience, usually predisposed toward him. This strategy was also an effective way to disconcert the missionaries, who traditionally based their salvos against Islam on a deep and thorough study of both the Quran and the *tafsir* literature. Deprived of this common ground, they floundered at Meherullah's sly challenges to their textual authority. The narrative of the self-taught tailor's moral and exegetical victory over the educated young native Christian convert may also be read as a coded triumph of Indian forms of knowledge over colonial texts of power. In such literature, Islam and Christianity are coded hierarchically as indigenous knowledge and colonial modern pedagogy, the values of which are decided by weighing textual purity. The struggle of establishing Jesus or Mohammad as the greater or truer prophet was also a struggle over the definition of the Bengali Muslim self. It was Meherullah's aim to establish this Muslim self as an authentic and immutable category and not a corrupted derivative of a centuries-long process of lower-class Hindu conversions.

In Meherullah's reformist program, we can see the emergence of a political Bengali Muslim selfhood—from the milieu of rural eastern Bengal, from the peasant class, which defined itself against evangelical Christianity. To fashion it, Meherullah creatively reformulated the search for self and community around the idea of religion as identity. This meant that rural peasants started presenting themselves more and more as Muslims of a particular kind—distinct from the four variations in the homogenized account presented by James Wise. This Bengali Muslim selfhood exhibited only tenuous links to the courtly culture of the *ashraf* landowning families of Calcutta and Dhaka and the great Muslim aristocratic traditions of Northern India. The reformist section of Bengal's Muslim intellectuals, who were at the forefront of this new understanding of self and sovereignty, stressed the authority of the Quran and advocated a purge of all syncretic elements of Hinduism and Christianity from Bengali Islam as a necessary step toward progress and modernization. This reformist agenda can be seen in Meherullah's pushback against missionaries, with his deep reliance on the textual purity of the Quran, which he used as a basis for his debate with Jamiruddin. In the religious apologias of the kind we see in the *Sudhakar*, *Akhbar'e Islamia* (News of the Islamic world), and the pamphlets penned by Meherullah, we can find, perhaps for the first time, a search for a Bengali Muslim *swajati* (community) and a Bengali Muslim *swadeshi* (nation). Meherullah articulated, for the Bengali Muslim peasantry, an authentic selfhood that emerged as a result of ideological debates between the Christian "Other" and the Muslim self. Therefore, this chapter offers an understanding of the liminal spaces of intellectual discourse aimed at the Bengali Muslim social imaginary and, in the process, complicates the notions of "good" versus "bad" Muslims in colonial India—an understanding that did not depend solely on colonial classification but also on internal divisions between Bengal's elite and non-elite, between the *ashraf* and the *atrap* Muslims, between Muslims and Christian missionaries.

The now-forgotten reform and apologetic program championed by Munshi Meherullah, and the residues of ephemeral life-worlds to which it poignantly attests, reflects a particularly *wayward* form of resistance to recognizable and predetermined modes of interactions between individuals, religious communities, and structures of political power. The accidental survival of archival ephemera—such as provincial periodicals and pamphlets like the *Sudhakar* and the *Akhbar'e Islamia*—sheds light on both ordinary life and the intellectual exchanges of the non-elite sections of South Asian society. They offer a richer understanding of communitarian identity-based politics at the non-central, non-elite levels of local and vernacular ecumenes in the late nineteenth century in colonial India. Closer examination of such archival ephemera can destabilize our accepted categories of historiographical analysis of religious communitarianism and communalism in colonial India. Above all, such analysis also illumines, perhaps inevitably, the tenaciously long-lived tragic genealogies of the ideologies of national belonging and otherness defined in religious terms, with eerie resonances for present-day postcolonial India.

CONCLUSION

Meherullah's intellectual world was one that looked to the social and religious reform of his fellow *atrap* Muslims of east Bengal. In his engagements with British and native Christian missionaries on issues of religious conversion, his intended audience were primarily members of his own social milieu. His emphasis on practical understanding and practice of the daily rituals of Islamic faith implies a movement toward a moral foundation of individual as well as communal religiosity, purged of extraneous syncretic elements. The political agenda is implicit in the registers of shifting dialects and genres, moving between textual exegesis, social belonging, and religious reform in this period of transition. Such an analysis of Meherullah's world and words serves the purpose of estranging the familiar terrain of South Asian historiography that would transpose Hindu for Indian and Calcutta for India. It is clear that in colonial east Bengal of the late nineteenth and early twentieth century, apologetic controversies about religious conversion enabled self-examination and analysis of one's immediate social milieu, just as Meherullah and his associates did. The threat, real or imagined, of mass Christian conversions helped social reformers like Meherullah to devise reformist agendas in order to resist the material lucrativeness of religious and political subordination by the ruling power of British imperialism and the intellectual and spiritual attack commenced by Christian apologetics. It also helped Meherullah to bring about these reforms from *within* his own social milieu, by creating a discursive space for the definition of the religious and communitarian self.

In his capacity to cross networks of information exchange—from the elite *ashraf* circles of the *Sudhakar* in Calcutta to the *bahas* and *waz-mahfils* of the villages and *mofussil* towns of rural Bengal—while remaining rooted in the sociopolitical reality of his milieu, Meherullah complicates our notions of who could speak for the community and the nation. In fact, his imagined community was envisioned as resisting Christianity and colonialism but also the inner corruption of Hindu syncretism. In doing so, Meherullah inspired rural peasants to claim an identity *as* Bengali Muslims. Meherullah's actions of resistance against Christian evangelism and his utopic vision wrought real social changes in terms of identity formation in the rural Muslim peasant milieu of Bengal, which cannot be drowned out by the larger intellectual currents of teleological structures of nationalist historiography. Meherullah, and those like him, constitute what Ranajit Guha called "the small voice[s] of history."[86] I have tried to recover the resonances of this voice from the ruins of the vernacular pasts barely acknowledged in the archives.

In Saidiya Hartman's words, Meherullah's resistance, expressed as *waywardness*, is "a social poesis that sustains the dispossessed."[87] How would such waywardness, embodied in rebellious marginal lives like that of Meherullah or Jamiruddin, help historians understand the entanglements between religion, politics, power, and liminality among subaltern groups in the colonial Indian context? As this chapter demonstrates, the idea of identity was sutured together with both the religious and the political in late nineteenth-century Bengal. It is worth considering, then, that a refiguration of the limits of Muslim identity as it pertains to religious faith and political affiliation had already emerged in the last three decades of the nineteenth century.[88] At the heart of the historiographical debates about this newly emergent Muslim identity, it is important to look beyond cultural and economic contingencies, framing the question of the religious *as* both the social and the political. Apologia, as a spirited defense of one's own faith and consequently one's understanding of one's own social network and moral capital, emerged in this period as neither partial nor luxurious.[89] It defined the ideal Bengali Muslim subject as operating beyond the limits of the conciliatory approaches that had been central to the interactions between an older generation of Muslim intellectuals and their Christian missionary counterparts. The understanding and definition of religion and religious action shifted from syncretic, private, everyday piety to textually approved performances of prayers and rituals. This reconfiguration of religious faith and political identity focused on the performance of social and cultural practices in the domain of the political. It was this performance of religious sensibility, dependent on strict exegesis of the Quran, that began to define a good Muslim in rural Bengal. In centering a particular understanding of the religious as inextricable from the political, this intellectual Muslim narrative broke with past syncretic accretion of pluralistic religious practices and conciliatory accommodations with Hinduism in eastern Bengal. It led subaltern Muslims to voice their own possibilities of other ways of belonging in the world. This was, ultimately, a refusal of erasure of Bengali Muslim voices from the emergent narratives of Indian nationalism.

CHAPTER SIX

The Elusive Legacies of Brahmabandhab Upadhyay

Douglas Kingsford, the feared and hated judge, presided over an astonishing scene in his court in September 1907. Judge Kingsford was already infamous for his merciless treatment of prominent Bengali politicians and ideologues during sedition trials. He had sentenced nationalist leaders like Bipin Chandra Pal and Bhupendranath Dutta to prison earlier in 1907. But on that hot autumn day, Kingsford found himself staring down a particularly intractable culprit, who was being represented by an even more obdurate barrister. The accused was a Brahmin convert to Catholicism, Bhabanicharan Banerjee, who self-styled himself as Brahmabandhab (Theophilus) Upadhyay. He was the editor of a rabble-rousing Bengali vernacular periodical called the *Sandhya*.[1] In this periodical, over its four-year print run from 1904 to 1908, Brahmabandhab Upadhyay espoused armed extremism as the most important and immediate form of resistance to colonial repression. The paper was very cheap and cost one paisa, and by 1906 it had reached a circulation of almost 7,000 copies a day. His editorials, written in colloquial idiomatic Bengali, had taken that message to every corner of Bengal, especially to the non-elite Bengalis.[2] His violent rhetoric was a response to the turbulent political atmosphere during the *swadeshi* or "own country" movement in Bengal and across India, which had emerged in protest of the partition of Bengal by the viceroy Lord Curzon on October 16, 1905.

Brahmabandhab found himself in a difficult situation, since Kingsford had often been the target of his revolutionary diatribes. He had smeared Kingsford with the appellation of *paji* or "wicked." He also frequently referred to Kingsford as the *kasai kazi*, or the "Butcher Judge." On August 28, 1907, a mere fortnight before his own arrest, Brahmabandhab learned that Kingsford had ordered the whipping of a fifteen-year-old boy named Sushil who was accused of brawling with the police. The magistrate turned a deaf ear to all pleas for clemency on account of the boy's youth. Brahmabandhab was furious: "The Government of Bengal has set up a *Kasai Kazi* (a butcher of a Magistrate) at Lal Bazar. . . . Sushil Chandra Sen was tried yesterday—one loathes to call it a trial—he was butchered; how to talk of a trial before a butcher!"[3] On September 21, 1907, as it became clear that Brahmabandhab faced a lengthy and rigorous prison term, the *Sandhya* printed a parody of folk singer *Pagla* Kanai's songs, heaping obloquies on Kingsford:

> The prison to me is Heaven.
> O it is the kind favor of the butcher Kazi.
> Whatever may be our fate, brothers,
> To the Andamans, if need be, we shall go![4]

Tempers were frayed inside the courtroom at Lal Bazar. Indecorous confrontations between Upadhyay, his legal team, and the magistrate were regular occurrences. The meanness of Kingsford's conduct weighed heavily on the trial. *The Bengalee,* a newspaper founded and edited by Surendranath Banerjee, a prominent leader of the "Moderate" old-school faction of the Indian National Congress, which was usually restrained in its reportage, recorded at least two such instances. On September 20, 1907, Brahmabandhab and his counsel J. N. Roy were "rudely" treated by a police constable, who hit and pushed them around repeatedly. Kingsford took notice of the incident and instructed the police to take steps to discipline the constable, but *The Bengalee* went on to say, "We are glad Mr. Kingsford took prompt notice of the man's conduct. But he must be very much mistaken if he thinks that mere departmental punishment can satisfy public opinion in such a case. Indeed, it is not enough that the man should be punished. The public must know what punishment he receives for his misconduct." Kingsford was rude and condescending to Brahmabandhab's legal counsel, the young barrister Chittaranjan Das, who would emerge as one of the most important nationalist politicians in India in the next two decades. On October 5, Chittaranjan had requested a short break in the court proceedings so he could eat lunch, being dizzy with hunger due to Kingsford only allowing a thirty-minute break during the day. Most barristers and lawyers usually went home for lunch in those days, making the half-hour break insufficient. Faced with Chittaranjan's polite request, Kingsford behaved as if his dignity as a judge had been affronted and accused him of purposefully wasting the court's time. The incident was, once again, reported widely in the Bengali press.[5] *The Bengalee* opined ruefully on the deteriorating relationships between the Indian barristers and the British judges and the judiciary's overt expression of racial prejudices: "Surely, Mr. Kingsford could easily have avoided being as discourteous as he was, without any detriment to the cause of justice. Mr. Kingsford is not only not cordial to Mr. Das, but is positively rude. . . . *Would he have treated it the way he did if it had proceeded from an English Barrister?*"[6] Noting the many daily humiliations the magistrate heaped on both the accused and his legal team, Chittaranjan Das was naturally worried about judicial impartiality. His daughter Aparna Devi left behind a poignant portrait of Chittaranjan and his client, exasperated by Kingsford's petty tyranny, lack of decorum, and refusal to maintain any pretension of impartiality or even civil behavior toward Indians:

> Father decided to represent Brahmabandhab Upadhyay. . . . During the trial, my father protested against the prejudiced conduct of Magistrate Kingsford. . . . My father said to Brahmabandhab, "I feel a great reluctance in going back to the court of that unreasonably behaved magistrate—I regret that it seems you may have to go to prison."
>
> Brahmabandhab smiled and replied, "I assure you—the English lack the power to imprison me."[7]

The case was temporarily adjourned while Das made an ultimately unsuccessful application in the Calcutta High Court to have the trial shifted to another judge. While Kingsford and the government attorney Mr. Gregory asked for a continuation of the trial, Brahmabandhab had already refused to defend himself in a judicial court administering British justice. To him, the British were an alien power, with no right of jurisdiction over Indian patriots. Brahmabandhab had always been an extraordinary prose stylist: the popularity of the *Sandhya,* and the unease that his fiery language caused among British administrators, reflects his charisma and the power of his stirring speeches. Standing on the dock, Brahmabandhab now made an impassioned plea that rocked the very foundation of the civilizing mission that purportedly justified British imperialism: the creation of Pax Britannica in India. In his statement, he said:

> I accept the entire responsibility of the publication, management and conduct of the newspaper, "*Sandhya*" and I say that I am the writer of the article, "Ekhane theke gechhi premer dai," which appeared in the *Sandhya* of the 13th August, 1907, being one of the articles forming the subject-matter of this prosecution. But I do not want to take any part in this trial, because I do not believe that in carrying out my humble share of the God-appointed mission of *Swaraj,* I am in any way accountable to the alien people who

happen to rule over us, and whose interest is and must necessarily be in the way of our true national development.[8]

This was a remarkable statement. To his contemporaries, both the young Bengali revolutionaries and the intelligentsia, Brahmabandhab's supreme defiance of the colonial law of sedition was a personal and national declaration of independence. For Brahmabandhab, authentic nationalism, and the creation of an ethical vision of *swaraj* (self-government) and *swadesh* (one's own country), depended on discrediting an alternate vision of colonial modernity's superiority. By refusing to be judged on racial and civilizational criteria thinly veiled as legal discourse, Brahmabandhab sought to delegitimize the ideological foundations of Anglo-Indian law and the politics of imperial liberalism that made British rule in India possible.

Brahmabandhab's alternate vision was for a modern, free nation that was strong in the power of arms to keep itself secure from foreign depredation, a nation where the dignity and self-respect of its people was unassailable. He recognized, as Elizabeth Kolsky has pointed out, that "the rule in India must be understood from its inception as integrally linked to a principle of racial inequality and to a practice of legal exceptionalism."[9] His statement before Kingsford at the trial, read out by Chittaranjan on September 23, 1907, is in many ways a political declaration of his patriotic ideology: we get a glimpse of the intellectual basis of his opposition to colonial rule through his comments before the "Butcher Judge." But it is also a glimpse into the soul of this enigmatic man. He defined his purpose in terms of love for his country, his patriotism, rather than the Brahminical Hindu faith of his birth or the Catholic Christianity that he had embraced.

This chapter examines this now forgotten self-styled patriot, who was a pioneer of the radical extremist ideology that characterized anticolonial politics in an era of anti-Bengal nationalist mass movements in the first decade of the twentieth century. His contribution to the politics of Indian nationalism was in the popularization of a particularly Hindu cultural apologetics that placed love of one's land, one's country, at the center of one's political ideology. The language of this new form of mass anticolonialism depended on creating a strong relationship that bound Indians to the cultural expressions of Hindu religiosity that could then be seamlessly transferred to the veneration of the nation and create an ideal imagined community that would fight against British colonial repression. This was both remarkable and unusual, given Brahmabandhab's own identity as a Christian convert.

Brahmabandhab's decision to overtly perform a deliberate public Hindu persona and keep his identity as a convert deeply though devoutly personal was the consequence of his own experiences—that of the marginalization and suspicions that Christian converts faced regarding their religious, social, and political affiliations. His story places pressure on familiar narratives of Indian nationalism during this period, which tend to emphasize the overwhelming Hindu affiliations of nationalist activists. Indeed, most non-Hindu figures have been erased from both the scholarship on Hindu nationalism and nationalist historiographies or their legacies have been appropriated to better fit with a majoritarian narrative about India's freedom struggle. This assumption about the Hindu faith of Indian revolutionaries has also been conflated with the secular liberal strand of nationalism in India. The result has been the minimization—and, at times, complete erasure—of the contributions of freedom fighters belonging to other minority faiths from the narrative of this early era of Indian anticolonial nationalism. Brahmabandhab's tense negotiation of his patriotism and his personal faith—evident in his identification of himself as "Hindu-Catholic," a dichotomy that is visible in his fiery Hindu revolutionary apologetics and his sober Catholic theological writings, and in the attempts at appropriations of his contested legacy—are the subjects of analysis in this chapter. His disinheritance and disappearance from the nationalist narratives of India's freedom struggle show us how attempts by India's Christians (and other minorities) to find a place within the broader nationalist discourse were (and are) thwarted.

This chapter thus sets out first to show how Hindu affective imagery became a normative part of the expression of this early outpouring of anticolonialism. The public political discourse, in which Brahmabandhab played a leading role, perpetuated this imagery through firebrand essays in vernacular periodicals and newspapers. These periodicals formed the basis of what the Anglo-Indian laws defined as seditious, a definition that has had surprising longevity in both colonial and postcolonial governmental repression of public sentiment to the present day. Second, this chapter analyzes the unique political and social conditions that had to be met by non-Hindu individuals when they participated in this nationalist movement. For Indian Catholic Christians like Brahmabandhab, whose faith was closely associated with first the Portuguese and then the British colonizers, it was especially difficult to express their patriotism and nationalism in the public sphere. Was it even possible to do so, while continuing a public avowal of their Christianity? Or would they have to find practices of accommodation to express their patriotic feelings within the idioms of Hindu affective imagery and practice their personal faith in the private domain, away from the glare of public attention? And if so, what did these practices of mental reservation, equivocation, and accommodation mean for personal identity and personal faith?

Postcolonial narratives of national belonging in India have often questioned the degree and value of various faith communities' contributions to the protracted struggle for independence. In the present day, majoritarian political parties in India often stake their claim of national identity on their real or imagined contributions to anticolonial protests in the early twentieth century. The life of Brahmabandhab and his untimely death led to a struggle to appropriate his political legacy by many revolutionary factions in Bengal—before he was forgotten almost entirely owing to the advent of nonviolent Gandhian civil resistance from 1917 onwards. His private faith as an observant Catholic was always in tension with his public persona, which he carefully presented as that of an ascetic, complete with the saffron garb and wooden sandals of a Hindu monk. Brahmabandhab clearly felt that his patriotism could not find full expression unless he affected a particular kind of Hindu persona publicly and used Hindu imagery in his seditious writings. The ideological foundations of Brahmabandhab's political thought and actions were deeply linked to the political circumstances in Bengal during the first decade of the twentieth century, and to developments in his own life, including his commitment to the extremist revolutionary politics of the *swadeshi* era. In this chapter, I analyze the career of Brahmabandhab as one of the pioneering ideologues of radical extremism, which was one of the most important strands of political rhetoric and action in Bengal during the events of the *swadeshi* movement.[10] His posthumous reputation is equally relevant to this chapter's story of the erasure of minority communities of faith from the nationalist discourse. His identity remained contested in death as in life, as important Indian intellectuals—most prominently, the politician Bipin Chandra Pal and the polymath Nobel recipient Rabindranath Tagore—sought to appropriate his legacy in the context of the anticolonial struggles of the *swadeshi* era.

THE *SWADESHI* MOVEMENT AND THE *SANDHYA* TRIAL

To understand his meteoric rise as one of the most famous patriotic figures in Bengal, it is necessary to first examine Brahmabandhab's personal history. Born into a Hindu Brahmin family in 1861, in the village of Khannyan in

Hooghly district, he subsequently underwent a series of spiritual and religious conversions that exemplified his restless and constant search for meaning. Brahmabandhab's uncle, Rev. Kalicharan Banerjee, had converted to Christianity in 1864, inspired by Alexander Duff and baptized by Lalbehari Dey. He served as a teacher and mentor for the young Brahmabandhab and taught him how to read and write. Brahmabandhab himself was first attracted to Brahmoism under the influence of Keshabchandra Sen and converted to the new dispensation in 1887, three years after Keshabchandra's death. Keshabchandra Sen was an admirer of Christian ethics and incorporated ideas of Christian liberal universalism within his own understanding of Brahmoism—which led to a schism in the Brahmo Church led by Debendranath Tagore and resulted in the new dispensation or *Naba Bidhan* of Brahmoism.[11]

Brahmabandhab, alongside his interests in Brahmoism, had also dabbled in Bengali Hindu mysticism based on the worship of the mother goddess Kali. This form of mysticism had gained widespread influence in Bengal in the latter half of the nineteenth century due to Ramkrishna Paramahansa's syncretic approach to Indian religious traditions (including Islam and Christianity) and his espousal of the simple, daily practices of Hindu religiosity.[12] Brahmabandhab started visiting Dakshineshwar, a riverside suburb that was the site of one of the most important temples for the goddess Kali in Bengal. Here he became close to Ramkrishna's most beloved disciple Narendranath Dutta, the future Swami Vivekananda. They had known of each other since his college days at the General Assembly's Institution, and this brief interlude strengthened their friendship. For Brahmabandhab, Vivekananda also became a figure of idolization later in his life. Vivekananda's own ambiguous relationship to Christianity and the figure of Christ would also affect Brahmabandhab.[13] After graduating from college, Brahmabandhab relocated to Western India in 1887 and lived and worked as a teacher of Sanskrit in Hyderabad and Karachi in Sindh province and briefly in Multan as well. In Multan, he was reunited with his father, who was terminally ill, and he nursed him until his death in 1888.

While keeping vigil at his father's sickbed, Upadhyay came across the Italian monk and mathematician Joseph Faà di Bruno's *Catholic Belief*.[14] Faà di Bruno's understanding of Catholicism was significantly inflected by his belief in the duty of believers to care for the poor and marginalized in society, including the destitute, servants, unwed mothers, and prostitutes. But more importantly, in Faà di Bruno's understanding, true belief in Catholicism required an "authentic interiorized sensitivity," which need not be publicly performed or proclaimed if political or social disadvantages would accrue to the convert as a result.[15] In other words, if there was a conflict between socially accepted public identity and inwardly held private faith, a convert to Catholicism could, in good faith, believe that his "real" self was defined by the latter. This is very much in keeping with the ethics of mental reservation or *mentalis restrictio,* a particular kind of omission of the entire truth in a situation where such equivocation might be more favorable to the upholding of faith, charity, or justice. Brahmabandhab was profoundly influenced by this idea, which certainly made social survival easier in inimical political and cultural climates, especially for revolutionary Indian subjects under brutal British repression. But we cannot discount the psychological trauma of the constant tension between "being" one self and performing another public self, as we will see demonstrated in Brahmabandhab's case.

Ashis Nandy speculates that it was Brahmabandhab's pious paternal grandmother, Chandramoni, who infused this sense of "affectionate self-sacrifice" in the young boy: "Her very life was an embodiment of the old Hindu ideal; Bhabani would never forget it."[16] Yet this is not quite accurate. Chandramoni had traveled all over India with Brahmabandhab's grandfather, who was an officer in William Sleeman's *Thugee* suppression force. These travels allowed her to glimpse other ways of being in the world, in a way that many Indian women could never experience, bound as they were to the *antahpur,* the inner domains of their households. Chandramoni's encounters with peoples of differing faiths, races, and social and political cultures contributed to her liberal outlook on life. Chandramoni was certainly not an orthodox embodiment of the old Hindu ideal of a woman, deeply concerned with honor and purity within the communitarian matrix. We can see this in her attitude toward one of her younger sons, Rev. Kalicharan Banerjee, who converted to Christianity and became a major pillar of native Bengali Christian society. The conversion had deeply hurt her. Yet she welcomed him to her home regularly and with real affection. Perhaps it was on her insistence that, surprisingly for a nineteenth-century Bengali Hindu household, Kalicharan Banerjee was not ostracized or outcasted by his family—although tensions remained within the household about how to treat him. It is within this familial web of liberal and forgiving tenderness that Kalicharan became a source of intellectual inspiration to his young nephew.[17] These two unorthodox figures shaped a young Brahmabandhab's intellect. Brahmabandhab may have felt encouraged in his attraction toward heterodoxy both by Chandramoni's liberal nature and by the tutelage of his rebellious uncle.[18]

Brahmabandhab, still known as Bhabanicharan, was first converted by the Church Missionary Society's Rev. Heaton in 1891, in Hyderabad—this was a Protestant conversion. The event revived old family anxieties about the destabilization of their caste and social status, already tainted by Kalicharan Banerjee's conversion. The news of Brahmabandhab's conversion, so soon after his father Debicharan's death, was a difficult blow for Chandramoni, although she seems to have reconciled herself to it relatively quickly. Despite familial remonstrances, Brahmabandhab remained stubborn. He then converted to Catholicism in Karachi, on September 1, 1891, and was baptized by a Jesuit priest called Theophilus Perrig. He was sponsored by another Jesuit named Bruder. Brahmabandhab adopted the name Theophilus after Bishop Theophilus of Antioch and to honor his baptizer, and would use the Bengali translation of this name—Brahmabandhab, "friend of God"—for the rest of his short life.[19] In his varied careers—as social reformer, political radical, heretic theologian denounced by the Catholic Church, and revolutionary against the British government—Brahmabandhab would self-fashion as the ideal Indian patriot. He would remain culturally connected to Hindu norms in order to better fit into the ways in which nationalist discourses were developing in the early twentieth century. But he would nonetheless hold on to his private faith as a Catholic Christian convert.

Amid the gathering momentum of the nationalist mass movement, which relied on Hindu affective imagery of the motherland—the kind popularized by Bankimchandra Chatterjee's *Anandamath* (Abbey of joy)—to express patriotic fervor, Brahmabandhab must have been in a difficult dilemma. For Brahmabandhab and others like him whose cultural and political affiliations were with their natal Hindu communities but whose chosen faith was Christianity, maintaining a Hindu ethnic identity in public must have seemed necessary in order to express their patriotism and be accepted within the fold of the emerging anticolonial mass agitation. The admiration for the figure of Christ that Rammohan Roy had expressed in the early nineteenth century was shared widely in India, echoed by later Indian intellectuals like Keshabchandra Sen and Vivekananda—both intellectual models for Brahmabandhab. Yet vituperation against Christian missionaries, Indian Christian converts, and the evangelical mission in India were just as commonly to be found in the writings of these great men. Vivekananda, for example, described Christ himself as an "oriental," Asiatic Yogi, or ascetic.[20] He was scathing, however, in his attitude toward Christian missionaries and conversion. In a lecture delivered in Detroit on March 11, 1894, Vivekananda said:

> The great heart of India is today absolutely untouched by missionary effort. The converts who are not kept in service in India, cease to be converts. That is about the entire matter in a nutshell. As to the way of converting, it is absolutely absurd. The money the missionaries bring is accepted. And so the young missionaries will hang about the end of a famine and give a starving native 5 shillings, and there you have him, a ready-made Christian; take him. . . . The only band of converts around each missionary is composed of those dependent upon him for a living. They have to be Christians or starve.[21]

This recognizable rhetoric about insincere conversions, supposedly for material benefits, had been circulating in the Indian public sphere from Rammohan Roy onwards. Brahmabandhab was profoundly aware of the constraints that his personal faith put on his desire to be an active and public part of the Indian nationalist movement. The knowledge that his one-time friend and idol Vivekananda believed that Indian Christian converts were merely performing conversion for material reasons must also have hurt him deeply.

Even for those revolutionaries who were in fact Hindu, the mere suggestion that they had Christian sympathies could be perceived as an act of treason against the motherland. For example, in the colonial intelligence officer Godfrey Denham's report on the Jugantar group of revolutionaries led by Aurobindo Ghosh and his younger brother Barin, we find mention of a curious incident that led to dissension. Aurobindo and Barin were called "'Christians,' in the heat of the argument" by the editor of the *Jugantar* periodical, Nikhileshwar Roy Moulik, which "caused a distinct coolness" and a rift in the ranks of the revolutionaries and their associates.[22] This was presumably a reference to Aurobindo's anglicized upbringing and education, because there is no evidence that he ever considered conversion to Christianity. In fact, in a recent (controversial) biography, Peter Heehs says that talk of Christian theology had bored a young Aurobindo to tears at his school in the hill station Darjeeling.[23] Calling him and, by association, his brother Christians was merely synonymous with calling them traitors to the cause of national independence. In order to find acceptance within this hostile environment for Christians in the emergent anticolonial movement while maintaining his own faith, Brahmabandhab must certainly have faced a crisis of identity.

Upadhyay's writings for the *Sandhya* consistently emphasized his driving conviction that Indian self-respect could only be regained through a relentless masculine espousal of violent resistance in service of the divine feminine figure of the country imagined as the Mother Goddess. Two events precipitated the changes that effectively made the monk into a Hindu-Catholic political theologian of armed violence. First, Brahmabandhab's friend Vivekananda—the inspiration for the national revival of masculine neo-Hinduism—died suddenly on July 4, 1902, at the age of thirty-nine. His death acutely affected Brahmabandhab, whose program of active involvement in Indian politics evolved partly from his desire to complete what he saw as Vivekananda's unfinished mission of spreading Vedanta in India and abroad. Manoranjan Guha quotes Brahmabandhab himself:

> As soon as I heard the news—it seemed as if a knife pierced me right in my heart. Once the profundity of grief had lessened somewhat, I thought, how will Vivekananda's mission be continued? . . . I would try to perform Vivekananda's *Feringhi-Joy-Brata* [literally ritual to gain victory over the *Feringhi*, i.e., the British]. It is at that moment that I decided to go to *Bilat* [Britain] and establish Vedanta there.[24]

Brahmabandhab recounted his journey to Britain via the continent in a series of delightful epistolary essays entitled *Letters from a Monk Travelling to Foreign Lands*.[25] The financial deprivations he suffered on the journey were offset by the experiences he had on his tour, which led to a renewed belief in the validity of his intellectual and political program. His observations of the British in their own country also cemented his conviction that Hindus still exhibited a superior civilizational quality when it came to interpersonal bonds and the bond of the individual with the soil, the nature, and the inner life of their country. He determined that the basis of British colonial repression in India was vicious racial discrimination. In his fifth letter from Oxford, dated January 16, 1903, Upadhyay wrote in apparent protest against British materialism and the effects of large-scale industrialization. He posited the Hindu ideal of *Niskam Karma* or selfless action, which enabled one to gain true mastery both over the nature of one's soul and the external natural world:

> The whole race is burning with the fires of avarice. Our reformers look at English sovereignty and denigrate their own country, ruing the ill-fated moment of their birth in India. They don't really understand what the Hindu's conquest of Nature [*prakriti*] is about. . . . The Hindu's principle ideal is withdrawal from action [*nibritti*]. The highest disciplined path [*sadhan*] for the Hindu is to conquer Nature without selfish desire [*niskam*].[26]

In the tenth epistle, "Letter from the Monk Returned from His Travels Abroad," written after his return to Calcutta and dated September 7, 1903, Brahmabandhab recounted his impressions of British mores and people:

> The belief is gradually taking hold among most Europeans that the white races (*svetanga jati*) are the best among humankind, that other peoples (*jati*)—the light-skinned, the dark and the black (*gaur, shyam o krishna*)—have been born to serve them. This desire for overlordship is gradually increasing, and betokens a demonic attitude. It has brought, and will bring, a great deal of harm to the world. And it is difficult to express how much damage it will cause to India if it gains in strength . . . because India has lost sight of herself (*atmabismriti*) at present. . . . Is there anything more shameful than this?[27]

The letters make it clear that Brahmabandhab had thought about developing a mechanism that could reverse the British intellectual colonialization of the Indians. This would be done, for example, through a sustained system of popularizing the teachings of Indian literature and philosophy to students at Oxford and Cambridge Universities. He tried hard to have a professorship of Indian philosophy established at the University of Cambridge, with the stipulation that the professor had to be of Indian nationality. The scheme ultimately failed because the funds could not be raised.[28] Reversing British racial discrimination (which Brahmabandhab felt was based on a false sense of civilizational superiority), along with ending the intellectual and political alienation of Indians, became one of the central tenets of Brahmabandhab's political ideology. He wanted to revive a sense of self-respect among Indians by removing all vestiges of legitimacy from Britain's rule of India, which had been justified as a civilizing mission. The effort to establish India's moral and civilizational superiority over Britain would pervade Brahmabandhab's political rhetoric in his subsequent career.

Brahmabandhab found his great purpose after the declaration of the partition of the Bengal Province into east (predominantly Muslim) and west (predominantly Hindu) Bengal in 1904. Although the British government justified the act on the basis of administrative efficiency, most Bengalis saw it as a move based on religious demographics and aimed at creating communal disharmony. The viceroy of India, Lord Curzon, had called the administrative measure a "settled fact," and despite a tumultuous public response carried it out in 1905. India's political leaders suspected that the partition was another colonial move to enforce the British political principle of divide et impera, undertaken to weaken the united voices of Bengalis. Bengalis protested en masse when the partition was declared. British administrators found that these Bengalis—especially from the middle, upper-middle, and upper classes, mostly urban, hitherto stereotyped as effeminate and sly, the most anglicized and modernized Indians—suddenly proved to be particularly unmanageable imperial subjects.[29] Curzon's home secretary Herbert Hope Risley more or less confirmed the move was political in two notes analyzing the critiques of the partition written on February 7 and December 6, 1904: "'Bengal united is a power; Bengal divided will pull in several different ways. . . . One of our main objects is to split up and thereby weaken a sold body of opponents to our rule.'—that is, curbing the growing dominance of middle-class Bengali Hindus in the British administration as well as in opposition to colonial rule."[30] The move was protested by the galaxy political leaders, including Surendranath Banerjee, Bipin Chandra Pal, Gopalkrishna Gokhale, Ashwinikumar Dutta, Motilal Ghosh, Rabindranath Tagore, and his niece Sarala Devi. Lokmanya Bal Gangadhar Tilak, Lala Lajpat Rai, Dinshaw Wacha, Madan Mohan Malviya, and other Congress leaders supported the move to boycott British goods and services and the programs of picketing and civil disobedience that Bengal's political leadership had undertaken to protest the partition. The period between 1904 and 1907, when Brahmabandhab charted the course of the anticolonial protests in Bengal through his editorials in *Sandhya,* was known as the *swadeshi* or "own country" movement. Characterized by revolutionary terrorist violence as well as boycotts and pickets, the participation of the common people of Bengal in this mass movement would foreshadow the mass nationalist movements of the later Gandhian era in terms of the sheer number of Indians who played a part in these anticolonial movements.

The revolutionary terrorism that began in Bengal as a form of protest against the partition, or the *Banga Bhanga,* slowly gained widespread support among educated Bengali youth.[31] It was an espousal of radical political extremism that depended on two different political ideologies. The first was an ideology of self-strengthening, or gaining *atmashakti,* which would enable Indians to offer passive resistance to British rule, a movement that could bring about the participation of India's masses.[32] The second involved armed resistance to British repression by a "daring minority" who would embrace violent means and not flinch from bloodshed in response to colonial violence. Brahmabandhab was one of the pioneering intellectuals who initiated this second ideology as a means of gaining *swaraj* or self-governance from the British colonizers. He worked closely with Aurobindo Ghose, the great ideologue of anticolonial resistance in Bengal, as well as with his younger brother Barin. Brahmabandhab was also friends with the extremist Congress politician Bipin Pal, Satish Chandra Mukherjee of the "Dawn Society," and Bhupendranath Dutta, who was Vivekananda's younger brother. All of these men were well known in British surveillance records as founding members of the radical extremist *samitis* or associations that believed in armed revolution as the only way to overthrow British rule in India.[33] For example, Bhupendranath (or Bhupen, as he was widely known) was suspected of having authored a series of widely circulated seditionist pamphlets titled *Sonar Bangla* (Golden Bengal), which exhorted the rural Bengali peasantry, both Hindu and Muslim, to rise together in armed insurrection against colonial rule. He had narrowly avoided prosecution for sedition in late 1906 and early 1907.[34]

The next person suspected of writing these incendiary pamphlets was Brahmabandhab Upadhyay himself. Their hypernationalistic and profoundly emotional rhetoric was very similar to his own prose style. Bhupendranath Dutta, Abinash Chandra Bhattacharya, and *Sandhya*'s manager Saradacharan Sen, all close associates of Brahmabandhab, refuted this suspicion. However, the incident clarifies that Brahmabandhab and the *Sandhya* had long been under surveillance for seditious activity. The British government had just been waiting for an opportune moment to arrest him under charges of sedition. Uma and Haridas Mukhopadhyay quote the chief secretary to the lieutenant governor of Bengal, the infamous Sir Andrew Fraser, advising against Brahmabandhab's prosecution for the *Sonar Bangla* pamphlets: "If we want to prosecute, I believe there is hardly a week in which the *Sandhya* does not publish an article which would justify our doing so."[35]

The colonial police officers charged with suppressing revolutionary activity in Bengal suspected Brahmabandhab of much more than writing seditious articles. Indeed, they clearly felt that Brahmabandhab was far more deeply and practically involved in acts of revolutionary terrorism in Bengal. This is made clear in Denham's report on the Jugantar group, compiled in 1908, almost a year after Brahmabandhab's death.[36] For example, Denham mentions Brahmabandhab's associate Kartik Chandra Dutta, who was in charge of recruiting members ready to commit dacoities on British treasuries and on arms depots in order to supply the revolutionaries of the Jugantar group. Brahmabandhab had presided over a ritual that celebrated the bonding in brotherhood of young revolutionaries at the *Sandhya* office in late 1906 and early 1907, in which he declared Kartik as the leader of the group and made the other participants swear to protect him with their lives. Kartik had printed the first recipes for making picric-acid bombs in the *Jugantar* periodical. According to Denham, Brahmabandhab incited Kartik to throw one at a railway booking clerk who had refused to support a strike by his fellow employees against the East Indian Railway in 1906. Kartik apparently refused to commit this murder, and Brahmabandhab handed the task to another revolutionary associate, Keshab Dey.[37] A large number of Brahmabandhab's close friends and associates were mentioned in Denham's report. It is impossible to say whether the colonial police's suspicions regarding Brahmabandhab's active participation in violent revolutionary activity beyond his editorial activism were in fact true. But it is clear that Brahmabandhab, for a period of five years, occupied an important position in the revolutionary networks of the Jugantar group and was respected and loved for his singular commitment to India's freedom.

THE APOLOGETICS OF HINDU NATIONALISM

Despite the suspicions of Denham and the Indian police and intelligence services, Brahmabandhab Upadhyay continued to write articles in *Sandhya* urging Bengalis to rise up in armed rebellion against the British. He used the language of the streets, not the chaste or *sadhu Bangla* that most mainstream vernacular periodicals used. One of the most recognizable aspects of his rhetoric and style was an almost obsessive pleasure in punning and onomatopoeia. The articles were deeply steeped in the ideology of worship of the motherland and took a martial attitude toward confrontation with the British authorities. His language was vituperative, shrill, arousing: in virtually every article written by him that I have found, he issued a direct threat against the British administration and threatened the use of sticks, stones, guns, and bombs to commit violence against the oppressive British and their treacherous Indian collaborators. His apologetics, as mentioned earlier, were also steeped in a Hindu social and cultural sensibility, with little of the nuance and sensitivity toward other religions and cultures found in his more refined essays and articles from an earlier period.

The Hindu scripture, the Gita, seems to have exerted a strong influence Brahmabandhab's political journalism and his personal ethos. One of the most famous stanzas in the Gita describes the body as a tattered cloth that covers the radiance of the soul. Just as old and used clothes are thrown away, the body can be discarded innumerable times within the Hindu cosmological cycle of rebirths. Therefore, Brahmabandhab saw the possibility of serving one's motherland with complete and reckless devotion through multiple lifetimes, and bearing multiple deaths, until one's destined work was complete. This ethics of loving self-sacrifice in the service of one's motherland was strengthened by the other influence on Brahmabandhab—that of Bankimchandra Chatterjee, who pioneered the Bengali Hindu ethos of masculine nationalism, which is espoused most famously in his novel *Anandamath.* In this path of service, the most important element was connection to one's motherland and one's own people. This was a connection that Brahmabandhab felt could only be realized through bonds of *jati* or community. This is why Brahmabandhab's self-identification as a Bengali Brahmin even after conversion is striking but not surprising. The cause of his motherland's liberty meant that he had to find his own place within the imagined community of both Bengali *bhadralok* and the less educated or ordinary *chotolok.* This community, in western Bengal, was predominantly Hindu. It seems that Brahmabandhab's imagined community and nation were, socioculturally if not demographically, Hindu. Therefore, even if he was a faithful Catholic and a celibate monk in his private life, he had to practice a strict mental reservation in order to sustain the original social and cultural bonds that tied him to his community of birth. Like Krishnamohan Banerjee and Gyanendramohan Tagore before him, Brahmabandhab may have been attempting to establish a hyphenated identity—one that would allow him, within certain constraints, to be both Brahmin and Catholic. The struggle, however, does not seem to have been resolved in his lifetime.

In particular, Brahmabandhab tried to renew close ties with the community of his birth and faith by undertaking a public performance of the ritual of *prayaschitta* in August 1907. Both Brahmachari Rewachand Animananda and Julius Lipner—his first and most recent biographers, respectively—stress that although he made a public performance of Indian belonging through modes of dress and the wearing of the sacred thread after his penance, he had not abandoned his personal faith in Christian salvation. Yet to many of his contemporary associates, like his colleague Kartik Nan and biographer Prabodh Chandra Singha, Brahmabandhab's act of penance meant that he had embraced his Indian and Hindu civilizational roots completely again. He seemed to have done so by tying his own performance of political allegiances and ideologies even closer to Hindu sociocultural norms, and by using Hindu affective imagery in his own patriotic writings. This return to his roots, for those who believed he had renounced Christianity, was signaled by his renewed wearing of the Brahminical sacred thread, which he had cast off many years ago, at his first conversion and baptism.[38] Brahmabandhab's penance, and his motivations in performing it, would later become highly contested among the crafters of his posthumous memory.

Rewachand was Brahmabandhab's student and disciple, one of his closest associates, who had observed firsthand his evolution from Catholic monk to firebrand Indian patriot. In his biography, he noted that in 1925—eighteen years after Brahmabandhab's death—he interviewed the two principal actors involved in Brahmabandhab's *prayaschitta* ritual of 1907. According to Rewachand, both of these men—Mokshadacharan Samadhyayi and Pandit Panchanan Tarkaratna—insisted that the penance was to atone not for his Christian faith but for his social transgressions: specifically, his 1903 crossing of the *kala pani* (black waters) in his journey from India to Europe and his breaking of commensality taboos by eating with the *mlechchha* British men and women. Tarkaratna, who presided over the ritual, was a Brahmin from Bhatpara and an authority on both the *Raghunandana* and *Mitakshara* norms of *prayaschitta.* When Rewachand asked if Upadhyay's ritual had included the formula of *Swadharma Tyagam* or "I renounce my [current] faith" based on the *Raghunandana* system, Tarkaratna reportedly said that "Upadhyay never spoke against Christianity nor had he any intention of giving up his faith."[39] Lipner supports this understanding of the penance, citing one of Upadhyay's own essays titled "Social Penance." Published in the *Twentieth Century* periodical on July 31, 1901, it read, "What is *Prayaschitta* or social penance according to Hindu law-givers? . . . If a Hindu enters into any social alliance with aliens calculated to injure the integrity of his race, society has every right to impose corrective chastisements on such a truant. . . . Social penances do not necessarily involve the questions of religious faith."[40] Of course, such theological hairsplitting was incomprehensible to Upadhyay's social and political network. Rewachand's own report of his investigations, undertaken almost two decades after Upadhyay's death and dependent on the unreliable memories of old men, expresses bewilderment about Brahmabandhab's reasons for performing the act and about the contents of the ritual. What we do know is that Brahmabandhab resumed wearing the sacred Brahminical thread that he had discarded on his first conversion in 1890. This shift in his public self-fashioning was reflected in his editorials for the *Sandhya,* especially the three articles that were officially cited as the cause for his indictment for sedition.[41]

Brahmabandhab's scornful rhetoric regarding British rule and British people was precisely calculated, as was his use of the impolite diction of the non-elite but literate Bengali section of the public sphere. According to Prabodh Singha, Brahmabandhab's use of the rustic language of rural Bengal was a calculated political move: the straightforward, unsophisticated diction was emblematic of the raw honesty of patriotism that Brahmabandhab practiced and hoped would be adopted by the common masses of India.[42] Even in his earliest writing for the *Sandhya,* he aimed to reverse the intellectual and spiritual alienation of Indians from their cultural traditions through 150 years of British colonial influence. By a liberal application of nationalist xenophobia, and the mythic reconstruction of a nationalist history of resistance, Brahmabandhab sought to realign Indians' relationship with their own land, their own society, their own nation. The rejuvenation of that nation, he argued, required Indians to drive out the British and proudly repossess their *desh,* which they would then defend by the strength of their arms.

For Brahmabandhab, India was the secure *kot* of and for Indians. This meant that one's country, one's *swadesh,* was one's own jurisdiction, which had to be guarded from unwanted insurrection by the alien powers of the British. Brahmabandhab characterized this space as one of belonging to and owning one's country in equal measure.[43] His belief in reaffirming and reemphasizing the relationship between Indians and their own land—the India of villages, where colonial modernity had not made a visible impression—is expressed beautifully in one of his articles for the *Sandhya.* Published on August 15, 1907, this piece was titled "The Proper Way to Meet an Antagonist." In it, he argued that it was in rural India, that India of the utopic village, which Brahmabandhab equates with the goddess Chandi (a form of Durga) herself—where the bond of men to their own country was a living, organic connection of love and devotion—that true resistance could be offered to British rule:

> A quarrel has broken between the *Feringhis* and ourselves. We did not bring on the quarrel; it is the *Feringhi* himself who has proclaimed war against *Swadeshi.* . . . But if in the halls and courtyards of our Chandimandaps (an outhouse where the goddess Durga is worshipped), we read the *Chandi* . . . who is like our Mother, whose water is sweet, whose fruits are sweet and who is dark green with crops, and if the *Feringhi* enters there and attacks us there, you will see whether or not a response is got from the country. Here it is the questions of our jurisdiction, our rights, and those rights were given us not by man but by God. If the *Feringhi* makes trouble inside this jurisdiction, in regard to these God-given rights, he will get thrashed and is sure to get worsted.[44]

In Brahmabandhab's eyes, the urban metropolis of Calcutta was far more emphatically marked by the colonial encounter than rural villages—and had therefore produced an elite Indian intelligentsia whose political rhetoric was shaped by the colonial influence. The stance of this modern and anglicized intelligentsia on nationalism was therefore merely reactionary and thus ineffective. Their anticolonial activism was corrupted by their very debts to the same colonial modernity from which they took their progressive ideologies. It was a project doomed to failure from its very inception. Rural India bore fainter external marks of the changes produced by the colonial governance project—and in its soul, this rural India retained an active link to older precolonial political and philosophical traditions. Brahmabandhab believed that a revival of those precolonial modes of political engagement would also revive Indians' latent powers of self-possession and self-respect.

Brahmabandhab's understanding of Bengal's history echoed Bankimchandra Chatterjee's insistence on *bahubol*—resistance to injustice through the power of arms, and the obtainment of social, religious, and political autonomy for Hindus through the exercise of that power. But for Bankimchandra, the operation of this power of arms was limited to the history of precolonial India and lost in the throes of colonial modernity, as Ranajit Guha has analyzed. Brahmabandhab, however, envisioned the rejuvenation of this power of *bahubol* in Bengalis in the immediate present, in resisting the alienating colonial force exerted by the British to enact a partition of Bengal.[45] His approach was an ethnography of the British imperialists, which slyly parodied colonial classification of India and Indians into many different groups with predetermined racial, social, and cultural characteristics, based predominantly on religion and caste distinctions. The acme of Brahmabandhab's racial classification of the alien colonizers can be found in his essay on the term *Feringhi,* a word he used consistently to refer to the British, singlehandedly transforming it into a pejorative racial slur that passed into common revolutionary idiom. In his article "The Meaning of the Word *Feringhi,*" in the *Sandhya* of November 23, 1906, ten months before his arrest for sedition, Brahmabandhab said:

> Take first the *fi;* the *Feringhis* are men who demand a fee (money) on any and every occasion, who send in bills to their parents (i.e., ask for a fee) for having boarded with them, who in return for a fee, write letters of release to men who have seduced their wives. Take next the *feri.* There is no nation of *feriwallas* (hawkers) on earth like the *Feringhis.* If you refuse to pay your fee, and to buy the goods he is hawking (*feri*-ing) about, he will make you go backwards and forwards (*fera-firi*) from death's door.... The *firanghis* have *rang* (fun) also in the sense they have a funny way of killing people off, and

> then they call that spreading the light. Under the stress of their funny way of spreading the light, the aborigines of America and Australia have attained eternal effulgence.[46]

Brahmabandhab's obsessive love of punning notwithstanding, the scathingly satirical article masks a comprehensive critique of colonial rule and the actors who enforced it in India. He heaped scorn on the commercial venality of the British, who masked motives of colonial expansion within the guise of the civilizing mission while enacting a program of global genocide in the name of enlightenment. Brahmabandhab enumerated these critiques in a language of crude derision and humor, one that could be appreciated by "the shopkeepers, traders, clerks, rent-collectors, teachers and students, laborers and coachmen, . . . landlords, tenants, the poor, the educated, the women in the zenana"—precisely those sections of the Bengali middle class who were not among the English-educated *bhadraloks*.[47]

It is through these non-elite Indians that Brahmabandhab saw the real force of resistance to colonialism working. They would be the foot soldiers who would build his cherished *swaraj-garh* or "fortress of independence."[48] Moreover, Brahmabandhab's critique of these colonial modes of intellectual and imperial domination made it clear that the Indian way of life held inherent moral and cultural superiority. This patriotic difference had to be reinforced for the illusion of colonial supremacy to break apart. Needless to say, this essay found its way into the *Reports on Native Newspapers* (hereafter *RNN*), that great official surveillance institution employed by the colonial state against the vernacular press in India. It alerted the colonial administration to the fact that Brahmabandhab's rabble-rousing was achieving new heights of mischief. These essays cemented his reputation as a great seditionist to the British and a great patriotic hero to the Indians.

In fact, his vituperative power reached a pinnacle of stunning intensity in two articles published on August 20 and 23, 1907, "The *Feringhi* Is Left Witless by the Booming of Sedition" and "The Darlings Will Surely Take Me to Sri Vrindaban."[49] In these articles, Brahmabandhab moved away from his usual depiction of the *Feringhi* in tones of condescending superiority. He usually branded the British as morally and culturally inferior to Indians and addressed them patronizingly as poor relations, often pejoratively calling them brother-in-law—*shala*. In these essays, however, Brahmabandhab now openly caricatured the British as bestial. In his article of August 20, he compared them to feral dogs who would wander into the devout Hindu householder's kitchen and despoil the food and cooking utensils. When threatened with sticks, the dogs barked and snapped at the householder but also ran away. Brahmabandhab said that the false bravado of the British, their efforts to despoil the economy and national life of Bengal through the partition of the province, had to be met with the sticks and stones of *swadeshi* boycott and picketing. He reasoned that the colonial administration was reinforcing the bogeyman of "sedition" because the British were terrified by the upsurge of anticolonial sentiments and acts of radical armed violence against the administration. It was both tragic and funny to Brahmabandhab that Bengalis were being repressed for merely trying to protect what was theirs from British thievery, as the British continued to pretend that they were civilizing the Indians. He warned the British administration that Bengalis would give up their bodies and souls, unafraid to die in the protection of their *kot,* their *desh*:[50]

> All this bustle and stir in making arrests, in the pretext of sedition is nothing but the dying grin of the wily *Feringhi.* We feel that our day is now come and that the day of *Feringhi*'s end is drawing near. We have all found out that the *Feringhi* has trespassed unnoticed into our jurisdiction and have all awoken and are serving him right by means of *Swadeshi* and boycott. This bustle of sedition has driven the *Feringhi* to his wit's end.

The article of August 23 expressed unremitting disgust at British pretensions of racial superiority. Brahmabandhab derided the opinion of English newspapers like *The Englishman* and *The Civil and Military Gazette* of Punjab, which suggested in their editorials that the British needed to practice strong racial apartheid against the seditious Bengalis. Bengalis needed to be barred and ostracized from administrative positions in the British colonial government, where they had enjoyed nearly unchallenged preference for almost a century and half, as punishment for their outrageous opposition. A precursor to these "seditious" articles, "Ekhane theke gechi premer daye" [Here we have been enmeshed by the bonds of love], offers a brief but startling glimpse of Brahmabandhab the sophisticated theologian, Brahmabandhab the friend of Vivekananda, and Brahmabandhab the ardent follower of Bankimchandra Chatterjee. Instead of the crude humor and rough and idiomatic style of his usual journalistic endeavors, Brahmabandhab here established a spiritual foundation to his program of *swaraj.* By this point the police had made several searches of the *Sandhya* office, and Brahmabandhab had already burned most of his correspondence and other sensitive materials relating to the periodical at the great cremation ground in Nimtala. It was a symbolic bonfire of any remaining vestige of fear at the colonial administration's effort to root out sedition in the vernacular press through coercion and repressive measures. So much of Brahmabandhab's public persona depended on his performance of a fearless and singular patriotic fervor. The bonfire at Nimtala, a symbolic ritual of purification, only enhanced his image as an ascetic patriot of the motherland.

Uma and Haridas Mukherjee, in their study of Brahmabandhab, drew a clear line connecting him to Aurobindo and Bipin Pal, noting that all three of these early heroes of the *swadeshi* movement defined anticolonial resistance as a "spiritual movement."[51] Brahmabandhab had himself written in the *Sandhya* that the hope of *swaraj* was also the hope of *Nirban,* the final liberation from the cycle of rebirth.[52] This is apparent in the article of August 13, 1907, the first "seditious" article:

> We have said over and over again that we are not *Swadeshi* only, so far as our salt and sugar are concerned. What we want is the emancipation of India. Our aim is how India may be free, how the stranger may be driven from our homes, how the continuity of learning, the civilization and the system of the *rishis* may be preserved. . . . Heaven we do not want; deliverance we seek not. Are we afraid of your cannons and guns? Arm, brothers, arm; the day of deliverance is near. We have heard the Voice, and we cannot fail to see the chains of India removed before we die.

Therefore, irrespective of his personal Christian faith, this affective bond tied Brahmabandhab to the wider cultural and social resources of his birth and his intellectual network. It was one that placed the highest demands on his loyalty and his allegiance. Within these numinous bonds, the superimposed nomos of Anglo-colonial law could find no place. Brahmabandhab wrote:

> Can you intimidate us? Our power is not human; it is divine. Your overweening pride is due to your possessing a few cannons and guns. This pride had led you to attempt to spoil our *Swadeshi* vow. Just see to what plight you are reduced. . . . We have all the advantages of the ancient greatness of India on our side. We are immortal.[53]

Brahmabandhab was charged with inciting sedition under the Indian Penal Code, section 124A, for these three editorials published on August 13, 20, and 23, 1907. There was no doubt among his readers, associates, or the colonial surveillance machinery that these articles had consciously sought to incite

Indians of all classes to hatred and contempt of the colonial powers. The articles in the *Sandhya* regularly found their way into the seditious newspapers section in the *RNN*.[54] Brahmabandhab's detention was inevitable. He was arrested on September 10 and put on trial immediately. A telegram from the viceroy in Simlah to the office in London succinctly summarizes the situation:

> From Viceroy, Simla 3rd September 1907, received at the London Office 2.41 PM: "*Sandhya* newspaper, Calcutta, is being prosecuted under section 124A of the Indian Penal Code for publishing articles entitled 'This time we are caught in the mesmerism of love'; 'The true significance of activity in making arrests for sedition'; and 'The *Feringhi*'s kindness,' in its issues of the 13th, 20th and 21st August respectively. The last two articles are reproduced on pages 860 to 862 of the Report on native papers in Bengal for the week ending 24th August."[55]

As the vehicle for his particular brand of nationalist apologetics, Brahmabandhab's journalism reflects his vision of the spirit and form of the *swadesh*—the Indian ethical polity. By 1904, he felt that this vision could be realized only with the intellectual alienation of occidental categories of modernity and enlightenment pedagogies, which he saw as antithetical to what Sugata Bose calls the "rich legacies of precolonial patriotism." Inspired by Bankimchandra Chatterjee's re-imagination of the nation as the (Hindu) motherland, revolutionaries and Bengali nationalists of the *swadeshi* era had accepted as a revolutionary tenet the identification of the nation as the Mother to be worshipped, protected, and saved. Brahmabandhab reconfigured the ethics and politics of violent resistance to colonial repression into an emotive, affectionate relationship of communitarian service that demanded the performance of sacrificial duties.[56] He defined one's allegiance to one's motherland as one's true personal faith, irrespective of religious or caste affiliations.

Bipin Pal, his closest associate in the years 1904–1907, defined this urgent new call of service to the motherland as one demanded by humanity. He said, echoing Brahmabandhab, "The new patriotism in India has become a new religion to vast numbers of its people."[57] In framing Bengalis' ethical duty to offer violent resistance to the partition of their homeland, Brahmabandhab adapted Bankimchandra's ideas about nation-making or *jati-pratisthan* to his political program, by squarely applying *bahubol,* or the strength of everyday resistance, to the *swadeshi* movement.[58]

However, Brahmabandhab's political theology also had another important dimension: it parlayed communitarian identity into the construction of an imagined community dedicated to anticolonial resistance, which would bring about self-rule or *swaraj.* This aspect of his political theology also appears in the *Sandhya,* in an article titled "Beware While There Is Yet Time":

> We want *Swaraj.* This *Swaraj* is not a *Swaraj* for Hindus only or for Musalmans [Muslims] or Buddhists or Parsis only. We want *Swaraj* for all the sons of Mother India that there are. If any race or community of the country is shut out from this treasure then we shall not have got genuine *Swaraj.* . . . We cannot promote the interests of the Hindus at the cost of those of the Musalmans, or the interests of the Musalmans at the cost of the Hindus. What we want is that Hindus and Musalmans both should bring about this *Swaraj* in unison and concert. We want *Swaraj,* we do not want subjection to the *Feringhis.* . . . We want *Swaraj* and we must have it.[59]

The repetition of the word *Swaraj* in this piece is a characteristic example of Brahmabandhab's rhetorical style: it is a chant of the desire for freedom, contrasted with the grief of unfreedom under British imperial rule. Brahmabandhab believed that this grief led to a soul bond among Indians, forged by the realities of a deep collective pain common to those who had been brutally colonized. In other words, all Indians, irrespective of personal faith, were actually a part of a community that found its political expressions in idioms of Hindu cultural norms. Perhaps this was also Brahmabandhab's way of resolving the disparity between his own personal faith and his expression of a particular kind of Hindu cultural belonging. Either way, he argued that the indignities Indians had suffered under British subjugation forged unity in a uniquely powerful way. The antidote to the psychological numbness that many Indians felt under the conditions of imperialism, he said, could only be found in revolutionary sacrifice performed by all Indians for the sake of the motherland. Emerging in the early days of extremist revolutionary terrorism in Bengal, his idea transformed how Indians understood both the wounds of political vulnerability under colonialism and the power of affectionate self-sacrifice:

> A powerful alien force has enchained all of India. The suffering caused by these chains is felt equally by all Indians. Formerly, there were many meeting grounds for Indians from different estates—pilgrimage sites, educational

> centers, places of collaborative businesses. Never before, however, was there such a union in shared grief—let our pains be manifested, our wounds show themselves—only the will our countrymen awake.[60]

On one hand, this claim valorized the motherland and the worship of one's own country as an embodiment of divinity. On the other, it was tempered by deeply felt affection and tenderness, which justified terrorist violence as a sanctified ritual sacrifice. This sacrifice was enabled by the familial tenderness one felt toward one's country. It must be remembered that Bengalis use the affectionate appellation of *Ma* to refer both to mothers and to young daughters in need of parental protection—a dimension that finds one of its rare subdued political expositions in some of Brahmabandhab's writings. One of the most poignant visual renditions of this tenderness can be seen in Abanindranath Tagore's famous 1905 portrayal of *Banga-mata* (Mother Bengal) or *Bharat-mata* (Mother India), which imagines the motherland as a young woman in the saffron clothing of a *sannyasi.* It was reportedly inspired by both his own daughter's face and the ascetic form of Sister Nivedita (Margaret Noble), who would also inspire Tagore's novel based on Brahmabandhab Upadhyay, *Gora,* as we will see later.[61] Patriotism was based on a love of one's country that echoed familial tenderness and therefore could be weaponized into self-sacrificial protectiveness as well. The depiction of this idealized vision of one's *swadesh* reminds us that it is familial love as well as a notion of honor that moved early revolutionaries to sing of the motherland and offer their lives in sacrifice. Brahmabandhab Upadhyay was the first Indian to popularize this vision of the motherland in which patriotic emotions merged with tenderness.[62]

THE MYTHOS OF BRAHMABANDHAB UPADHYAY

Returning to the chaotic scenes of the courthouse where he was on trial for sedition, we find Brahmabandhab completely exhausted. The physical and mental trauma of standing in the docks for almost six hours a day in enervating heat had aggravated his health issues. He was suffering from a hernia, which now took an acute turn. Magistrate Kingsford had not offered his nemesis the courtesy of a chair, and Brahmabandhab found it beneath his dignity to request one from the *kasai kazi.* He fainted in the streets one day due to the unbearable pain. The decision was made to operate on the hernia, a major surgery in those days. He left the home of his friend Kartik Chandra Nan on the evening of October 21, 1907, to be admitted to Campbell Medical Hospital. Barefooted, bareheaded, and wearing the Hindu sacred thread, he entered "Brahmin" in the hospital register under the column for caste. The entry for religion was left empty. "Three times he was asked to state his religion, but he refused to comply with the request," his biographer Rewachand wrote in 1940—perhaps echoing the trials of Peter during the betrayal of Jesus at the Garden of Gethsemane.[63] The operation, performed by Dr. Mrigendralal Mitra, was deemed a success, and for the first few days of his convalescence Brahmabandhab seemed to be on the mend.

Magistrate Douglas Kingsford asked for the opinion of the superintendent of Campbell Medical Hospital on how soon Brahmabandhab could return to court and was advised that the patient would not be able to attend his trial for at least thirty days. Kingsford was compelled to postpone the trial until November 19, 1907. In the meantime, further searches of the *Sandhya* office were ordered, and Brahmabandhab's manager Saradacharan Sen and his printer Haricharan Das were remanded to custody without bail. The radical newspaper *Bande Mataram* (I Praise the Mother[land]) reported on October 25, 1907, "This is the first time in the history of sedition trials in Bengal that the accused are refused bail."[64] The second sedition case was lodged against the *Sandhya* on the October 26. Brahmabandhab found a police guard attending his hospital bed. He was restless and saddened by the treatment of the *Sandhya* employees—especially Saradacharan Sen, who was devoted to Brahmabandhab and to the periodical, even though he suffered from abject poverty and earned nothing from his service. His tenacious selflessness had won him Brahmabandhab's love and admiration. These troubles took their toll on Brahmabandhab's mental and physical health. Rewachand reported that Brahmabandhab seemed increasingly fatigued, although he still conversed cheerfully with visitors. Rewachand added that Brahmabandhab said to his friend Vaswani, reflecting on his checkered career, "Wonderful have been the vicissitudes of my life: wonderful has been my faith."[65]

Brahmabandhab soon began to display symptoms of tetanus or lockjaw, including seizures that began on the fourth day after the surgery. Possibly due to infection at the incision site, his case worsened, despite some efforts by attendant doctors to administer medication—and soon the presence of trismus confirmed that this was a death sentence; he would not recover. According to Rewachand, Brahmabandhab, in the unbearable agonies of lockjaw, kept murmuring, "O Thakur," or "Oh God."[66] Rewachand insisted that "Thakur" was Upadhyay's characteristic way of referring to Jesus Christ. He cites Kartik

Nan and other worshippers who had seen Brahmabandhab at his habitual devotions to emphasize Brahmabandhab's continuing private fealty to his Catholicism to the end of his life.[67] Seeing his agony, the doctors wished to administer chloroform. Brahmabandhab said he wanted to die while fully conscious and refused palliatives. Trying to introduce a catheter, the doctors inadvertently broke his teeth. Blood poured over his face and hands, as the muscle spasms continued to worsen. Brahmabandhab was pronounced dead at 8:30 a.m. on Sunday, October 27, 1907. He was forty-six years, eight months, and fourteen days old.

The hospital administration required Upadhyay's body to be moved, as tense rumors about foul play by the British government and doctors began circulating on the streets of Calcutta.[68] If last rites are an indicator of the deceased's religious faith, Brahmabandhab did not die the death of a true Catholic. The manner of his death, the absence of the rites of extreme unction, and the public cremation of his body with all due Hindu rituals reinforce the image of him as a man who had renounced his Christian faith and had reentered the fold of Hindu *Varnashrama Dharma.* The contemporary narratives celebrate his last journey to the great Hindu cremation ground of Nimtala—where he had previously consigned the sensitive documents of his journal *Sandhya.* Brahmabandhab's body was consumed by the flames of a Hindu cremation instead of being laid to rest in a Christian believer's grave. These narratives are also the first records of a battle that was brewing for the appropriation of his legacies, as they offered competing ideological justifications for Brahmabandhab's last rites: some asserted that he died in the socially accepted faith of his ancestors, while others found him steadfast in his privately observed Christian faith. For example, Rewachand's biography blamed the performance of Hindu cremation rites on the mounting confusion and the frenzy of mass mourning that took place after Brahmabandhab's death. Just as Brahmabandhab's body was being carried out, the Catholic parish priest Friar Berghmans arrived to aid Rewachand in performing the last rites. Brahmabandhab had been staying at Kartik Chandra Nan's home before his hospitalization. Nan and Vaswani, another follower of Brahmabandhab, apparently took control of his mortal remains and stopped Berghmans and Rewachand from performing the burial rites.

According to Rewachand, Vaswani called him a troublemaker in front of the already emotional crowd that had gathered at the gates of the hospital, where Brahmabandhab's body lay in the shade of a tree. They asked Rewachand, "Have you any writ from him [i.e., Brahmabandhab] that he died a Catholic?"[69] This was a particularly manipulative question under the circumstances. It capitalized on the majoritarian sentiment that already saw Brahmabandhab as a Hindu monk, a successor to Vivekananda, and quietly erased his Catholic identity in death. Although Brahmabandhab himself had never hidden his Catholicism in life, he had never expressed it publicly either. His performance of a patriotic saffron-clad ascetic had been so convincing to those who only saw his public persona that, before any of his Christian associates could intervene, the mourning public had taken away his mortal remains in grand procession. The bier was decked with flowers and carried to the *Sandhya* office on Cornwallis Street, where the crowd swelled to about 5,000 people chanting the revolutionary *swadeshi* slogan, "Bande Mataram" (I praise the mother[land]). The funeral procession then proceeded from Sibnarayan Das Lane, merged onto Cornwallis Street, went past Beadon Street and Bethune Row, where Brahmabandhab had often made speeches, and finally arrived at the great Hindu cremation ground Nimtala *Ghat*. The flame to the pyre was lit by a nephew, Jyoti, and following Hindu funerary customs, ghee and sandalwood were fed to the flames, as befitted the last rites of a great and holy Hindu man.

The news of his death evoked a strange mix of elation and grief in the Bengali public sphere. Brahmabandhab had been a political pioneer in demanding *swaraj* or self-rule for Indians. Brahmabandhab's general attitude of brash opposition to colonial norms, both before and during his trial, combined with his sudden and tragic death, made him an emblem of the national striving toward independence and self-rule. He had declared, when his trial began, that he would not suffer prison at the hands of the British. Prabodh Chandra Singha, who taught at Saraswat Ayatan, the school founded by Brahmabandhab, wrote in his biography of the monk, "The day before he died, he had said to one of his visiting friends, 'The *Feringhi* has no such powers that they can constrain me in jail. I have been called away.'"[70] Aparna Devi, Chittaranjan Das's daughter, reported a similar conversation between him and Brahmabandhab.[71]

This rumor spread like fire. Posthumous narratives repeatedly said that Brahmabandhab, through his great patriotism and the power of his ascetic love for his motherland, had willed himself to death instead of allowing British chains to imprison him. Bhupendranath Dutta, younger brother of Swami Vivekananda, heard the news of Brahmabandhab's death while in Presidency Jail on charges of sedition as one of the editors of the *Jugantar* periodical, the mouthpiece of the revolutionary terrorist organization Anushilan Samiti.

Bipin Chandra Pal was Brahmabandhab's friend but is better known today as one of the triumvirate of the radical faction of Congress leaders known as "Lal Bal Pal." He advocated the boycotting of British goods and pickets and strikes in a bid to economically drain British interests in India, and he had been imprisoned in 1907 for six months for his involvement with the periodical edited by Aurobindo Ghosh, the *Bande Mataram,* and for refusing to testify against Aurobindo. Bipin Pal worked closely with Brahmabandhab, and Brahmabandhab in turn identified with Pal's political views about self-rule. When Pal heard the news of Brahmabandhab's tragic passing, Bhupendranath Dutta writes, he flinched and then quietly said, "Upadhyay *Mahashay* has not died—he has merely discarded this mortal body."[72]

Nationalist newspapers made much of Brahmabandhab's death as well. Rewachand records that Sisir Ghosh, proprietor and editor of the *Amrita Bazar Patrika,* danced with joy when he heard the news: "He has taught the enemies of our freedom a good lesson. He has won a great victory." The *Amrita Bazar Patrika* went on to compare Brahmabandhab to Bhisma, the grand patriarch of the great Indian epic *Mahabharata,* who had the boon of willing his own death—*Ichhya Mrityu.*[73] Brahmabandhab's own periodical, mourning its late editor, printed some of his earlier ruminations on a death proper to an Indian and Hindu Brahmin patriot. These reflections found their way into the *RNN* in due course: "Who can oppress a people in whose view the physical body is so contemptible as to be fit to be thrown away like a piece of a torn rag? Those who think that the body is everything are afraid of oppression. What need I fear as I am a *Bengali Brahmin?*"[74] Reuters reported on the funeral, and it was printed in the evening edition of *The Times* in London on October 28 as well as in its morning edition on October 29, 1907: "Pandit Upadhyay, editor of the *Sandhya,* against whom two charges of sedition were pending, has died. . . . Handbills notifying his death were distributed and broadcast. . . . Never before has a burning *ghat* been a scene of such a demonstration."[75]

The British-Indian colonial press was less charitable about Upadhyay but also relieved at his death. *The Empire* wrote, "With the death of the editor of the *Sandhya,* it is probable that the organ of extremism will promptly cease to pour out its denunciation of the government and of everything that is British. He was the life and soul of that vitriolic publication."[76] Brahmabandhab Upadhyay's polemical writings remade sedition and revolution into seraph lances of political responsibility and spiritual urgency for Bengalis. However, just as in life, his posthumous reputation was divisive. Patriotic mythologies about him began circulating immediately after his death. He was not easily pigeonholed: the paradox of his private Christian faith and public performance as an ascetic and militant Hindu persona left his character as an elusive cipher. Perhaps that is why his legacy has been so amenable to appropriation. His program of reviving a masculine, martial Bengali—and, more broadly, Indian—imagined community did not have a lasting effect on the Indian anticolonial imaginary. The hidden thread of tender love and self-sacrifice in Brahmabandhab's ideology that enabled a devoted service of the motherland was refashioned by Gandhi into a far more acceptable nonviolent ideology of civil resistance in the 1910s, with far more transformative effect. By the 1920s, when Gandhian nonviolence was beginning to gain acceptance as the method of mass anticolonial protest, his ideas were mostly cast aside.

THE POSTHUMOUS LIFE OF BRAHMABANDHAB UPADHYAY

Unlike Vivekananda, Brahmabandhab had not left behind disciples of or adherents to his particular school of thought. Revolutionaries who had worked closely with him and, after his death, with Aurobindo and Barin Ghosh found themselves embroiled in a political firestorm of colonial suppression. As the Denham report on the Jugantar group shows, the young revolutionaries who had accepted the call to arms preached by radical extremist periodicals like the *Jugantar*, the *Bande Mataram*, and the *Sandhya* soon found themselves implicated in either the sedition trials of the Alipore Bomb Conspiracy or the political assassination trial of the Muzaffarpur Case of 1908–1909.[77] Many of these young men (including Kshudiram Bose) were given capital punishment, while others were sentenced to life imprisonment with rigorous labor in the infamous Cellular Jail of Andaman Island (the fate of Barin Ghose, Ullaskar Dutta, and the expert bombmaker Hem Chandra Kanungo). The harsh penitentiary conditions and the torture of prisoners led to suicides, deaths, or insanity, as in the case of Ullaskar.[78] They returned to India after decades, transformed by their suffering under the terrible conditions. Aurobindo himself retired to the French colony of Pondicherry in 1910 to evade capture by the British. The remaining few who remembered Brahmabandhab's contribution to the *swadeshi* movement had either never supported armed extremism and chauvinistic nationalism as viable models of anticolonial political action, like Rabindranath Tagore, or had shifted in their own ideological leanings toward a less strident form of a federal nation, like Bipin

Pal. For this reason, it is instructive to compare how Tagore and Pal in particular narrated Brahmabandhab's life. Their assessments of Brahmabandhab's contributions to the anticolonial struggle in Bengal are diametrically opposed and paint radically different pictures of Brahmabandhab as a person, while also claiming his posthumous legacy to suit their own political opinions. Pal considered Brahmabandhab to be a pioneering figure of Indian nationalism of the *swadeshi* era who had advocated a move away from Western notions of patriotism preferred by Indian intellectuals of the late nineteenth century, in favor of a truly genuine Hindu social reformism based on a familial love of the motherland. Tagore, on the other hand, was mindful of the ways in which Brahmabandhab's violent revolutionary approach to anticolonial protests and his dependence on radical Hindu affective imagery in his editorials and articles obscured his privately gentle and devoted love of the nation. Tagore did not believe in obscuring Brahmabandhab's personal Christian faith, and he was deeply aware of the psychological damage Brahmabandhab had wrought upon himself by separating his public persona as a Hindu revolutionary ascetic and his privately held Christian beliefs, and that this double consciousness had left Brahmabandhab desolate, exhausted, and profoundly alienated from his own sense of moral integrity. Between Pal and Tagore, we can see the tensions regarding the paradoxes of Brahmabandhab's identity—as both a Christian convert and a devoted patriot championing a Hindu religious nationalist discourse—begin to emerge. These two distinct identities, one public and one private, both belonging to the same man, remained for Pal and others like him an irreconcilable enigma. Brahmabandhab could either be one or the other, and given his patriotism it was much easier to accept his Hindu cultural affiliations than his private Christian devotions. For Tagore, in contrast, Brahmabandhab's efforts at reconciling his faith and his patriotism were unsuccessful, and this led to an unceasing mental torment that haunted Brahmabandhab to his death.

Bipin Pal on Brahmabandhab

Bipin Pal featured Brahmabandhab in a compilation of short essays on politically influential figures of Bengal that he published in 1917. The essay on Brahmabandhab opens with a lament on the fickleness of public memory:

> The people of this country seem to have developed a particular amnesia about our debt to Brahmabandhab Upadhyay Mahashay in his contribution toward our present understanding of the ideals of *Swadeshi* (*Swadeshikata*).

> Otherwise, why is it that so much effort is being made to preserve the memories of such a variety of people, but there is not even one annual memorial meeting organized for Upadhyay Mahashay?[79]

It is clear from Pal's sorrowful and frustrated tone that, a mere decade after his passing, Brahmabandhab was already a half-forgotten figure in Bengal. Pal then went on to analyze the form of Upadhyay's patriotism, which he found to be a unique and profoundly important influence on the rhetoric of self-governance and independence in colonial Indian politics. Pal attributed to Brahmabandhab a profound and almost spiritual respect for Hindu society. This faith in the cultural life of the nation also set him apart from the kind of asceticism that paid lip service to human relations out of a desire to convert, preach, and gather a following among men.

Pal attributed this attachment of Brahmabandhab to an unfettered devotion for his country: Brahmabandhab's patriotism was uniquely built on a foundation of nonjudgmental love for the land and her people exactly as they were, faults and all. For Bipin Pal, this was an intellectual achievement that was neither conservative nor reactionary but came from a deeper place of knowing the true reality of the soul of India—it was entirely inspired by his commitment to his country and his people. This was a self-aware patriotism, one that knew the external sorrows and blemishes, the backwardness, the political repression, and the poverty of the Indian people would fade away with time. In a poignant passage, Pal tries to articulate whether Brahmabandhab could be termed a social reformer:

> He could not be called a "Reformer" in the true sense of the word. The reason of course is that he loved his country, was devoted to his country. . . . Upadhyay Mahashay had realized the essential truth of India. . . . Our present *Swadeshikata* differs from the "patriotism" of our English-educated forefathers from forty years ago. Their patriotism lacked this profound respect for *Swadeshi* civilization and self-realization; they lacked this unshakable faith in the latent inner spiritual power of the national community. Our patriotism and national-reform efforts were extroversions, turned toward Britain for inspiration and evaluation. . . . This led to a terrible self-forgetting (*atmasbismriti*) in us. Upadhyay Mahashay strongly protested against the poisonous fruit of this extroverted and alien form of patriotism.[80]

Pal, by resurrecting the memory of this forgotten hero, revived the ways in which Brahmabandhab pioneered a vision of one's own land, one's *swadesh*, that was motivated by tenderness rather than religious adoration or nationalism based on Western modes of thought. The argument rested on defining an Indian vision of patriotism that would work for Indians. This act of seeing was also not what Dipesh Chakrabarty has called *darshan*—this mode of "piercing the veil of the real" was not compensatory, in any sense.[81] According to Pal, Brahmabandhab understood that the only way for Indians to regain a sense of self-respect, of their own *bahubol*, was through violent resistance to British attempts at partitioning the land.

For Pal, Brahmabandhab's repudiation of a patriotism that was outwardly focused and influenced by Western notions of nationalism was a decisive and extraordinarily important intervention in the new methods of Bengali political activism. Pal's own political ideologies aligned with what Brahmabandhab had advocated—which was a turning away from older supplicatory political tactics of "prayer and petition" favored by the nationalist leaders of the late nineteenth century.[82] Brahmabandhab's belief in the efficacy of boycotts and picketing (which offered economic violence to the colonial body politic) and actual acts of terrorism (bombs, assassinations, and robbery of armaments and resources belonging to the colonial government) also allied with Pal and his associates' interests in propagating an active and masculine indigenous Hindu anticolonial resistance. However, through this framing of Brahmabandhab's memory and politics, Pal erased an important dimension of his identity: his Christian faith. Pal made him an exemplar of the traditionalist revolutionary patriot who fought to preserve Hindu cultural practices from the depredation of British colonialism. Pal posited that Brahmabandhab was worth remembering and emulating as a patriot because his ideology prioritized Indian tradition against colonial modernity. Brahmabandhab focused on self-strengthening, a program of *atmashakti*. Unless this strength could be achieved, a program of modernization compatible with Indian and specifically Hindu social mores could not be initiated.[83] In Pal's elegiac resurrection of Brahmabandhab's memory, it is clear that for him Brahmabandhab was a patriot only because Brahmabandhab was a devout and reconverted Hindu.

If Brahmabandhab was the person who had indeed redefined and reshaped the definition of Indian patriotism of the *swadeshi* era, according to Pal, his place in contemporary Hindu Bengali society was that of a true saint, better than the reformers and political leaders of old. This is a stunning attempt to appropriate Brahmabandhab's political and intellectual legacy for the majoritarian nationalist narrative of India's independence movement. Pal clearly felt deep unease about Brahmabandhab's private faith, as evidenced by its complete absence from his account. For political leaders like Pal, Brahmabandhab's public Hindu persona became the only acceptable version of his memory.

Rabindranath Tagore on Brahmabandhab

Rabindranath Tagore offered an almost diametrically opposite view, wherein Brahmabandhab's private faith and public persona became emblematic of the conflict between narrow religious extremism and a liberal, unprejudiced, and tolerant patriotism. It was a conflict that Tagore also viewed as a battle for the political future of India. His relationship with Brahmabandhab was one of mutual respect and understanding, despite widely differing ideological beliefs. The relationship was also a socially and culturally collaborative one, rather than a political association of the kind that Upadhyay shared with Bipin Pal. Tagore nurtured close personal connections with Brahmabandhab.[84] The two had epistolary interactions, and Brahmabandhab wrote four of his most important essays for *Banga-Darshan* (A vision of Bengal), edited by Tagore, in April–May 1901.[85] The chief of these essays was "Hindu-Jati'r Eknisthatha" (the singular devotions of the Hindus), which outlined his evolving views on India's political destiny against the lived realities of everyday colonial repression.

Tagore took special notice of Brahmabandhab after Brahmabandhab wrote a glowing review of Tagore's poetry collection *Naibedya* (Sacred offerings). The review was published in July 1901, in the periodical *The Twentieth Century*.[86] What brought these two men together was their shared love for their *swadesh,* although they differed immensely in their personal, intellectual, and political stances. They did, however, have similar ideas about social reconstruction through pedagogy. This resulted in a collaboration that has now been largely forgotten. The experimental school at Santiniketan founded by Tagore, which would later grow into the Viswa-Bharati University, began with Brahmabandhab and Rewachand bringing boys from their own Calcutta school to Bolpur in 1901–1902. Rewachand briefly worked as the headmaster of this new institution.[87] Tagore's two sons, Rathindranath and Shamindranath, joined this school as pupils as well. It was Brahmabandhab who first asked the students at the school to refer to Tagore as *Gurudev,* an affectionate and respectful title that Tagore bore for the rest of his life.[88] The boys were educated according to the strictest conditions of Vedic asceticism or *brahmacharya,* and the curriculum was modeled on the Indian tradition of *Gurukul* training.[89]

This moment of collaboration was brief. Brahmabandhab and Rewachand soon left Santiniketan, ostensibly because of disagreements with Tagore on the daily running of the school. But the real reason was Tagore's father, the formidable Debendranath. Debendranath did not want two convert Indian Christians to have so much power to influence the young students, especially when two of his own grandsons were being taught by them. Debendranath obviously still harbored deep suspicion of Christian missionaries as teachers, and he had already made clear his abhorrence of Christianity and conversions decades earlier, as we have seen in Chapters 2 and 3. Manoranjan Guha, in his memoir of Brahmabandhab, quotes Jitendralal Bandopadhyay's article "Rabindranath in Santiniketan" (Santiniketan'e Rabindranath), published in the *Suprabhat* (Good Morning) periodical in 1910, as evidence of Debendranath's continued hostility toward Christian converts, like Brahmabandhab. Rabindranath himself verified Debendranath's role in the ouster of Upadhyay and Rewachand:

> It is not true that my father objected merely because Upadhyay and Rewachand were Christians. . . . When their religion became widely known locally, many of the inhabitants were disturbed that Santiniketan may turn into a gathering of Christians—this attitude of the inhabitants and the possibility deeply hurt my father's heart. . . . The fact that the boys were in the care of a Christian teacher made many parents anxious as well. My father heard about this, and on his orders and the request of the parents, the relationship between Upadhyay and the school was ended. I was left alone again.[90]

Yet Rabindranath, unlike his beloved father, had a far more liberal and catholic view of religion and personal faith, and he retained an interest in Brahmabandhab's life and career.[91] Tagore's fascination with the intellectually brilliant, intensely charismatic, and characteristically restless Brahmabandhab left a deep impression on his own literary creativity.[92] Brahmabandhab's memory would haunt Tagore's literary output for the next three decades. For one, Brahmabandhab's redoubtable grandmother Chandramoni resembles quite closely and may be the inspiration for the extraordinary Anandamoyi in Tagore's most powerful novel on religious faith and political affiliation, *Gora,* first published in 1910.[93] It is the first of Tagore's "political" novels, followed by *Ghare Baire* (*The Home and the World,* 1916) and *Char Adhyay* (*Four Chapters,* 1934). In *Gora,* Anandamoyi is portrayed as a study in contradictions, as the liberal and loving protagonist to her son's narrow and rigid orthodoxies.

Though she is a pious and orthodox Brahmin's daughter, her adamantine personal faith is unbound by religious taboos, ritualism, or traditionalism. Instead, she has a refreshing and liberal outlook fostered by travels across British India with her civil servant husband. Immediately after the Mutiny of 1857, she adopts the orphaned infant son of a dead Irish (and Catholic Christian) soldier and brings him up as her own child. She appoints a low-caste Christian convert woman, Lachhmia, as the baby's wet nurse and has no qualms about accepting food or water from Lachhmia, an act that violates the taboos of caste purity. Anandamoyi's supposed eccentricities evoke horror and dismay from everyone in her family, even Gora. Gora, who does not know the secrets of his own origin, grows up to be an orthodox Hindu with deeply partisan ideologies. As an adult, he refuses to accept water contaminated by his nurse's touch and wants Lachhmia to leave their home as soon as possible—an attitude that hurts both Anandamoyi and Lachhmia deeply. Anandamoyi seemingly does not care that her liberal outlook and complete disregard of caste taboos have alienated her from Gora, her family, and other Hindus in her social community. Gora tries to get her to follow at least some of the caste taboos of a Brahmin household. Anandamoyi answers, with a deep irony based on her knowledge of Gora's true origins:

> My husband, my sons, if they are so troubled by me at every moment, do you think that leaves me happy? But the moment I took you in my arms, I let go of all my rituals and taboos. When you take a baby in your lap, you immediately understand that no one is born bearing caste marks. From the day I felt that truth, I have also known, if I despise someone just because they're Christians or from a lower caste, God will rip you away from me as well. Stay as you are, filling up my heart and lighting up my home; I will accept water from all *jatis* in the world.[94]

Anandamoyi's maternal love for an abandoned white Christian child, coupled with her wide travels, seems to have washed away all vestiges of narrow belief in casteism. The rest of her family does not express such liberalism. For her husband and her older son, having a Western education and affecting an anglicized modern outlook is important only outside the home. Within the *antahpur* and in the circle of Hindu friends and relations, they are orthodox Brahmins, a dichotomy that does not seem to trouble their conscience. Gora is the way he is because he has no knowledge of his own true identity. Anandamoyi is deeply lonely in this environment. Because she does not perform any of the outward rituals of belonging or caste exclusions, no one in her immediate vicinity seems to comprehend her deeply felt personal faith. The Hindu ideal, in Anandamoyi at least, reforms into an affectionate and liberal outlook, an entirely quiet and private but unbreakable moral certitude, which is not bound by the narrowness of communal faith-based identity.[95]

There is a consensus in literary history that Tagore modeled the character of Gora on Brahmabandhab Upadhyay. Anandamoyi's moral certitude, which Tagore contrasted positively with Gora's intellectual, physical, and political restlessness and his violent orthodoxies of faith and political ideology, show us Tagore's own commitments to a vision of religious belonging in India that was unjudgmental, liberal, and constructively critical of the Indian nationalist movement. Anandamoyi's mental fortitude and her profoundly tender acceptance of the equality of all Indians, regardless of their caste or religion, is a product of her travels across the breadth of India in her own youth and is contrasted in the novel with her confinement within the home in her middle age. Her son experiences a different discovery of India. Gora, who is violently orthodox in his understanding of Hinduism, decides to understand his motherland through restless travels across Bengal and, in this restlessness, very much resembles Brahmabandhab's own constant travels across India. Gora is tormented by the demands of the rituals of purity demanded by his Hindu faith and by the Hindu Bengali society he thinks he has been born into. Yet during his travels, especially in Chawr Ghosepur, Gora realizes the deep devastation wrought by poverty and lack of education among not only Hindus but Muslims as well. He realizes that religion created a particular kind of division within Indian society, one that made it almost impossible to achieve the dream of national independence. In the last few pages of the novel, Gora confesses to his mentor Paresh Babu. Once he learns the truth of his own parentage—that he is the orphaned son of a dead Irish Christian couple, brought up with great tenderness by a Hindu Brahmin mother—he realizes that he is at once unmoored and excluded from Hindu society, whose caste and purity rituals had grounded his sense of belonging. This violent unmooring is tempered, however, by Anandamoyi's desperate love for him, which helps him to realize that his exclusion is also a form of independence:

> "I am free today, Paresh Babu," Gora said. "I no longer have to be afraid that I may Fall from caste. I have tried so hard to find the real *Bharatbarsha* in all my devotions; yet, there has always been some obstacle within me. Though I have worked day and night, I have not been able to resolve this tension. . . . Today I am truly Indian. There is no opposition in my heart about Hindu,

Muslim, or Christian communities. . . . Paresh Babu, today morning I have been born anew into the lap of India with my unadorned pure soul."[96]

Gora returns home, and after a long time lays his weary head in Anandamoyi's lap and asks Lachhmia to bring him a glass of water. The characters of Anandamoyi and Gora represent the two contrasting aspects of Brahmabandhab's persona. Tagore seemed to feel that the personal rectitude of Brahmabandhab's private faith and the rhetorical excess of his persona as the *Sandhya*'s firebrand editor resolved themselves in a paradoxical fashion distinctive of his strange duality. This resolution could be found in his tender and affectionate political vision of his motherland, which could be protected only through an armed revolution against the colonizers. Tagore does not look into the future or examine how Gora's violent orthodoxies could transmute into his nationalism. But Tagore clearly recognizes that the violence of extremist terrorism, for Brahmabandhab, was enabled by and in proportion to the great bond of love for the motherland.

This tenderness became the cornerstone of Brahmabandhab's political belief, as Tagore astutely understood it. The mental reservations that Brahmabandhab had to practice in order to express his patriotism meant that he could preserve the core of his personal faith as a devout Christian. It did not preclude an accommodation of his political loyalties, which were based on his Hindu ethnic identity or Bengali Hindu cultural moorings. Brahmabandhab's patriotism, Tagore seemed to suggest, had everything to do with sociopolitical relationships rather than religious ones. Tagore's clearest exposition of this idea appears in a 1912 essay titled "Atmaparichay" (Self-identity). Published in the *Tattvabodhini Patrika* in Baishakh, it offers an extraordinary analysis of the distinctions between communitarian social ties and personal religious faith:

> Sectarian ties cannot take the place of societal relationships. . . . If I wish, I can easily convert to the beliefs of another sect, but how will I find my place in another society? The history of that society can never be my own. If you convert to Islam or Christianity, can you still be a part of Hindu society? . . . Christianity was the outer coloring; substantively they were Hindus. Just because they converted to Christianity, are we to think of Kalicharan Banerjee, Gyanendramohan Tagore and Krishnamohan Banerjee as divorced from this profound philosophical stream? Community is much greater and much more of an inwardly held conviction than mere opinion and belief. Opinions and beliefs can change, communitarian ties [*jati*] cannot.[97]

Brahmabandhab is surprisingly absent from Tagore's illustrious list of converted Bengali Christians, which included Brahmabandhab's uncle Kalicharan Banerjee. And yet, echoes of Brahmabandhab's essay "Are We Hindu" are clear in Tagore's writing as well.[98] In this essay, published in the *Sophia* in July 1898, Brahmabandhab had written:

> By birth we are and shall remain Hindu till death. But as *dvija* [twice-born], by virtue of our sacrament rebirth, we are Catholic. In customs and manners, in observing caste or social distinctions, in eating and drinking, in our life and living, we are genuine Hindus; but in our faith, we are neither Hindu, nor European, nor American, nor Chinese, but all-inclusive. . . . In short, we are Hindus so far as our physical and mental constitution is concerned, but in regard to our immortal souls we are Catholic. We are *Hindu-Catholic.*[99]

Brahmabandhab also seems to be directly echoing his uncle here. One of the first articles to appear in the *Bengal Christian Herald,* a periodical founded and edited by Rev. Kalicharan Banerjee and Joygovinda Shome, announced: "In having become Christians, we have not ceased to be Hindus. We are Hindu Christian, as thoroughly Hindu as Christian. We have embraced Christianity but we have not discarded our nationality."[100] Whether Tagore ever read the *Sophia* is impossible to discern. However, his cousin Gyanendramohan Tagore had made similar arguments after his own conversion in 1851, when he declared himself a Brahmin Christian. In *Gora,* ultimately, Tagore reimagines Brahmabandhab's legacy: his private faith and his public political persona, though initially in deep conflict with each other, are partially resolved in the realization of a constructive and unchauvinistic patriotism.[101] This preoccupation would again return in Tagore's novel *Ghare Baire,* in which the two friends Nikhil and Sandeep embody fictionally Tagore and Upadhyay's public intellectual and political preoccupations.[102]

The specter of Brahmabandhab continued to haunt Tagore for many years to come, and his recollections of the Hindu-Catholic revolutionary monk created a firestorm of controversy when his last novel was published in 1934. *Char Adhyay* focused on the terrorist movement in India. Its preface recorded Tagore's final encounter with Brahmabandhab, an event that had occurred twenty-seven years earlier.[103] Tagore wrote:

> He [i.e., Brahmabandhab] was a Roman Catholic monk and a Vedantist—radiant, fearless, self-sacrificing, immensely learned, and singularly influential. His dedication to spiritual knowledge and his intellect attracted my

deepest respect toward him. It is around this time that Lord Curzon determined to partition Bengal. I observed this *sannyasi* immerse himself in the ripples of the country-wide emotional turmoil. He himself published the *Sandhya* periodical, and his intense language set an intoxicating fire to the bloodstream of the nation. It was in this periodical that the first subtle hints of radical terrorism in Bengal were intimated.

During this period, we lost contact for a long while. I assumed that it was the differences between his and my own political ideologies for national agitation that made him turn away from me. During one of those days of blind madness, I was sitting alone in my third-floor room of our Jorasanko home when Upadhyay came to meet me. At the time of leave-taking, he went up to the threshold and then turned back to face me. He said, "Rabi-Babu, I have fallen perilously."[104] He went away immediately. I clearly understood that he had only come to say those heart-wrenching words. By then, the net of his activities had entangled him, there was no deliverance possible. This was my last conversation and last meeting with him.[105]

Tagore's own affection and respect for Brahmabandhab is easily discernible here, as is his deep ambiguity about the strand of radical extremist terrorism that characterized Brahmabandhab's political ideology. It is certainly possible that Tagore, at an interval of almost three decades, partly misremembered his discussion with Brahmabandhab. But this seems unlikely, given the startling nature of that last poignant confession and Tagore's own prodigious memory. Was Tagore trying to justify his own ambivalence about armed extremism, by imputing to Brahmabandhab his own feelings about the effects of violence both on victims and perpetrators? That too seems unlikely: Brahmabandhab, as we have already seen, was largely forgotten in the narrative of India's freedom, which had already entered the last fateful decade of political maneuvering for *swaraj* or self-rule under the leadership of Mahatma Gandhi and the Congress. Tagore by this time was a Nobel Prize recipient and a public intellectual with global renown, universally respected as one of the founding fathers of Indian nationalism. He really did not need external support to strengthen his position on anticolonialism as a cosmopolitan, humanitarian, nonviolent enterprise.

The outrage on publication of the novel was immediate and virulent. Young politically involved Indians, as well as the older generation of radical ex-extremists, felt betrayed by the novel, which openly criticized their seasoned leadership for emotionally and intellectually manipulating young revolutionaries. The novel made it clear that this bankrupt leadership endangered the very souls of young revolutionaries by compelling them to undertake morally and ethically inadmissible actions, including murder, robberies, and thefts from common Indian people. But those who had lived and worked during the *swadeshi* era and had suffered horrible repression and torture for their part in the "own country" movement were devastated by Tagore's insistence that Brahmabandhab regretted his involvement in the *swadeshi* movement. Tagore presented him as ruefully penitent about the inherent violence of the political extremism he preached and popularized, which he came to view as a slow-acting corruption debasing his soul. For the revolutionaries who had idolized Brahmabandhab and suffered immense cruelties in the colonial state's infamous Andaman Islands prison, Rabindranath's portrait of Brahmabandhab recanting his patriotic beliefs was the ultimate betrayal.[106]

So why did Tagore feel the need to remember Brahmabandhab in this manner? He removed the controversial preface in the second edition of the novel but added an interesting clarification. Although Tagore insisted that the novel was centrally a love story between the two main characters, Atin and Ela, he also insisted that the novel's depiction of the *swadeshi* movement arose from his own direct experiences during that turbulent period. He maintained that personal memories of a particular historical event could very well be diverse but argued that popular opinions of his novel largely fell outside the boundaries of literary criticism. And curiously he also referred to an unnamed female reader who had written to him to express "her" opinion that the character of the antagonist—the cruel, manipulative, pragmatic, and violent Indranath—was an expression of the outward actions of Brahmabandhab's character, while the morally conflicted, romantic, and tender Atin manifested Brahmabandhab's inner nature.[107] The opinions of this reader, if "she" did indeed exist, must have been very similar to Tagore's own views.

In his fiction, Tagore returned repeatedly to what he saw as the contradictions in Brahmabandhab's political ideology, personal faith, and intellectual legacy. These contradictions emerged in at least three important novels: in *Gora* and the eponymous protagonist of the novel; in *Home and the World,* in which the protagonist and antagonist seem to echo Tagore's and Brahmabandhab's respective political positions on patriotism; and finally in *Four Chapters,* in the contest of character between the revolutionary demagogue Indranath and the conscientious patriot Atin. In these novels he repeatedly explores the viability of patriotism, self-sacrifice, and radical extremism as ideologies for anticolonial politics, as well as the ethical and moral costs to the individual's soul on choosing each of these paths.

APPROPRIATIONS OF BRAHMABANDHAB'S LEGACIES

Scholars like Julius Lipner have noted the complexity inherent in Brahmabandhab's character. This was largely the result of his public performance of the persona of a Hindu patriot, committed to the experimental extremist political rhetoric and revolutionary actions of the anticolonial movement. This public persona was anchored in the Hindu cultural and communitarian identity that was a hallmark of the *swadeshi* movement heralded by the partition of Bengal in 1905. At the same time, Brahmabandhab privately and devoutly maintained his Catholic faith. While seeking to unite all Indians in an imagined community of brotherhood, the appeal to Hindu affective imagery—along with a disregard for the economic and social conditions of the non-Hindu classes of Bengal, including its Muslim peasantry and Christian converts—opened up certain fault lines that would keep widening in the decades ahead (despite momentary rapprochements, for example during the Khilafat Movement).[108] Brahmabandhab embodies this contested zone of identity politics in his own life, where he was torn between his patriotism, which was suffused by a Hindu cultural and political ideology, and his personal Catholic Christian faith. In death he was forgotten because the contradictions between his affectionate self-sacrificing inner life and the rigid, violent politics of Hindu anticolonial resistance that he preached were not easily amenable to incorporation within simpler majoritarian narratives about Indian nationalism and Indian patriots. Brahmabandhab's essay "Swaraj-Garh" (Fortress of independence) begins with a confession:

> I have neither sons nor a partner in life. I have roamed from place to place. At last exhausted and diminished, I thought of setting up an *ashrama* on the banks of the river Narmada—in that secluded desolate spot, I would spend my days in meditation.[109] But in the depths of heart and soul, I heard a call—India would be independent again. . . . I have heard the message of deliverance—my devotion, my prayer, everything is gone now. Anxious, fervent, eager, like a man struck with insanity, I restlessly wander about. I do not want to remain caged anymore in the fortress of slavery (*Golam-Garh'e thakite chai na*)—I want to build that fortress of independence (*Swaraj-Garh*)—my heart yearns to be a citizen of independent India. Come . . . let us progress on the path of *Mukti*.[110]

The poignant urgency of this epiphany reflects Brahmabandhab's loneliness and sense of estrangement from the elite society of Bengal. Of course, by the time of his death, he was very much accepted as a member of that intelligentsia—the result of his intense charisma and his self-fashioning as the voice of the common people of Bengal, who were invited to be a part of the anticolonial nationalist movement in an unprecedented program of mass mobilization. As "Swaraj-Garh" illustrates, Brahmabandhab obviously felt deeply alienated from his personal faith, at least for a time. His private beliefs were profoundly overwritten by his sense of patriotism, though one can sense that this self-alienation, toward the end of his brief life, seemed to him an act of insanity. Brahmabandhab almost equated the intensity of his patriotic fervor with a loss of his rationality and his contemplative inner life.[111] He seemed to have loved his motherland to the point of madness. The deeply emotional and affective nature of this bond to his country was at odds with his critical and intellectual mind. Perhaps this is why his biographer Prabodh Singha remembered Brahmabandhab violently recoiling when he contemplated his career during the *swadeshi* movement:

> He [Brahmabandhab] was a truly great philosopher, and it is a matter of profound regret that he was known in society only as a reactionary political theologian. He had once said with regret, "God, how did this happen? Leaving the path of true spiritual joy, how did I, after so many years, decide to sift through the mud and refuse of the world?"[112]

Singha's memory must be weighed carefully, knowing that he single-mindedly narrated Brahmabandhab's legacy as a reconverted and reconciled Hindu nationalist leader in his biography. However, it is striking that Tagore used the theologically loaded word "Fall," evocative of the final expulsion of humans from a Christian heaven and the birth of the idea of sin, in memoriam of Brahmabandhab's last encounter with him.[113] Singha, meanwhile, speaks of Brahmabandhab using the concept of ritual pollution, with decidedly Hindu orthodox connotations. He describes Brahmabandhab praying at the Kalighat temple a month before his demise, asking the goddess Kali to relieve him from the burden of carrying a polluted and blemished body. Brahmabandhab here is presented as having discarded his Christian faith. This penitent Brahmabandhab asks a boon of rebirth from the deity who was Time herself:

> Send me to the home of a righteous Brahmin family. Grant me a Brahmin's body again, so that twenty years from now, I am reborn in this same land, Mother, where I can take a renewed part in observing your rituals of faith. Grant me this prayer, that while working for my country, while preaching

> the truth, my body is annihilated into the five elements, before the British can jail me.[114]

The faith of Brahmabandhab Upadhyay, patriot, enigmatic theologian and nationalist leader, heretic and revolutionary, Hindu-Catholic monk, enigma, and paradox, eluded everyone—his friends, his collaborators, his followers, and British administrators alike.[115] The mythologization of his death by all his biographers reflects this fundamental lack of understanding of the complicated motives that drove him. If some biographers read his invocation to a *Thakur* or *Ishta Devata* on his deathbed as evidence of his unshakable private Christian faith, others took his acts of penance and his prayers to a Hindu goddess—as well as his worship of the image of the motherland as a deity in his violent apologetic tirades against British oppression—as incontrovertible proof that he died a true Hindu. Perhaps the true location of Brahmabandhab's faith, the specific nature of his intellectual and spiritual quest, eluded him as well. The performance of a public persona as a Hindu revolutionary exhausted him, and yet, as Tagore so perceptively noted, he could not escape the bonds that he himself had created in order to preach a different path to true independence. He held his personal faith in strict mental reservation, perhaps knowing that it would be difficult to reconcile with the militant Hindu patriotic persona that inspired respect and confidence from his associates and followers.

Brahmabandhab experienced many different conversions and performed a particular outward form of Hindu religiosity to claim authority as a champion of Indian nationalist aspirations in his short and troubled life. His negotiations of his patriotic identity found resonances among prominent Indian Christian leaders and politicians in the later period of nationalist agitation. Brahmabandhab's maneuvers around his personal faith foreshadowed the registers of religious, social, and national belonging that Christian converts would have to deftly negotiate in the period between his death in 1907 and independence in 1947. Among those Indian Christians were nationalists like S. K. Datta, the president of the All India Conference of Indian Christians and the YMCA, and Bishop V. S. Azariah, who had a deeply hostile relationship with Mahatma Gandhi and was referred to as his "Enemy Number One."[116] Both Datta and Azariah found themselves at the center of the nationalist movement, and Datta participated in the Round Table Conferences in the 1930s.[117] They soon realized that upholding nationalist allegiances required compromises that were deeply alienating to their sense of self, to their identity as Christians, and to their freedom and safety to evangelize in postcolonial India. They also realized that minorities would always have to prove that they were Indians in their loyalties first. Their allegiances to their Christian faith could only hinder them and count as a very distant second in nationalist aspirations in postcolonial India. In this sense, Brahmabandhab's story is a precursor to the political compromises of later Indian Christian intellectuals—and to broader negotiations around the place of minority communities of faith in the Indian nationalist discourse. Brahmabandhab made one of the most important, though short-lived, efforts by an Indian Christian convert to resolve the dichotomy between private faith and public political allegiance in the context of the Indian anticolonial struggle. His disappearance from the narrative of nationalist historiography, and the many attempts to appropriate his legacy, point to a fundamental failure to heal that wound.

Epilogue

Mohandas Karamchand Gandhi, better known as the Mahatma, had his own encounters with Christian apologetics during his visit to Calcutta in the early twentieth century. He met with the well-known native convert and Indian Congress leader Rev. Kalicharan Banerjee in 1901, to learn more about Christian ethics.[1] Gandhi explained why he sought out Rev. Banerjee: "I had heard of Babu Kalicharan Banerji and held him in high regard. He took a prominent part in the Congress, and I had none of the misgivings about him that I had about the average Christian Indian, who stood aloof from the Congress and isolated himself from Hindus and Musalmans." This was part of his search for what Gandhi referred to as the Truth, though the meeting with Rev. Banerjee left him unsatisfied.[2] Gandhi, always a pragmatist who knew how closely religious identity was tied to politics in India, would claim in his famous autobiography, "I can say without the slightest hesitation, and yet in all humility, that those who say that religion has nothing to do with politics do not know what religion means."[3] In an interview with the American missionary and Nobel Peace Prize recipient John Mott in 1929, Gandhi made clear that to him the legacy of Christianity in India had been tainted by its association with British colonial rule, and that he did not believe in conversion at all:

> Christianity in India has been inextricably mixed up for the last one hundred and fifty years with British rule. It appears to us as synonymous with materialistic civilization and imperialistic exploitation by the stronger white races of the weaker races of the world. Its contribution to India has been therefore largely of a negative character. . . . I disbelieve in the conversion of one person by another.[4]

This book has sought to weave together an intellectual and political history of the creation of the Indian political self, which emerged through an often oppositional relationship with evangelical Christianity and the apologetic debates arising from this relationship. South Asian material and intellectual history, if divorced from the religious catalysts of sociopolitical action, both impoverishes and reifies the lives of Indians in the nineteenth century. By filling in a history of forgotten people and erased narratives, I have endeavored to provide a historical genealogy of the politics of religion and its evolution in the nineteenth century and into the *Swadeshi* era of the twentieth. Apologetic debates about Christianity and conversion were always about defining the self against the Other and defining personal faith against communal political identities. These issues remain highly and often violently contested today, a reflection of the enduring centrality of religious faith in the modern public sphere and the political domain in South Asia.

By the early twentieth century, the definition of the Hindu and Muslim political self, in opposition to that of the Christian convert, created an impossible situation for the converts themselves. The divided loyalties they had been accused of as a result of their conversion now created political difficulties in terms of engaging in the broader anticolonial mass movements beginning to take shape in Bengal and in India. They now had to face a difficult choice. In a situation where Hindu identity lent authenticity to one's patriotic fervor, Christian converts now often had to hide or temper their love and devotion toward their personal faith and publicly perform a cultural and political affiliation to the religious identity they had discarded. In order to find a place within the matrix of the anticolonial nationalist movement, this was a necessary political maneuver. But it complicated their relationships to both their communities of birth and their communities of choice through conversion.

In the two decades before India's independence in 1947, a number of princely states, mostly with Hindu rulers, passed anti-conversion laws, including Raigarh (1936), Sarguja (1945), and Udaipur (1946).[5] These laws were purportedly enacted to stop "forcible" conversions. In reality, these laws allowed the rulers of these princely states to control evangelical activities in their domains and practice widespread repression of converts, who mostly belonged to India's impoverished tribal Indigenous peoples. In the period after India gained freedom, Indians belonging to the majority religious communities continued to maintain a paranoid and suspicious attitude toward India's convert Christian population. Political scientist Nalin Mehta has shed light on an ongoing debate about missionary activity and conversions in India between 1947 and 1955, which saw India's first prime minister, Jawaharlal Nehru, pitted against

India's first president, Rajendra Prasad. While Nehru assured India's minority communities of their rights, Prasad warned against conversion activities by missionaries twice in 1954. Prasad was supported against Nehru by the more orthodox Hindu members of the Indian Congress Party.[6] In 1954, the Bharatiya Jana Sangh (BJS) called for observation of an "Anti–Foreign Missionary Week." The BJS was the political arm of the Rashtriya Swayamsevak Sangh (RSS) and the parent party to today's Bharatiya Janata Party (BJP). In response, the Congress Party–led state government in Madhya Pradesh called for the setting up of the Niyogi Committee, chaired by a retired judge, to carry out an extensive inquiry into evangelical activities in the state.[7] This led to the publication of the controversial *Niyogi Committee Report on Christian Missionary Activities* in 1956, which was described later variously as "a fishing expedition on the supposition that something discreditable can be discovered," "an inquisition," and "an accusation."[8] Despite the fact that religious liberty was enshrined as a fundamental right in India's constitution, and despite Nehru's avowal that India was a secular state and "an equal space," where "minority communities were free to practice their religions," the debate ended with the Indian government instituting multiple curbs on activities by "foreign" missionaries in India in 1955, especially in the sensitive border regions.[9] Multiple Indian states also subsequently passed what were known as "Freedom of Religion" acts. These legal provisions were ostensibly aimed at preventing supposed "forcible" conversions, especially conversions to Christianity. But they were and are often used arbitrarily, and with undue force, to spread an atmosphere of fear among India's minority communities. These acts were passed, for example, in Odisha (1967), Madhya Pradesh (1968), Arunachal Pradesh (1978), Chhattisgarh (2000 and 2006), Gujarat (2003), Himachal Pradesh (2006 and 2019), Jharkhand (2017), and Uttarakhand (2018).[10] Where these acts have received the approval of the state governor or the president of India and are ratified, the penalties for carrying out "forcible" conversions can be one to five years of imprisonment and/or up to Rs. 300,000 in monetary fines. In India's most populous state of Uttar Pradesh, which has given India nine of its eighteen prime ministers since 1947, the Prohibition of Unlawful Conversion of Religion Ordinance was passed in January 2021. The Uttarakhand Freedom of Religion Act of 2018 defined "unlawful" conversion as follows:

> (a) "Allurement" means and includes offer of any temptation in the form of any gift or gratification or material benefit, either in cash or kind or

> employment, free education in reputed school run by any religious body, easy money, better lifestyle, divine pleasure or otherwise; (b) "Convincing for conversion" means to make one person agree to renounce one's religion and adopt another religion; (c) "Undue influence" means the unconscientious use by one person of his power or influence over another.[11]

Allegations of such allegedly forced conversions could, in the form of legal complaints, be made by the convert's parents or siblings to a court of law. Commenting on the widespread violence against India's minority communities, including Christians, as a result of state oppression through legal, political, and social means, the United States Commission on International Religious Freedom (USCIRF) report for 2023 stated:

> At the end of the reporting period, 12 of India's 28 states had legislation that criminalized religious conversion in various circumstances (Arunachal Pradesh, Chhattisgarh, Gujarat, Haryana, Himachal Pradesh, Jharkhand, Karnataka, Madhya Pradesh, Odisha, Rajasthan, Uttarakhand, and Uttar Pradesh). . . . Common features of these laws include prohibitions on conversions, requirements to notify the government of one's intent to convert. . . . These laws . . . disproportionately target Christians and Muslims. Increasingly, anti-conversion laws are used to prevent interfaith marriages or relationships.[12]

By now, these definitions of what constitutes "forcible" conversion should be familiar to the readers of this book: after all, this is the same language that has been used by majority communities to prevent conversion and surveil younger (and therefore supposedly more impressionable) members of their social matrix since Raja Rammohan Roy. Heated discussions on what constitutes "forcible" conversion have been prevalent in the Indian public sphere for the last two centuries and continue in the present day. These anti-conversion laws do face resistance, both legally and through public protests as well. For example, Madhya Pradesh's anti-conversion laws were challenged in India's Supreme Court in the 1977 *Rev. Stanislaus v. Madhya Pradesh* case. However, in its judgment, the highest court in India stated that the constitutional fundamental right to practice and propagate one's religion did not extend to the right to convert, and therefore upheld the constitutional validity of Madhya Pradesh's anti-conversion laws. It should also be noted that most of these contemporary "anti-conversion" laws were passed after the BJP-led political alliance came to power in India in 2014.

I would like to end on a personal note. On the night of January 23, 1999, Australian missionary Graham Staines was sleeping with his two young sons, Philip and Timothy, aged ten and six, in the family's car, outside a church in Keonjhar, in the eastern Indian state of Orissa. Staines and his wife Gladys had spent more than thirty years working to care for leprosy patients in the region. They were well known and well regarded by the local population, who counted among the most destitute of India's tribal populations. A local strongman, Ravinder Kumar Pal, better known as Dara Singh, with close ties to the militant right-wing Hindu nationalist group Bajrang Dal and with a prior history of violence toward and murder of Christian converts in Mayurbhanj and Keonjhar districts, had heard of the Staineses' arrival and their participation in a local church festival. The local branch of the Bajrang Dal, and Dara Singh himself, believed the Staines had been actively working to convert the Indigenous tribal population of the area, the Adivasis, to Christianity. He gathered a mob, which flocked to the spot where Staines and his sons were sleeping, surrounded the car, poured gasoline on it, and set it on fire. The mob effectively prevented Staines and his sons from escaping the car and watched while they burned in a gruesome death.[13] The violence against the Staines was only one of many attacks on Christians and churches in India, though the savagery of the attack set it apart. In that year, as the then home minister Lal Krishna Advani stated in February, there had already been 116 attacks on Christians, more than in the previous fifty-one years combined.[14] Churches had been demolished in the Dangs tribal area of the western Indian state of Gujarat, and ritual purification events called *ghar wapasi,* or a return and reconversion to Hinduism, had been held across India by the country's premier right-wing Hindu nationalist group, the RSS, and its auxiliary offshoots, such as the Bajrang Dal.

I was fifteen years old in 1999, attending a missionary school, when the Staineses' murder happened. The language of instruction was English, deemed by my mother, like many other parents in India, to be indispensable for future opportunities. This had been the case for the last two centuries, as a result of the conditions of British colonial rule. Most of my closest friends were either Indian Christians or descendants of Anglo-Indian officers who had stayed back in Purulia, my home district, and had intermarried with the Bengali and tribal population who inhabited this corner of Bengal's Jungle Mahals. I went to chapel service every morning, took part in Christmas and Easter celebrations, and could, of course, recite the Lord's Prayer from memory. I had never felt myself to be distinctive in any way from my Christian friends, and neither, I think, did they feel any such overt difference. The very rituals of ordinary everyday life and our youth had smoothed away these differences and the long existent tensions around political identity and religious faith in the South Asian subcontinent, which had resulted in the Partition and then in regular religious violence and rioting for the next half a century.

It all changed for me and my classmates with the Staineses' murder. Suddenly, there was a fissure that created a sense of "us and them" in the school. And there was deep anxiety among the Christian families of my hometown, Purulia, who were worried for their safety. I was too young when the Babri Masjid destruction and the Bombay riots occurred in 1992–1993, but the tragedy of the Staineses' murder was my political awakening. I might have been a sheltered teenage girl, but that was the moment when my knowledge of the religious differences between India's many communities of faith took on a political significance. Just before the murder of Staines and his sons, in the wake of tribal violence in the Dangs region in Gujarat, India's then prime minister Atal Bihari Vajpayee had been asked about his opinions on conversions to Christianity. In his inimitable way, this witty and charismatic politician and poet, the public face of the right-wing BJP, shifted the discourse on religiously motivated political violence against minority communities of faith by declaring that there needed to be "a national debate on conversions."[15] He of course later condemned the murder of Graham Staines and his sons, as well as the communal attacks on churches, just as he would go on to criticize the state government of Gujarat, and the then chief minister, a man named Narendra Modi, during the Gujarat riots of 2002.

But Vajpayee's comments about the necessity of a national debate on conversion had already subtly shifted the blame onto India's minority communities, including Indian Christians, for the violence that was perpetrated against them. It is worth noting that the RSS and the Bajrang Dal, which had been accused of collusion in the Staineses' murder and for the wave of religious violence perpetrated against India's Christian minorities, were affiliated with Vajpayee's party, the BJP, which is also currently in power at the center. Since 1998 and the gruesome murder of Staines and his sons, again and again in the last twenty-five years, widespread atrocities have been committed against Christian and Muslim minorities in India, including the horrific communal violence in the state of Gujarat in 2002.[16] The USCIRF report for 2023 said, "In 2022, religious freedom conditions in India continued to worsen. Throughout the year, the Indian government at the national, state, and local levels promoted and enforced religiously discriminatory policies, including laws targeting religious conversion."[17] The liberal, secular strands of India's political and social discourse have continuously strived to weave a nation from the immense ethnographic, linguistic, religious, political, and social diversities of the Indian subcontinent. But it should also be clear that the illiberal, communal, and profoundly violent tendencies within that same social, political, and national matrix have riven India with hate and prejudice based on religious faith and religious identity, leading to the regular eruption of ferocious carnage. Depending on the political context, sometimes the secular has submerged and overpowered the communal, but it has never ever been able to suppress or eliminate this dark shadow beneath the illuminated lamp of Indian democracy. In the last ten years, such religious violence has become a part of the daily fabric of Indian life, like never before.[18]

This book has been the result of my effort to understand the social, political, and religious tensions that led to my devastating political awakening at age fifteen, when I began to recognize the realities of communal violence in India. I wanted to understand the ways in which religious faith not only dominates our social and political identity but also creates immense disparities in how a supposedly secular state treats its minority citizens. Like all Indians of my generation, I have lived through this unresolved trauma of a secular, democratic nation's tendency of suspicion and violence toward its own minority citizens. The roots of that dark mirror to a "shining India" lie in the colonial past, in the Bengal Province, where a new awakening, a Renaissance for Indians, began in the nineteenth century. I have tried to excavate and bring into the light the unremembered fault lines that slowly widened within that birthplace of a vaunted liberal and secular Indian political tradition. The roots of communalism sprouted in that same ground in the early nineteenth century, with devastating consequences across the next two centuries for those who were considered to be outside the majoritarian fold.

Conversion, either as a realized threat or as a far more terrifying but politically effective phantasmagoria, spurred the need in colonial India in the nineteenth century for the creation of a nationalist narrative of a cohesive and monolithic Hindu or Muslim identity. It unfortunately continues to serve the same political purpose in postcolonial India with the rise of Hindu majoritarianism. The politics of conversion therefore rooted within the very concept of Indian liberal secularism its inevitable failure.

Archival Sources

BANGLADESH

Dhaka University Library, Archives, Rare Books and Special Collections Reading Room, Dhaka University, Dhaka

National Archives of Bangladesh, Dhaka

INDIA

Asiatic Society of India, Calcutta

Bangiya Sahitya Parishat, Calcutta

Carey Library and Resource Center, Serampore

Goethals Indian Library and Research Society, St. Xavier's College, Calcutta

The National Library, Calcutta

Private collection, Pathuriaghata Tagore family, courtesy of Srijit Tagore and Pramantha Tagore

Rammohan Library and Free Reading Room, Calcutta

West Bengal State Archives, Bhawani Dutta Lane, Calcutta

West Bengal State Archives, Writers' Buildings, Calcutta

UNITED KINGDOM

The Angus Library and Archive, Regent's Park College, University of Oxford, Oxford

British Library, India Office Records (IOR) and Private Papers, London

British Library, Newspaper Archives, Newsroom, St. Pancras, London

The Cambridge South Asian Archive, Centre of South Asian Studies, University of Cambridge, Cambridge

Cambridge University Library, University of Cambridge, Cambridge

The National Archives (United Kingdom), Kew, London

SOAS Library, Archives and Special Collections, School of Oriental and African Studies (SOAS), University of London, London

The University of Manchester Library, Raymond English Anti-Slavery (REAS) Collection, The University of Manchester, Manchester

UNITED STATES

The Center for Research Library, University of Chicago, Chicago

Harvard Divinity School Library; Harvard University Archives; Houghton Library; Law School Library; Lamont Library Microfilm Collections; Widener Library, Harvard University, Cambridge, MA

The Joseph Regenstein Library, University of Chicago, Chicago

Memorial Library, University of Wisconsin-Madison, Madison, WI

Notes

ABBREVIATIONS

BJP	Bharatiya Janata Party, India
BJS	Bharatiya Jana Sangh, India
IOR	India Office Records and Private Papers, British Library, London
REAS	Raymond English Anti-Slavery Collection, 1824–1886, GB 133 REAS 1–14, the University of Manchester, Manchester
RNN	*Reports on Native Newspapers,* a compendium of abstracts in English of articles in vernacular Indian newspapers, from the Bengal, Madras, Bombay, and Allahabad Presidencies, 1868–1942, University of Birmingham, Cadbury Research Library, Special Collections
RSS	Rashtriya Swayamsevak Sangh, the volunteer core of the BJP
SPFEE	The Society for Promoting Female Education in the East
USCIRF	United States Commission on International Religious Freedom

INTRODUCTION

1. Though "Kolkata" is the spelling used since 2001, I have deliberately used the older colonial spelling Calcutta for the name of the city throughout this book, to reflect the fact that this was the official name of the city since its founding by the British trader Job Charnock in the late seventeenth century, and that this is the spelling used in all archival sources consulted.

2. *Dansagar* (ocean of alms) was the most ruinously expensive and difficult of the *sraddha* rites, involving the distribution of immense quantities of gold, silver, clothing, cattle, and money among the attendees. For more on the three such *Dansagar* rituals of the Dev family preceding that of the dowager Maharani's described in this chapter, see Brajendranath Bandopadhyay, ed., *Sambadpatre Sekaler Katha* [Yesteryears in newspapers and periodicals],

2nd ed., 3 vols. (Calcutta: Bangiya Sahitya Parishat Mandir, 1933–1936), 1:294–295; Bandopadhyay, *Sambadpatre Sekaler Katha,* 3:378–379.

3. William Hastie, *Hindu Idolatry and English Enlightenment . . . Letters Addressed to Educated Hindus Containing a Practical Discussion of Hinduism* (Calcutta: Thacker, Spink & Company, 1882), 1–5.

4. Kalikrishna Dev (1808–1872), scholar of English and Sanskrit, was the grandson of Nabakrishna Dev and after 1867 the president of the Sanatan Dharma Rakshini Sabha or Association for the Protection of Orthodox Dharma. See Lokanātha Ghosa, *The Modern History of the Indian Chiefs, Rajas, Zamindars, & Etc. . . . Down to the Present Time* (Calcutta: J. N. Ghose, 1881), 120–121, 124.

5. Hastie, *Hindu Idolatry and English Enlightenment,* 2–3.

6. Bepin Bihary Mitra, *The Life of Maharaja Nabakrishna Dev Bahadur of Sovabazar, Calcutta* (Calcutta: I. C. Bose and Company, Stanhope Press, 1879).

7. Sushanta Krishna Dev, *Tin Shatabdir Sovabazar Rajbari* [Three centuries of the Sovabazar Raj family] (Calcutta: Sarat Book House, 2000).

8. *A Rapid Sketch of the Life of Raja Radhakanta Dev Bahadur, with Some Notices of His Ancestors and Testimonials to His Character and Learning* (Calcutta: J. M. Gaumiss, Englishman Press, 1859). See also Ghosa, *Modern History of the Indian Chiefs,* 95–118.

9. Alexander Duff, *The Intolerant and Persecuting Section of the Calcutta Baboos Exposed!!!* (Calcutta: J. Thomas at the Baptist Mission Press, 1847).

10. Hastie, *Hindu Idolatry and English Enlightenment,* 8.

11. Hastie, *Hindu Idolatry and English Enlightenment,* 10.

12. Hastie, *Hindu Idolatry and English Enlightenment,* 126.

13. It was the government's displeasure at Bankimchandra's novel *Anandamath* that resulted in his demotion and temporary exile. See Amitrasudan Bhattacharya, *Bankimchandra Jibani: The Life of Bankimchandra* (Calcutta: Ananda Publishers, 1991), 564–565.

14. Chandra Mallampalli, "British Missions and Indian Nationalism, 1880–1908: Imitation and Autonomy in Calcutta and Madras," in *The Imperial Horizons of British Protestant Missions,* ed. Andrew N. Porter (Grand Rapids, MI: Eerdmans, 2003), 158–181.

15. Dipesh Chakrabarty, *Provincializing Europe: Postcolonial Thought and Historical Difference,* new ed. (Princeton, NJ: Princeton University Press, 2009), 8–10.

16. Partha Chatterjee, "The Moment of Departure: Culture and Power in the Thought of Bankimchandra," in *Nationalist Thought and the Colonial World: A Derivative Discourse* (London: Zed Books for the United Nations University, 1986), 75–76.

17. Tapan Raychaudhuri, *Europe Reconsidered: Perceptions of the West in Nineteenth-Century Bengal,* 2nd ed. (Delhi: Oxford University Press, 2002), 146.

18. Partha Chatterjee, "The Fruits of Macaulay's Poison Tree (1985)," in *Empire and Nation: Selected Essays* (New York: Columbia University Press, 2010), 91–110.

19. This religious definition of identity was a direct result of the colonial policy of defining demographics on the basis of religious majority and minority from the census of 1872 onward.

20. C. A. Bayly, introduction to *Recovering Liberties: Indian Thought in the Age of Liberalism and Empire* (Cambridge: Cambridge University Press, 2011), 3.

21. Sir Syed Ahmed Khan, *Asbab-e-Baghawat-e-Hind* (1858), trans. His American Well-Wisher [pseud.] as *The Causes of the Rebellion of India* (2005), http://www.columbia.edu/itc/mealac/pritchett/00urdu/asbab/translation2005.html.

22. Eric Stokes, *The English Utilitarians and India* (New York: Oxford University Press, 1989). See also Boyd Hilton, *The Age of Atonement: The Influence of Evangelicalism on Social and Economic Thought, 1795–1865* (New York: Oxford University Press, 1988).

23. Christopher Leslie Brown, *Moral Capital: Foundations of British Abolitionism* (Chapel Hill: University of North Carolina Press, 2012).

24. Kālīprasanna Siṃha, "Khristiani Hujoog," in *Hutoma Pyāñcāra Nakśā,* ed. Rajendranath Bandopadhyay and Sajanikanta Das (Calcutta: Bangiya Sahitya Parishat, 1956), 53–54.

25. According to the 2011 census of India, the numbers hover around 2 percent. Stephanie Kramer, "Population Growth and Religious Composition," Pew Research Center, September 21, 2021, https://www.pewresearch.org/religion/2021/09/21/population-growth-and-religious-composition.

26. Christopher Alan Bayly, *Empire and Information: Intelligence Gathering and Social Communication in India, 1780–1870,* vol. 1, *Print* (New York: Cambridge University Press, 1996); Susan Mary Bayly, *Saints, Goddesses and Kings: Muslims and Christians in South Indian Society, 1700–1900* (New York: Cambridge University Press, 1989); Ayesha Jalal, *Self and Sovereignty: Individual and Community in South Asian Islam since 1850* (New York: Routledge, 2002); Sugata Bose, "Nation, Reason and Religion: India's Independence in International Perspective," *Economic and Political Weekly* 33 (1998): 2090–2097.

27. Gauri Viswanathan, *Outside the Fold: Conversion, Modernity, and Belief* (Princeton, NJ: Princeton University Press, 2021); Chandra Mallampalli, *A Muslim Conspiracy in British India? Politics and Paranoia in the Early Nineteenth-Century Deccan* (Cambridge: Cambridge University Press, 2017), and *Christians and Public Life in Colonial South India* (London: Routledge Curzon, 2004), 2, 8–9; Nandini Chatterjee, *The Making of Indian Secularism: Empire, Law and Christianity, 1830–1960* (New York: Palgrave Macmillan, 2011); Shabnum

Tejani, *Indian Secularism: A Social and Intellectual History, 1890–1950* (Bloomington: Indiana University Press, 2021). Mallampalli says, "Debates concerning the place of Christians within British India were . . . that of the beleaguered convert who, on account of his or her apostasy from Hinduism, was . . . cut off from family and caste and denied inheritance and other familial rights."

28. Viswanathan, *Outside the Fold,* 16.

29. Soldiers were required to bite the cartridge, an act that would bring the taboo pig fat in contact with their mouths and lead to an immediate excommunication from their respective religions—and therefore they would have no choice but to convert to Christianity.

30. Khan, *Asbab-e-Baghawat-e-Hind.*

31. *Proclamation by the Queen in Council, to the Princes, Chiefs, and People of India, 1858,* British Library, accessed June 15, 2014, https://www.bl.uk/collection-items/proclamation-by-the-queen-in-council-to-the-princes-chiefs-and-people-of-india.

32. *Oxford English Dictionary* (*OED*), s.v. "apologia," accessed March 30, 2024, https://www.oed.com/dictionary/apologia_n.

33. *OED,* s.v. "apology," https://www.oed.com/dictionary/apology_n?tab=meaning_and_use#767477.

34. C. A. Bayly, *Empire and Information: Intelligence Gathering and Social Communication in India, 1780–1870* (New York: Cambridge University Press, 1996), 180–182.

35. Bayly, *Saints, Goddesses, and Kings,* 241–463.

36. Christopher Harding, *Religious Transformation in South Asia: The Meanings of Conversion in Colonial Punjab* (New York: Oxford University Press, 2008).

37. Ananya Chakravarti, *The Empire of Apostles: Religion, Accommodatio, and the Imagination of Empire in Early Modern Brazil and India* (New Delhi: Oxford University Press, 2018).

38. Kōji Kawashima, *Missionaries and a Hindu State: Travancore, 1858–1936* (Delhi: Oxford University Press, 1998).

39. Bose, "Nation, Reason and Religion," 2091.

40. Viswanathan, *Outside the Fold,* 118–152.

41. Duncan B. Forrester, *Caste and Christianity: Attitudes and Policies on Caste of Anglo-Saxon Protestant Missions in India* (London: Curzon Press, 1979). See also Kawashima, *Missionaries and a Hindu State.*

42. Jeffrey Cox, *Imperial Fault Lines: Christianity and Colonial Power in India, 1818–1940* (Stanford, CA: Stanford University Press, 2002). For nonofficial

white violence, see Elizabeth Kolsky, *Colonial Justice in British India: White Violence and the Rule of Law* (New York: Cambridge University Press, 2011).

43. Geoffrey A. Oddie, *Imagined Hinduism: British Protestant Missionary Constructions of Hinduism, 1793–1900* (New Delhi: Sage, 2006).

44. Robert Eric Frykenberg, *Christianity in India: From Beginnings to the Present* (Oxford: Oxford University Press, 2008); Penelope Carson, *The East India Company and Religion, 1698–1858* (Martlesham, UK: Boydell Press, 2012); Geoffrey Oddie, ed., *Religious Conversion Movements in South Asia: Continuities and Change, 1800–1990* (Abingdon, UK: Taylor & Francis, 2013); Geoffrey A. Oddie, *Missionaries, Rebellion and Proto-Nationalism: James Long of Bengal* (Abingdon, UK: Taylor & Francis, 2014); Eliza F. Kent, *Converting Women: Gender and Protestant Christianity in Colonial South India* (New York: Oxford University Press, 2004).

45. Parna Sengupta, *Pedagogy for Religion: Missionary Education and the Fashioning of Hindus and Muslims in Bengal* (Berkeley: University of California Press, 2011).

46. Alexander Duff and William Howard Pearce, *Observations on the Hindoo and Moohummudan Laws of Inheritance, as Affecting Converts to Christianity in India* (Calcutta: The Baptist Mission Press, 1831).

47. Gaṇendramohaṇa Ṭhākura, *Thoughts by a Christian Brahmin on the Position and Prospects of Religion in India* (London: Hamilton, Adams & Co., 1871).

48. Carlo Ginzburg, "In History as in Cinema, Every Close-Up Implies an Off-Screen Scene," interview by Nicholas Weill for *Le monde des livres,* October 3, 2022, trans. for Verso Books blog by David Fernbach, June 6, 2023, https://www.versobooks.com/en-gb/blogs/news/5536-carlo-ginzburg-in-history-as-in-cinema-every-close-up-implies-an-off-screen-scene.

49. Francesca Trivellato, "Microstoria / Microhistoire / Microhistory," *French Politics, Culture & Society* 33, no. 1 (2015): 122–134.

50. Saidiya Hartman, *Wayward Lives, Beautiful Experiments: Intimate Histories of Riotous Black Girls, Troublesome Women and Queer Radicals* (New York: W. W. Norton, 2020).

51. Hartman, "Wayward: A Short Entry on the Possible," in *Wayward Lives, Beautiful Experiments.*

ONE CONVERSION AND THE BIRTH OF MODERN APOLOGETICS IN INDIA

1. James R. Fichter, "Death of the India Monopoly," in *So Great a Proffit: How the East Indies Trade Transformed Anglo-American Capitalism* (Cambridge, MA: Harvard University Press, 2010), 232–251.

2. Bhabanicharan Bandopadhyay, *Kalikata Kamalalaya* (Calcutta: Samachar Chandrika Press, 1823).

3. Penelope Carson, *The East India Company and Religion, 1698–1858* (Rochester, NY: Boydell Press, 2012).

4. Carson, *East India Company*, 1–3.

5. Thomas Twining, quoted in John William Kaye, *Christianity in India: An Historical Narrative* (London: Smith, Elder and Company, 1859), 153–154.

6. William Ward, *Farewell Letters to a Few Friends in Britain and America, on Returning to Bengal in 1821* (New York: E. Bliss and E. White, 1821), 149.

7. Chandra Mallampalli, "Jesuits and the Emperor Akbar, 1580–3," in *South Asia's Christians: Between Hindu and Muslim* (Oxford: Oxford University Press, 2023), 40–61.

8. Avril A. Powell, "Muslim-Christian Debate: The Medieval Legacy of the Munazara," in *Muslims and Missionaries in Pre-Mutiny India* (Richmond, Surrey, UK: Curzon, 1993), 6–7.

9. For the different forms of apologetics, from the *munazara* and *bahas* to written correspondence and in the handwritten *akhbars* and printed periodicals, see C. A. Bayly, *Empire and Information: Intelligence Gathering and Social Communication in India, 1780–1870* (Cambridge: Cambridge University Press, 1996).

10. For example, see Lynn Zastoupil, "Defining Christians, Making Britons: Rammohun Roy and the Unitarians," *Victorian Studies* 44, no. 2 (2002): 215–243, http://www.jstor.org/stable/3830327; Sumit Sarkar, "Rammohun Roy and the Break with the Past," in *Rammohun Roy and the Process of Modernization in India,* ed. V. C. Joshi (Delhi: Vikas Publishing House, 1975), 46–68; Dermot Killingley, *Rammohun Roy in Hindu and Christian Tradition: The Teape Lectures 1990* (Newcastle upon Tyne, UK: Grevatt & Grevatt, 1993); Bruce Carlisle Robertson, *Raja Rammohan Ray: The Father of Modern India* (Delhi: Oxford University Press, 1995); David Kopf, *The Brahmo Samaj and the Shaping of the Modern Indian Mind* (Princeton, NJ: Princeton University Press, 1979).

11. Editors of Encyclopedia Britannica, "Clapham Sect," *Encyclopedia Britannica,* August 4, 2016, https://www.britannica.com/topic/Clapham-Sect.

12. Carson, *East India Company,* 4–5, 140–142.

13. Homi K. Bhabha, *The Location of Culture* (New York: Routledge, 1994), 124.

14. Stephen Tomkins and Clapham Society, *The Clapham Sect: How Wilberforce's Circle Transformed Britain* (Oxford: Lion Hudson, 2010).

15. Charles Grant, *Observations on the State of Society among the Asiatic Subjects of Great Britain: Particularly with Respect to Morals; and on the Means of Improving It* (London: House of Commons, 1813), 26.

16. Grant, *Observations on the State of Society,* 44.

17. Grant, *Observations on the State of Society,* 86. Emphasis added.

18. James Mills, *History of British India* (London: Baldwin, Cradock, and Joy, 1817).

19. William Ward, *Extracts from an Account of the Writings, Religion, and Manners of the Hindoos, Including Translations from Their Principal Works, in Four Volumes Quarto* (London: J. Haddon, 1813).

20. Eli Daniel Potts, *British Baptist Missionaries in India, 1793–1837: The History of Serampore and Its Missions* (London: Cambridge University Press, 1967), 6–9. For more on Carey, Marshman, and Ward, the richest source is John Clarke Marshman, *The Life and Times of Carey, Marshman, and Ward: Embracing the History of the Serampore Mission,* 2 vols. (London: Longman, Brown, Green, Longmans, & Roberts, 1859). See also Potts, *British Baptist Missionaries in India.*

21. Boyd Hilton, *A Mad, Bad and Dangerous People? England 1783–1946* (Oxford: Oxford University Press, 2006), 174–184.

22. Eric Stokes, *The English Utilitarians and India* (Oxford: Oxford University Press, 1959), 27.

23. Stokes, *English Utilitarians,* xii. See also Carson, *East India Company.*

24. Stokes, *English Utilitarians,* 30.

25. Shibnath Sastri, *Ramtanu Lahiri o Tatkaleen Bangasamaj,* ed. Baridbaran Ghosh (Calcutta: New Age Publishers, 2009), 48–49.

26. Quoted in George Smith, *The Life of William Carey, D.D.: Shoemaker and Missionary, Professor of Sanskrit, Bengali, and Marathi in the College of Fort William, Calcutta* (London: J. Murray, 1885), 88.

27. Penelope Carson's work reorients the history of the East India Company's rule in India from 1757 to 1858 to argue that the colonization of India depended on deployment of religious diplomacy. See Carson, *East India Company.* Chapters 8, 9, and 10 are of particular importance.

28. Bernard S. Cohn, *Colonialism and Its Forms of Knowledge: The British in India* (Princeton, NJ: Princeton University Press, 1996).

29. The order in which their names are presented is also a conscious reflection of their importance to the phenomenon of the achievements of the Serampore Baptists.

30. For details on the early East India Company chaplains working in Bengal, see Daniel O'Connor, "Garrison," in *The Chaplains of the East India Company, 1601–1858* (London: Continuum, 2012), 95–118.

31. Quoted in C. H. Philips, "The India House Divided against Itself, 1806–1912," in *The East India Company, 1784–1834* (Manchester: Manchester University Press, 1961), 171.

32. Carson, *East India Company,* 73–74.

33. Headed by Sir Francis Baring, director and a partner of the John and Francis Baring Company bank, Baring was one of the City's greatest financiers and a director of the English East India Company. See Peter E. Austin, *Baring Brothers and the Birth of Modern Finance* (London: Pickering & Chatto, 2007), 14–20.

34. Claudius Buchanan, *Memoir of the Expediency of an Ecclesiastical Establishment for British India: Both as the Means of Perpetuating the Christian Religion among Our Own Countrymen; and as a Foundation for the Ultimate Civilization of the Natives* (London: T. Cadell and W. Davies, 1805), 31. Emphasis added.

35. Buchanan, *Memoir of the Expediency,* 28–41.

36. Thomas Twining, *A Letter, to the Chairman of the East India Company: On the Danger of Interfering in the Religious Opinions of the Natives of India; and on the Views of the British and Foreign Bible Society, as Directed to India* (London: J. Ridgway, 1807).

37. Twining, *A Letter, to the Chairman,* 27–31.

38. Marshman, *Life and Times,* 1:122–123.

39. Marshman, *Life and Times,* 1:266–267.

40. Cohn, *Colonialism and Its Forms of Knowledge,* xiii.

41. Bhavani Raman, *Document Raj: Writing and Scribes in Early Colonial South India* (Chicago: University of Chicago Press, 2012).

42. David Kopf, "Fort William College and the Origins of the Bengal Renaissance," *Proceedings of the Indian History Congress* 24 (1961): 296–303, http://www.jstor.org/stable/44140769.

43. Brian A. Hatcher, "Remembering Rammohan: An Essay on the (Re-) Emergence of Modern Hinduism," *History of Religions* 46, no. 1 (2006): 58, https://doi.org/10.1086/507928. See also Amiya P. Sen, *Rammohan Roy: A Critical Biography* (New Delhi: Penguin, 2012).

44. Carson, *East India Company,* 3.

45. Rammohan Roy has been written about extensively and it is not within the scope of this chapter to give a detailed account of his life and work. The best nineteenth-century accounts of his life are as follows: Mary Carpenter, *The Last Days in England of the Rajah Rammohan Roy* (London: Trubner & Co., R. C. Lepage, 1866); Sophia Dobson Collet, *The Life and Letters of Raja*

Rammohan Roy (Calcutta: A. C. Sarkar, 1913); Nagendranath Chattopadhyay, *Mahatma Rammohan Roy'er Jiban-charit* (Calcutta: Brahmo Mission Press, 1911). On the history of the abolition of *sati* as a religious custom, and Rammohan's role in it, see Lata Mani, *Contentious Traditions: The Debate on Sati in Colonial India* (Berkeley: University of California Press, 1998).

46. Chattopadhyay, *Mahatma Rammohan Roy'er Jiban-charit*, 7–12. Chattopadhyay quoted Mary Carpenter, who surmised that the letter, containing a brief autobiography, had been written by Rammohan in London to his friend in Calcutta, Mr. Gordon.

47. Brian A. Hatcher, "Upcountry with Rammohan," in *Hinduism before Reform* (Cambridge, MA: Harvard University Press, 2020), 126–150.

48. C. A. Bayly, "Rammohan Roy and the Advent of Constitutional Liberalism in India, 1800–30," *Modern Intellectual History* 4, no. 1 (2007): 25–41, http://doi.org/10.1017/S1479244306001028.

49. Marshman, *Life and Times*, 2:127–130. Marshman made a small mistake about Rammohan's age—he was about forty-two years old when he settled in Calcutta, not thirty-six. It is extraordinary that Rammohan entirely remade both himself and Indian society when he was approaching late middle age (average life expectancy at birth in India was twenty-five years in 1881).

50. Lynn Zastoupil, *Rammohan Roy and the Making of Victorian Britain* (New York: Palgrave Macmillan, 2010), 73–76.

51. Quoted in Dobson Collet, *Life and Letters*, 26–29.

52. George Augustus Frederick FitzClarence, *Journal of a Route Across India, Through Egypt, to England, in the Latter End of the Year 1817, and the Beginning of 1818* (London: J. Murray, 1819), 106–107.

53. Dobson Collet, *Life and Letters*, 29–34.

54. Jatindra Kumar Majumdar, *Raja Rammohan Roy and Progressive Movements in India: A Selection from Records, 1775–1845* (Calcutta: Brahmo Mission Press, 1983), 16–17.

55. Hatcher, *Hinduism before Reform*, 142.

56. Hatcher, *Hinduism before Reform*, 144.

57. Kopf, *Brahmo Samaj*.

58. Rammohan Roy and Joshua Marshman, *The Precepts of Jesus: The Guide to Peace and Happiness, Extracted from the Books of the New Testament Ascribed to the Four Evangelists. To Which Are Added the First, Second, and Final Appeal to the Christian Public, in Reply to the Observations of Dr. Marshman* (New York: B. Bates, 1825).

59. Chattopadhyay, *Mahatma Rammohan Roy'er Jiban-charit,* 104–105.

60. Roy and Marshman, *Precepts of Jesus,* xxv–xxviii.

61. Roy and Marshman, *Precepts of Jesus,* xxviii. Rammohan mirrored another "notorious and convicted mutilator"—Thomas Jefferson, who was also interested in Unitarianism and infamously experimented with physically altering the Bible, in his *The Life and Morals of Jesus of Nazareth,* also published in 1820. See Lynn Zastoupil, "'Notorious and Convicted Mutilators': Rammohun Roy, Thomas Jefferson, and the Bible," *Journal of World History* 20, no. 3 (2009): 399–434, http://www.jstor.org/stable/40542805.

62. Roy and Marshman, *Precepts of Jesus,* xviii. Emphasis mine.

63. Rammohan Roy, *Rammohan Rachanaboli,* ed. Ajit Kumar Ghosh (Calcutta: Haraf Prakashani, 1973), 452. "Extract from a Letter Addressed to a Gentleman of Baltimore, Dated Calcutta, October 27th, 1822." Emphasis mine.

64. Joshua Marshman, *A Defence of the Deity and Atonement of Jesus Christ: In Reply to Ram Mohun Roy of Calcutta* (London: Kingsbury, Parbury, and Allen, 1822), 3. Emphasis Added.

65. Roy, *Rammohan Rachanaboli,* 451. "Extract from a Letter Dated September 5th, 1820."

66. Rammohan castigated Marshman and Schmidt for falling very short of the true Christian values of liberality and charity. See Roy and Marshman, *Precepts of Jesus,* 104–105.

67. See Geoffrey Oddie, "Constructing 'Hinduism': The Impact of the Protestant Missionary Movement on Hindu Self-Understanding," in *Christians and Missionaries in India: Cross-Cultural Communication since 1500, with Special Reference to Caste, Conversion, and Colonialism,* ed. Robert E. Frykenberg and Alaine Lowe (Grand Rapids, MI: W. B. Eerdmans, 2003), 155–182.

68. Rammohan Roy, *Second Appeal to the Christian Public* (New York: B. Bates, 1825), 120.

69. Roy, *Second Appeal,* 120.

70. Roy, *Rammohan Rachanaboli,* 451. "Extract from a Letter Addressed to a Gentleman of Baltimore, Dated Calcutta, October 27th, 1822."

71. *The English Works of Raja Rammohan Roy,* vol. 1, ed. Jogendra Chunder Ghose and Eshan Chunder Bose (Calcutta: The Oriental Press, 1885), 169.

72. Dobson Collet, "Cause of the Failure of Christian Missions," in *Life and Letters,* 63.

73. Roy and Marshman, *Precepts of Jesus,* 118–120.

74. W. W. Wroth and Penelope Carson, "Middleton, Thomas Fanshaw (1769–1822), Bishop of Calcutta," *Oxford Dictionary of National Biography,* Sep-

tember 23, 2004, https://www.oxforddnb.com/view/10.1093/ref:odnb/9780198614128.001.0001/odnb-9780198614128-e-18683.

75. See Dobson Collet, *Life and Letters,* 68–69. "Mr. William Adam to Mr. N. Wright. Calcutta, May 7, 1821—It is now several months since I began to entertain some doubts respecting the Supreme Deity of Jesus Christ, suggested by frequent discussions with Ram Mohun Roy." William Adam was one of the supporters of Rammohan in establishing the Atmiya Sabha, instrumental in the establishment of the Brahmo Samaj. He features in Benjamin Robert Haydon's famous portrait of the World Anti-Slavery Convention of 1840, now in the National Portrait Gallery. *The Anti-Slavery Society Convention, 1840* (1841), National Portrait Gallery, https://www.npg.org.uk/collections/search/portrait/mw00028/The-Anti-Slavery-Society-Convention-1840.

76. Charles Webb Le Bas, *The Life of the Right Reverend Thomas Fanshaw Middleton, D.D.: Late Lord Bishop of Calcutta* (London: C. J. G. and F. Rivington, 1831), 178–180.

77. Le Bas, *Life of the Right Reverend Thomas Fanshaw Middleton,* 420–421.

78. Dobson Collet, *Life and Letters,* 70.

79. Roy, "Brahman Sevadhi," in *Rammohan Rachanaboli,* 235.

80. *The English Works of Raja Rammohan Roy, with an English Translation of the "Tuhfatul Muwahhiddin"* (Allahabad: The Panini Office, 1906), 145–146.

81. Roy, *Rammohan Rachanaboli,* 233.

82. For Henry Ware Sr., see "Papers of Henry Ware, Sr.," Harvard University Archives, accessed March 25, 2024, https://hollisarchives.lib.harvard.edu/repositories/4/resources/4198. The famed *Glass Flowers* exhibit at Harvard was sponsored by his granddaughter, Mary Lee Ware. For Rammohan's transcontinental Anglo-American Unitarian networks, see Lynn Zastoupil, "Rammohan Roy, Celebrity Unitarian," in *Rammohan Roy and the Making of Victorian Britain,* 41–56.

83. Henry Ware, *Correspondence Relative to the Prospects of Christianity, and the Means of Promoting Its Reception in India,* ed. William Adam (London: C. Fox & Company, 1825).

84. Ware, *Correspondence Relative to the Prospects of Christianity,* 2–4.

85. Ware, *Correspondence Relative to the Prospects of Christianity,* 122.

86. Ware, *Correspondence Relative to the Prospects of Christianity,* 122.

87. Ware, *Correspondence Relative to the Prospects of Christianity,* 129–130.

88. Ware, *Correspondence Relative to the Prospects of Christianity,* 135.

89. Alexander Duff (1806–1878), born in Perthshire, studied at St. Andrews University, where he was inspired in ministry and evangelism by a visit from the Serampore missionary Joshua Marshman.

90. *Merriam-Webster,* s.v. "rice Christian," accessed April 29, 2022, https://www.merriam-webster.com/dictionary/rice%20Christian.

91. Bayly, "Rammohan Roy and the Advent of Constitutional Liberalism in India," 25–41.

92. Bayly, "Rammohan Roy and the Advent of Constitutional Liberalism in India."

93. Partha Chatterjee, *The Black Hole of Empire: History of a Global Practice of Power* (Princeton, NJ: Princeton University Press, 2012).

94. James Jaffe, "Custom, Identity, and the Jury in India, 1800–1832," *The Historical Journal* 57, no. 1 (2014): 131–155, http://www.jstor.org/stable/24528913.

95. Jaffe, "Custom, Identity, and the Jury in India."

96. Jaffe, "Custom, Identity, and the Jury in India."

97. Roy, *Rammohan Rachanaboli,* 468. "Letter to J. Crawford, Dated August 18, 1828."

98. Chatterjee, *Black Hole of Empire,* 150. Emphasis added.

99. Zastoupil, "Defining Christians, Making Britons."

100. Chatterjee, *Black Hole of Empire,* 157.

101. C. A. Bayly, "The Pre-History of 'Communalism'? Religious Conflict in India, 1700–1860," *Modern Asian Studies* 19, no. 2 (1985): 177–203, http://www.jstor.org/stable/312153. See also the critique of Bayly's argument by Ayesha Jalal, "Exploding Communalism: The Politics of Muslim Identity in South Asia," in *Nationalism, Democracy and Development: State and Politics in India,* ed. Sugata Bose and Ayesha Jalal (Delhi: Oxford University Press, 1997), 9–10.

102. Partha Chatterjee, *Texts of Power: Emerging Disciplines in Colonial Bengal* (Minneapolis: University of Minnesota Press, 1995).

103. Quoted in George Smith, *The Life of Alexander Duff,* vol. 1 (New York: American Tract Society, 1879), 118.

104. Syed Ahmed Khan, *Asbāb-i baghāvat-i Hind or Causes of the Indian Revolt: Three Essays,* ed. Salim al-Din Quraishi (Lahore: Sang-e-Meel Publications, 2009). See also Charles Trevelyan, *The Letters of Indophilus to the Times* (London: Longman, Brown, Green, Longmans, and Roberts, 1858).

TWO THE CONTEST OVER HIGH-CASTE CONVERSIONS

1. Ishwar Chandra Gupta, "Ingraji Nobo-Borsho" [English New Year], in *Ishwar Gupter Granthabali,* 2 vols. (Calcutta: Basumati Sahitya Mandir, n.d.), 1:113.

2. For more on Gupta, see Bankim Chandra Chattopadhyay, *Ishwar Chandra Gupter Jiban-Charit o Kabitwa Bishoyok Prabandha* (Calcutta: Gopal Chandra Mukhopadhyay, 1885).

3. Gupta, "Ingraji Nobo-Borsho," 1:113.

4. Gupta, "Ingraji Nobo-Borsho," 1:113–114.

5. Jatindra Kumar Majumdar, ed., *Indian Speeches and Documents on British Rule, 1821–1918* (Calcutta: Longmans & Company, 1937), 49–50. Emphasis added.

6. Rosinka Chaudhuri, *Freedom and Beef Steaks: Colonial Calcutta Culture* (New Delhi: Orient Blackswan, 2012); Parna Sengupta, *Pedagogy for Religion: Missionary Education and the Fashioning of Hindus and Muslims in Bengal* (Berkeley: University of California Press, 2011); Hayden J. A. Bellenoit, *Missionary Education and Empire in Late Colonial India, 1860–1920* (Abingdon, UK: Taylor & Francis, 2015).

7. Ishwar Chandra Gupta, "Babu Chandicharan Singher Khristadharmanurokti" [Babu Chandicharan Singha's Love for the Christian Religion], in *Ishwar Gupter Granthabali,* 1:120.

8. For details on Alexander Duff, see George Smith, *The Life of Alexander Duff,* 2 vols. (New York: American Tract Society, 1879).

9. Ishwar Chandra Gupta, "Bodo-Din" [Christmas], in *Ishwar Chandra Gupter Shreshtha Kabita,* ed. Alok Ray (Calcutta: Bharabi, 2002), 86–90. "A B pora Duffy chele, proti ghare" (89). By "AB Learning," Gupta meant a knowledge of the English language (i.e., a knowledge of the alphabet or A and B).

10. Ishwar Chandra Gupta, "Choddo-Missionary" [The false missionary], in Ray, *Ishwar Chandra Gupter Shreshtha Kabita,* 118. The tub was of course the receptacle used for the act of baptism.

11. Ishwar Chandra Gupta, "Durbhikkha" [Famine], in Ray, *Ishwar Chandra Gupter Shreshtha Kabita,* 76–83.

12. Martin Moir and Lynn Zastoupil, eds., *The Great Indian Education Debate: Documents Relating to the Orientalist-Anglicist Controversy, 1781–1843* (London: Routledge, 2016).

13. For more on Macaulay's "Minute" and the debates on new directions in Indian education, see Moir and Zastoupil, *Great Indian Education Debate,* 162–172.

14. "Minute by the Hon'ble T.B. Macaulay," Columbia University website, February 2, 1835, http://www.columbia.edu/itc/mealac/pritchett/00generallinks/macaulay/txt_minute_education_1835.html.

15. Elmer H. Cutts, "The Background of Macaulay's Minute," *American Historical Review* 58, no. 4 (1953): 824–853, https://doi.org/10.2307/1842459.

16. Moir and Zastoupil, *Great Indian Education Debate,* 162–172.

17. "Minute by the Hon'ble T.B. Macaulay."

18. Moir and Zastoupil, *Great Indian Education Debate,* 170.

19. Quoted in Moir and Zastoupil, *Great Indian Education Debate,* 170. Emphasis added.

20. "Minute by the Hon'ble T.B. Macaulay."

21. William Clarkson, *India and the Gospel: Or, An Empire for the Messiah* (London: J. Snow, 1851), 205, 242–247.

22. S. N. Mukherjee, "Daladali in Calcutta in the Nineteenth Century," *Modern Asian Studies* 1, no. 9 (1975): 59–80. The four factions or *dals,* as they were called in 1845, are described by Mukherjee on p. 76.

23. Thomas Edwards, *Henry Derozio, the Eurasian Poet, Teacher, and Journalist* (Calcutta: W. Newman, 1884). See also Abirlal Mukhopadhyay, Henry Derozio, and Derozio Commemoration Committee, eds., *Song of the Stormy Petrel: Complete Works of Henry Louis Vivian Derozio* (Calcutta: Progressive Publishers, 2001), appendix IX.

24. Ramchandra Ghosh, *A Biographical Sketch of the Rev. K.M. Banerjee: Missionary, Scholar and Patriot* (Calcutta: Samya Press, 1893), 9.

25. *Hindu College Theke Hindu School: Dwishatabarshiki Smarak Grantha* (Calcutta: Dey's Publishing, 2017), "Shikshak," 126. See also Shibnath Shastri, *Ramtanu Lahiri o Tatkaleen Bangasamaj,* ed. Baridbaran Ghosh, 3rd reprint (Calcutta: New Age Publishers, 2009), 69–75.

26. Shibnath Shastri and Roper Lethbridge, *Rāmtanu Lahiri, Brahman and Reformer: A History of the Renaissance in Bengal, from the Bengali of Pandit Sivanath Sastri* (London: Swan Sonnenchein & Co., 1907), 69.

27. *Hindu College Theke Hindu School,* 71.

28. Shastri and Lethbridge, *Rāmtanu Lahiri,* 80.

29. Smith, *Life of Alexander Duff,* 1:145–147.

30. Shastri, *Ramtanu Lahiri o Tatkaleen Bangasamaj,* 73.

31. Shastri, *Ramtanu Lahiri o Tatkaleen Bangasamaj,* 73.

32. Pallab Sengupta, *Derozio* (Calcutta: Sahitya Academy, 2000), 9.

33. Shastri, *Ramtanu Lahiri o Tatkaleen Bangasamaj,* 55.

34. Susobhan Chandra Sarkar, *On the Bengal Renaissance* (Calcutta: Papyrus, 1979), 105–106.

35. Edwards, *Henry Derozio,* letter, sections 82–89, section 84. Emphasis added.

36. Rudrangshu Mukherjee, "The Derozio Affair: An Annal of Early Calcutta," *Economic and Political Weekly* 52, no. 36 (2017): 54–60, http://www.jstor.org/stable/26697559.

37. *Converts from the Government and Missionary Schools in India* (Calcutta: J. Thomas, Baptist Mission Press, 1852), 10–11. For details on the circumstances of the conversions, see Alexander Duff, *India and India Missions: Including Sketches of the Gigantic System of Hinduism, Both in Theory and Practice; Also Notices of Some of the Principal Agencies Employed in Conducting the Process of Indian Evangelization* (Edinburgh: J. Johnstone, 1840), 673–683.

38. Lalbehari Dey, another of Duff's converts, reported on Nandy's flight from Fatehpur in 1857, and his safe arrival in Calcutta, in *Arunodaya* 2 (1857), http://crossasia-repository.ub.uni-heidelberg.de/475.

39. Duff, *India and India Missions,* 675–676.

40. Mukherjee, "Daladali in Calcutta in the Nineteenth Century," 59–80. *Daladali* is factionalism. Mukherjee quotes an anonymous source who wrote of four factions in Calcutta in 1845—the missionary *dal,* the Nastik *dal* (agnostic members of Young Bengal), the Brahmo *dal* (Debendranath Tagore and others), and the Dharma Sabha *dal* (of Raja Radhakanta Deb). The Brahmo *dal* and the Dharma Sabha *dal* had close kinship and social ties, even if the Brahmos espoused monotheistic Vedantism and the Dharma Sabha *dal,* as is evident from its name, considered itself the representative of orthodox Hindu society.

41. "The Tagore Family: The Rothschilds of Bengal," *The Oriental Miscellany: A Monthly Journal of Politics, Literature, Science and Arts* 2, no. 16 (July 1880): 241–250.

42. Debendranath Tagore (1817–1905), eldest son of Dwarkanath Tagore and father of Rabindranath. He founded the Brahmo Samaj, by merging Rammohan Roy's Brahmo Sabha with his own Tattvabodhini Sabha. The mouthpiece of the Tattvabodhini Sabha, the *Tattvabodhini Patrika,* took an important early role in the second wave of anti-missionary apologetics in Bengal, as I discuss in this chapter. See Debendranath Tagore, *The Auto-Biography of Maharashi Debendranath Tagore with Portraits,* trans. Satyendranath Tagore and Indira Devi (Calcutta: S. K. Lahiri, 1909).

43. James Wyburd Furrell, *The Tagore Family: A Memoir* (London: Kegan Paul, Trench & Co., 1892), 14–18.

44. "Puja," February 16, 1822. Among his many other charities, Gopimohan Tagore, Prosonnocoomar's father, made the largest donation of gold to the temple at Kalighat in its history, surpassing the fabled donation a generation earlier by Raja Nabakrishna Dev of Sovabazar. See Brajendranath Bandyopadhyay, ed., *Sambadpatre Sekaler Katha* [Yesteryears in newspapers and periodicals], 2nd ed., 3 vols. (Calcutta: Bangiya Sahitya Parishat Mandir, 1933–1936), 1:263.

45. "His professional income at the Bar is said to have averaged two lakhs (two hundred thousand) of rupees a year, but he was a man of private means and retired while still in the prime of life in order to devote himself to public matters." For details, see Evan Cotton, *Calcutta, Old and New: A Historical and Descriptive Handbook to the City* (Calcutta: General Printers & Publishers, 1980), 344–345.

46. "Prosonnocoomar Tagore, C.S.I.," *The Oriental Miscellany: A Monthly Journal of Politics, Literature, Science and Arts* 2, no. 19 (October 1880): 361–374. The Indian Penal Code (IPC) came into force as Act XLV under Lord Canning, the first viceroy of India, on January 1, 1862. It is clear from the *Oriental Miscellany* article that Tagore was deeply involved in the process from the beginning to the successful completion and implementation of the IPC. For details, see Barry Wright, "Macaulay's Indian Penal Code: Historical Context and Originating Principles," in *Codification, Macaulay and the Indian Penal Code: The Legacies and Modern Challenges of Criminal Law Reform,* ed. Chan Wing-Cheong, Barry Wright, and Stanley Yeo (Aldershot, UK: Ashgate, 2011), 19–58.

47. Vācaspatimiśra and Prosonnocoomar Tagore, *Vivada Chintamani: A Succinct Commentary on the Hindoo Law Prevalent in Mithila* (Madras: Printed by A. D'Rozario, 1863).

48. In a collection of brief legal opinions, printed in 1868 as *Loose Papers,* Tagore put forward his opinions on the *Dayabhaga* and on alienation of ancestral property in the essays titled "Alienation of Immovable Ancestral Property" and "Property according to the Hindu Law." For details on the *Dayabhaga,* see Ludo Rocher, *Jimutavahana's Dayabhaga: The Hindu Law of Inheritance in Bengal* (New York: Oxford University Press, 2002).

49. Edmund Ronald Leach and S. N. Mukherjee, eds., *Elites in South Asia* (Cambridge: Cambridge University Press, 1970), 32–78.

50. Radhakanta Dev (1784–1867) was the leader of the so-called orthodox faction in Calcutta. He was a pioneer in promoting female education and was a noted Sanskrit scholar. He was the grandson of Raja Nabakrishna Dev.

51. For a general example of popular public opinion about conversion, see Binaya Ghosha, ed., *Selections from English Periodicals of 19th Century Bengal,* vol. 1 (Calcutta: Papyrus, 1978), 88–89.

52. *Padri:* Bengali loan word from the Portuguese *padre.*

53. Ghosha, *Selections from English Periodicals,* 89. Emphasis added.

54. For an illustrative article on the benefits of female education in *The Reformer,* see Ghosha, *Selections from English Periodicals,* 89–92.

55. The name of Krishnamohan's journal is suggestive of his intellectual inclinations. Derozio's approach to pedagogy was influenced by William Godwin. Godwin's *The Enquirer* was published in 1797.

56. Ghosh, *Biographical Sketch of the Rev. K.M. Banerjee,* 18.

57. Prosonnocoomar Tagore, "Baboo Prosunno Koomar Thakoor," *The Reformer,* September 12, 1831, in Ghosha, *Selections from English Periodicals,* 89–90.

58. Krishnamohan Banerjee, "Prospects of Hindoo Improvement," *The Enquirer,* February 4, 1832, in Ghosha, *Selections from English Periodicals,* 106–108.

59. Shastri and Lethbridge, *Rāmtanu Lahiri,* 86–87.

60. Shastri and Lethbridge, *Rāmtanu Lahiri,* 86–87.

61. Krishnamohan Banerjee, *The Persecuted: Or Dramatic Scenes Illustrative of the Present State of Hindu Society in Calcutta* (Calcutta: Printed by A. Morriro and Co., East Indian Press, 1831).

62. Quoted in Suranjan Middye, ed., *Krishnamohan Banerjee's "The Persecuted": The First Modern Bengali Play* (Calcutta: Anjali Publishers, 2012), 73.

63. Middye, *The Persecuted,* 73.

64. Ananda Lal, "The Persecuted," in *Indian Drama in English: The Beginnings,* ed. Ananda Lal (Calcutta: Jadavpur University Press, 2019), 29.

65. Lal, "The Persecuted," 49.

66. Lal, "The Persecuted," 50.

67. Lal, "The Persecuted," 44–45.

68. Sugata Bose contends that there needs to be "a dynamic and historicized conception of religion" that goes beyond the prevalent historiographic trend of asserting that Indian religious and faith systems were, in the colonial era, seen as the "Other" to colonial conceptions of Enlightenment reason and rationality, by both British political thinkers and Indian intellectuals. "Nation, Reason and Religion: India's Independence in International Perspective," *Economic and Political Weekly* 33, no. 31 (1998): 2092.

69. Thomas Spring (Lord Monteagle) Rice, *A Reply to the Rev. K. M. Banerjea's Remarks on the Speech of the Earl of Ellenborough, in the House of Lords . . . against Act. XXI. of 1850, of the Government of India. With an Appendix Containing the Speeches of Lord Monteagle and the Earl of Ellenborough. By A*

Member of the Committee Appointed by the Hindu Inhabitants of Bengal, Behar and Orissa, for Petitioning Parliament against the Aforesaid Act (Calcutta: Printed by D'Rozario and Co., 1853), 10.

70. Harihar Das, *The Rev. Krishnamohan Banerjea, D.L., C.I.E.: Parts 1–3, Bengal Past and Present,* vols. 37–38 (Calcutta: Journal of the Calcutta Historical Society, 1929).

71. *Converts from the Government and Missionary Schools,* 11–14.

72. Dutta's *Meghnadbadh Kavya* won praise as the Indian *Paradise Lost*—the celebration of the will to rebel against the established order—and as such was read also as a critique of British colonial rule. See Rosinka Chaudhuri, *Gentlemen Poets in Colonial Bengal: Emergent Nationalism and the Orientalist Project* (Calcutta: Seagull Books, 2002), 101–167.

73. Golam Murshid, "Shadhite Moner Shadh," in *Ashar Chalane Bhuli* [Deceived by hope] (Calcutta: Ananda Publishers, 1994), 60–67. See also Rosinka Chaudhuri, *Freedom and Beef Steaks: Colonial Calcutta Culture* (Delhi: Orient Blackswan, 2012).

74. Murshid, *Ashar Chalane Bhuli,* 310–312.

75. This description of factionalism in Calcutta was provided by Bhabanicharan Bandyopadhyay, editor of Rammohan Roy's paper *Sambad Kaumudi* [The Sun News] and then his own paper, more aligned to the ideals of the so-called orthodox faction, called *Samachar Chandrika* [The Moon News]. See Bhabanicharan Bandyopadhyay, *Kalikata Kamalalaya* (Calcutta: Samachar Chandrika Press, 1823), 15–18, 47–62.

76. "Minute by the Hon'ble T.B. Macaulay."

77. For the details of Krishnamohan's expulsion, see Shastri, *Ramtanu Lahiri o Tatkaleen Bangasamaj,* 74–75.

78. Paul D. Halliday, introduction to *Habeas Corpus: From England to Empire* (Cambridge, MA: Belknap Press of Harvard University Press, 2010), 1–2.

79. Ernest John Trevelyan, "Lecture I," in *The Law Relating to Minors in the Presidency of Bengal* (London: Thacker, Spink and Company, 1878), 1–35.

80. Muhammad Mohar Ali, "The Reaction to Specific Conversions to Christianity," in *The Bengali Reaction to Christian Missionary Activities 1833–1857* (Chittagong: The Mehrub Publications, 1965), 78–160.

81. William Smithers Church, *A Treatise of the Writ of Habeas Corpus: Including Jurisdiction, False Imprisonment, Writ of Error, Extradiction, Mandamus, Certiorari, Judgments, Etc. With Practice and Forms* (San Francisco: A. L. Bancroft, 1884), 555–566; "In the Court of Queen's Bench: Reg. *vs.* Maria Clarke in re Alicia Race," *The American Law Register (1852–1891)* 5, no. 9 (1857): 537–551, https://www.jstor.org/stable/3301780.

82. Calcutta Missionary Conference, *Statement Concerning Sir Mordaunt Wells's Judgment in the Case of Hema Nath Bose: By the Calcutta Missionary Conference. With Notes and Appendices* (Calcutta: The Baptist Mission Press, 1863), 8–9, 12.

83. *Converts from the Government and Missionary Schools,* 16–17.

84. "The Case of Brijonath Ghose," *Asiatic Journal and Monthly Miscellany* 13 (1834): 82–88.

85. Josiah Bateman, *The Life of Daniel Wilson, D.D., Bishop of Calcutta and Metropolitan of India* (Boston: Gould and Lincoln, 1860), 262–263.

86. Quoted in Stephen Neill, *A History of Christianity in India, 1707–1858* (Cambridge: Cambridge University Press, 1985), 378.

87. Bateman, *Life of Daniel Wilson,* 262–263.

88. "Case of Brijonath Ghose," 68–72.

89. "Case of Brijonath Ghose," 82–88.

90. Rev. James Long, *Handbook of Bengal Missions in Connexion with the Church of England Together with an Account of General Educational Efforts in North India* (London: John Farquhar Shaw, 1848), 111.

91. See Kissory Chand Mittra, *DvāRakānāTha ṬhāKura* (Kalikātā: Sambodhi PāBalikeśāNa, 1962). On his pioneering entrepreneurial role in colonial Bengal, see Blair B. Kling, *Partner in Empire: Dwarkanath Tagore and the Age of Enterprise in Eastern India* (Berkeley: University of California Press, 1976).

92. Dwarkanath Tagore to Debendranath Tagore, May 22, 1845, Rabindra Sadhana, Tagore Family Papers. Quoted in Kling, *Partner in Empire,* 236n. Emphasis added.

93. See Alexander Duff and Thomas Smith, *Work of Grace at Calcutta: Being a Narrative of the Circumstances Attending the Recent Conversions There* (Edinburgh: W. P. Kennedy, 1845), 30–31.

94. For a detailed report, see *Tattvabodhini Patrika* 3, no. 22 (Jaishtha edition, 1845): 172–177. The article was written by the rationalist Akshay Kumar Dutta at Debendranath Tagore's request.

95. Article dated December 4, 1845, in *The Friend of India,* quoted in S. R. Mehrotra, *The Emergence of the Indian National Congress* (Delhi: Vikas Publications, 1971), 38–39.

96. Duff and Smith, *Work of Grace at Calcutta.*

97. Duff and Smith, *Work of Grace at Calcutta,* 10.

98. Duff and Smith, *Work of Grace at Calcutta,* 9.

99. Duff and Smith, *Work of Grace at Calcutta,* 9.

100. Referred to as the young Raja K* by Duff, grandson of Nabakrishna Dev. Kalikrishna's first cousin was Radhakanta Dev, the titular head or *kulapati* of the orthodox Bengali Hindu elites of Calcutta. Kalikrishna would later succeed to this position.

101. Duff and Smith, *Work of Grace at Calcutta,* 15–16.

102. Debendranātha Ṭhākura and Indirā Debī Caudhurāṇī, *The Autobiography of Maharshi Devendranath Tagore* (London: Macmillan, 1914).

103. Ajit Kumar Chakrabarty, *Maharshi Devendranātha Ṭhākura* (Allahabad: Indian Press, 1916).

104. Chakrabarty, *Maharshi Devendranātha Ṭhākura,* 130–135.

105. Duff and Smith, *Work of Grace at Calcutta,* 15.

106. Duff and Smith, *Work of Grace at Calcutta,* 30–31.

107. For a detailed report, see *Tattvabodhini Patrika* 3, no. 22 (Jaishtha edition, 1845): 172–177. *Converts from the Government and Missionary Schools,* 20–21. See also Chakrabarty, *Maharshi Devendranātha Ṭhākura,* 138–140.

108. Chakrabarty, "Khristan Sanghat: Hindu-hitarthi bidyalay," in *Maharshi Devendranātha Ṭhākura,* 111–114.

109. Duff and Smith, *Work of Grace at Calcutta,* 19.

110. Duff and Smith, *Work of Grace at Calcutta,* 25–33.

111. Alexander Duff, *The Intolerant and Persecuting Section of the Calcutta Baboos Exposed!!!* (Calcutta: J. Thomas at the Baptist Mission Press, 1847), 19–21. "That men are to be found among the Orthodox Baboos of Calcutta, who would . . . readily employ their clubmen to fell a Missionary."

112. *Intolerant and Persecuting Section,* 22.

113. *Converts from the Government and Missionary Schools,* 20–21.

114. Lalbehari Dey, *Recollections of Alexander Duff, D.D., LL.D., and of the Mission College Which He Founded in Calcutta* (London: T. Nelson and Sons, 1879), 183–184.

115. Lucy Carroll, "Law, Custom, and Statutory Social Reform: The Hindu Widows' Remarriage Act of 1856," *Indian Economic & Social History Review* 20, no. 4 (1983): 363–388, https://doi.org/10.1177/001946468302000401.

116. *The Children's Missionary Newspaper: Designed to Communicate Interesting Intelligence Respecting the Missionary Efforts of All Evangelical Denominations in Language Adapted to the Capacities of Children,* vol. 16, no. 3 (Edinburgh: James Gall, Inglis and Son, 1857), 19–22.

117. This was a legal fiction under Hindu personal law, something that Gauri Viswanathan explains as a "civil death." See Gauri Vishwanath, "Coping with

(Civil) Death: The Christian Convert's Rights of Passage in Colonial India," in *After Colonialism: Imperial Histories and Postcolonial Displacements,* ed. Gyan Prakash (Princeton, NJ: Princeton University Press, 1995), 183–210.

118. William Hough, *Law of Inheritance, Etc., India as It Ought to Be under the New Charter Act: Improvements Suggested* (London: Thacker and Co., 1853), 5–7.

119. See for example the Parsi convert's case, "The Queen vs. Shapurji Bezonji and Bezanji Edalji," in T. A. Venkasawmy Row, *The Indian Decisions (Old Series): Being a Verbatim Reprint of the Reports of Cases Decided by the Late Supreme Courts and the Sudder Dewanny Adawluts in India,* 17 vols. (Madras: The Law Printing House, 1912), 4:84–94.

120. Krishna Mohan Banerjee, *Sanctity of Conjugal Relations: Reasons for Signing the Clerical Petition against the Remarriage of Converts Bill: By Rev. K.M. Banerjea* (London: Thacker, Spink & Company, 1865), 3.

121. Nandini Chatterjee, *The Making of Indian Secularism: Empire, Law and Christianity, 1830–1960* (New York: Palgrave Macmillan, 2011), 101–102.

122. Smith, *Life of Alexander Duff,* 2:248–249.

123. The senior branch of the family, sons of India's first native puisne judge Rasamay Dutt, had all converted to Christianity in 1862. See Harihar Das, *The Dutt Family, Life and Letters of Toru Dutt* (London: Humphrey Milford, Oxford University Press, 1921), 1–16.

124. Smith, *Life of Alexander Duff,* 2:248–249.

125. "The Hindu Convert to His Wife," in *The Dutt Family Album* (London: Longmans, Green & Co., 1870), 28–31. For the attribution of the poem to Govin Chunder Dutt, see Das, *Dutt Family, Life and Letters of Toru Dutt,* 10–11.

126. Thomas Sergeant and John C. Lowber, *Reports of Cases Argued and Determined in the English Courts of Common Law: With Tables of the Cases and Principal Matters,* vol. 31 (Philadelphia: T. and J. W. Johnson Law Booksellers, Publishers and Importers, 1853), 623–643. "When an infant is brought before the Court by Habeas Corpus, if he be of an age to exercise a choice, the Court leaves him to elect where he will go" (285).

127. George Taylor, *The Queen vs. Ogilvie, Reports of Cases Heard and Determined in the Supreme Court of Judicature at the Fort William in Bengal from January 1847 to December 1848, Both Inclusive* (Calcutta: P. S. D'Rozario and Co., 1851), 140–141.

128. Row, *Indian Decisions (Old Series),* vol. 2, "The Queen vs. Ogilvie, in Re Radacaunt Dutt, 1847, 8th July, Thursday: Habeas Corpus, the right of Hindu father to the custody of the infant child," 83–87.

129. *Allen's Indian Mail, and Register of Intelligence for British and Foreign India, China, and All Parts of the East,* vol. 5 (London: Wm. H. Allen and Company, 1845), 611.

130. Duleep wore the famous Kohinoor diamond in his armlet. Login ceded the diamond to the governor-general of India, Lord Dalhousie, after convincing Duleep to give it up. Dalhousie ultimately sent it to Queen Victoria as a gift in 1849. Danielle C. Kinsey, "Koh-i-Noor: Empire, Diamonds, and the Performance of British Material Culture," *Journal of British Studies* 48, no. 2 (2009): 391–419, http://www.jstor.org/stable/25483040.

131. Quoted in Rice, *Reply to the Rev. K. M. Banerjea's Remarks,* 8.

132. Rice, *Reply to the Rev. K. M. Banerjea's Remarks,* 7–10.

133. Duleep's conversion made waves in Calcutta as well. Kālīprasanna Simha, "Khristiani Hujoog," in *Hutoma pyāñcāra nakśā,* ed. Arun Nag (Calcutta: Subarnarekha, 1991), 131–132. Simha, who wrote the *nakśā* in the aftermath of the uprising of 1857 and published it between 1861 and 1863, mentioned that the conversion of Duleep caused widespread amazement, anger, and unrest. Rumors abounded that the elite Hindus and Sikhs of India would all be forced to convert to Christianity, following his example.

134. "In the Court of Queen's Bench."

135. Calcutta Missionary Conference, *Statement Concerning Sir Mordaunt Wells's Judgment,* 12.

136. Calcutta Missionary Conference, *Statement Concerning Sir Mordaunt Wells's Judgment,* 11.

137. Edgar Hyde, *Reports of Cases Argued and Determined During the Years 1862 & 1864: In the High Court of Judicature at Fort William in Bengal in Its Ordinary Original Jurisdiction and on Appeal Therefrom,* vol. 1 (Calcutta: E. W. Elloy at the Law-Publishing Press, 1897), 119. Emphasis added.

138. *Sir Mordaunt Wells and Public Opinion in India* (Calcutta: Printed by C. H. Manuel, Scott & Co.'s Press, 1863), 19.

139. Blair B. Kling, *The Blue Mutiny: The Indigo Disturbances in Bengal, 1859–1862* (Philadelphia: University of Pennsylvania Press, 2016). For Rev. James Long, see Geoffrey A. Oddie, *Missionaries, Rebellion, and Proto-Nationalism: James Long of Bengal* (Richmond, Surrey, UK: Taylor & Francis, 2016).

140. *Sir Mordaunt Wells and Public Opinion in India,* 3.

141. *Sir Mordaunt Wells and Public Opinion in India,* 32.

142. Calcutta Missionary Conference, *Statement Concerning Sir Mordaunt Wells.*

143. Calcutta Missionary Conference, *Statement Concerning Sir Mordaunt Wells,* 7.

144. "Youthful Converts in India," *The Missionary Herald* (London: Pewtress & Company, 1864), n.s., 186.

145. "Youthful Converts in India," 185–187.

146. Trevelyan, "Lecture VI," in *The Law Relating to Minors,* 239–243.

147. Quoted in Trevelyan, "Lecture VI," 241.

148. Quoted in Trevelyan, "Lecture VI," 242.

149. William Smithers Church, *A Treatise on the Writ of Habeas Corpus, including Jurisdiction, False Imprisonment, Writ of Error, Extradition, Mandamus, Certiorai, Judgements, etc.: With Practice and Forms* (San Francicso: Bancroft and Whitney, 1893), 671–675.

150. Trevelyan, "Lecture I." See also *Indian Jurist: A Journal and Law Reports* (Madras: Vest and Company, 1887), 370–373.

151. Neera Chandhoke, "Exploring the Mythology of the Public Sphere," in *Civil Society, Public Sphere and Citizenship: Dialogues and Perceptions,* ed. Rajeev Bhargava and Helmut Reifeld (New Delhi: Sage, 2005), 334. Chandhoke references Jürgen Habermas's "Discourse Ethics: Notes on a Program of Philosophical Justification."

152. Shakespeare, *The Tempest,* act 1, scene 2, 366–368. See also Partha Chatterjee's analysis of the famous exchange between the Derozian Tarachand Chakrabarti and the principal of Hindu College, D. L. Richardson, on free speech. Partha Chatterjee, *Texts of Power: Emerging Disciplines in Colonial Bengal* (Minneapolis: University of Minnesota Press, 1995), 13–14.

THREE THE GREAT TAGORE WILL CASE

1. Kālīprasanna Siṃha, "Khristiani Hujoog," in *Hutoma Pyāñcāra Nakśā,* ed. Rajendranath Bandopadhyay and Sajanikanta Das (Kalikata: Bangiya Sahitya Parishat, 1956), 53–54. See also Priyanka Basu, "The Observant Owl: Sensory Worlds of Colonial Calcutta in Hutom's Vignettes," *South Asia: Journal of South Asian Studies* 44, no. 5 (2021): 948–965, https://doi.org/10.1080/00856401.2021.1966170.

2. Gyanendramohan was the first Indian barrister also admitted as the advocate of the Calcutta High Court.

3. Alexander Duff and William Howard Pearce, *Observations on the Hindoo and Muhammedan Laws of Inheritance, as affecting Converts to Christianity in India* (Calcutta: Baptist Mission Press, 1831).

4. Duff and Pearce, *Observations on the Hindoo and Muhammedan Laws.*

5. Chandra Mallampalli, *Christians and Public Life in Colonial South India, 1863–1937* (London: Routledge, 2012), 2, 8–9. Mallampalli's work first noted the effacement of Christian converts from family and community, and the denial of inheritance rights to them.

6. Ludo Rocher and Donald R. Davis, eds., *Studies in Hindu Law and Dharmaśāstra* (London: Anthem, 2012), 191.

7. S. R. Mehrotra, *The Emergence of the Indian National Congress* (Delhi: Vikas Publications, 1971), 35–40.

8. *Hansard Parliamentary Debates,* HL Deb., August 12, 1853, vol. 129, cc. 1675–1679, UK Parliament website, https://api.parliament.uk/historic-hansard/lords/1853/aug/12/protest.

9. *Hansard Parliamentary Debates,* HL Deb., August 12, 1853. Emphasis added.

10. Thomas Spring Rice, *A Reply to the Rev. K. M. Banerjea's Remarks on the Speech of the Earl of Ellenborough, in the House of Lords . . . against Act. XXI. of 1850, of the Government of India. With an Appendix Containing the Speeches of Lord Monteagle and the Earl of Ellenborough. By a Member of the Committee Appointed by the Hindu Inhabitants of Bengal, Behar and Orissa, for Petitioning Parliament against the Aforesaid Act* (Calcutta: Printed by D'Rozario and Co., 1853), 2.

11. Ludo Rocher, introduction to *Jimutavahana's Dayabhaga: The Hindu Law of Inheritance in Bengal* (New York: Oxford University Press, 2002), 1–50.

12. Rice, *Reply to the Rev. K. M. Banerjea's Remarks,* 33.

13. "The Accounts of All Respectable and Opulent Natives of the Presidency," compiled by Raja Radhakanta Dev at the request of H. T. Prinsep in 1822, revised and extended in 1839. In S. N. Mukherjee, "Class, Caste, and Politics in Calcutta, 1815–38," in *Elites in South Asia,* ed. Edmund Leach and S. N. Mukherjee (Cambridge: Cambridge University Press, 1970), 46–49.

14. Reported July 17, 1851. Quoted in Mehrotra, *Emergence of the Indian National Congress,* 51.

15. Sir Syed Ahmed Khan, *Asbab-e-Baghawat-e-Hind* (1858), trans. His American Well-Wisher [pseud.] as *The Causes of the Rebellion of India* (2005), http://www.columbia.edu/itc/mealac/pritchett/00urdu/asbab/translation2005.html. "Act 21 of 1850 was a clear case of the disturbance of religious rules. Then, because of this Act, for one thing people suspected that the Act had been issued specially to encourage people to accept the Christian religion. Because it was clear that no person from another religion can be admitted among the Hindus, the Hindus were deprived of any benefit from this law. If some man from another religion would become a Muslim, then from the practice of the religion that he has adopted, he is forbidden to take any inheritance from his bequeathers who were of another religion. But indeed, whoever accepted the Christian religion, he could obtain advantage. For this reason, people thought that in addition to religious intervention, this Act was a clear enticement."

16. Khan, *Asbab-e-Baghawat-e-Hind.*

17. Siṃha, "Khristiani Hujoog," 10–11.

18. *Zenana* (pl. *zenanas*) (in India and Iran): the part of a house for the seclusion of women. From Persian and Urdu *zanānah,* from *zan,* "woman." In the

Bengali Hindu and Brahmo context, this part of the house would be called *antahpur.*

19. Raj Jogeshur Mitter, ed., *Speeches by Mr. George Thompson: Father of Political Education in India* (Calcutta: Messrs. S. K. Lahiri and Company, 1895), 5–8.

20. Mehrotra, *History of the Indian National Congress,* 25–26. See also S. R. Mehrotra, "The British India Society and Its Bengal Branch, 1839–46," *Indian Economic & Social History Review* 4, no. 2 (1967): 131–154, https://doi.org/10.1177/001946466700400203.

21. Mehrotra, *History of the Indian National Congress,* 28–33.

22. Amelia married Frederick William Chesson, who was secretary to the Aborigines Protection Society. For details, see S. J. Morgan, "Thompson, George Donisthorpe (1804–1878)," ed. Rev. Matthew Lee, in *Oxford Dictionary of National Biography* (Oxford: Oxford University Press, 2004); online ed., October 2016, http://www.oxforddnb.com/view/article/27261.

23. REAS/2/2/54, Raymond English Anti-Slavery Collection (REAS), University of Manchester Library.

24. For comparison, this amount would be about £3,847,619 in 2014. The per annum income of Jane Austen's fabulously rich Mr. Darcy was £10,000. A table of typical annual incomes for the Victorian age, adapted from Sally Mitchell's *Daily Life in Victorian England,* puts the average annual income of the richest aristocratic landowners at about £30,000. Sally Mitchell, *Daily Life in Victorian England* (London: Bloomsbury Academic, 2009), 33.

25. *Debottar* land is land held in stewardship for a deity to whom the land belongs in fact as well as legally. See Arjun Appadurai and Carol Appadurai Breckenridge, "The South Indian Temple: Authority, Honour and Redistribution," *Contributions to Indian Sociology* 10, no. 2 (1976): 187–211.

26. Thompson was mistaken in his calculation. Born in 1826, Gyanendramohan would have been about seventeen years old during Thompson's first visit.

27. "Puja," February 16, 1822, in *Sambadpatre Sekaler Katha* [Yesteryears in newspapers and periodicals], 2nd ed., vol. 1, ed. Brajendranath Bandopadhyay (Calcutta: Bangiya Sahitya Parishat Mandir, 1937), 263.

28. Thompson says she was eleven years old at her marriage; Storrow and the pamphlet published by the Society for Promoting Female Education in the East (SPFEE) put her at nine years old. Storrow first published his account of Bala's life in 1852, Thompson wrote his letter to Amelia Chesson in 1856, and the SPFEE pamphlet was published in 1856 as well.

29. Priyanath Shastri, ed., *Maharshi Debendranath'er Patrabali* (Calcutta, n.d.), 40–41.

30. Gyanadanandini Devi, *Puratani* [Those old days] (Calcutta: Indian Associated Publishing Co., 1957). For women's education in colonial Bengal, see Geraldine Forbes, "Education for Women," in *Women and Social Reform in Modern India: A Reader,* ed. Sumit Sarkar and Tanika Sarkar (Bloomington: Indiana University Press, 2008), 58–77.

31. REAS/2/2/54, 21. Underlining in the original text.

32. Alexander Duff and Thomas Smith, *Work of Grace at Calcutta: Being a Narrative of the Circumstances Attending the Recent Conversions There* (Edinburgh: W. P. Kennedy; London: J. Nisbet and Company, 1845), 4–18.

33. Edward Storrow, *The Eastern Lily Gathered: A Memoir of Bala Shoondoree Tagore* (London: John Snow, 1852), 41–42.

34. Storrow, *Eastern Lily Gathered,* 41–42.

35. Gyanadanandini had a "Bibi" to teach her to speak in English and to play the piano to her and her sister-in-law Swarnakumari Debi Tagore. Devi, *Puratani.*

36. Storrow, *Eastern Lily Gathered,* 31.

37. REAS/2/2/54, 29.

38. REAS/2/2/54, 32. Underlining in the original text.

39. See Tinkori Chattopadhyay, *Shantishojja: The Peaceful Deathbed Scenes of Indian Christians* (Calcutta: Baptist Mission Press and the Bengal Branch of the Christian Vernacular Education Society, 1880).

40. REAS/2/2/54, 36–37. Underlining in the original text.

41. REAS/2/2/57, 5.

42. This perceived disloyalty brought about bloody retribution of Indian converts to Christianity by the Indian rebels during the uprising of 1857. The murder of Dr. Chaman Lal, converted Christian and physician to the last Mughal emperor, Bahadur Shah Zafar, was well known. See William Darlymple, "The Sword of the Lord of Fury," in *The Last Mughal: The Fall of a Dynasty: Delhi, 1857* (New York: Vintage Books, 2008), 134–179. Rev. Lalbehari Dey, another prominent Bengali converted by Alexander Duff, reported some of these outrages in his periodical *Arunodaya* (Sunrise). The fact that the native Christian community was a target of attack is clear from such reportage. See *Arunodaya* (1857), http://crossasia-repository.ub.uni-heidelberg.de/475.

43. The early account of the conversion of three Parsi boys in Bombay in 1840, by Rev. John Wilson, is a good example. *Conversion of Two Parsis and Prosecution of the Rev. John Wilson, on a Writ of Habeas Corpus, Before the Supreme Court of Judicature at Bombay* (Bombay: High Court of Judicature, 1840).

44. REAS/2/2/57, 8. Emphasis added.

45. John Cochrane, *Hindoo Law: Defence of the Daya Bhaga: Notice of the Case on Prosonnocoomar Tagore's Will* (London: W. H. Allen and Company, 1872), 114–115. This sentence is the fourth clause in Prosonnocoomar Tagore's will and forms the basis for the interpretation of the disinheritance of Gyanendramohan.

46. *The Great Tagore Will Case: G.M. Tagore versus Woopendermohun Tagore, and Others, Being a Full Report of the Proceedings* (Calcutta: Indian Mirror Press, 1872).

47. Devi, *Puratani.* This is according to Professor Projit Bihari Mukharji, whose mother was from the Pathuriaghata family and therefore had heard tales of Gyanendramohan (and the curse) since her childhood.

48. Chitra Dev, *Thakurbari'r Bahir Mahal* (Calcutta: Ananda Publishers, 2016), 266. Chitra Dev had access to family lore about Gyanendramohan, which she documented alongside the usual missionary sources on pp. 244–274. She is, however, misinformed on the question of Gyanendramohan's sons—his will specifies that his only son to survive to adulthood was Prossonnomohan. Gyanendramohan outlived this son. British India Office Wills & Probate, *Birth, Marriage & Death (Parish Registers),* L-AG-34-29-136, folio number: 82; catalog description: Wills—Bengal 1780–1938.

49. Anna Johnston, *Missionary Writing and Empire, 1800–1860* (New York: Cambridge University Press, 2003), 84–85.

50. Susie Tharu and K. Lalita, eds., *Women Writing in India: 600 B.C. to the Present* (New York: Feminist Press at the City University of New York, 1991), 203–210. Hannah was the daughter of a Swiss missionary, Father Francois Lacroix, who was based in Chinsurah, the Dutch colonial domain in Bengal. She married Joseph Mullens, a London Missionary Society missionary, and the couple settled and worked in Calcutta. Subodh Sengupta and Anjali Bose, eds., *Samsad Bangla Charitavidhan,* vol. 1 (Calcutta: Aava Press, 1960), 423.

51. Storrow, *Eastern Lily Gathered.*

52. Quoted in Storrow, *Eastern Lily Gathered,* 42–43. Emphasis added.

53. Quoted in *The Evangelical Magazine and Missionary Chronicle* 29 (1851): 680.

54. Ram Gopal Sanyal, *Calcutta: Additional Converts to the Christian Faith, Reminiscences and Anecdotes of Great Men of India* (Calcutta: Herald Printing Press, 1894), 675–680.

55. This was a legal fiction under Hindu personal law. See Gauri Viswanathan, "Coping with (Civil) Death: The Christian Convert's Rights of Passage in Colonial India," in *After Colonialism: Imperial Histories and Postcolonial Displacements,* ed. Gyan Prakash (Princeton, NJ: Princeton University Press, 1995), 183.

56. James Wyburd Furrell, *The Tagore Family: A Memoir* (Calcutta: Thacker, Spink & Company, 1892), 147. Prosonnocoomar's biography takes up seventy pages, ending with this stark sentence: "He left one son, Gyanendramohan Tagore, who is a convert to Christianity and was disinherited by his father."

57. Quoted in Storrow, *Eastern Lily Gathered,* 43.

58. *The Evangelical Magazine and Missionary Chronicle* 29 (1851): 680.

59. The Society for Promoting Female Education in the East (SPFEE), *The History of a Converted Hindoo Lady* (Edinburgh: Oliver and Boyd, 1857).

60. Furrell, *Tagore Family,* 129.

61. Shibnath Shastri and Roper Lethbridge, *Rāmtanu Lahiri, Brahman and Reformer: A History of the Renaissance in Bengal, from the Bengali of Pandit Sivanath Sastri* (London: Swan Sonnenchein & Co., 1907); Rajnarayan Bose, *Rājanārāyaṇa Basura ātma-carita* (Calcutta: Kuntaline Press, 1909); Bhudev Mukherjee, *Bhudev Carita,* 3 vols. (Calcutta: India Press, n.d.).

62. Edward Jewitt Robinson, *The Daughters of India: Their Social Condition, Religion, Literature, Obligations, and Prospects* (Glasgow: Thomas Murray and Son, 1860), 242–251.

63. Anna Johnston, "The London Missionary Society in India," in *Missionary Writing and Empire* (Cambridge: Cambridge University Press, 2009), 84–91; Deepra Dandekar, "Translation and the Christian Conversion of Women in Colonial India: Rev. Sheshadri and Bāḷā Sundarābāī Ṭhākūr," *Journal of South Asian Studies* 41, no. 2 (2018): 366–383.

64. SPFEE, *History of a Converted Hindoo Lady.*

65. British India Office, Marriages, *Parish Register Transcripts from the Presidency of Bengal: 1713–1948,* archive reference: N-1-8, folio number: 347.

66. Pran Nath Chopra, Prabha Chopra, and Padmsha Jha, *Secret Papers from British Royal Archives* (Delhi: Konark, 1998), 68–69. Emphasis added.

67. SPFEE, *History of a Converted Hindoo Lady.*

68. SPFEE, *History of a Converted Hindoo Lady,* 27–29.

69. British India Office Wills & Probate, *Birth, Marriage & Death (Parish Registers),* L-AG-34-29-136, folio number: 82, catalog description: Wills—Bengal 1780–1938.

70. Krishnamohan's experiences bear out the threats of physical violence directed toward converts. An account of the Parsi Dhunjibhai's conversion gives a vivid description of the mob frenzy: "They shouted, 'Seize! Kill him!'" William Clarkson, *India and the Gospel; or an Empire for the Messiah* (London: John Snow, 1851), 243–244.

71. *Tattvabodhini Patrika* 4, no. 33 (Baishakh ed., 1846), 379–384.

72. Quoted in Shastri, *Maharshi Debendranath'er Patrabali,* 40–41.

73. Sanyal, *Reminiscences and Anecdotes of Great Men of India,* 25.

74. Sanyal, *Reminiscences and Anecdotes of Great Men of India,* 11.

75. *Christian Examiner* 5 (1851): 470–472. Some of the *vyavasthas* inspired later commentary as well—of the few that still exist among the Vernacular Tract (VT) collections of the India Office Library, titles such as "Khristianer Hindu-Samaj'e punah-pravesh sambandhiya vyavastha" (Rules for the re-entry of Christians into Hindu society) are quite common (VT 1729).

76. The revived Sanjaya, chronicler of the great Mahabharata war to the blind king Dhritarashtra.

77. Sanjay Redivivus [Krishnamohan Banerjee], *Report of a Grand Brahminical Meeting on Behalf of Brahminical Rights and against the Lex Loci etc.* (Calcutta: Messrs. P. S. D'Rozario and Company, 1850).

78. Dev, *Thakurbari'r Bahir Mahal,* 164.

79. Prosonnocoomar Tagore, trans., *Vivada Chintamani: A Succinct Commentary on the Hindoo Law Prevalent in Mithila, from the Original Sanskrit of Vachaspati Misra* (Calcutta: The Albion Press, 1863).

80. Rocher, introduction to *Jimutavahana's Dayabhaga.*

81. Prosonnocoomar Tagore, *Table of Succession under the Hindu Law as Prevalent in Bengal* (Calcutta: A. D'Rozario at the Albion Press, 1864).

82. Cochrane, *Hindoo Law,* 1–3.

83. Prosonnocoomar Tagore, *Loose Papers By P.C.T CSI* (Calcutta: Bengal Superior Press, 1868), 1–33.

84. Cochrane, *Hindoo Law,* 113–131.

85. *Great Tagore Will Case.* The Privy Council ruled that Jatindramohan would enjoy the estates of Prosonnocoomar Tagore for his natural lifespan, at the end of which the estates would revert to Gyanendramohan.

86. *In the High Court of Judicature: At Fort William in Bengal Ordinary Original Civil Jurisdiction, Present the Hon'ble Mr. Justice Phear, Gyanendramohan Tagore vs. Woopendramohan Tagore and Others, 1st April 1869,* 13–15.

87. *In the High Court of Judicature,* 20–23.

88. Jogendra Chunder Ghose, *The Principles of Hindu Law,* 3rd ed. (Calcutta: S. C. Auddy & Co., 1917), 886–892. In the matter of "unborn generations," see the reminiscences of the positivist legal scholar Krishnakamal Bhattacharyya in Bipina Bihārī Gupta, *Purātana Prasaṅga [Bhūmikā: Pramathanātha Biśī,*

Bidyābhāratī Saṃskaraṇa], 2nd ed., ed. Biśu Mukhopādhyāẏa (Kalikata: Bidyābhāratī, 1966), 321–324.

89. *Ijlas* (from Arabic): a session, an official meeting, a sitting of a law court, an assembly session, the sitting of a court of justice.

90. Gyanendramohan returned to India from England in 1864, and his name was entered into the rolls of the original side of the Calcutta High Court in either March or November 1865. B. K. Acharya, "Annals of the Bengal Bar, Continued," *Calcutta Law Journal* 19, no. 5 (March 1914): 55. I am grateful to James Jaffe for the reference. The *Friend of India* reported on November 16, 1865, that "this [was] the first instance of an Asian practicing as a barrister in India." Golam Murshid in his biography of Michael Madhusudan Dutta writes that Gyanendramohan did have a flourishing practice in Calcutta, earning about Rs. 200 or £20 per day. According to sources I can find, Gyanendramohan remained and practiced in Calcutta until 1869 and returned to England with his children after Kamala Banerjee's death.

91. "Appellate Jurisdiction: Present The Hon'ble Sir Barnes Peacock, Knight, Chief Justice, and the Hon'ble Mr. Justice Norman," appended to *In the High Court of Judicature*, 57–58.

92. "Appellate Jurisdiction," 77.

93. "Appellate Jurisdiction," 99–104, 131–134.

94. *Tyajja putra:* A son disowned and disinherited by his father. ত্যাজ্যপুত্র করা: to disown or disinherit a son; to cut off.

95. Cochrane, *Hindoo Law*, 346.

96. Rocher, introduction to *Jimutavahana's Dayabhaga*, 28.

97. Raymond West, Georg Bühler, and Abdul Majid, *A Digest of the Hindu Law of Inheritance, Partition, and Adoption, Embodying the Replies of the Sâstris* (London: Sweet and Maxwell, 1919), 59. Quote from Willes's opinion in the case of *Ganendro Mohun Tagore v. Rajah Juttendro Mohun Tagore.*

98. Mr. Sreejit Tagore, current scion of the Pathuriaghata Tagore family, email message to author, March 29, 2014.

99. Sreejit Tagore, email message to author, March 29, 2014.

100. Tagore, *Table of Succession under the Hindu Law.*

101. Rabindranath Tagore wrote to Jatindramohan in a letter, "You're the most honored head of the family for all of us now." Quoted in Dev, *Thakurbari'r Bahir Mahal*, 322.

102. "*Sreemutty Soorjeemoney Dossee v. Denobundoo Mullick and Others*, 1857," in *Moore's Indian Appeals*, vol. 6 (London, 1857), 526–556.

103. *Judgment of the Lords of the Judicial Committee of the Privy Council on the Appeals of Jatindramohan Tagore and Another v. Gyanendramohan Tagore, and Cross Appeal from the High Court of Judicature at Calcutta; Delivered 5th July 1872*, 10–14.

104. *The Bengal Law Reports of Decisions of the High Court at Fort William Civil and Criminal in Its Original and Appellate Jurisdictions: Privy Council Decisions on Indian Appeals; Orders and Rules of the High Court; and Revenue Circular Orders. . . .* (Bangalore: Printed and published for the Bengal Council of Law Reporting by Thacker, Spink & Company, 1874), 8.

105. I am grateful to T. C. A. Achintya and several audience members at a panel I presented at ASLH 2022, who pointed out the profound cruelty of converts having no access to their own inheritances and having to fight protracted legal battles to secure their rights against their relatives.

106. *Great Tagore Will Case.*

107. Mitra Sharafi, *Law and Identity in Colonial South Asia: Parsi Legal Culture, 1772–1947* (New York: Cambridge University Press, 2014), 140.

108. Hugh Roper Lethbridge, *The Golden Book of India: A Genealogical and Biographical Dictionary of the Ruling Princes, Chiefs, Nobles, and Other Personages, Titled or Decorated of the Indian Empire* (London: Macmillan & Co., 1893), 527–528.

109. J. Duncan M. Derrett, "Factum Valet: The Adventures of a Maxim," *International and Comparative Law Quarterly* 7, no. 2 (1958): 294, http://www.jstor.org/stable/755499.

110. Rocher and Davis, *Studies in Hindu Law and Dharmaśāstra*, 639.

111. I'm grateful to Hayden Bellenoit for the scalpel metaphor!

112. "Tagore v. Tagore," *Law Magazine and Review* 2, no. 9 (September 1873): 824.

113. *Bengal Law Reports of Decisions of the High Court at Fort William*, 1–34.

114. For example, this is how he signed his name in a memorial to Lord Dufferin on the Bengal Tenancy Act Debates, on July 6, 1884. See India Office Records (IOR) at the British Library, IOR/L/PJ/6/157, file 1204.

115. Gyanendramohan Tagore, *Thoughts of a Christian Brahmin on the Position and Prospects of Religion in India* (London: Hamilton, Adams and Co., 1871), 5.

116. British India Office Wills & Probate, *Birth, Marriage & Death (Parish Registers)*, L-AG-34-29-136, folio number: 82; catalog description: Wills—Bengal 1780–1938.

117. British India Office Wills & Probate, *Birth, Marriage & Death (Parish Registers)*, L-AG-34-29-136.

118. Rakhaldas Haldar, *The English Diary of an Indian Student, 1861–62: Being the Scribbling Journal of the Late Rakhaldas Haldar* (Dhaka: Ashutosh Library, 1903).

119. Dev, *Thakurbari'r Bahir Mahal,* 270.

120. Chopra, Chopra, and Jha, *Secret Papers from British Royal Archives,* 68–69. Emphasis added.

121. *Atmaparichay* is a compound Bengali word of Sanskrit origin that means "self-identity."

122. Rabindranath Tagore, *Rabindra Racanabali,* vol. 9 (Kalikata: Bisvabharati, 1995), 599.

123. Chandra Mallampalli, *Race, Religion, and Law in Colonial India: Trials of an Interracial Family* (Cambridge: Cambridge University Press, 2011), 231.

124. Mallampalli, *Race, Religion, and Law.*

FOUR CONVERSION AND THE POLITICS OF LAND OWNERSHIP IN COLONIAL BENGAL

1. John William Kaye, *A History of the Sepoy War in India, 1857–1858,* vol. 1 (London: Longmans, Green and Co., 1906). See also Syed Ahmed Khan, *The Causes of the Indian Revolt, Written by Sir Syed Ahmed Khan Bahadur in 1858, and Translated into English by His Two European Friends* (Banaras: Medical Hall Press, 1873).

2. C. A. Bayly, *Empire and Information: Intelligence Gathering and Social Communication in India, 1780–1870* (New York: Cambridge University Press, 1996), 244. Bayly quotes the missionary C. B. Leupolt, who was told by his Indian interlocutors with great bitterness, "You have already conquered our bodies and you are in a fair way to conquering our minds."

3. Kaye, *History of the Sepoy War in India,* 364–365.

4. Blair B. Kling, *The Blue Mutiny: The Indigo Disturbances in Bengal, 1859–1862* (Philadelphia: University of Pennsylvania Press, 1966).

5. Sisirkumar Ghose, *Peasant Revolution in Bengal* (Calcutta: Bharati Library, 1953), e.g., 42–47.

6. Katherine Prior, "Bethune, John Elliot Drinkwater (1801–1851)," in *Oxford Dictionary of National Biography* (Oxford: Oxford University Press, 2004); online ed., September 2004, http://www.oxforddnb.com/view/article/2310.

7. Edwin Hirschmann, *"White Mutiny": The Ilbert Bill Crisis in India and Genesis of the Indian National Congress* (New Delhi: Heritage, 1980).

8. Dinabandhu Mitra, *Nil Darpan,* ed. Sasankhasekhar Bagchi (Calcutta: Modern Book Agency, 1961), 43.

9. A *ryot* is an Indian peasant or tenant farmer.

10. See Kling, *Blue Mutiny.*

11. William Theobald, *Summary of Statements and Arguments [on the Administration of the Law in the Lower Provinces of Bengal]: Submitted to the Right Honorable the President of the Board of Control, and Some Other Gentlemen* (London: W. Benning, 1857), 25.

12. James Charles Jack, *Bakarganj* (Calcutta: Bengal Secretariat Book Depot, 1918), 1–2.

13. A. Z. M Iftikhar-ul-Awwal, "Murder in the District of Bakarganj in the Late Nineteenth Century," *Journal of the Asiatic Society of Bangladesh (Humanities)* 32, no. 2 (December 1987): 167–168.

14. Quoted in Muhammad Mohar Ali, *The Bengali Reactions to Christian Missionary Activities, 1833–1857* (Chittagong: The Mehrab Publications, 1965), 146.

15. *The Friend of India,* February 25, 1841. Quoted in Ali, *Bengali Reactions to Christian Missionary Activities,* 146.

16. Henry Beveridge, *The District of Bákarganj: Its History and Statistics* (London: Trübner & Co., 1876), 247–248.

17. Jack, *Bakarganj,* 32–33.

18. Jack, *Bakarganj,* 31.

19. Beveridge, "Physical Features," in *District of Bákarganj,* 23. In terms of the number of converts in Barisal, Gordon Soddy gave a figure of 192 in 1851. To have thirty-five new recruits represents a surge of almost 18 percent. Gordon Soddy, *Baptists in Bangladesh: An Historical Sketch of More than One Hundred Years' Work of the Baptist Missionary Society in Bengal* (Khulna: Literature Committee, National Council of Churches, Bangladesh Baptist Sangha, 1987), 137.

20. Details discussed here are from the aforementioned pamphlet by the missionary Edward B. Underhill, the secretary of the Baptist Society of England, which is hereafter referred to as the "Underhill pamphlet." Ali, the only other South Asian historian to discuss this case in detail, remarked that this pamphlet was most possibly authored by J. C. Page, whose converts had been attacked. Underhill, *Case of the Baropakhya Christians.* See also Ali, *Bengali Reactions to Christian Missionary Activities,* 151–157.

21. Underhill, *Case of the Baropakhya Christians,* 17, from the reproduced judgment of Hon. F. B. Kemp, who overturned the magistrate H. A. R. Alexander's ruling on the case.

22. This violence was "nonofficial"—perpetrated by white Britons who were not connected to the official administrative machinery of either the East India

Company before 1857 or the Raj thereafter. This nonofficial white population of India enjoyed significant immunity from prosecution. See Elizabeth Kolsky, *Colonial Justice in British India* (New York: Cambridge University Press, 2011).

23. Iftikhar-ul-Awwal, "Murder in the District of Bakargunj," 180.

24. Baptist Wriothesly Noel, *On Public Immoralities: Speech by the Hon'ble Arthur Kinnaird, June 11, 1857, England and India, an Essay on the Duty of Englishmen towards the Hindoos* (London: J. Nisbet and Company, 1859), 125–126.

25. Arthur Kinnaird, *Bengal, Its Landed Tenure and Police System: Speech on a Motion for Inquiry in the House of Commons, June 11, 1857* (London: James Ridgway, 1857), 13–14.

26. Manuscript copy of "History of the Beel Churches," 24.9.1890, Baptist Missionary Society Archives, Box India, Barisal etc., 1847, The Angus Library and Archive, Regent's Park College, Oxford University. I am profoundly grateful to the archivist Emily Burgoyne for locating the material and providing me access to it.

27. *The Barisal Mission, Containing "The Epitome of My Life" by John Sircar, The Missionary Herald: Containing Intelligence, at Large, of the Proceedings and Operations of the Baptist Missionary Society* (United Kingdom: G. Wightman, 1883), 284–286.

28. "History of the Beel Churches," 6–8.

29. Quoted in Ali, *Bengali Reactions to Christian Missionary Activities,* 150–151.

30. Quoted in Ali, *Bengali Reactions to Christian Missionary Activities,* 136–157.

31. F. Schurr, "On the Influence of the System of Indigo Planting on the Spread of Christianity," in *Proceedings of a Conference Held at Calcutta, Sept. 4–7, 1855,* General Conference of Protestant Missionaries (Calcutta: Baptist Mission Press, 1855), 86.

32. For Edward Underhill and his activities in India and Jamaica, see "Edward Bean Underhill," in *Oxford Dictionary of National Biography* (Oxford: Oxford University Press, 2004); online ed., 2004, https://www.oxforddnb.com/view/10.1093/ref:odnb/9780198614128.001.0001/odnb-9780198614128-e-1002794.

33. Underhill, *Case of the Baropakhya Christians.*

34. Underhill, *Case of the Baropakhya Christians,* 8.

35. Underhill, *Case of the Baropakhya Christians,* 38–40, 56–57.

36. Underhill, *Case of the Baropakhya Christians,* 40–42, 54–56.

37. Underhill, *Case of the Baropakhya Christians,* 4.

38. Elizabeth Kolsky, "'The Body Evidencing the Crime': Rape on Trial in Colonial India, 1860–1947," *Gender & History* 22, no. 1 (2010): 109–130,

https://doi.org/10.1111/j.1468-0424.2009.01581.x. The Latin *rapere* means equally to abduct or to commit sexual violence.

39. "History of the Beel Churches," 17.

40. Underhill, *Case of the Baropakhya Christians,* 48.

41. Underhill, *Case of the Baropakhya Christians,* 49.

42. Underhill, *Case of the Baropakhya Christians,* 55.

43. Underhill, *Case of the Baropakhya Christians,* 2.

44. Madhupasha / Madhubpasha—as it is variously spelled in the Underhill pamphlet—refers to the small distributary channel that fed during the monsoons from the Madhabpasha lake Durga Sagar, situated about seven kilometers (i.e., about 4.3 miles) from modern-day Barisal town.

45. Underhill, *Case of the Baropakhya Christians,* 6–7.

46. "History of the Beel Churches," 9.

47. Underhill, *Case of the Baropakhya Christians,* 7.

48. Underhill, *Case of the Baropakhya Christians,* 49–56.

49. Underhill, *Case of the Baropakhya Christians,* 55–57. From the testimonies of Gauri, Janoo's wife, and Roso, Ledoo's wife.

50. Underhill, *Case of the Baropakhya Christians,* 12–14.

51. *Naib:* officer in charge of revenue collection. *Gomastha:* agents of the planters and *zamindars,* with coercive powers to compel signing bonds ensuring plantation of indigo.

52. Underhill, *Case of the Baropakhya Christians,* 14–15.

53. Underhill, *Case of the Baropakhya Christians,* 14–15.

54. Underhill, *Case of the Baropakhya Christians,* 14–15.

55. Quoted in Wriothesly, *On Public Immoralities,* 124.

56. Underhill, *Case of the Baropakhya Christians,* 25–26. Emphasis added.

57. Underhill, *Case of the Baropakhya Christians,* 30–32.

58. Underhill, *Case of the Baropakhya Christians,* 23. Emphasis added.

59. Underhill interjected in the pamphlet to ask whether it was possible to apostatize from heathenism.

60. Underhill, *Case of the Baropakhya Christians,* 36.

61. Schurr, "On the Influence of the System of Indigo Planting," 93.

62. *Haftam* laws: Regulation VII of 1799, commonly known as *haftam* or seventh, which armed the *zamindars* with despotic powers over their defaulting *ryots*. The *zamindars* could now distrain their crops, cattle, and other properties and sell them, in the name of recovering rents. *Zamindars*, as absolute proprietors, could summon the defaulting *ryots* to their *cutcherry* and keep them confined in fetters until the arrears were paid. They could impose community fines on the whole village if any of the defaulting *ryots* ran away to safety with his family and property.

63. Rev. J. C. Page, "The Zamindary System and Christianity," in *Proceedings of a Conference Held at Calcutta, Sept. 4–7, 1855*.

64. Charles Trevelyan, *The Baropakhya Christians and Judge Kemp's Unrighteous Decision*, republished from the *Calcutta Christian Observer*, September 1856, Council for World Mission Library B.3/16, Archives and Special Collections, School of Oriental and African Studies, London, 16–17.

65. Trevelyan, *Baropakhya Christians*, 22–23. Emphasis added.

66. Trevelyan, *Baropakhya Christians*, 23–25.

67. Trevelyan, *Baropakhya Christians*, 27–28.

68. *The Home and Foreign Record of the Free Church of Scotland: New Series, August 1856–July 1857*, vol. 1 (Edinburgh: James Nichol, 1857), 97–99.

69. Ali, *Bengali Reactions to Christian Missionary Activities*, 155–157.

70. Ram Gopal Sanyal, *Reminiscences and Anecdotes of Great Men of India: Both Official and Non-Official for the Last One Hundred Years* (Calcutta: Herald Printing Press, 1894), 140–141.

71. Edward Bean Underhill, *A Report Presented to the Committee of the Baptist Missionary Society, on His Return from India* (London: Reed and Pardon, 1857), 28–30.

72. "History of the Beel Churches," 9.

73. "History of the Beel Churches," 9–11.

FIVE THE WORLD OF MUNSHI MEHERULLAH

1. L. S. S. O'Malley, *Jessore District Gazetteers* (Calcutta: Bengal Secretariat Book Depot, 1912), 45.

2. *Murid:* Arabic Sufi term meaning "disciple."

3. Anne M. Blackburn, *Locations of Buddhism: Colonialism and Modernity in Sri Lanka* (Chicago: University of Chicago Press, 2010), 13.

4. Muhammada Ābū Tāliba, *Munaśī Mohāmmada Meheraullāha, deśa, kāla, samāja* (Dhaka: Isalāmika Phāuṇḍeśana Bāṃlādeśa, 1983), 204–205.

5. Tāliba, *Munaśī Mohāmmada Meheraullāha,* 204–205.

6. Rafiuddin Ahmed, "Muslim-Christian Polemics and Religious Reform in 19th Century Bengal: Munshi Meher'ullah of Jessore," in *Religious Controversy in British India: Dialogues in South Asian Languages,* ed. Kenneth W. Jones (Albany: State University of New York Press, 1992), 94–96. The veteran civil surgeon James Wise's classic article divided the Muslims of eastern Bengal into these three groups, along with the *Rafi'yadain,* whom he called the "real Wahabbis" of Bengal. See James Wise, "The Mohammadans of Eastern Bengal," *Journal of the Asiatic Society of Bengal* 63 (1894): 33.

7. Anisujjamana, *Musalimamānasa O Bāṃlā Sāhitya* (Dhaka: Lekhak Sangha Prakasani, 1964), 347–360.

8. *Waz-mahfil:* propagatory meetings. *Bahas:* debate, especially to discuss religious and sectarian theological issues.

9. For an in-depth discussion of the term *ecumene,* see C. A. Bayly, "The Indian Ecumene: An Indigenous Public Sphere," in *Empire and Information: Intelligence Gathering and Social Communication in India, 1780–1870* (Cambridge: Cambridge University Press, 1996), 180–211.

10. Mustafa Nur'ul Islam, ed., *Samayik-Patr'e Jiban o Janamat* (Dhaka: Bangla Academy, 1977), 95.

11. Islam, *Samayik-Patr'e Jiban o Janamat,* 110–111. Meherullah wrote a pamphlet, *Vidhava Ganjana o Bishad Bhandar* [The abuse suffered by widows and their storehouse of sorrows], poignantly chronicling the state of poor young Muslim and Hindu widows.

12. Originally from Sheikh Jamiruddin's *Meher Charit,* which was the earliest biography of Meherullah. Quoted in Rafiuddin Ahmed, "Muslim-Christian Polemics and Religious Reform," 265.

13. Better known as Karamat Ali Jaunpuri, the founder of the Tariqah-i-Muhammadiya in Bengal.

14. Islam, *Samayik-patr'e Jiban o Janamat,* 111.

15. Ābū Tāliba, *Munaśī Mohāmmada Meheraullāha,* 204–205.

16. See the introduction to Meherullah's biography written by one of his admirers—Sheikh Habibur Rahman, *Karmabir Munshi Meherullah* (Calcutta: Muhammadi Press, 1934).

17. Andrew Sartori, *Liberalism in Empire: An Alternative History* (Berkeley: University of California Press, 2014).

18. Sartori, "Peasant Property and Muslim Freedom," in *Liberalism in Empire,* 136–198.

19. Dipesh Chakrabarty, "Nation and Imagination," in *Provincializing Europe: Postcolonial Thought and Historical Difference,* new ed. (Princeton, NJ: Princeton University Press, 2008), 149–179.

20. Saidiya Hartman, *Wayward Lives, Beautiful Experiments: Intimate Histories of Riotous Black Girls, Troublesome Women and Queer Radicals* (New York: W. W. Norton, 2020).

21. Mou Banerjee, "The Tale of the Tailor: Munshi Mohammad Meherullah and Muslim-Christian Apologetics in Bengal, 1885–1907," *South Asian Studies* 33, no. 2 (2017): 122–136.

22. Faisal Devji, "Apologetic Modernity," *Modern Intellectual History* 4, no. 1 (2007): 61–76, http://doi.org/10.1017/S1479244306001041.

23. James Hugh Eliot Garrett, "Natural Calamities," chap. 6 in *Bengal District Gazetteers: Nadia* (Calcutta: Bengal Secretariat Book Depot, 1910), 98.

24. Garett, "Public Health," chap. 4 in *Bengal District Gazetteers,* 57–66.

25. Garett, "Christian Missions," chap. 14 in *Bengal District Gazetteers,* 145.

26. Garett, "Education," chap. 13 in *Bengal District Gazetteers,* 134. See also Nilanjana Paul, *Bengal Muslims and Colonial Education, 1854–1947: A Study of Curriculum, Educational Institutions, and Communal Politics* (New Delhi: Taylor & Francis, 2022).

27. Abul Ahsan Chaudhuri, *Munshi Sheikh Jamiruddin* (Dhaka: Bangla Academy, 1953), 14–16.

28. Chaudhuri, *Munshi Sheikh Jamiruddin,* 14. Chaudhuri mentions the district magistrate of Meherpur donating a substantial sum to the Church Missionary Society's funds in 1904.

29. Garett, "The People," chap. 3 in *Bengal District Gazetteers,* 44.

30. Garett, "People," 52.

31. Garett, "People," 56.

32. Ahmed, "Muslim-Christian Polemics and Religious Reform," 97–98.

33. O'Malley, *Jessore District Gazetteers,* 40–43.

34. For the colonial suspicions regarding *Wahhabis* as a result of the Great *Wahhabi* Case that roiled British India from 1869 to 1877, see Julia Stephens, "The Phantom Wahhabi: Liberalism and the Muslim Fanatic in Mid-Victorian India," *Modern Asian Studies* 47, no. 1 (2013): 22–52; James Wise, *Notes on the Races, Castes and Trades of Eastern Bengal* (London: Harrison and Sons, 1883), 44.

35. Wise, *Notes on the Races, Castes and Trades,* 45.

36. Haram: forbidden or proscribed by Islamic law. *Haram-khor:* one who eats haram food, since an observant Muslim is forbidden from eating pork.

37. Kazi Nazrul Islam, *Mrityu-Khuda,* 4th ed. (Calcutta: Gopaldas Publishers, 1958), 4.

38. Islam, *Samayik-patr'e Jiban o Janamat,* 95. *Isa'i Din* is the religion of Isa Masih or Jesus the Messiah.

39. Quoted in Chaudhuri, *Munshi Sheikh Jamiruddin,* 15.

40. Muin-ud-din Ahmad Khan, *History of the Fara'idi Movement in Bengal, 1818–1906* (Karachi: Pakistan Historical Society, 1965), 50–56.

41. Nabīnacandra Sena, *Āmāra Jībana,* 2nd Saṃskaraṇa ed., vol. 3 (Kalikata: Sānyāla Eṇḍa Kompānī, 1912), 142–155.

42. Sugata Bose, *Peasant Labour and Colonial Capital: Rural Bengal since 1770* (Cambridge: Cambridge University Press, 1993), 81.

43. Shaikh Jamiruddin, *Meher Charit/Meherul Islam,* 7th ed. (Jessore, 1967); Mohammad Asiruddin Pradhan, *Meherulla'r Jibani* (Jalpaiguri: Printed by M. L. Datta at Jalpaiguri Press, 1909); Rahman, *Karmabir Munshi Meherullah.*

44. Following John and Jean Comaroff, who describe life history as "patently ideological modes of inscription." Quoted in David Arnold and Stuart Blackburn, eds., introduction to *Telling Lives in India: Biography, Autobiography, and Life History* (Bloomington: Indiana University Press, 2004), 5.

45. Jamiruddin, *Meherul Islam,* 9.

46. Parts 1 and 2 of *Barna Parichay* were written in 1854 and 1855. *Bodhoday* was written in 1851.

47. Ābū Tāliba, *Munaśī Mohāmmada Meheraullāha,* chap. 1.

48. For discussion of *akhlaq* literature, see Muzaffar Alam, "Sharia, Akhlaq and Governance," in *The Languages of Political Islam: India, 1200–1800* (Chicago: University of Chicago Press, 2004), 26–69.

49. Kartikeya Chandra Roy, *Dewan Kartikeya Chandra Rayer Atma Jiban Charit* (Calcutta: Indian Mirror, 1897); Satish Chandra Chakrabarti, ed., *Debendranath Thakur: Atmajibani* (Santiniketan: Biswabharati, 1927). They were the fathers of Rabindranath Tagore and D. L. Roy, respectively.

50. Quoted in David Kopf, *The Brahmo Samaj and the Shaping of the Modern Indian Mind* (Princeton, NJ: Princeton University Press, 2015), 353n89.

51. Ayesha A. Irani, *The Muhammad Avatāra: Salvation History, Translation, and the Making of Bengali Islam* (New York: Oxford University Press, 2021). Irani discusses how the *Nabi Vamsa* became the prime source of knowledge about

Islam and the Prophet in Bengal and often provided a template for other authors working on *sirat* literature.

52. For a detailed discussion, see the seminal work by Anisujjamana, *Musalimamānasa O Bāṃlā Sāhitya,* 234–239. Saymon Zakaria has found evidence of *Bishad Sindhu* being adapted into cycles of Jari-Gaan in Netrakona district. Sāimana Jākāriẏā, *Pronomohi Bongomata: Indigenous Cultural Forms of Bangladesh* (Dhaka: Nymphea Publications, 2011), 31–44. Abul Bashar writes poignantly of the many ways of reading, listening to, and loving the novel in rural peasant and middle-class Hanafi Muslim communities in Bengal. See "Bishad Sindhur Bishadmoy Torongo" [The sorrowful waves of the sea of sorrows] [in Bengali], Amarboi.com, September 9, 2019, http://www.amarboi.com/2015/11/bishad-sindhur-bishadmoy-torongo-abul-bashar.html. Bashar says, "In my childhood I saw pious Muslims display *Bishad Sindhu* in bamboo caskets specially used for storing religious texts with other books."

53. Wise, *Notes on the Races, Castes and Trades,* 44.

54. For details, see Rahman, "Mohd. Meherullah the Orator," in *Karmabir Munshi Meherullah,* 44–63.

55. See Chaudhuri, *Munshi Sheikh Jamiruddin,* 17–19. Jamiruddin studied at the Allahabad St. Paul's Divinity College and graduated with a first-class Bachelor of Theology or BTh degree, with added honors as an HGR, or high-grade reader.

56. Pradhan, *Meherulla'r Jibani,* 13–14.

57. "Religions," in *Census of India, vol. 1 of 1901* (Calcutta: Government of India Central Printing Office, 1904), section 318, 175. Also quoted in Sufia Ahmed, *Muslim Community in Bengal, 1884–1912* (Dhaka: S. Ahmed, distributed by Oxford University Press, 1974), 311: "In November last a Muhammadan reformer, Munshi Meherullah of Jessore, was invited by the Hanafis to deliver lectures on the superiority of the Muhammadan religion in general, and more especially on that of the Hanafi doctrine. The Munshi . . . delivered excellent lectures on the necessity for reform of the Musalman community and gave offence to none. Now and then he threw a word at the Hindus telling them that the Muhammadan religion does not inculcate the duty of making war for the spread of religion or of killing the Kafir if he would not accept 'the true faith.'"

58. Rahman, *Karmabir Munshi Meherullah,* 46–48.

59. Rahman, *Karmabir Munshi Meherullah,* 17–18.

60. Pradhan, *Meherulla'r Jibani,* 9.

61. Pradhan, *Meherulla'r Jibani,* 9–10. For details, see Gordon Soddy, *Baptists in Bangladesh: An Historical Sketch of More than One Hundred Years' Work of the Baptist Missionary Society in Bengal* (Khulna: Literature Committee, National Council of Churches, Bangladesh, 1987), 61.

62. Rahman, *Karmabir Munshi Meherullah,* 20.

63. Rahman, *Karmabir Munshi Meherullah,* 22–24.

64. T. W. Norledge, "Missionary Work in Jessore, Bengal," July 1, 1897, in *The Missionary Herald of the Baptist Missionary Society* (London: Alexander and Shepheard, 1897), 368–370.

65. Ābū Tāliba, *Munaśī Mohāmmada Meheraullāha,* 27.

66. Anisujjamana, *Musalimamānasa O Bāṃlā Sāhitya,* 354.

67. Ābū Tāliba, *Munaśī Mohāmmada Meheraullāha,* 28.

68. Ābū Tāliba, *Munaśī Mohāmmada Meheraullāha,* 44–45.

69. Ābū Tāliba, *Munaśī Mohāmmada Meheraullāha,* 43–48.

70. Ābū Tāliba, *Munaśī Mohāmmada Meheraullāha,* 49–50. Talib claims that these events were verified by Meherullah's youngest son, Mokhlesar Rahman. The description given by Habibur Rahman is slightly different, making no mention of Monroe's incendiary comments on the Prophet. Rahman, *Karmabir Munshi Meherullah,* 35–36.

71. Quoted in Ābū Tāliba, *Munaśī Mohāmmada Meheraullāha,* 49–50.

72. Munshi Meherullah, *Jawabunnesara* [Exchanges of questions and answers with Christians] (Dhaka: Muslim Anushilan Sanstha, 1898).

73. Meherullah, *Jawabunnesara.*

74. I follow Nile Green, *Bombay Islam: The Religious Economy of the West Indian Ocean, 1840–1915* (New York: Cambridge University Press, 2011), 18. On Meherullah's opinions on the performance of miracles, see *Radde Khr̥shṭāna o dalilula Isalāma, ba, Khr̥shṭāna dharmera asāratā* (Dhaka: Āñjumāne Tāmarinula Musalimina, Musalima Anuśīlana Saṃsthā, 1976), 25–29.

75. Meherullah, *Radde Khr̥shṭāna,* 2. William Henry Quilliam (1856–1932), later Abdullah Quilliam and then Haroun Mustapha Leon, was one of the earliest converts to Islam from Methodism. See Ron Geaves, *Islam in Victorian Britain: The Life and Times of Abdullah Quilliam* (Markfield: Kube Publishing, 2010). Mohammed Alexander Russell Webb (1846–1916) converted to Islam in 1888 (in Manila, where he was the consular representative appointed by President Cleveland), influenced by the Indian founder of the Ahmadiyya sect, Mirza Ghulam Ahmad of Qadian. Webb is considered to be the earliest American convert. For details see Umar F. Abd-Allah, *A Muslim in Victorian America: The Life of Alexander Russell Webb* (New York: Oxford University Press, 2006).

76. Meherullah, *Radde Khr̥shṭāna,* 37–40. Meherullah quoted from the *Parasar Samhita* to strengthen his case against the divine paternity of Jesus.

77. Quoted in Chaudhuri, *Munshi Sheikh Jamiruddin*, 26.

78. Chaudhuri, *Munshi Sheikh Jamiruddin*, 25–27.

79. Nilkantha Nehemiah Goreh (1825–1895) was a Maharashtrian Chitpavan Brahmin by birth. He is remembered for his fierce debates with the Brahmos on the debate between trinitarianism and unitarianism—encapsulated in his treatise *A Rational Refutation of Hindu Philosophical Systems.* He was a mentor to Pandita Ramabai. See Meera Kosambi, *Pandita Ramabai through Her Own Words: Selected Works* (New York: Oxford University Press, 2000).

80. For interactions between Muslims and missionaries in pre-Mutiny India, see Avril Powell, *Muslims and Missionaries in Pre-Mutiny India* (Richmond, Surrey, UK: Curzon, 1993), 132–157.

81. Powell, "New Focus on Islam: The Reverend Carl Pfander and the *Mizan-ul-Haq*," in *Muslims and Missionaries in Pre-Mutiny India*, 132–157. See also Sir William Muir, *The Mohammedan Controversy: Biographies of Mohammed, Sprenger on Tradition, the Indian Liturgy, and the Psalter* (Edinburgh: T. & T. Clark, 1897).

82. Ābū Tāliba, *Munaśī Mohāmmada Meheraullāha*, 171–172.

83. Ābū Tāliba, *Munaśī Mohāmmada Meheraullāha*, 178. Translation mine.

84. Chaudhuri, *Munshi Sheikh Jamiruddin*, 26–28.

85. Chaudhuri, *Munshi Sheikh Jamiruddin*, 26–29.

86. Ranajit Guha and Partha Chatterjee, *The Small Voice of History: Collected Essays* (Ranikhet: Permanent Black, distributed by Orient Blackswan, 2009).

87. Wayward: "Willful, reckless, troublesome, riotous, tumultuous, rebellious, and wild. To inhabit the world in ways inimical to those deemed proper and respectable, to be deeply aware of the gulf between where you stayed and how you might live. Waywardness: the avid longing for a world not ruled by master, man, or the police." Hartman, *Wayward Lives, Beautiful Experiments.*

88. Banerjee, "Tale of the Tailor."

89. Devji, "Apologetic Modernity."

SIX THE ELUSIVE LEGACIES OF BRAHMABANDHAB UPADHYAY

1. The word has various meanings depending on the context. *Sandhya* means twilight, but it can also mean a ritual of worship and meditation performed three times a day by Hindus of the higher castes. In this context both are applicable, given the nature and content of the periodical.

2. Brahmachari Rewachand Animananda, *The Blade: Life and Work of Brahmabandhab Upadhyay* (Calcutta: Roy, 1940), 167. Rewachand Animananda estimated 12,000 copies being sold daily.

3. Amiya K. Samanta, *Terrorism in Bengal,* 6 vols. (Calcutta: Government of West Bengal, 1995–1996), 4:628–631. Lal Bazar is a neighborhood in central Calcutta where the headquarters of the Calcutta Police is situated. The police headquarters are now synonymous with the name of the neighborhood.

4. Quoted in Samanta, *Terrorism in Bengal,* 4:628–631.

5. Chittaranjan Das or Deshbandhu (friend of the nation) (1870–1925) would go on to become one of the greatest of India's political leading lights in the independence movement, the founder of Bengal's Swaraj Party, and a mentor to the young Subhas Chandra Bose.

6. IOR/L/PJ/869, file 1909: "The *Sandhya* Case"—Prosecution under Section 124 A, IPC: Newspaper cuttings. Emphasis added. The quoted sections from *The Bengalee* are from newspaper clippings preserved with the file.

7. Aparna Devi, *Manush Chittaranjan* (Calcutta: Indian Associated Publishing Company, 1955), 67–70.

8. IOR/L/PJ/869, 91.

9. Elizabeth Kolsky, "A Note on the Study of Indian Legal History," *Law and History Review* 23, no. 3 (2005): 704, http://www.jstor.org/stable/30042903.

10. Sumit Sarkar, *The Swadeshi Movement in Bengal, 1903–1908* (New Delhi: People's Publishing House, 1973). See chap. 2, "Trends in Bengal's Swadeshi," 31–91.

11. John A. Stevens, *Keshab: Bengal's Forgotten Prophet* (New York: Oxford University Press, 2018), 3.

12. Sumit Sarkar, "'Kaliyuga,' 'Chakri' and 'Bhakti': Ramakrishna and His Times," *Economic and Political Weekly* 27, no. 29 (1992): 1543–1566, http://www.jstor.org/stable/4398664.

13. Vivekananda, *Christ, The Messenger: Lecture* (Boston: The Vedanta Centre, 1900); Ruth Harris, *Guru to the World: The Life and Legacy of Vivekananda* (Cambridge, MA: Belknap Press of Harvard University Press, 2022), 8–9.

14. Joseph Faà di Bruno, *Catholic Belief; or, A Short and Simple Exposition of Catholic Doctrine,* ed. Louis A. Lambert, American ed. (New York: Benziger Brothers, 1884). The book had been granted an imprimatur by Cardinal Manning and went through twenty editions by 1902.

15. For an interesting reading of Faà di Bruno and the implications of his precept of "authentic interiorized sensitivity" for the epistemology of queer Catholicism, see P. R. O'Malley, "Epistemology of the Cloister: Victorian England's Queer Catholicism," *GLQ: A Journal of Lesbian and Gay Studies* 15, no. 4 (2009): 535–564, https://muse.jhu.edu/article/316565. I certainly do not mean to suggest that Brahmabandhab was gay, and there is no evidence to suggest any such possibility. But being a converted Catholic Christian in colonial Bengal

and being a participant in the *swadeshi* movement, which privileged Hindu affective imagery for political mass mobilization, must have seemed somewhat similar to being in the closet. The attractions of Faà di Bruno's formulations for someone like Brahmabandhab become clearer on such considerations.

16. Ashis Nandy, *The Illegitimacy of Nationalism* (New Delhi: Oxford University Press, 1994). See the essay "Brahmabandhab Upadhyay: Tagore's Political Double," 52–53.

17. For more on Rev. Kalicharan Banerjee, see B. R. Barber, *Kali Charan Banurji: Brahmin, Christian, Saint* (London: Christian Literature Society of India, 1912).

18. Barber, *Kali Charan Banurji*, 20–22.

19. For the many shifts in Brahmabandhab's spiritual and intellectual positions from 1880 to 1891, see Julius J. Lipner, "Faith's Brave Spark," in *Brahmabandhab Upadhyay: The Life and Thought of a Revolutionary* (Delhi: Oxford University Press, 1999), 72–99.

20. David J. Neumann, "Christ as Yogi: The Jesus of Vivekananda and Modern Hinduism," *Church History* 90, no. 1 (2021): 117–140, https://doi.org/10.1017/S0009640721000767.

21. "Kananda, the Pagan Attacked Christian Missions in Last Night's Lecture," *Detroit Tribune*, March 11, 1894, https://www.ramakrishnavivekananda.info/vivekananda/volume_9/newspaper_reports/part_i_american_newspaper_reports/19_detroit_tribune_mar_11_1894.htm.

22. Samanta, *Terrorism in Bengal*, 2:655. The report by Denham was extremely important in the trial of the so-called Alipore Bomb Case of 1908.

23. Peter Heehs, *The Lives of Sri Aurobindo* (New York: Columbia University Press, 2008), 67.

24. Quoted in Suman Bhowmik, ed., *Brahmabandhab Upadhyay: Tyagi Jiban, Teji Jaban* (Calcutta: Sutanuti Boimela, 2011); *Brahmabāndhaba Upādhyāẏa* (Bardhamāna: Śikshā-Niketana, 1976), 43.

25. Bhowmik, *Brahmabandhab Upadhyay*. Manoranjan Guha, "Bilat-Jatri Sannyasi'r Chithi," in Bhowmik, *Brahmabandhab Upadhyay*, 79–131.

26. Brahmabāndhaba Upādhyāẏa, *The Writings of Brahmabandhab Upadhyay: Including a Resume of His Life and Thought*, ed. Julius Lipner and George Gispért-Sauch, 2 vols. (Bangalore: United Theological College, 1991), 2:510.

27. Upādhyāẏa, *Writings of Brahmabandhab Upadhyay*, 2:532–537.

28. Bhowmik, *Brahmabandhab Upadhyay*, 45–48.

29. See, for example, Mrinalini Sinha, *Colonial Masculinity: The "Manly Englishman" and the "Effeminate Bengali" in the Late Nineteenth Century* (New York: Manchester University Press, 1995).

30. Sugata Bose and Ayesha Jalal, *Modern South Asia: History, Culture, Political Economy,* 3rd ed. (New York: Routledge, 2004), 103.

31. Durba Ghosh, *Gentlemanly Terrorists: Political Violence and the Colonial State in India, 1919–1947* (New York: Cambridge University Press, 2017).

32. See Aurobindo Ghosh, "The Doctrine of Passive Resistance" (published in *Bande Mataram,* April 13, 1907): "Where the oppression is legal and subtle in its methods and respects life, liberty and property and there is still breathing time, the circumstances demand that we should make the experiment of a method of resolute but peaceful resistance. . . . *In other methods, a daring minority purchase with their blood the freedom of the millions; but for passive resistance it is necessary that all should share in the struggle and the privation.*" Emphasis added.

33. Sarkar, *Swadeshi Movement in Bengal.* See chap. 9, "Early Revolutionary Terrorism," 465–492.

34. Sarkar, *Swadeshi Movement in Bengal,* 477. See also the discussion by Haridas Mukhopadhyay and Uma Mukhopadhyay, *Upadhyay Brahmabandhab o Bharatiya Jatiyatabad* (Calcutta: K. L. Mukhopadhyay, Firma, 1961), 165–179. For a discussion on Indian "ethical polity," see Sugata Bose, "The Spirit and Form of an Ethical Polity: A Meditation on Aurobindo's Thought," *Modern Intellectual History* 4, no. 1 (2007): 129–144, doi:10.1017/S1479244306001089.

35. Mukhopadhyay and Mukhopadhyay, *Upadhyay Brahmabandhab,* 165–179.

36. Samanta, *Terrorism in Bengal,* 2:657–658.

37. Samanta, *Terrorism in Bengal,* 2:664.

38. Prabodh Chandra Singha, *Upadhyay Brahmabandhab* (Calcutta: Amarendranath Chattopadhyay, Cherry Press, n.d.), 97–99.

39. Animananda, *Blade,* 162–167.

40. Upādhyāẏa, *Writings of Brahmabandhab Upadhyay,* 2:130–132. Condensed form of the article presented here.

41. In the *Anushthan Patra* or "Ceremonial Introduction" published in the short-lived *Swaraj* periodical, Upadhyay offered up a description of what *swaraj* or self-rule meant to him. It was being established in one's own land, under one's own jurisdiction, aware of the glory of one's own self, looking inwards to meditate on the possibilities of tomorrow. Mukhopadhyay and Mukhopadhyay, *Upadhyay Brahmabandhab,* 188–193.

42. Singha, *Upadhyay Brahmabandhab,* 88–89.

43. *Kot:* According to the Samsad Bengali Dictionary, the meanings of this now rarely used Bengali word are as follows: কোট (p. 256)—a fort, a fortress (রাজকোট); a town, a city (পাঠানকোট); control, power, jurisdiction

(কোটে পাওয়া); one's area (নিজের কোটে থাকা); bounds (কোটের বাইরে যাওয়া); position, resolve, claim (কোট বজায় রাখা) ।.

44. From the *Reports on Native Newspapers* (hereafter *RNN*), *Sandhya,* August 15, 1907.

45. Ranajit Guha, *Dominance without Hegemony: History and Power in Colonial India* (Cambridge, MA: Harvard University Press, 1997), 203–210.

46. The translation is from the *RNN.* The essay was republished in Sajanikanta Das, "Phiringibhay-hari Brahmabandhab" [Brahmabandhab the destroyer of our fear of the Feringhi], in *Sanibarer Chithi,* October 1961.

47. Quoted in Lipner, *Brahmabandhab Upadhyay,* 347.

48. Singha, *Upadhyay Brahmabandhab,* 84–85.

49. Sri Vrindaban, the birthplace of Krishna, was also a humorous way to refer to the fearsome colonial prisons. Brahmabandhab had two summonses issued against him by this point in August 1907, and knew he would be arrested any day.

50. *RNN, Sandhya,* August 20, 1907.

51. Mukhopadhyay and Mukhopadhyay, *Upadhyay Brahmabandhab,* 108–110.

52. Mukhopadhyay and Mukhopadhyay, *Upadhyay Brahmabandhab,* 110.

53. *RNN, Sandhya,* August 13, 1907.

54. Samanta, *Terrorism in Bengal,* 4:609–631, "Seditious Newspaper Articles."

55. IOR/L/PJ/6/826, file 3002, September 4, 1907, seen in Council on September 18, 1907.

56. Sugata Bose, "Nation as Mother: Representations and Contestations of 'India' in Bengali Literature and Culture," in Bose and Jalal, *Modern South Asia,* 50–75.

57. Bipin Chandra Pal, *The Spirit of Indian Nationalism by Bipin Chandra Pal: With an Introduction by W.T. Stead* (London: Hind Nationalist Agency, 1910), 14.

58. Bose, "Spirit and Form of an Ethical Polity," 131.

59. Samanta, *Terrorism in Bengal,* 4: 622–624, "Seditious Newspaper Articles."

60. Bhowmik, *Brahmabandhab Upadhyay,* 64.

61. Nivedita, Vivekananda's Irish Christian disciple, had "converted" to "Hindu-dharma" and was a leading figure of the revolutionary movement, knew both Aurobindo and Barin Ghosh intimately, and may also have been familiar with Brahmabandhab himself. For further details, see Reba Som, "Nationalism," in *Margot: Sister Nivedita of Swami Vivekananda* (New York: Viking, 2017).

62. Bose, "Nation as Mother."

63. Animananda, *Blade.*

64. Quoted in Mukhopadhyay and Mukhopadhyay, *Upadhyay Brahmabandhab,* 146.

65. Quoted in Mukhopadhyay and Mukhopadhyay, *Upadhyay Brahmabandhab,* 174.

66. See Animananda, *Blade,* 175.

67. Animananda, *Blade,* 180–186. See also Lipner, *Brahmabandhab Upadhyay,* 385–386. In Manomohan Gangopadhyay's *Shruti-Smriti* [Hearsay and memories] he reported Brahmabandhab telling him in 1904 that Christ was his *Ishta Devata* or personal deity of choice—Brahmabandhab saw no inner contradiction in praying to Christ in private and maintaining a Hindu public identity. Manomohan Gangopadhyay, *Shruti-Smriti* (Calcutta: Rajlakshmi Pustakalaya, 1928), 14–16.

68. The sudden and incredibly painful death Brahmabandhab suffered, combined with Indian mistrust of British colonial motives, led to the circulation of a number of conspiracy theories, including, but not limited to, his having died of medically induced hydrophobia, strychnine poisoning, and medical negligence. On the other side of the spectrum were tall tales of his ascetic powers, leading to a willed suicide or *Ichhya Mrityu.* See Animananda, *Blade,* 178–179.

69. Animananda, *Blade,* 177.

70. Singha, *Upadhyay Brahmabandhab.*

71. Devi, *Manush Chittaranjan,* 67–70.

72. Bhupendranath Dutta in the introduction to Balai Debasharmana, *Brahmabandhab Upadhyay* (Calcutta: Radharaman Choudhury for Prabartak Publishers, 1961), 16–17.

73. Animananda, *Blade,* 176–180.

74. *RNN,* October–December 1907, 1197–1198; "Sayings of the Late Brahmabandhab Upadhyay," *Sandhya,* October 29, 1907. Emphasis added.

75. Bhowmik, *Brahmabandhab Upadhyay,* 75–76.

76. Quoted in Animananda, *Blade,* 180.

77. A sixteen-year-old boy, Kshudiram Bose, killed the wife and daughter of an English barrister, Mr. Pringle-Kennedy, by bombing their carriage, which he had mistaken as that of Magistrate Kingsford.

78. On the harshness of prison internment, forced labor extracted from political prisoners, and repeated use of torture both by British officers and Indian

constabulary and prison guards, see Ullaskar Dutta, *Twelve Years of Prison Life* (Calcutta: Arya Publishing House, 1924), 65–70; Barindra Kumar Ghosh, *The Tale of My Exile* (Pondicherry: Arya Publishing House, 1922). The accounts of Indubhushan's suicide and Ullaskar's madness are on pp. 97–99. See also Ghosh, *Gentlemanly Terrorists.*

79. Bipin Chandra Pal, *Charit-Katha* (Calcutta: Bhattacharyya and Sons, printed by Shri Debendranath Bhattacharyya, 1917), 124.

80. Pal, *Charit-Katha,* 129–130.

81. Dipesh Chakrabarty, *Provincializing Europe: Postcolonial Thought and Historical Difference—New Edition* (Princeton, NJ: Princeton University Press, 2009), 172–174.

82. Bose and Jalal, *Modern South Asia,* 103.

83. Bose and Jalal, *Modern South Asia,* 104.

84. Nandy, "Brahmabandhab Upadhyay: Tagore's Political Double," in *Illegitimacy of Nationalism,* 51–67.

85. Lipner, *Brahmabandhab Upadhyay,* 281–284.

86. Lipner, *Brahmabandhab Upadhyay,* 284.

87. See Kartik Chandra Nan's letter to Rabindranath Tagore and Tagore's reply on August 8, 1933, quoted in the appendix of Mukhopadhyay and Mukhopadhyay, *Upadhyay Brahmabandhab,* 151–152.

88. Mukhopadhyay and Mukhopadhyay, *Upadhyay Brahmabandhab,* 155. The Mukhopadhyays quote Tagore's long article, "Ashram Bidyalayer Suchana" [The beginning of our Ashrama-school], published in the *Prabasi* magazine in September 1934. It was therefore Brahmabandhab and not Mahatma Gandhi who first gave Tagore the name *Gurudev* or "Revered Teacher."

89. *Gurukul:* an ancient system, wherein (male) students lived in the house of their guru (teacher), practicing the strictest code of celibacy and moral probity of conduct. *Brahmacharya:* the condition of being celibate, mentally and physically, devoting oneself to study and contemplation.

90. Bhowmik, *Brahmabandhab Upadhyay,* 42.

91. See Kartik Chandra Nan's follow-up letter to Tagore about the reasons for the end of the Santiniketan collaboration between him, Brahmabandhab, and Rewachand. Nan clearly states that Debendranath's objections to the presence of Christians at Santiniketan forced a profoundly reluctant Rabindranath to curtail his relationship with Upadhyay and Rewachand. In fact, Tagore then engaged Rewachand as a tutor for his sons Rathi and Shami at his Jorasanko

home in Calcutta. Mukhopadhyay and Mukhopadhyay, *Upadhyay Brahmabandhab,* 158–161.

92. Nandy, "The Novels," in *Illegitimacy of Nationalism,* 9–50.

93. Rabindranath had first conceived of the novel's plot when he recounted the story to Vivekananda's Irish disciple Margaret Noble, who was known in India as Sister Nivedita. She had been one of the major figures in connecting Indian revolutionaries of the *swadeshi* period to a wider cosmopolitan anticolonial revolutionary network, which spanned from Russia to Germany via Turkey. For more on Nivedita, see Śaṅkarīprasāda Basu, *Nibeditā Lokamātā* (Kalikata: Ānanda Pābaliśārs, 1987) and Reba Som, *Margot: Sister Nivedita of Vivekananda* (New York: Viking, 2017).

94. Rabindranath Tagore, *Gora* (Santiniketan: Visva Bharati Press, 1951), 25.

95. See Rabindranath Tagore, *Gora,* trans. Radha Chakravarty (New Delhi: Penguin Books India, 2009). *Gora* was first published in 1910.

96. Tagore, *Gora* (1951), 611–614.

97. Rabindranath Tagore, *Rabindra Racanabali,* vol. 9 (Kalikata: Bisvabharati, 1402), 599.

98. Upādhyāẏa, *Writings of Brahmabandhab Upadhyay,* 1:24–25.

99. Upādhyāẏa, *Writings of Brahmabandhab Upadhyay,* 1:24–25.

100. Quoted in Kaj Baagø, *Pioneers of Indigenous Christianity* (Bangalore: Christian Institute for the Study of Religion and Society and the Christian Literature Society, 1969), 3.

101. On languages of violence, see Veena Das, "Language of Sacrifice," *Man,* n.s., 18, no. 3 (1983): 445–462, http://www.jstor.org/stable/2801591.

102. Rabindranath Tagore, *The Home and the World,* trans. Surendranath Tagore (New York: Penguin, 1985).

103. Shuddhasatva Basu, *Rabindranather Char Adhyay* (Calcutta: Bharati Prakasani, 1979), 7–10.

104. "Rabi-Babu, aamar khub patan hoyechey." *Patan* is the Bengali word for "moral fall."

105. Basu, *Rabindranather Char Adhyay,* 7–10.

106. For details, see Chinmohan Sehanobis, *Rabindranath O Biplabī Samaja* (Calcutta: Visvabharati Granthan Bibhag, 1985), 134–140.

107. Basu, *Rabindranather Char Adhyay,* 7–10.

108. Sugata Bose, "Nation, Reason and Religion: India's Independence in International Perspective," *Economic and Political Weekly* 33, no. 31 (1998): 2090–2097, http://www.jstor.org/stable/4407049.

109. *Ashrama* (Sanskrit origin): the dwelling of a Hindu sage; a religious or monastic retreat.

110. Baridbaran Ghosh, ed., *Brahmabandhab Upadhyayer Rachana Sangraha* (Calcutta: De Book Store, 1987), 55–57.

111. Amales Tripathi quoted W. B. Yeats's poem on the 1916 Easter Rising in Ireland to explain this irrational attachment to one's land of birth: "And what if excess of love / Bewildered them till they died?" Amales Tripathi, *The Extremist Challenge: India between 1890 and 1910* (Bombay: Orient Longman, 1967), 117.

112. Bhowmik, *Brahmabandhab Upadhyay,* 67.

113. Basu, *Rabindranather Char Adhyay,* 6.

114. Singha, *Upadhyay Brahmabandhab,* 106–107.

115. Mukhopadhyay and Mukhopadhyay, *Upadhyay Brahmabandhab,* 193–195. In the article "Amader Swarajneeti" (Our self-rule policy), Brahmabandhab says the British could not possibly be the rulers (literally *Raja* or kings) of India, since they had not been sanctified by anointed coronation ceremonies. "They were interloping tyrants, unjustly ruling India. To accept them as such would be against *Dharma,* against righteousness."

116. Susan Billington Harper, *In the Shadow of the Mahatma: Bishop Azariah and the Travails of Christianity in British India* (Abingdon, UK: Taylor & Francis, 2019), 59.

117. Geoffrey A. Oddie, "Indian Christians and National Identity, 1870–1947," *Journal of Religious History* 25, no. 3 (2001): 346. See also Harper, *In the Shadow of the Mahatma,* 291–350.

EPILOGUE

1. See M. K. Gandhi, "A Month with Gokhale-II," in *An Autobiography or The Story of My Experiments with Truth,* ed. Shriman Narayan, trans. Mahadev Desai (Ahemadabad: Navajivan Mudranalaya, n.d.), accessed November 2, 2023, http://www.mkgandhi.org/autobio/chap72.htm.

2. C. F. Andrews, *Mahatma Gandhi's Ideas (1929): Including Selections from His Writings,* Routledge Revivals (London: Routledge, 2016), 72–73.

3. Mohandas K. Gandhi, *Autobiography: The Story of My Experiments with Truth* (Garden City, NY: Dover, 2012), 454.

4. Mahatma Gandhi, "Interview to Dr. John Mott, before March 1, 1929," in *The Collected Works of Mahatma Gandhi,* vol. 45 (New Delhi: Publications Division,

Government of India, 1999), 142–145, http://www.gandhiashramsevagram.org/gandhi-literature/mahatma-gandhi-collected-works-volume-45.pdf.

5. Goldie Osuri, "The Concern for Sovereignty in the Politics of Anti-Conversion," *Religion Compass,* no. 7 (2013): 385–393, https://doi.org/10.1111/rec3.12064.

6. Nalin Mehta, "The Sangh Parivar and Education: Tribal Communities, Vanvasi Kalyan Ashram and Christian Missionaries," in *The New BJP: Modi and the Making of the World's Largest Political Party* (Chennai: Westland Non-Fiction, 2022), chap. 14.

7. Christophe Jaffrelot, *The Hindu Nationalist Movement and Indian Politics: 1925 to the 1990s: Strategies of Identity-Building, Implantation and Mobilisation (with Special Reference to Central India)* (London: Hurst & Company, 1993), 164, Hurst eBooks.

8. Abraham Vazhayil Thomas, *Christians in Secular India* (Madison, NJ: Fairleigh Dickinson University Press, 1974), 133–136.

9. Mehta, "Sangh Parivar and Education."

10. "Religious Freedom and the Anti-Conversion Statute in India," *South Asia@LSE* (blog), November 8, 2021, https://blogs.lse.ac.uk/southasia/2021/11/08/religious-freedom-and-the-anti-conversion-statute-in-india.

11. The Uttarakhand Freedom of Religion Act, 2018, Act 28 of 2018, India, PRS Legislative Research, https://prsindia.org/files/bills_acts/acts_states/uttarakhand/2018/Act%2028%20of%202018%20UKD.pdf.

12. United States Commission on International Religious Freedom (USCIRF), *Annual Report of the U.S. Commission on International Religious Freedom* (Washington, DC: USCIRF, April 2023), 24–25, https://www.uscirf.gov/sites/default/files/2023-05/2023%20Annual%20Report_1.pdf.

13. Akash Joshi, "Remembering Graham Staines, 18 Years after His Murder," *The Quint,* January 22, 2017, https://www.thequint.com/india/2016/01/22/remembering-graham-staines-17-years-after-his-murder.

14. "Crime and Punishment," *Economic and Political Weekly* 38, no. 38 (2003): 3949, http://www.jstor.org/stable/4414035.

15. Harsh Mander, "The Conversion Crusade: Competing for People's Souls," *Hindustan Times,* January 15, 2015, http://www.hindustantimes.com/ht-view/the-conversion-crusade-competing-for-people-s-souls/story-E3Y6cZmGs9Ih9JsgO1v22I.html.

16. Jeffrey Gettleman and Suhasini Raj, "Arrests, Beatings and Secret Prayers: Inside the Persecution of India's Christians," *New York Times,* December 22, 2021, https://www.nytimes.com/2021/12/22/world/asia/india-christians-attacked.html.

17. USCIRF, *Annual Report of the U.S. Commission on International Religious Freedom, 2023*, 24.
18. Outlook Web Desk, "A Look at Recent Attacks against Christians in India," *Outlook*, March 13, 2023, https://www.outlookindia.com/national/a-look-at-recent-attacks-against-christians-in-india-news-269813.

Acknowledgments

This book has lived with me for almost fifteen years now. I have navigated three continents, personal and family illness, multiple academic institutions as a graduate student and as an assistant professor, and a pandemic in these years. It has been a very long journey from Purulia, the small dusty town in India I call home, to Harvard and beyond. There have been many people and many institutions that have supported and encouraged me in my meandering and difficult path toward the completion of this book, and to all of them I owe a profound debt of gratitude.

I thank the Social Science Research Council Mellon International Dissertation Research Fellowship, the Harvard University History Department, the South Asia Institute, and the Asia Center at Harvard, which supported the research for my dissertation. The joint Center for History and Economics (CHE) at Harvard University and the University of Cambridge funded a visiting fellowship at Magdalene College, Cambridge, that made research in England easier. Support from the Clemson University History Department was invaluable in the beginning stages of writing. The University of Wisconsin-Madison (UW-Madison) History Department, the Wisconsin Alumni Research Foundation, the Office of the Vice Chancellor for Research and Graduate Education at UW-Madison, and the UW-Madison Center for South Asia all helped me continue my research and writing through the COVID-19 pandemic. The Center for the Humanities at UW-Madison organized a "First Book Workshop" for my book. I am grateful to Durba Ghosh, Julia Stephens, Chandra Mallampalli, and my colleagues who participated in the workshop and provided me with invaluable advice to convert the manuscript into an academic monograph. The American Institute of Indian Studies' "Dissertation to Book" workshop, Anand Yang, and Projit

Mukharji similarly provided much-needed guidance. I also thank Rochona Majumdar for her encouragement and advice. The UW-Madison Institute for Research in the Humanities awarded me a residential fellowship and relieved me of my teaching and service duties for a semester, thereby allowing me the time to write. I thank Steven Nadler, Katie Apsey, Elizabeth Neary, and the IRH fellows.

I owe my deepest gratitude to my teachers, whose intellectual generosity and unstinting support have sustained me. Sugata Bose has been the best of mentors. His care was sometimes all that kept me going. Everything that is good in me and in this book, I owe to his generosity, kindness, and support. Emma Rothschild, David Armitage, and Sunil Amrith continue to influence and shape my work. Ayesha Jalal's formidable intellect and warm affection have inspired me and made me think more carefully about historical narratives of marginalized communities of faith in South Asia.

This book was greatly improved by the generous feedback provided by the anonymous reviewers of Harvard University Press. I thank Sharmila Sen for her generous support and unerring advice, and for introducing me to my extraordinary editor, Emily Silk, who has been an unwavering champion of this book from the beginning. This book is so much better for Emily's involvement and guidance. I am grateful to Jillian Quigley, Stephanie Vyce, Katrina Vassallo, and everyone at Harvard University Press who assisted in the publication of this book. I also thank John Donohue and Westchester Publishing Services for their work on the book.

I have worked at multiple archives and libraries in India, Bangladesh, the United Kingdom, and the United States. I want to extend my gratitude to Monohar'da and the staff at the Netaji Research Bureau, the late Richard Bingle and the desk staff at the British Library, Fred Burchsted and Richard Lesage at Harvard, S. M. Zabed Ahmed at the Dhaka University Library, and Emily Burgoyne at the Angus Pusey Library at Oxford, who all went above and beyond in helping me. Last but not least, I extend my profound gratitude to Todd Michelson Ambelang and the interlibrary loan staff at UW-Madison, who heroically sourced and provided me with the rare documents I needed to write during the pandemic. This book literally would not exist without their extraordinary support.

I owe my gratitude to Alison Johnson, Ann Blair, Sven Beckert, Lisa McGirr, Andy Gordon, Sidney Chalhoub, Ajantha Subramanian, Tim Harper, and Sumantra Bose for a multitude of reasons, intellectual and personal. I would be very remiss if I did not extend my gratitude to Mary McConell and Laura Johnson, who have been pillars of strength and loving support. Kimberly O'Hagan, Daniel Bertwell, Mathew Corcoran, and Nora Maginn Fame repeatedly came to my aid. I also thank Inga Markan Huld and Mary-Rose Cheadle at CHE Cambridge.

From Michael Silvestri and Stephanie Barczewski I learned how to be a good teacher, a conscientious scholar, and a supportive colleague. I miss their company and conversation every day. Kathryn Langenfeld, Stephanie Hassell, Steven Marks, Lee Wilson, Criss Smith, and Rachel Moore were wonderful friends and colleagues at Clemson.

UW-Madison has been home for the past five years, and I have found a community here that has been an unwavering source of intellectual inspiration. Louise Young, Jennifer Ratner-Rosenhagen, and Mitra Sharafi have provided generous advice, love, support, and care throughout these five years in profound abundance—I am truly fortunate to know them. Alexandra Mountain and Kacie Lucchini Butcher have filled my life with joy. Susan Zaeske and Viren Murthy have given me the gift of music. Anne Hansen, Sarah Thal, Anthony Cerulli, Ulrich Rosenhagen, Florence Hsia, Daniel Ussishkin, Steve Kantrowitz, Kathryn Ciancia, Karl Shoemaker, Laird Boswell, Pablo Gomez, James Sweet, Neil Kodesh, Francine Hirsch, Leonora Neville, Lee Palmer-Wandel, Nan Enstad, Finn Enke, April Haynes, Gloria Whiting, Brandon Bloch, Allison Powers Useche, Marla Ramirez, Paige Glotzer, Sumudu Atapattu, Preeti Chopra, Patrick Iber, Marc Kleijwegt, Joe Dennis, Judd Kinzley, Charles Kim, Elizabeth Lapina, Bala Venkat Mani, Priya Mukherjee, Darshana Mini, and Zara Choudhary have at many moments held my hand and provided support, care, and advice. Muhammad Farooq Asif patiently taught me how to read and write Urdu, and Mary Farooq opened her home to me. Tony and John Jensen provided loving companionship. Todd Anderson, Leslie Abadie, Scott Burckhardt, Lisa Normand, Sophie Olson, Jenn Schumacher, Amelia Zurcher, Yasi Rezai, Davis Fugate, and Iain McLoughlin have provided invaluable teaching advice and administrative support. Sarah Beckham and Andrea Fowler have helped me in myriad ways and have supported my work. Christina Matta has supported my digital humanities project with undergraduate students on civil activism and nonviolence and has often made impossible things happen. Andrea Schnell, Rebecca Sippel, and Jack Nitschke provided care and compassion during serious health crises.

The camaraderie of my friends and colleagues at Harvard and elsewhere has greatly enriched the process of research and writing. Julia Stephens, Johan

Mathew, Sana Aiyar, Neeti Nair, Geetanjali Surendran, Antara Datta, Tariq Omar Ali, Benjamin Siegel, Mircea Raianu, Mridu Rai, Hardeep Dhillon, and Nikhita Obeegadoo have all, in their own ways, made this book better. Julie Miller has been a sister and companion in both my best and worst moments. Guillaume Wadia has seen this project evolve into a book and has been my intellectual sounding board, voice of reason, cheerleader, and writing companion. Nicolas Roth, Reihan Nadarajah, Swati Moitra, Priyanka Basu, Cynthia Farid, and Sumona Chakravarty have been constant friends, and I cannot thank them enough for being in my life.

Semanti Ghosh, Betsy More, Heidi and Michael Tworek, Elizabeth Cross, James McSpadden, Josh Ehrlich, Tomasz Blusiewicz, Andrew Bellisari, Michael Thornton, Shane Bobrycki, Jake Ransahoff, Carla Heelan, Maria Blackwood, Kyle Shernuk, Elise Burton, Arafat Razzaque, Abbas Jaffer, Namita Dharia, Neelam Khoja, Namita Wahi, Neelum Sohail, Satgin Hamrah, Nabil Ahmad Khan, Magda Mohammad, Michal Hasson, Andy McDowell, Rahul Kulka, Daniel Majchrowicz, Rohit De, Aditya Balasubramaniam, Tara Suri, Andrew Amstutz, Shaheen Kachwala, Francesca Fuoli, Sarah Shehabuddin, Sharmeen Shehabuddin, Barnali Chanda, Ahona Panda, and Thomas James Newbold have all influenced my intellectual trajectory in their own inimitable ways. Satyasri Ukil Barishkar helped me source an important illustration for the book. Firdous Azim and the late Bashirul Haq were the most affectionate and generous of hosts during my two visits to Dhaka. Firdous Mashi and Bashirul Mesho filled my days at their home with laughter, great conversation, and wonderful food.

I have been fortunate to work with many brilliant students over half a lifetime as a teacher. I thank them all—Sayan Bhattacharjee, Aaisha Sikander Shah, Aditya Agrawal, Madhavi Narayanan, Vimal Konduri, Lena Simon, Kayla Parker, Gabe Sanders, Nadya Hayasi, Chloe Foor, Rae Kalscheuer, Simran Bedi, Braden Longstreth, Tyler Lehrer, Shatrunjay Mall, Ujaan Ghosh, Cameron Daddis, Amrita Chowdhury, Srotaswini Bhowmick, Yue Qiu, and many others. Srotaswini painstakingly edited my endnotes, and to her I owe an extra dose of gratitude!

The late Krishna Bose was a source of loving encouragement through the many years that I have worked on this book. I am profoundly sad that she will not see it published, and I miss her all the time. My thanks to my aunt Arundhati, my late beloved uncle Amit Sarkhel, and my cousin Anjana for providing a home away from home. My grandmother, my Dida, Bina Bandopadhyay, saw me leave for the United States but passed away shortly afterward. I hope she is proud of me and of my work.

My sister Mimi Banerjee has been my best friend and strictest critic. She has sustained me and shouldered many responsibilities on my behalf, and she has made me laugh. My mother, Dr. Madhusree Chattopadhyay, taught me to dream beyond the possibilities offered by my immediate social and personal circumstances. When I look back, I find it is their courage that inspired mine. Thank you, Ma; thank you, Mimi.

I dedicate this book to the wonderful women in my life who have given me wings—Ma, Mimi, Dida, and Krishna Mashi. You have made immensities possible.

Index

Note: page numbers in *italics* indicate figures.